THE PSYCHODYNAMICS AND PSYCHOLOGY OF GAMBLING

ABOUT THE AUTHOR

Mikal Aasved is a Research Associate at the Center for Addiction Studies for the School of Medicine and an Adjunct Assistant Professor in the Department of Sociology and Anthropology at the University of Minnesota in Duluth. He has degrees in the behavioral and social sciences with academic specializations including human motivational theory, human social theory, and addiction studies. The findings of his gambling, alcohol, and barroom behavior research have been presented as papers read at professional conferences and as articles published in scholarly journals. This is his second book.

Cover art by Lin Tuschong, www.typewitch.com.

The Gambling Theory and Research Series

THE PSYCHODYNAMICS AND PSYCHOLOGY OF GAMBLING

The Gambler's Mind

Volume 1

By

MIKAL AASVED, PH.D.

Center for Addiction Studies
University of Minnesota, Duluth

Charles C Thomas
PUBLISHER • LTD.
SPRINGFIELD • ILLINOIS • U.S.A.

Published and Distributed Throughout the World by

CHARLES C THOMAS • PUBLISHER, LTD.
2600 South First Street
Springfield, Illinois 62704

ISBN 0-398-07276-0 (hard)
ISBN 0-398-07277-9 (paper)

Library of Congress Catalog Card Number: 2002020649

With THOMAS BOOKS *careful attention is given to all details of manufacturing and design. It is the Publisher's desire to present books that are satisfactory as to their physical qualities and artistic possibilities and appropriate for their particular use.* THOMAS BOOKS *will be true to those laws of quality that assure a good name and good will.*

Printed in the United States of America
MM-R-3

Library of Congress Cataloging-in-Publication Data

Aasved, Mikal J.
The psychodynamics and psychology of gambling / by Mikal Aasved.
p. cm. -- (Gambling theory and research series; v. 1)
ISBN 0-398-07276-0 -- ISBN 0-398-07277-9 (pbk.)
1. Gambling--Psychological aspects. 2. Compulsive gambling I. Title. II. Series.

RC569.5.G35 A25 2002
616.85'841--dc21 2002020649

To the memory of my Father

This one's for you, Dad

PREFACE TO THE SERIES

This series of books was written primarily to fill what I perceived as a conspicuous gap in the gambling literature: some years ago when I first entered the field of gambling studies and tried to locate a single source which would provide the necessary background on the motivations for normative and excessive gambling, no such source existed. For some puzzling reason, no similarly extensive review and synthesis of the voluminous published materials on gambling theory and research had ever been undertaken. With the exception of a few "handbooks" on gambling and some hard-to-find anthologies of papers presented at various symposia, the necessary source materials were scattered throughout a plethora of academic journals and books. Moreover, most existing reviews of the gambling literature are far from exhaustive. Instead, they are all too often cursory overviews appearing either as relatively brief journal articles or as chapters or even smaller sections of books whose authors usually then go on to profess the superiority of their own favored theory.

This series therefore represents a synthesis of the major ideas and findings of leading theoreticians and researchers in their quest to discover and explain the human propensity for gambling. It is evident that just as many writers in the field of alcohol studies often fail to distinguish among drinking, drunkenness, and alcoholism, so do many writers in the field of gambling studies fail to acknowledge that there are also different degrees of gambling involvement. It is therefore extremely important to distinguish among normal or moderate recreational gambling which is harmful to none, heavy or immoderate gambling which may or may not be harmful to a particular gambler, and compulsive or pathological gambling which is generally harmful not only to all those who are afflicted with it but also to their families, friends, and sometimes even to the greater society in which they live. Addressing primarily the etiological issues related to both normative and excessive gambling, this series includes the speculative thoughts of armchair scholars as well as the empirical findings of front-line scientific researchers in all disciplines including the behavioral, social, and medical sciences.

It is intended to benefit both students and professionals. One goal is to provide students with the introductory background they need to embark on a career in gambling studies. A second is to remind those who are already established in the field not only that many possible explanations for normative and pathological gambling have been proposed, but also that the authority of those who have advanced them should always be questioned. Toward this end, another aim of this more extensive review is objectivity. Rather than champion a particular theoretical orientation as so many others have done, it includes critical assessments of many of the theoretical ideas and research findings that are reviewed. This has been done to help readers become more critical not only in their appraisal of the ideas of others but also in their own thinking. Many of the "experts" in any field are firmly convinced that they have discovered the absolute truth and then write as though their explanation for any phenomenon constitutes the final, definitive answer to that particular question. Many such explanations have an initial intuitive appeal that may "sound good" but that can blind the unwary reader to all other possibilities. In this way some theories have become very much like religions that are sustained more by the faith of the zealots who follow them than by any unbiased scientific observations. Since so many different and competing final "truths" have been propounded, it is clear that not all of them can claim the prize. This is particularly evident in the field of addiction studies, but it is also true of other disciplines. Occasionally a purportedly scientific treatise or explanation will turn out to be merely a guise that its author has used to promote some hidden agenda. The propagandistic tracts of the "creation scientists" are prime examples of this. Readers of all scientific works–including those by reputable authors–are therefore strongly encouraged always to question their validity and never to accept any idea or argument solely on the basis of its author's credentials, reputation, position, or salesmanship since it may turn out to be entirely baseless. The ultimate truth or falsity of any proposition must always be determined by empirically derived facts.

MIKAL AASVED

ACKNOWLEDGMENTS

A work of this nature and scope is clearly not the product of a single author but of many, all of whom deserve credit. I therefore want to thank all the theoreticians and researchers in gambling studies upon whose ideas, analyses, and conclusions the entire contents of this series are based.

I am especially grateful to my parents, Harry and Lucille Aasved, for their undying encouragement and support throughout this project. Although severely tried, they were never wanting.

William Madsen, my mentor, friend, and author of the highly popular *The American Alcoholic*, not only introduced me to addiction studies but also provided the inspiration necessary to undertake this work. Thanks for everything, Bill, including all those prime rib dinners.

I would also like to thank a number of friends and colleagues including Jim Schaefer, with whom I first entered into gambling studies, who introduced me to the hidden world of pull tab gambling, and who demonstrated that it can sometimes be more profitable not to raise when you are holding a nut hand; J. Clark Laundergan not only for his help and encouragement but also for making this work possible; Ken Winters for sharing his collection of professional journals; and Henry Lesieur for his sage advice, assistance, direction, and willingness to share any information he has.

I am also indebted to the entire staff of the University of Minnesota/Twin Cities interlibrary loan office for tracking down countless source materials and to my friend Merlin Spillars, thespian, terpsichorean, and librarian extraordinaire, who generously provided me with source materials I would not otherwise have been able to review.

Finally, but foremost in my life and thoughts, my beloved Star, my soulmate and lifemate, gave me all the love and support necessary to see this endeavor through to its completion. Mo grá thu, my Goddess.

CONTENTS

PART III: COGNITIVE-BEHAVIORAL PSYCHOLOGY
The Role of Expectancy and Belief

THE PSYCHODYNAMICS AND PSYCHOLOGY OF GAMBLING

INTRODUCTION TO THE SERIES

Why do people gamble? Why do some continue to gamble even when they consistently lose more than they win? Why do some continue to gamble even when they have lost everything they have? Many theories have been proposed by various clinicians, laboratory and field researchers, and participant observers in their attempts to discover and explain the reasons for gambling. This series of books was written to review and evaluate the most popular and influential of these explanations and the extensive amount of research that has been undertaken to test them.

Gambling, according to most definitions, means risking something of value on the unknown outcome of some future event. The ultimate goal–or, more accurately, the ultimate hope–of gambling is to realize a value greater than that risked. When we hear the word most of us think of a friendly (or not so friendly) poker game, or of betting on competitive events like horse racing or football games, or of casino games like roulette, blackjack, and slot machines. However, gambling also has other guises. Any speculative business venture, commodities investment, or insurance purchase is just as much a "crap shoot" as playing the dice tables in Las Vegas. Historical and archaeological records provide ample evidence that gambling has also been popular throughout the world for a very long time. Almost since the dawn of human existence people have gambled for the possessions of their dead, for the possessions of their living friends and relatives, to settle legal disputes and establish rights to various resources, and on the outcome of athletic contests and other competitive events.

Gambling is increasingly being recognized by national and local governments throughout the United States and the world as an effective means of generating revenues. Whereas most gambling activities were unlawful in many states and countries until quite recently, many forms of gambling are now becoming accepted and, as a result, national trends toward the legalization of gambling in one form or another are on the rise. Not only has "lottery fever" swept many nations, but many are also allowing on- and off-track parimutuel betting, video gambling machines, and other forms of lawful gambling. In the United States, as some of the states along the Mississippi River and other major waterways began to legalize riverboat gambling as it existed in the nineteenth century, others quickly followed suit. Indian reservations across the country and rural communities in such states as Colorado and South Dakota are now offering Las Vegas, Atlantic City, and even Monte Carlo some stiff competition for the tourist's discretionary income.

Many specialists are convinced that as opportunities for gambling continue to increase, so will the problems associated with it. Salient among these potential problems is the anticipated increase in the incidence of excessive or problem gambling which is commonly referred to as *compulsive* or *pathological gambling*. Whether one considers pathological gambling to be an individual, social, or public health problem, it is one that must be confronted if it is to be prevented and treated. To do so effectively will of course require a thorough understanding of the phenomenon. Unfortunately, with our currently limited knowledge of the mechanisms and motivations underlying gambling, we have a long way to go before achieving this goal.

While our current understanding of the causes of pathological gambling is insufficient, its ramifications are well known. It can have disastrous consequences not only for the individual, but also for his or her immediate family, employer, and society. Among its most well-known consequences are the calamitous losses and severe personal and family debts it can cause. Individual debts for pathological gamblers seeking help have been reported to average from about $53,000 to $92,000.[1] Considered together, the sum of individual gambling debts can be extraordinary. One estimate placed the annual debt accrued by pathological gamblers in New Jersey alone at $514 million.[2] The debt levels of many pathological gamblers can become so high at the individual level that the stress and depression they produce can cause actual physical ailments that require medical treatment. At the domestic level pathological gambling and its consequences can disrupt home life to such an extent that it causes the breakup of families. In its more advanced stages pathological gambling frequently results in absenteeism and loss of productivity on the job. Eventually the need for gambling money can lead to such crimes as theft, embezzlement, insurance fraud, and other kinds of illegal activities. In its final stages the only apparent course of action remaining is all too often suicide.[3]

Because gambling usually involves money, many people believe that therein lies the answer to its attraction and popularity—that this motivation alone explains why people gamble. People are thought to gamble in the hope of winning money they don't already have, of winning more money than they already have, or, in the case of insurance, of protecting what money they already have. But is acquisitiveness really the only reason for gambling? While many card games are played for money, many people play these same games among friends purely for enjoyment or as an opportunity to socialize with friends and relatives, often with no money involved. While many adults become mesmerized by the electronic gambling games they play in casinos in hopes of winning money, countless children and adolescents become equally mesmerized by electronic video games in public arcades and on home computers that are played for amusement only. Technically, friendly card parties and children's video games do not constitute gambling since they do not involve money, but they certainly have many other elements in common with gambling. On the other hand, many risky behaviors like sky-diving, auto racing, Russian roulette, motorcycle jumping, and driving while intoxicated do not involve money but they certainly constitute gambling. There may very well be more to gambling than just the prospect of monetary gain.

A number of competing theories have been proposed by various psychiatrists, psychologists, sociologists, economists, anthropologists, and laypeople in their attempts to explain the "real" motivations for gambling. A number of the more popular and influential of these approaches will be reviewed in this series. Theories, it will be seen, are often little more than opinions, and nearly everyone who studies gambling behavior has a favored opinion. It will be clear that many of those that have been advanced are frequently little more than the standard, stock-in-trade ideologically inspired answers that specialists in various disciplines typically call upon to explain all behavioral phenomena. Thus, in the past and sometimes even today it has generally been assumed that all instances of gambling–normal and pathological–have the same underlying cause irrespective of individual preferences. Many authorities have even proposed single, monolithic explanations to account for excessive or uncontrolled behaviors of all kinds, and a number of the approaches that will be discussed reflect this tendency toward "grand theorizing." It should be obvious that some of these theories may, indeed, offer some insights into certain instances of gambling behavior while the utility of others may be extremely limited. Most importantly, however, since the individual motivations for gambling appear to be so many and varied, it should also be obvious that no single theoretical approach, despite the most fervent aspirations, proselytizations, and diatribes of its adherents, will ever be able to account for all cases.

A QUESTION OF MORALS?

The earliest theoretical approach viewed drinking, drug use, and gambling from a moral perspective.[4] Throughout most of human history the social mores, religious doctrines, and ethical standards of a society have provided the only criteria by which to gauge the behavior of its members. Islamic tradition forbade drinking alcohol and gambling at the same time since both were regarded as tools of Satan. In India the great spiritual leader Mahatma Ghandi also compared the habit of gambling to that of drinking: it is a vice that destroys men's souls and makes them a burden on the earth.[5] Similar views have a long standing in the Western cultural and Judeo-Christian religious traditions. Aristotle himself equated gamblers with thieves and plunderers in his treatise on ethics. In describing those who take what they are not entitled to he wrote:

> meanness is not the term we apply to those who operate in this way on a grand scale–high and mighty persons, for example who sack cities and plunder temples. Such we prefer to call wicked or impious and unrighteous. But the dicer, the thief, the footpad may be reckoned among the mean, because their own hope is to turn a dishonest penny. That is why they labour in their vocation regardless of the world's reproach; the thieves running the greatest risk for the sake of the haul, the gamblers by skinning their friends, who ought rather to benefit by their connexion. Both sorts are unscrupulous profit-hunters, looking to the main chance in discreditable circumstances.[6]

In fourteenth-century England Geoffrey Chaucer's Pardoner condemned gambling as

> . . . the very mother of all lies,
> And of deceit, and cursed false swearing,
> Blasphemy of Christ, manslaughter, and
> waste also
> Of property and of time; and furthermore,
> It is shameful and dishonorable
> To be known as a common gambler.[7]

In the American colonies Cotton Mather censured gambling as "unquestionably immoral and, as such, displeasing to God."[8] Despite a remarkable lack of any concrete evidence, both legal and illegal forms of gambling in the modern United States are commonly believed to be under the firm control of vast organized criminal networks. According to a sociologist who has thoroughly examined the issue, this myth is often perpetuated, exaggerated, and exploited by self-serving politicians and other government officials whose public support and personal fortunes are predicated on an illusory commitment and adherence to the principles of law, order, capitalism, and Christianity.[9]

These moralistic attitudes persist because one of the most cherished core values in Western European Protestant capitalistic societies is that wealth should be acquired only through hard work, sacrifice, and frugality. Any money that has been acquired through other means such as theft or gambling was considered to be ill-gotten and tainted, the cause of hardship and ruin for others, and thus a blemish on the Puritan complexion. Indeed, criminologists, treatment providers, and other gambling researchers have often claimed an association between pathological gambling and criminal activities of one form or another[10] although this is rarely the case among non-problem or normal gamblers. Nevertheless, gambling, whether pathological or non-pathological, has therefore been condemned as an un-Christian and uncapitalistic tool of the devil.

Interestingly, gambling has been denounced as an agent of moral decay equally by representatives of both capital and labor. Since winning eliminates the need for honest labor as a means for social advancement, the religious and ruling elite have seen gambling as a threat to the existing "divinely instituted" social order. Since losing what wealth one does manage to accumulate through wage labor eliminates all chances for honest social advancement, labor leaders have seen gambling as a greater enemy of the working classes than capitalism itself. Thus, "To the guardians of public morality gambling is Gambling and Wrong; so labeled it has been filed safely away, along with Drugs and Homosexuality, under the headings of 'Vice' and 'Deviance.'"[11]

A fundamental assumption of this "simplistic"[12] prescientific "moral model" of human behavior is that gambling, drinking, and other "degenerate" behaviors are solely a matter of willpower. In the traditional popular view, any activity that does not conform to established behavioral norms and conventions is often condemned as a deliberately deviant and immoral flouting of the standards and values of propriety. Thus, the gambler, drinker, drug user, roué, or homosexual, always in full control of himself (women were generally excluded from considerations of such possibilities), is a willful sinner who, owing to his spiritual weakness and moral depravity, freely chooses to indulge himself for his own hedonistic pleasures. Since he is entirely responsible for his "vice" he must be held fully accountable for any and all consequences that may ensue, and should expect no help or sympathy from others. In the past, "treatment" for these self-indulgences consisted of spiritual, moral, and theological counseling and exhortation. When these methods failed, the individual was often subjected to such secular punishments as public ridicule, restraint, corporal punishment, and imprisonment to insure his future conformity to accepted social conventions.

The moralistic view of gambling has the longest history of any approach and is still held by large segments of the general public.[13] Although this attitude predates the development of the scientific method by millennia it is still very much alive in the popular press and today's cultural moralist continues to regard excessive, and even nonexcessive, gambling as a moral deficiency rather than a consequence of cultural, social, psychological, and/or biological factors over which the individual may or may not have any personal control. Nevertheless, owing to the widespread popularity and acceptance of gambling, others argue that it is a normal, everyday psychologically beneficial activity which should be regarded as neither socially or personally harmful.[14] For those who prefer to view gambling from a more scientific perspective, all moral, religious, and ethical arguments against it "are essentially matters of belief and, as such, unanswerable."[15]

AN ADDICTION?

Many specialists in the field feel that pathological gambling, like alcohol and other drug dependence, is an addiction and therefore a major public mental health problem which must be dealt with by medically trained personnel.[16] The inclusion of pathological gambling in the 1980 and subsequent editions of the *Diagnostic and Statistical Manual of Mental Disorders* (DSM-III, DSM-III-R, DSM-IV), published by the American Psychiatric Association,[17] and the *International Classification of Disease* (ICD-9-CM; ICD-10) of the World Health Organization,[18] is responsible for much of this agreement.

The Definitional Issue in Addiction Research

It is important to note, however, that the conception of pathological gambling as an addiction is not universally shared, especially since the DSM and the ICD have always classified pathological gambling as a disorder of impulse control rather than an addiction. Nevertheless, many authorities from many different disciplines tend to agree that compulsive or pathological gambling is, indeed, an addiction. However, there is relatively little agreement as to what this term signifies. Among professionals in the field the definitional issue alone is therefore monumental but relatively few find it necessary to provide a formal definition of what they mean by "addiction." Many simply leave it to their readers to infer their intended meanings from the contexts in which the term is used.[19] Apparently, most feel that a formal definition is unnecessary since they seem to assume that their own particular use of the term enjoys universal acceptance even though this is clearly not the case. Moreover, many specialists are convinced that the idea that gamblers can be neatly dichotomized as either "normal" or "pathological" is entirely groundless since, apart from their differing levels of involvement, there are no observable qualitative differences between them. They argue that excessive or problem gambling is that point along a continuum of involvement–progressing from zero, through light and moderate, to extremely heavy involvement–at which an individual begins to encounter negative consequences. Since people live in a wide variety of financial and social circumstances, some will reach this point much sooner than others.

Not only are existing terms being used inconsistently to convey different meanings for different addiction specialists, but new terms are continually being coined in the hope that taxonomy alone might somehow resolve the issue. Many specialists in the field of substance abuse adhere to a narrow definition in which "addiction" refers only to physiological dependence on a chemical substance, as in cases of nicotine or opiate addiction. On the other hand are those who hold an equally narrow definition by seeing it as an entirely psychological phenomena with no physiological basis whatsoever. Thus, the expressions "monopolistic activities"[20] and "addictive-like preoccupations"[21] have been proposed to describe such behaviors as pathological gambling, compulsive hair pulling (trichotillomania), nail biting, and even such involuntary non-goal-directed behavioral phenomena as facial tics. Advocates of this view refer to these and other nonchemical dependencies as "pure addictions" since the addict's functioning is not influenced by the effects of chemical substances.[22] However, some specialists prefer a less restricted usage in which the term refers to physiological and psychological dependence, or to persistent behaviors which are in any way harmful to the "addict" irrespective of the presence or absence of physical dependence as in "problem drinking" and certain eating disorders. Those who wish to avoid taking sides in the debate suggest the term "driven behaviors"[23] or "appetitive behaviour problems"[24] to account for all types of behavioral excesses irrespective of whether they are psychological or physiological in origin.

A number of authorities feel there is no need to distinguish chemical from behavioral addictions since they have so much in common that no distinction is necessary. (One cannot help but wonder if they might also suggest that arson be regarded and treated the same as spontaneous combustion since they also have so much in common.) Still others, including many laypeople, have adopted a very broad definition in which "addiction" includes indulgence in any behavior, whether goal-oriented or not, which is thought to exceed culturally normative standards, as in the case of "workaholics," "exercise nuts," and blues or bluegrass music "junkies." While one specialist in the field distinguishes "positive addictions" such as jogging and meditation which are deemed to have beneficial effects from "negative addictions" which have harmful consequences,[25] another feels that the term is being used so broadly and inclusively that it is in danger of becoming meaningless[26] since even such hobbies as hang gliding, racing, painting, poetry, gardening, needlepoint, knitting, and reading are sometimes referred to as "addictions." Perhaps none trivialize the concept so much as those who speak of individual and societal addictions to other people, love, pets, religion, music, television programming, coin and stamp collecting, a particular standard of living, and externally structured lives.[27] This situation has been characterized as follows:

> . . . it is not impossible to see two [addiction] researchers using the same terms but coming to entirely different conclusions about the same subject. There is, consequently, no accumulated body of knowledge informed by previous research in the field. Hence the fundamental purpose of the scientific process, the accumulation of a body of knowledge based on systematic and consistent research, is largely unfulfilled in this field.[28]

Among gambling specialists there is little agreement not only as to how "addiction" should be defined, but also as to what constitutes an addiction or how addictions of any sort originate and develop.[29] One addiction specialist has referred to this unfortunate situation as a "conceptual crisis" which plagues the entire field of addiction studies.[30] Consequently, some gambling authorities, particularly those with moralistic inclinations, fail to distinguish normal or nonharmful gambling from that which is excessive or harmful by treating all degrees of gambling as equivalents. Others, who see no qualitative difference between compulsive gambling and any other form of steady and harmful or potentially harmful gambling, prefer to speak of "immoderate,"[31] "heavy,"[32] "excessive,"[33] "intensive,"[34] "troubled,"[35] "habitual,"[36] "high-frequency," "persistent,"[37] "dysfunctional,"[38] "dysfunctionally persistent,"[39] or "disordered"[40] gamblers in their research and writing. Those who dispute the validity of such concepts as "compulsive" or "pathological" gambling speak only of "problem" or "problematic" gambling,[41] a term that has been described as a semantic "wastebasket" since it has been invested with so many different meanings.[42] Likewise, steady but nonpathological gamblers have been referred to by a variety of designations including "obsessive,"[43] "habitual" or "control,"[44] and "serious social"[45] gamblers. Finally, at the low end of the spectrum, those- who gamble only lightly and periodically have been called "casual,"[46] "social,"[47] "occasional,"[48] and "infrequent"[49] or "low-frequency"[50] gamblers.

Unfortunately, politics rather than scientific objectivity often determines which particular definition is adopted for which particular addiction by which particular interest group at which particular time under which particular set of circumstances. These choices are more than occasionally influenced by the researcher's need for funding, a highly competitive funding process, and the perspectives of particular funding agencies or government administrations. Thus, it has been observed that

> Drug abuse is viewed, even by professionals as a crime, alcoholism as a disease, smoking as a bad habit, and obesity [i.e., compulsive overeating] as either simple gluttony and laziness, a learned behavior pattern, or a metabolic disorder. These different ways of conceptualizing addictive behavior patterns are more related to historical/political phenomena than to factual information.[51]

As will be shown, gambling has been, and often still is, considered in the same light as all of the above. Since the course of addiction research often appears to be guided by the same tides of emotionalism that currently surround human fetal tissue research, the definitional question will no doubt remain unresolved for a long time to come, just as it has in the past.

Co-Addiction

A large number of empirical studies have confirmed the existence–though not necessarily the cause–of a strong association between pathological gambling and other addictions, a phenomenon known as co-addiction, cross-addiction, multi-addiction, or poly-addiction. However, this association was not always evident. One of the first studies to investigate this phenomenon found that 8 percent of a sample of Gamblers Anonymous members were alcoholic and 2 percent were addicted to other drugs. It also found that 4 percent of a sample of hospitalized pathological gamblers were also alcoholic and 6 percent were addicted to other drugs.[52] Although the low frequencies that were initially reported did not arouse much concern, many later studies employing modern screening techniques have reported much higher occurrences of co-addiction.

More recent studies have reported that rates of problem gambling (7% to 64%) among adult substance abusers are much higher than those (.23% to 3%) which have been reported for general adult populations.[53] For example, an earlier study of seventy alcoholics reported that 17 percent also admitted having "gambling difficulties" as opposed to only 3 percent of an equal number of nonalcoholic controls.[54] A later study of 100 substance abusers reported 14 percent rates of both pathological and problem gambling.[55] A much larger survey of 458 patients undergoing treatment for substance abuse found that nearly one-fifth of these subjects also had gambling difficulties: 40 (8.7%) were diagnosed as pathological and 47 others (10.3%) were problem gamblers.[56] An even larger and more recent study of 2,171 substance abusers reported that 7.2 percent were also probable and 5.8 percent were severe pathological gamblers.[57] A smaller study of 85 males found that 21.3 percent of the Caucasians and 41 percent of the Native Americans who had entered a U.S. Veterans Administration treatment center for alcohol dependence also had gambling problems.[58] After 100 alcoholic prisoners were screened for gambling problems, 18 were referred to Gamblers Anonymous.[59] Recent studies of heroin addicts enrolled in methadone maintenance treatment programs have reported similar findings. One of these found that 3 percent of the 220 methadone patients sampled were problem gamblers while 7 percent were classed as probable pathological gamblers.[60] Substantially higher rates were reported in a similar study of 117 methadone patients which found that nineteen or 16 percent of those sampled were probable pathological gamblers and another eighteen or 15 percent were potential pathological or problem gamblers.[61] Two years later a larger study of 462 methadone patients identified 21.4 percent as probable pathological gamblers and 8.9 percent as potential problem gamblers.[62] Likewise, of 93 homeless veterans admitted to an outpatient treatment program for alcohol and heroin addiction, 17 percent were diagnosed as probable pathological gamblers and 34 percent as potential problem gamblers. This study also made the interesting observation that those who were addicted to both heroin and alcohol were even more likely to have a gambling problem than those who were addicted to only one of these substances.[63] A third study of military veterans admitted for substance abuse treatment reported that fully one-third (33.3%) were also pathological gamblers.[64] A fourth found that 25 percent of the veterans admitted to a substance abuse treatment center in Minnesota had mild gambling problems while 15 percent were pathological gamblers, a rate that is approximately ten times that of the state's general population.[65]

Rates of psychoactive substance abuse among problem gamblers are also inordinately high. Modern research has found that from 36 percent[66] to 88 percent[67] of the pathological gamblers studied also abused alcohol and/or other drugs. One recent survey of 246 mostly male (85%) pathological gamblers found that more than one-quarter (26 percent) of the sample had a concurrent drug problem while more than half (50.8%) admitted that they also had an alcohol problem.[68] Studies of co-addiction among female compulsive gamblers reported that well over half (56%) of those who were members of Gamblers Anonymous either abused or were dependent upon alcohol and/or other drugs[69] and that nearly all (88%) of a sample of female prisoners who were pathological gamblers were also chemically dependent.[70] As many as 52 percent of the members of two additional Gamblers Anonymous groups demonstrated evidence of alcohol and other drug addiction.[71] In one of these, a group of fifty females, 24 percent also considered themselves to be compulsive spenders, 20 percent admitted they were also compulsive overeaters, and 12 percent claimed to be sexually addicted.[72] Of fifty one successive males admitted for inpatient treatment for pathological gambling at the Veterans Administration Hospital in Brecksville, Ohio, nearly half (47%) met the medical criteria for chemical dependency at some time in their lives and nearly two-fifths (39%) met these criteria within the previous year.[73] A similar study reported that more than one-third (36%) of a separate group of fifty consecutively admitted male pathological gamblers were also chemically dependent (32% alcoholics; 4% drug abusers).[74] A later study of one hundred pathological gamblers admitted to this program reported that 14 percent were also diagnosed as sex addicts.[75]

In another gambling treatment center 34 percent of those enrolled also were alcoholics, 6 percent were drug addicts, and 31 percent abused both alcohol and drugs.[76] A subsequent study of prison inmates found that 30 percent of this population exhibited clear signs of pathological gambling. Of this sample population, more than half (58%) the women and nearly half (44%) the men were also alcoholics. Two-fifths of both the men (39%) and women (40%) who were drug addicts, and nearly two-thirds of the men (64%) and two-fifths (39%) of the women who were alcoholics, were also pathological gamblers.[77] A study of 136 hospitalized male pathological gamblers found that 81, or 60 percent, were also diagnosed as alcoholic.[78] Of 58 patients admitted to a pathological treatment unit in Germany 29 (50 percent) were also addicted to alcohol while another 8 (13.8%) were addicted to more than one drug; only two (3.4%) did not smoke.[79] An epidemiological survey of the general population of Edmonton, Alberta reported that 63.3 percent of those identified as pathological gamblers were also alcoholics and 23.3 percent were also drug addicts.[80] A study of 298 patients receiving treatment for cocaine abuse found that 15 percent (n=44) were also pathological gamblers. The authors noted that this frequency was ten times that reported in general population studies.[81] Likewise, of 64 veterans seeking treatment for chemical dependency, 17 percent were diagnosed as probable and 14% as potential pathological gamblers.[82] A study of 25 male and 14 female pathological gamblers receiving outpatient treatment in Minnesota found that 60 percent of both sexes also had a substance abuse or dependence disorder of some kind, the most common of which was alcoholism.[83] Similar findings have been reported by many other researchers.[84] However, some who have found no co-addictive relationship between substance abuse and pathological gambling in clinical populations have suggested that they are independent addictions.[85]

One of the more interesting studies to posit an association between problem gambling and other addictions employed an epidemiological approach: it reported that those cities in Galicia (northwestern Spain) which have the highest rates of pathological gambling also have the highest rates of addictive substance consumption.[86] However, a study of 46 patients admitted to a German gambling treatment facility suggested that substance abuse may be differentially associated with different types of gambling. Although twenty-two or nearly half (48%) of these patients were either periodic or chronic substance abusers, only two (4.3%) subjects in the entire sample were diagnosed as alcohol dependent or addicted. Nevertheless, far more slot machine players (42%) than roulette players (16%) abused alcohol while more roulette players (21%) than machine players (4%) abused pain killers or sleeping medicines after gambling.[87] While this hypothesis is intriguing, it will require further testing with larger samples.

Some findings suggest that among alcoholics and drug addicts, gambling that was once merely problematic often becomes fully pathological when they quit drinking and using drugs. For this reason one treatment specialist warns that "One should always be cautious of the recovering alcoholic who starts to gamble."[88] A previously mentioned study of incarcerated female gamblers also found an interesting pattern of drug use and gambling among these women: although the majority used these substances while they gambled, they tended to gamble less when drugs were available but to gamble more when they were not. This pattern suggested that these individuals simply alternated between drugs and gambling to satisfy a generalized addictive drive.[89] A somewhat similar pattern was reported in a study which found a low (8%) incidence of drinking among pathological gamblers before treatment but an increase in alcohol use after they had stopped gambling.[90] Similar reciprocal patterns of drug use have also been reported among substance abusers.[91]

Although the authors of some of these studies have interpreted their findings to mean that the source of all addictive and polyaddictive behaviors can be traced to the same underlying personality and/or learning factors, this same body of evidence could also point to the influence of genetic, biological, or sociocultural factors as common causes.[92] However, one medical researcher has suggested two other possibilities for this association: if gambling is primary, chemical dependency may represent the gambler's means of mustering the courage necessary to continue gambling; conversely, if chemical dependency is primary, gambling may represent the addict's means of obtaining the money necessary to continue drinking or using drugs.[93] Due to the lack of certainty, some investigators feel that further research will be required before this evidence can be considered conclusive.[94] Nevertheless, no matter what its cause may be, "multiple addiction appears to be a fact of life for many pathological gamblers."[95]

THE NATURE-NURTURE CONTROVERSY IN MENTAL HEALTH AND ADDICTION STUDIES

Developments in addiction theory appear to be based on those which have taken place in the study of other psychiatric disorders. For example, the search for the cause of schizophrenia has led to the emergence of countless theoretical explanations. However, more than a generation ago all of these approaches were seen to fall into three broad categories which were referred to as life-experience theories, monogenic-biochemical theories, and diathesis-stress theories.[96] Essentially, the first referred to explanations that attributed the disorder to environmental causes, the second to biological or genetic causes, and the third to a combination of biological and environmental influences. More specifically, diathesis-stress theory maintains that it is not the abnormality *per se* that is inherited, but merely a predisposition for it. Thus, development of the latent disorder must be triggered by a sufficiently stressful experience. Each of these major categories has its analogue in theories that attempt to explain addictive behaviors.

Despite the many different views of addiction, modern etiological or causal theories of gambling are also of several major types, each of which claims explanatory primacy. As has been the case among students of other addictions,[97] the "nature-nurture" controversy over why human beings behave as they do has not bypassed the field of gambling studies. Consequently, many researchers have tended to align themselves with one or the other of these two camps. On one hand are those who believe that all addictive behaviors are purely a matter of "nurture," or of learning and experience; on the other are those who are equally convinced that all addictions are largely a consequence of "nature," or of biology and genetically determined predisposition. It has generally been the case that most "talk therapists," behavioral psychologists, and sociologists who see these behaviors as lying along a continuum from moderate to severe align themselves with the first camp. This viewpoint assumes that, biologically, all people are basically the same and that pathological gambling and other addictive behaviors are essentially a matter of degree commensurate with one's life experiences. Conversely, medical professionals who endorse the precepts of biopsychiatry and biopharmacology tend to favor the second approach since they regard addicts as qualitatively (physiologically and/or genetically) different from social or occasional participants in these behaviors. Members of Gamblers Anonymous, Alcoholics Anonymous, and other self-help groups which have come into being to provide help and understanding for addicts of all kinds also tend to regard addictions as organically-based illnesses.

The strength of the convictions of some of those in either camp that theirs is the only valid approach sometimes borders on the religious. It has therefore been suggested that

> The most serious problem of definition seems to be its usual sequel–an attempt to provide **the** explanation of gambling, that is to seek a single underlying process, mechanism, set of factors or whatever that accounts for gambling in all its manifestations. This is a well known state of affairs in Psychology, and can often be misguided.[98]

For this reason gambling researchers have been warned that theories can act as perceptual filters which serve to limit our research and treatment options: exclusive adherence to any single theory can not only lead to misconceptions concerning the nature of gambling but can also blind one to the value of any other approach.[99] More recently, therefore, a number of researchers and clinicians from both camps have begun to regard addiction as the consequence of a combination of environmental and biological influences.

SCIENTIFIC APPROACHES

Whether "it" is merely a form of entertainment, a habit, an impulse disorder, a form of physiological dependence, a combination of these factors, or something else entirely has yet to be decided. Nevertheless, in the face of this confusion a number of scientific approaches to gambling and pathological gambling have emerged.

Most theories seeking to explain pathological gambling define it as symptomatic of either a sick mind, a sick body, or a sick society; more recent approaches attribute it to various combinations of these causes. One of the earliest and most persistent theoretical explanations for pathological gambling is the psychoanalytic, psychodynamic, or Freudian model which regards all addictions, including pathological gambling, as a deep-seated intrapsychic or basic personality problem.[100] Learning, behavioral, or reinforcement models regard all behaviors, whether excessive or not, as a matter of learning or habituation and explain persistent gambling in terms of rewards, reinforcements, and learned associations.[101] Cognitive psychological models explain gambling persistence as a consequence of the erroneous beliefs gamblers have about gambling and the false hopes they have about their ability to win.[102] The sociological, environmental, or subcultural model postulates that all potentially addictive behaviors, whether "normal" or pathological, result from the temporary pleasure, satisfaction, or relief they provide the participant in the face of stressful crisis situations,[103] or as the result of social expectations where such behaviors are accepted and encouraged.[104] The medical, disease, or physiological model seeks the cause in human biology.[105] The most recent multicausal, multifactorial, or biopsychosocial, approach attributes pathological gambling and other addictive disorders to various combinations of endogenous and exogenous factors.[106]

Statistical models employ mathematical methods for measuring and ascertaining the nature and extent of various behaviors including normative and pathological gambling. Some statistical studies such as prevalence surveys are primarily descriptive in nature since they focus almost exclusively on the frequencies of these behaviors in a given population.[107] Others such as risk factor analyses are primarily correlational in that they attempt to ascertain which psychological, personality, demographic, social, and other environmental variables are associated with these behaviors and may therefore be considered at least partially responsible for them.[108] Still other statistical studies are undertaken to test hypotheses that have been advanced by others.[109]

The general features of each of these approaches and a number of specific examples will be reviewed in this series. Many of these theories will strike the reader as highly plausible, some as questionable, and others as patently ludicrous. Since each of these approaches has had its vociferous and highly persuasive champions, all competing with one another to attract the greatest number of adherents, all have at one time or another gained wide but often uncritical acceptance as entirely valid explanations. Consequently, many of the more popular theories, as well as some of the research studies designed to test them, will also be critically examined to point out some of their more obvious weaknesses and strengths.

The goal of this endeavor is to draw the reader's attention to the many divergent explanations that have been proposed to account for both moderate and immoderate gambling and, hopefully, to equip the reader to avoid some of the hazards of blind adherence to any single approach. It will be seen that gambling theorists can be every bit as partisan and intolerant of opposing viewpoints as any politician or preacher. In the past the explanations of many were derived almost exclusively from the precepts of their own particular field. Thus, behavioral scientists tended to look for and find answers to the phenomena they investigated in psychological maladaptations, social scientists attributed theirs to various social forces, and medical scientists contended that biological factors lay at the heart of these matters. As a consequence, many specialists were often reluctant to see any value in those coming from any other discipline. Fortunately, however, recent years have seen a move away from such parochialism.

A NOTE ON GENDER BIAS

The male orientated gender bias which has tended to dominate gambling research, particularly in its earlier days, has been justifiably criticized.[110] Apparently, many early clinicians, researchers, and other authorities believed either that most women avoided potentially addictive behaviors, or that they were somehow immune to many addictive disorders, or that the occurrence of these disorders among women was so rare as to be negligible. In fact, one early psychologist and gambling researcher reflected the strong gender bias of his day by attributing the differences he observed in the willingness of young males and females to take risks to their inherent evolutionary biological differences:

> The fact that the boys' curve rises, as the ages approach those of maturity, we believe to be in line with the general biological thesis of the male being the more iconoclastic, exploiting and venturesome element, while the fact, that the curve of the girls falls, is, on the other hand, in line with the biological thesis, that woman is the conservative and cautious element.[111]

In reality, as many women gamble as men. Although women tend to gamble less frequently than men overall, certain forms of gambling such as electronic machines attract high-frequency gamblers in equal numbers from both sexes[112] while bingo and video poker machines appear to be particularly attractive to women. Moreover, population studies have determined that at least one-third of all pathological gamblers are women.[113] In Las Vegas, the traditional gambling capital of the United States, more than half the members of Gamblers Anonymous are women.[114] Nevertheless, the gender bias of many gambling researchers, particularly those of earlier generations, will be reflected in the extensive use of male pronouns throughout much of the discussion. This bias has been retained so that the original tenor of the ideas, perspectives, and thought processes of the various theoreticians under discussion might be more accurately conveyed.

INTRODUCTION TO THIS VOLUME

The present volume focuses on the various motivational theories that have been advanced by specialists in the psychological sciences, most of whom are convinced that gambling is a consequence of the gambler's individual life experiences. Psychoanalytic theory, the brainchild of Sigmund Freud, is probably the most complex explanation for human behavior that has ever been conceived. Nevertheless, psychoanalytic theory dominated psychological thought throughout much of the twentieth century. Many psychoanalytically-based explanations for gambling have been proposed, all of which trace the motivation for gambling and other maladaptive behaviors to one or more unconsciously felt sources of guilt stemming from some traumatic emotional experience in infancy or early childhood. Although this once highly popular approach has not yet been relegated to the scrap heap of history, it has been superseded by developments in behavioral and cognitive psychology.

Personality theorists are closely aligned with the psychoanalysts. In general, personality theorists contend that gambling represents a coping mechanism for those who are either born with or develop a particular basic personality type, or who possess a particular constellation of personality traits. They have subjected countless gamblers to an array of standardized psychometric tests in their efforts to discover which basic personality traits are peculiar to the gambler.

The explanations of various learning theorists began to supplant those of the psychoanalysts in the middle of the twentieth century. Following the lead of such pioneers as I. P. Pavlov and B. F. Skinner, today's learning theorists continue to explore the processes through which such behavioral responses as gambling and drinking are reinforced and maintained through the influence of certain rewards and associations.

Cognitive psychology, a relatively recent development, explains gambling behavior and persistence as a consequence of flawed thinking and erroneous beliefs about the gambler's ability to win. This approach is rapidly growing in popularity as it continues to attract ever increasing numbers of adherents.

Part I

PSYCHODYNAMIC APPROACHES

The Role of Early Childhood Experiences

1

PSYCHOANALYTIC THEORY: EARLY VIEWS

Psychoanalytic theorists have always thought of excessive gambling as a disease or pathology, but not of the body: it indicates a psychopathology or disease of the mind. Psychoanalytic theory was developed in the late nineteenth and early twentieth centuries by the renowned Viennese physician Sigmund Freud,[1] most of whose ideas are based only on a relatively small number of clinical observations and a great deal of speculation. Nevertheless, throughout the first half of the twentieth century, Freud's explanations for human behavior attracted a very large following and permeated both the behavioral and social sciences.

Few psychoanalytic theorists bothered to distinguish between normal or social gambling of the kind enjoyed by the vast majority of people and abnormal compulsive or "neurotic" gambling of the kind that affects only a small minority of gamblers. Consequently, many psychoanalysts viewed all manifestations of gambling in the same way. The essence of all psychoanalytic approaches to gambling has been crystallized in a single sentence: "Compulsive gambling is a symptom of a mental disease caused by an intense feeling of inferiority and inadequacy."[2] However, the explanations proposed by various theorists are far more elaborate than this simple statement suggests.

General Assumptions

Psychoanalytic theory is characterized by several fundamental general–and generally untestable, therefore, undemonstrable and indefensible–assumptions, all of which have been thought to play their part in the development of compulsive or pathological gambling. In order to appreciate the individual psychoanalytic theories that will be discussed, at least a rudimentary understanding of these ideas is necessary. Their brief discussion below will make them more recognizable when they are encountered in the individual theories that follow.

One fundamental assumption of psychoanalytic theory is that much of the activity of the human mind takes place subliminally, at the level of unconsciousness, so that the individual has no discernable knowledge of it. According to the psychoanalysts, this means that gamblers themselves are often entirely unaware of their own "true" motivations for gambling.

A second basic assumption is the existence of a "collective unconscious" or "racial memory," that part of the unconscious mind which is thought to contain certain biologically inherited memories. Freud was convinced that much of human behavior was instinctive[3] and most of his contemporaries adopted this position. They therefore felt that all members of the human species share genetically transmitted sets of unconscious memories which originated in the experiences of our earliest human ancestors and have been handed down to all subsequent generations ever since. The seat of this racial memory, the *id*, stores all our baser instincts and bestial impulses which are responsible for our neurotic conflicts and the intense guilt feelings they can generate. Another part of the unconscious, the *superego*, is the seat of the conscience where all parental admonitions and social conventions, instilled to counteract the instinctive, antisocial id impulses, are housed. It is these internalizations that plague the individual with guilt whenever one of the id impulses threatens to surface and a breach of parental teachings is contemplated.

Freud regarded mythology, particularly that of ancient Greece, as a window into the human phylogenetic past. He obtained the idea of the Oedipus complex, for example, from the Greek myth of the Theban king of that name who unwittingly killed his father, then married, cohabited with, and had children with his own mother. Freud assumed that this myth embodied the racial memory of a devastating human family trauma that had actually occurred at some point in our distant ancestral past. According to Freud,[4] our earliest male progenitors must have committed the genuine original sin when, in a jealous rage, they actually did kill the archetypal tribal patriarch and took his women, their own mothers, for themselves. The psychological trauma and guilt resulting from these avowed parricidal and incestuous acts was so intense, Freud insisted, that they became deeply etched into the human collective unconscious and have plagued each new generation ever since. Of course, no real evidence whatsoever exists to support this fantastic scenario or any other mythical family drama that has ever been contrived to explain modern human behavior. Nevertheless, since mythology was believed to reveal the contents of the putative collective unconscious, Freud and his followers eagerly seized upon such "evidence" as proof of their theoretical formulations. In the words of one of his early disciples, "The deeper psycho-analysis penetrates into the knowledge of social-psychological productions (myths, fairy-tales, folklore), the stronger becomes the confirmation of the phylogenetic origin of symbols, which stand out as a precipitate of the experiences of previous generations."[5] As will be shown, a number of committed psychoanalysts have argued that the passion some people have for gambling is a direct consequence of this archaic source of guilt.

A third assumption is the notion of infantile sexuality, the belief that strong sexual sensations and Oedipal desires are experienced even in infancy and early childhood. According to Freud and other psychoanalytic theorists, infants derive sexual pleasure when certain parts of the body are stimulated. These "erogenous zones" include the lips and anus as well as the genitals.

A fourth fundamental assumption of psychoanalytic theory is that nearly all mental illnesses or neuroses can be traced to some childhood trauma, generally involving the frustration of specific libidinous or sexual impulses associated with one or more of the erogenous zones. Freud assumed that in the course of maturation, all human beings pass through a series of psychosexual or libidinal developmental stages, each of which can profoundly influence later personality development. The *oral* stage is associated with breast feeding which is synonymous with acceptance and love, and weaning which is equated with the rejection and the withholding of love. The *anal* stage is associated with defecation which is believed to provide anal-erotic gratification and toilet training which involves frustration of and punishment for an uncontrolled eliminative drive. The *phallic* stage is associated with the child's discovery of the genitals and the pleasurable sensations obtained from them during infantile "masturbatory" activities. Then, from about the age of four or five to puberty, children experience a sexual *latency* period during which all libidinous urges lie dormant. Finally, the *genital* stage is associated with the onset of puberty and the emergence of the adult sex drive. Any psychological trauma that is experienced in association with any of these stages can result in an arrested or "fixated" personality development.

The child's first truly libidinous or sexually oriented id impulses, the well-known Oedipus and Electra complexes, are normally directed toward the parent of the opposite sex. In essence, psychoanalytic theory postulates that Oedipal feelings arise during the phallic stage of psychosexual development from the unconsciously harbored desires of all young boys to eliminate the father and possess the mother–sexually and otherwise–for themselves. At the same time, however, they love and admire the father and want to emulate him. Since no child can have it both ways, all young boys are torn by the intense ambivalent emotions of love and hatred that they feel for their fathers. Normally, a boy eventually realizes that if he ever does attempt to eliminate and replace his father he will be punished by castration at the hands of his much larger and stronger rival. To preserve his masculinity he abandons these childish wishes and the Oedipal conflict is resolved. However, if a boy does not eventually outgrow or resolve the desires and conflicts that are aroused by his infantile sexual fantasies, his personality development will become fixated at the phallic stage and his Oedipal desires and fantasies will persist into adolescence and adulthood. Since desires of this sort are socially reprehensible and shameful, he will be plagued with severe though unconsciously felt guilt feelings for the rest of his life–guilt which some men, it has been proposed, attempt to expiate through the losses they sustain while gambling.

Although the circumstances under which personality development becomes arrested at any stage may vary, the basic psychoanalytic formula employed to explain any fixation or regressive neurosis is nearly always the same. As children mature, their narcissistic demands for immediate gratification of their own wants, desires, and id impulses are thwarted by parental interference. Denied the immediate gratification they previously enjoyed or are just beginning to experience, they become enraged at their parent(s) whom they soon grow to hate as well as love. In the process of normal maturation and socialization, children will abandon their infantile desires and conform to those of their parents, thereby resolving any emotional conflicts. Sometimes, however, in cases of arrested development, a child is unable to relinquish his own wishes and "work through" his feelings of ambivalence. The emotional conflicts that persist into adulthood are thought to arouse strong feelings of anxiety and guilt with which the neurotic attempts to cope in any of a number of maladaptive ways. Psychoanalysts therefore believe that the particular stage at which the personality development of adult neurotics became fixated is revealed in their language and repetitive behaviors, such as compulsive hand washing, drinking, or gambling, and sometimes even in their everyday occupations and the jargon they entail.

A fifth basic assumption of psychoanalytic theory is that all human beings are born inherently bisexual. They have the potential to become either heterosexual or homosexual depending on the particular environmental influences to which they are exposed during the childhood socialization process. Normally, with maturity and proper socialization, this poses no problems in later life since the inappropriate tendencies are successfully repressed as the appropriate sexual orientation is being learned. However, developmentally fixated individuals often fail to repress their inherent homosexual tendencies completely. In later life these dormant tendencies can then surface in a variety of ways ranging from the expression of latent or unconscious, to blatant homosexuality.

Depending on their particular way of dealing with the Oedipal situation, some boys will follow an entirely different course of development. In most cases, when they are faced with the father's hatred and possible castration that their rivalry for the mother's affection threatens, boys will normally abandon their Oedipal wishes and parricidal fantasies as they begin to identify with and emulate the fathers. In some cases, however, a boy will choose to alter his sexual orientation and allow the feminine side of his personality to surface. This abnormal response is believed to represent a maladaptive effort to regain the affections of the father by identifying with and emulating the mother whom the father loves because of her femininity. Those who experience this confusion in sexual orientation will begin to encourage and exhibit, rather than deny and repress, the homosexual tendencies that all children are supposed to feel. In these cases, any later attempts to re-identify with the father will be profoundly affected by this early experience. For example, psychoanalysts believe that if the father was a harsh, demanding, brutal, and sadistic disciplinarian, the feminine passivity that was poorly repressed in childhood will resurface as a masochistic need for punishment in adulthood. Psychoanalytic theorists hold that many of the emotional disorders that emerge in adulthood can be traced to this biologically based infantile bisexuality, the homosexual side of which was unsuccessfully or incompletely repressed in childhood. Thus, many psychoanalysts have come to believe that compulsive gambling, despite severe losses, constitutes proof of the gambler's early feminine identification and presently latent homosexuality.

Finally, a sixth fundamental assumption of psychoanalytic theory involves the phenomenon of sublimation, the substitution of covertly desired but socially unacceptable behaviors with overt activities that are similar but more socially and culturally acceptable. For example, mature adults might vent their frustrations on a punching bag instead of another person. However, psychoanalysts generally use the term in reference to neurotic immature expressions of the various id instincts. In times of stress, they contend, a seemingly mature personality can regress to an earlier developmental stage during which any unresolved libidinal impulses are sublimated, "acted out," and satisfied in a variety of alternative ways. Psychoanalysts have therefore explained alcoholism as the manifestation of an oral fixation brought about by the trauma of weaning: the bottle is thought to be a symbolic substitute for the mother's breast, the beverage represents her milk, and the state of intoxication is equated with the gratification of a full stomach.[6] Some explanations, involving substitutions of substitutions, are even more convoluted. Thus, alcoholism has also been explained as an overt manifestation of latent male homosexual tendencies: the bottle represents the penis which, in turn, is actually a substitute for the mother's breast[7] while the beverage represents the ejaculate which, in turn, is said to be substitute for the mother's milk.[8] Since the entire psychodynamic process is said to take place unconsciously, neurotics would never be aware of their underlying feelings and motivations, or that their overt behaviors are actually sublimated expressions of their poorly repressed id impulses. The ideas of a number of influential psychoanalysts are summarized below. It will be seen that many of them saw gambling–both normal and pathological–as a substitute for other secretly desired but socially reprehensible behaviors and attributed it to the same underlying psychodynamic processes.

Hans Von Hattingberg: A Pioneering Effort

Even before Freud offered his own explanation for gambling, some his followers had anticipated a number of their mentor's ideas and pronouncements. The earliest known psychoanalytic treatment of gambling was undertaken by Hans Von Hattingberg[9] who suggested that the fear, tension, and anxiety that always accompany gambling make it a libidinous or sexually pleasurable activity, and that inadequate psychosexual functioning is therefore its most fundamental cause. Although his original writings have never been translated, Von Hattingberg's contributions have been outlined by numerous reviewers. One of the more comprehensive summaries of his ideas was that of psychiatrist Richard Rosenthal[10] who attributed several distinct lines of later psychoanalytic thought on the subject to Von Hattingberg's seminal explorations.[11]

In typical psychoanalytic fashion, Von Hattingberg traced the love of gambling to a personality fixation at an early pregenital stage of psychosexual development. For Von Hattingberg this was the crucial toilet training period during which an infant's previously unchecked eliminative functions of urination and defecation are for the first time met with disapproval and punishment at the hands of the parents. In adulthood, gambling becomes a maladaptive means of coping with the anger and guilt engendered by the frustration of these childish eliminative desires.

Freud,[12] Von Hattingberg, and other psychoanalytic theorists,[13] contended that infants derive autoerotic pleasure from the acts of urination and defecation. They believed that children like to hold their urine and feces and delay elimination until such time as they can derive the greatest urethral- and anal-erotic pleasure from their forceful, explosive expulsion. Afterward, in the case of defecation, they derive additional pleasure from manipulating and playing with the soft, warm mass. In the mind of the psychoanalyst, then, the infant's retention of the feces constitutes a form of anal masturbation, the act of defecation is an anal-orgasmic experience, and the feces itself, an early love-object, represents every individual's first "savings" and first "toy." Those who advocated this approach maintained that during the toilet training and socialization processes, the socially unacceptable childish interest in defecation and feces is discouraged and repressed but it never really disappears: in adulthood it is merely replaced by an equally intense obsessive interest in acquiring money, hoarding it, and enjoying the things it will buy. Gambling, as one way of acquiring and playing with money, is therefore merely a sublimation of the early narcissistic drive for anal-erotic gratification which, in the anally-fixated neurotic, becomes compulsive.

Since unrestricted elimination is forcefully and painfully checked in childhood, gambling, an activity in which the flow of money is unrestricted, becomes for the adult a more appropriate substitute for this previously pleasurable childhood experience. Nevertheless, since gambling is unconsciously equated with elimination, gamblers also view it as an aggressively rebellious act directed against their authoritarian parents who had originally denied them their infantile eliminative pleasures. For this reason, gambling is also fraught with strong feelings of guilt for this act of willful disobedience and fear of parental chastisement for this unacceptable behavior. Von Hattingberg therefore concluded that the eroticization of gambling stems from the participants' inherent masochism, or the pleasure they derive from fear of the anticipated punishment they will receive. As Rosenthal[14] observed, Von Hattingberg's notions that gambling is a substitute for sexual behavior, that it represents a developmental fixation which can be traced to elimination and toilet training, and that it is a manifestation of the gambler's inherent masochism was embraced, elaborated, and elucidated by a number of later writers, including Freud himself.

Ernst Simmel: An Anal-Erotic Manifestation of Dependency Conflict

Perhaps no other psychoanalytic theorist carried psychoanalytical speculation on addiction to such extremes as Ernst Simmel[15] who saw in it evidence of several pregenital traits. For the alcoholic, Simmel claimed, drinking represents unfulfilled orally aggressive cannibalistic urges, masturbatory needs, Oedipal longings, and homosexual tendencies, all of which were said to be universally felt id impulses. Because of their strong unpalatable taste, he ventured, the beverages the alcoholic ingests represent "the wishful fantasies of urinating and defecating into one's own mouth."[16] Simmel was equally fervent in his assessment of the gambling addiction which he, like Von Hattingberg, interpreted as a fixation at the anal stage of psychosexual development. It should be noted that Simmel's ideas on the causes of gambling were founded on a single case history.

Pathological gambling, Simmel proclaimed, is a manifestation of a repressed anal-erotic narcissistic bisexual wish-fulfillment fantasy in which the gambler acts out his unresolved dependency needs. Like Von Hattingberg, Simmel explained gambling in terms of anal-autoeroticism. Furthermore, if gambling is the sublimated expression of an unresolved anal fixation, then the money that is used in gambling is the symbolic equivalent of feces. Thus, the act of gambling constitutes stimulation (anal-masturbation), winning is equated with orgasm, and losing represents both castration and defecation (giving up the feces). In Simmel's interpretation the continuous exchange of money through winning and losing has tremendous additional significance: it represents the gambler's unconscious desire to impregnate himself anally, to give birth to himself anally, and to nurture himself anally. In this way, he maintained, the gambler fancifully eliminates parental involvement and interference, thereby revealing his unfulfilled desire for independence.[17]

While Von Hattingberg saw gambling as an expression of the gambler's masochistic desires, Simmel saw it as an expression of sadism as well as masochism. For him the gambler's unconscious wish to eliminate the parents was proof enough of his anal-sadistic tendencies. Simmel also interpreted the symbolic replacement through gambling of both the mother and the father as evidence of the gambler's inherent bisexual nature. However, since Freud had attributed criminality to unconscious masochistic desires for punishment, Simmel did likewise when he interpreted the criminal activities that some gamblers pursue as their means of obtaining punishment from a vindictive father figure who appears in the guise of a stern, reproachful judge. Neurotic dependency conflict has also been proposed as an explanation for alcoholism[18] though not as a manifestation of an anal fixation.

Wilhelm Stekel: Escape, Excitement, Latent Homosexuality, and Sadism

Other early psychoanalysts, while not so zealous or extreme, nevertheless continued to promulgate these ideas. Wilhelm Stekel,[19] for example, also saw similarities between the "gambling mania" and alcoholism since, in his view, both are motivated by escapism, regression to childhood, exhibitionism, power concerns, and various id impulses including repressed sexuality, latent homosexuality, sadism, and fantasies of incest. However, Stekel's analyses were far more superficial than those of other psychoanalysts.

Stekel distinguished the "real gambler," for whom gambling represents "a flight to another realm," from the "professional player" who is "not a gambler in the true sense of the word."[20] The real gambler plays only for the sake of playing and not for monetary gain; for him gambling is "a disease."[21] The professional gambler plays only for money and not for recreation; for him gambling is a livelihood. Stekel described the gambling mania as a form of paraphilia, the love of play. The predisposition to gamble, Stekel believed, was therefore universally shared by all people as it represents a regression to childhood during which the gambler can temporarily avoid all adult cares and responsibilities. Artists, he maintained, often fall victim to the gambling mania since they already "dwell in a make-believe realm" and "are always prone to exchange play and reality."[22]

He also anticipated a number of the ideas of later interactional theorists when he wrote that gambling allows an individual to reveal his hidden qualities. Like alcohol, it enables all gamblers to exhibit the repressed character traits they secretly harbor but ordinarily conceal from public scrutiny. Thus, gambling represents "a fight for one's personality, for the supremacy of one's selfhood, for superiority"[23] when there are no other ways of doing so. Stekel felt that the hidden personality fantasies of most gamblers are grandiose in nature and that card playing in particular has the ability to transform even the humblest of clerks and most henpecked of husbands into brilliant, courageous, and similarly outstanding individuals.

Stekel was the first to recognize the ability of gambling to produce alternating emotional states. Man's "craving for excitement" and need for "tension and release," he claimed,[24] lies at the heart of the gambling mania since it arouses intense feelings of expectation, hope, and joy as well as severe disappointment, humiliation, and anxiety. Owing to the uncertainty that gambling entails, "It is a play with fear. Depressive and manic states succeed one another."[25] The ability of gambling to reduce tension as well as to induce states of emotional arousal or "affect intoxication"[26] were taken up and elucidated by later behavioral psychologists.

He was also the first to highlight the gambler's faith in superstitious beliefs and ritualistic behaviors, points which were elaborated by later cognitive psychologists. Good luck, which is "appraised as a personal merit,"[27] is believed to be granted by supernatural powers who are thought to favor the better man. However, gamblers often attempt to influence the outcome of a game by appealing to these supernaturals through prayers and other superstitious rituals in which gambling paraphernalia become fetishes: "The dice are treated as living things, they are kissed, praised, and punished."[28] Moreover, since winning is taken as a sign of supernatural favor, many gamblers interpret the outcome of a game as an "oracle" or predictor of future events and tell themselves, "If you win this game, you will attain also your other secret wish."[29] Stekel felt that the gambler's superstitious behaviors and other mannerisms–including speech, tics, motions, habits, and eternal optimism even in the face of heavy losses–are all indications of a basic infantile nature. Stekel's idea that gambling represents a childish challenge to Fate itself may well have been influenced by a description of Fyodor Dostoevsky, the noted Russian novelist who was himself a compulsive gambler, of some of the emotions he had personally experienced while gambling:

> I think I must have picked up about four thousand gulden in five minutes or so. This is where I should have quit, but some kind of strange sensation built up in me, a kind of challenge to fate, a kind of desire to give it a flick on the nose, or stick my tongue out at it. I placed the largest bet allowed, four thousand gulden, and lost. Then flushed with my loss, I took out all the money I still had left, staked it on the same spot, and lost again, after which I walked away from the table stunned. I actually couldn't comprehend that it was I to whom this had happened. . . .[30]

As will be seen, the ideas that Fate is an oracle which is challenged through gambling was to become quite popular among later psychoanalytic theorists.[31]

Like Freud, Von Hattingberg, and others, however, Stekel saw the expression of sublimated sexuality as the most important aspect of gambling. This view was quite common among psychoanalysts of the time since some of their disciples and colleagues compared each phase of betting to an analogous phase of sexual stimulation.[32] One of them expressed his unqualified agreement in such statements as, "To win is to achieve an orgasm, to attain the potent manhood of ejaculation."[33] Dostoevsky himself came close to doing in a particularly poignant passage:

> fear cast its spell over me . . . for with horror I realized that I must win, and that upon that stake there depended all my life. "Rouge" called the croupier. I drew a long breath, and hot shivers went coursing over my body.[34]

In Stekel's view, money symbolizes love since it provides the means of obtaining and holding love. As evidence, he cited "the well-known fact that persons who are really in love lose all interest in games."[35] Conversely, he noted that many people who are unlucky in love find consolation in gambling. As one disciple put it: "The expression 'lucky in cards, unlucky in love,' is a striking testimonial to the fact that neurotics with unresolved conflicts regarding homo- and heterosexuality find gambling an appropriate outlet for their frustrations."[36] A more recent psychiatrist also asserted that "it is a clinical fact that some compulsive gamblers suffer from potency disturbances; others, although capable of performance, seem relatively uninterested in sex."[37] But because even married gamblers spend so much time at gaming houses in the company of other men rather than at home with their wives, Stekel postulated that latent homosexual desires must be one of the primary motivations for gambling. By the same token, gamblers who are also womanizers are "disguised homosexuals" since they are merely masking their true (though unconsciously harbored) homosexual inclinations through their sexual conquests of women.[38]

Stekel was convinced that even the paraphernalia and language employed by gamblers constituted proof of their unconscious desires and motivations. For card players, he insisted, "Every card is already linked with certain cryptic unconscious thoughts, which find current expression in the art of laying out the cards."[39] Card players reveal their inherent sadistic nature by "cutting" cards, "mixing" the deck, and "beating" their opponents. Sadism is also apparent in the joy that all gamblers take in the losses suffered by others.[40] Stekel's only evidence for the incestuous desires with which he charged all gamblers was derived from a single case history in which one of his patients, a man who was disinterested in sex with his unfaithful wife and who happened to be a gambler, obtained his most gratifying sexual experiences while masturbating with his sister's and mother's used underwear. Nevertheless, like so many of his other ideas, these notions were also adopted and developed by later writers.

Sigmund Freud: Unfulfilled Oedipal Desires

Although Freud was the principal architect of psychoanalytic theory, his own explanation for gambling appeared after those of some of his disciples. When Freud encountered compulsive gambling in the life and work of Fyodor Dostoevsky he looked to his earlier ideas on infantile sexuality to explain the phenomenon. In a letter to a friend and colleague written in 1897, Freud expressed the opinion that "masturbation is the one great habit that is a 'primary addiction,' and that the other addictions . . . only enter into life as a substitute and replacement for it."[41] Later psychoanalysts continued to explain all addictions as direct or indirect substitutes for sexual satisfaction and even today some contemporary psychoanalysts persist in regarding masturbation as an "addiction."[42]

In the case of Dostoevsky, Freud[43] was particularly struck by the observation that although the epileptic novelist repeatedly promised his young wife that he would quit soon or never gamble again, his promises were inevitably broken. Freud noted further that Dostoevsky was never more productive than when he had lost all his money, pawned all his possessions, and was completely destitute. In a letter to a friend, Dostoevsky had once indicated that he was not driven to gamble so much by the need for money, though he could certainly use it, as by the thrill of the "play" itself. Thus, Freud did not see gambling as a quest for money, but for what is now commonly referred to as "action."

Freud, seeing a causal relationship between Dostoevsky's masochistically self-destructive behavior and his subsequent brilliant creativity, was convinced that this association must originate in a deeply unconscious part of the mind. Because Dostoevsky's gambling always resulted in his near ruin, Freud reasoned that "For him gambling was a method of self-punishment."[44] He therefore postulated that the damage that inevitably resulted from gambling must arise from deep-seated, pervasive, anxiety-arousing guilt feelings which at other times interfered with the author's innate artistic and expressive abilities: "When his sense of guilt was satisfied by the punishments he had inflicted upon himself, the inhibitions on his work became less severe and he allowed himself to take a few steps along the road to success."[45]

When the question arose as to what might be the cause of so much guilt, psychoanalytic theory, with its emphasis on infantile sexuality, provided a ready answer: the secret is revealed in the gambler's use of the hands. The activity of the hands in gambling, Freud reasoned, must act as a substitute for some previously gratifying though tremendously guilt-laden experience. In the case of compulsive gambling, he ventured, the source of these guilt feelings can be traced to the act of masturbation in childhood:

> The "vice" of masturbation is replaced by the mania for gambling; and the emphasis

> laid upon the passionate activity of the hands betrays that derivation. The passion for play is an equivalent of the old compulsion to masturbate; "playing" is the actual word used in the nursery to describe the activity of the hands on the genitals. The irresistible nature of the temptation, the solemn resolutions, which are nevertheless invariably broken, never to do it again, the numbing pleasure and the bad conscience which tells the subject he is ruining himself, (committing suicide)–all these elements remain unaltered in the process of substitution.[46]

In their efforts to emulate and even transcend the insights of their mentor, many of Freud's later disciples developed this idea even further. In their own psychoanalytic interpretations of gambling, some compared "the superficial resemblance of this rhythmical, repetitive series of tension, excitement, and subsequent discharge with the foreplay, crescendo, and ejaculatory release of masturbation and sexual intercourse."[47] Another saw sublimated masturbatory activity not only in those who actually "play" the horses or "play" the stock market,[48] but also in those who are employed in these arenas: "The masturbatory use of the hands in a gambling situation can readily be seen in the manual language of racing's 'tic-tac' signalling code and the complex finger-talk of commodity speculators in the broking exchanges."[49] Thus, according to one of his more enthusiastic disciples, "Freud's remarkable discovery relating masturbation to gambling stands unimpeachable."[50]

Although the act of masturbation itself was thought to provide an important source of guilt and anxiety at the conscious level, Freud located the primary source at the unconscious level in the incestuous masturbatory fantasies and parricidal death wishes that invariably accompany the Oedipal situation. Freud ventured that Dostoevsky's unconscious death wishes and ensuing guilt would have been especially strong since his father was an uncommonly domineering, violent, and sadistic man who he would have been most eager to replace. Freud then postulated a causal association between the strength of Dostoevsky's Oedipal guilt feelings and his epileptic episodes which, like masturbation, he also regarded as a mechanism for the discharge of excessive instinctive sexual energy.

In the Freudian view, then, gambling is displaced masturbation. Since the act of masturbation in infancy was always accompanied by incestuous fantasies and parricidal death wishes, it was also accompanied by intense feelings of guilt. Normally, these desires and emotions are put aside and all memory of them is repressed and forgotten as children grow up. However, this is not the case among those who were unable to "work through" the Oedipal situation. For them, the act of gambling in adulthood, which is merely a thinly disguised sublimation of masturbation, dredges up the same poorly repressed Oedipal memories, desires, and attendant guilt feelings that they experienced in childhood. Neurotic or compulsive gambling, as an uncontrollable passion for this kind of "play," is therefore symptomatic of a fixation at the phallic stage of psychosexual development. It is held to be an overt manifestation of the intolerably stressful guilt- and anxiety-arousing covert intrapsychic situation that accompanies an unresolved Oedipal conflict. In the words of Ralph Greenson, another of Freud's more ardent disciples,

> The unconscious fantasies of the neurotic gambler are identical with the masturbation fantasies of the individual and are responsible in part for the guilt feelings in regard to gambling. Masturbation and gambling both start out as play. A play begins as an attempt

> to discharge tension in regulated dosage at a specific time. In masturbation and gambling, the stirring up of unconscious oedipus fantasies destroys the playful character of the act. The ego is overwhelmed by anxiety and guilt, and what started out as play is no longer play or pleasurable, but becomes a threat to mental equilibrium. . . . The forbidden nature of the fantasies stirred up in gambling are responsible for the fact that these fantasies must be maintained in repression.[51]

In his attempt to expiate these intense (though unconscious) feelings of guilt through masochistic self-punishment, Freud ventured, the gambler plays not to win but to lose. As noted, gambling arouses the same forbidden sexual desires and fantasies that were felt in childhood and generates the same strong guilt feelings that infantile masturbation aroused. However, through the losses it entails, neurotic gambling also provides a means of atoning for these transgressions and expiating the guilt. He took this line of reasoning even further when he insisted, "we find no cases of severe neurosis in which the autoerotic satisfaction of early childhood and puberty has not played a part."[52] Freud attracted many disciples, some of whom carried his ideas far beyond anything he had originally intended.

Otto Fenichel: Father Fate and Lady Luck, Sublimated Parental Figures

Somewhat later Otto Fenichel,[53] another prominent psychoanalyst, also explained habitual gambling as a fixation at the phallic stage of psychosexual development. Like others before him, Fenichel attributed the apparently self-destructive activity of uncontrollable gambling to the unconscious masturbatory and parricidal fantasies that produce the feelings of guilt which underlie an intense, masochistic need for self-punishment. However, rather than view it as an obsessive-compulsive disorder, he saw it as an impulse disorder. The difference is that obsessive-compulsive people obtain no enjoyment from their behavior but see it as a burden they would like to eliminate but cannot; conversely, those with impulse disorders find them pleasurable and exciting and do not want to give them up. While the gambler dislikes losing, he thoroughly enjoys the act of gambling.[54]

Fenichel enlarged somewhat upon the ideas of his predecessors by comparing the excitement of gambling to sexual arousal (sublimated masturbation), of winning to orgasm and the symbolic killing of the father (Oedipal victory), and of losing to punishment by castration or death at the hands of the father (Oedipal defeat involving the imagined punishments which allegedly threaten all young boys should their hidden desires be discovered).[55] Although he acknowledged his predecessors' anal-erotic components to gambling and the symbolic association between money and feces, he declined to elaborate on their importance.

Fenichel went on to describe the apparent narcissistic personality characteristics exhibited by many compulsive gamblers. This quality was thought to be evident in the gambler's expectation of winning despite the statistical odds against it. According to a later colleague, the first thing one notices about gamblers is their sense of false optimism: gamblers are convinced that "things will work out because it is important that they work out."[56] These unrealistic expectations were thought to be sustained by the belief that through gambling one can contend with and ultimately triumph over Fate, which for the gambler, Fenichel maintained, symbolizes a powerful father figure and chief rival for the mother's affections and sexual favors. Fenichel was clearly influenced by Stekel in this matter.

He also saw Fate as an oracle through which the gambler attempts to divine by winning whether his playing (i.e., sublimated masturbation and incestuous Oedipal fantasies) will be deemed acceptable to, and therefore rewarded by, this ultimate father surrogate or whether it will be judged unacceptable and punished by loss (i.e., symbolic castration).[57] One of Fenichel's contemporaries took this line of reasoning several steps further when he described the gambler's mental masturbation as a paradoxical situation having no possible resolution: both winning and losing are fraught with conflict since both result in psychic victory and defeat. Should the gambler win it means that his secret incestuous desires are approved and rewarded but also that he is then culpable of the unconscious murder of his father. Thus, while he gains psychic omnipotence he must suffer the guilt of psychic parricide. Should he lose it means that he avoids psychic parricide but that he is then denied psychic omnipotence, becomes guilty of psychic incest, and must suffer the pain of psychic castration. The gambler therefore strives to accomplish the impossible feat of winning *and* losing at the same time and it is his ceaseless quest to resolve this no-win situation that keeps the gambler bound to the gaming table.[58] It should be noted that this interpretation, like those of many other psychoanalysts, was formulated on the basis of a single case history.

A number of later psychoanalysts also attributed pathological or "neurotic" gambling to a personality fixation brought about by childhood traumas and deprivations. Some, like Fenichel, also saw gambling as a manifestation of the conflicting "primal and inevitable" wishes to kill the father and at the same time to be loved and accepted by him. Gambling serves not only as punishment for these ambivalent feelings and their associated guilt feelings, but also as a means of questioning Destiny or Fate, the symbolic father figure. Answers to various questions are, of course, divined through winning or losing. Thus, some maintained that losing signifies that the anticipated punishment–death or castration at the hands of the father–is justified and will be carried out while winning means that the gambler's Oedipal sins are forgiven.[59] Others contended that winning and losing signify the force and effectiveness of the gambler's paternal death wishes: winning signifies victory over the father while losing means defeat.[60] In contrast, others saw gambling as an appeal for the love and approval of Lady Luck, the symbolic mother figure. Because of the gambler's psychological insecurities, his luck, which represents[61] the mother's love–specifically her breast which is presented in the form of money–must be continually tested and sought through repetitive gambling.[62] At times, however, some psychoanalysts were not really sure if Fortune, the parental surrogate to whom the gambler appeals for love, acceptance, and approval, is a mother or a father surrogate.[63]

Edmund Bergler: Orality, Infantile Omnipotence, and Psychic Masochism

Edmund Bergler, a contemporary of Fenichel, also insisted that "the gambler is . . . *a neurotic with the unconscious wish to lose.*"[64] However, Bergler was adamant about distinguishing the "clinical" or pathological gambler from the nonclinical or occasional gambler and insisted that his discussion referred only to the former. In identifying the key signs and symptoms of the pathological gambler Bergler appears to have anticipated some of the essentials of the later medical model. The characteristics that he identified include the gambler's habitual risk-taking, his preoccupation with gambling to the exclusion of all other interests, his persistent optimism and failure to learn from defeat, his inability to stop when winning (or losing), his wagering of too much money, and the "pleasurable-painful tension" or thrill that the gambler experiences between the time a bet is placed and its outcome.

As a treatment specialist, Bergler found that pathological gamblers always give one or the other of two standard replies whenever they are asked to explain their behavior. They invariably claim that they gamble either to win money or to relieve boredom through the thrill and excitement that it provides. As a dedicated psychoanalyst, however, Bergler was convinced that these stock answers were merely rationalizations for their true motivations which, he insisted, could never be understood without a thorough knowledge of the gambler's unconscious mental processes.[65]

To explain the unconscious motivations involved in pathological gambling Bergler[66] provided a classic frustration-aggression model which became one of the most comprehensive and influential psychoanalytic explanations since Freud's. For Bergler, gambling represented both the aggressive impulses directed against one's parents and a self-punishing reaction to the intense feelings of guilt that this aggressive drive arouses. Like Fenichel, Bergler believed that the pathological gambler sees Fate as a symbolic representation of the parental figures–both mother and father–which must be constantly tested. Focusing on the gambler's continuing play despite chronic losses, he agreed with Freud and Fenichel that the driving force behind this compulsion is a desire for defeat, humiliation, rejection, and pain through loss, a neurotic condition he described as "psychic masochism." The need for this kind of self-punishment, he also reasoned, must be the product of a profound sense of guilt and anxiety a gambler feels. For Bergler, however, these emotions arise not from an unresolved Oedipal conflict, but from the unconsciously felt hostility and aggression the gambler directs toward a refusing, demanding, and punishing parental figure.[67]

In Bergler's scheme the compulsion to gamble does not originate in the infantile phallic stage of psychosexual development as Freud and Stekel had suggested, but in the earlier oral stage associated with nurturance and weaning and, to a somewhat lesser degree, in the anal stage associated with elimination and toilet training as Von Hattingberg and Simmel maintained. This, he reasoned, is because throughout the demanding and punishing socialization process the parents frustrate not only the infant's selfish demands for oral gratification during the weaning period, but also his needs for anal gratification during the harsh, punitive period of toilet training.

From the day of their birth until the weaning and toilet training period, all infants enjoy a period of unlimited freedom and omnipotence in which no restrictions are imposed on their behavior and all their demands are met by doting parents. But this situation is dramatically and traumatically reversed when their freedom to nurse and defecate at will are abruptly curtailed by withholding, castigation, and threats. Now it is no longer the child who is omnipotent, but the parents.[68] The terrible hostility and rage a child develops for such refusing, rejecting, demanding, and punishing parents–who are the primary objects of his hatred as well as his love–cause him to suffer the anguish of guilt. Should these same unconsciously harbored guilt feelings persist or become reactivated in adulthood, the individual may masochistically and self-destructively punish himself through his persistent gambling losses, thereby deriving pleasure from displeasure. Bergler acknowledged that not all orally fixated neurotics become gamblers, but all gamblers, he insisted, are orally fixated. A similar self-destructive explanation for alcoholism was also attributed to an oral fixation at about the same time.[69]

Despite its tremendous importance, psychic masochism alone does not provide a complete answer to the problem since it does not explain the specificity of gambling. That is, why should a person choose gambling over any other self-effacing behavior which would serve the same end? For Bergler, the answer to this question lay in the gambler's megalomaniacal narcissism, his need to recapture the feelings of unlimited freedom and power he once enjoyed in infancy. He therefore added a regressive component to the equation by claiming that gambling rekindles the latent and unconscious megalomaniacal desire for unlimited power that affects all people but which is especially strong in gamblers. Everyone secretly wishes to return to the blissful state of infantile omnipotence, and gambling provides the ideal vehicle for acting out this wish-fulfillment fantasy. In the words of a later psychoanalyst, "Gambling in the adult . . . is an attempt to regain symbolically the ever-flowing breast–to get the supplies unconditionally, that is, without doing what is classified as *work*."[70] At the same time that gambling revives the old desire for infantile omnipotence, it also revives the parental hatred and guilt that arose when it was originally lost.

Bergler explained that since Fate is the definitive parental surrogate, gambling is a symbolic act of rebellion against the parents as well as a test of the gambler's power over them. Since winning would constitute evidence of this power, all gamblers consciously hope to win. Unconsciously, however, they know they are destined to lose since their life experiences have taught them that denial, rejection, and defeat is all they can ever expect from their withholding, punishing parents and the frustrating conditions they have always imposed. According to one review of his ideas, "Compulsive gamblers are involved in an adversarial relationship with the world. Their opponents at the poker table, the dealer in the casino, the roulette wheel or stock exchange are unconsciously identified with the refusing mother or rejecting father."[71]

Compulsive gamblers persist despite constant loss because their megalomaniacal desire to regain the omnipotence they once enjoyed in infancy is still so strong that it becomes confused with the feeling that they really are omnipotent and cannot possibly lose. Fate is tested again and again in a futile effort to confirm this irrational belief. In this way the gambler becomes caught up in a vicious circle of appealing to and aggressively rebelling against the parents, and the need to punish himself for doing so.

Thus, Bergler felt that gambling is at once (1) an attempt by the neurotic to regain and reassert his infantile omnipotence by denying reality, (2) a constant demand for his parents' reassuring confirmation of this, and (3) a means of self-punishment for the aggressive anger and hostility he feels toward them.[72] He also felt that the "pleasurable-painful tension" or thrill of gambling is a direct consequence of these events. Pleasure is derived from the aggressive act of rebellion against the parents and the optimistic certainty of winning that accompanies the renewed feelings of infantile omnipotence. At the same time, however, the gambler is painfully aware of the punishment that he can expect for his "naughty" recalcitrant behavior. As always, of course, the entire process is presumed to take place on the unconscious level so that in adulthood the gambler is never aware of his "true" motivations.

Unlike his predecessors, Bergler[73] was among the first to acknowledge that women, too, could be neurotic gamblers. He was also one of the first to attempt to classify various types of gamblers. In Bergler's scheme (a) the **classical gambler**, the most common type, is the orally fixated masochist described above; (b) **passive-feminine male gamblers** are bisexual or latently homosexual men who, because of their strong feminine identification, unconsciously play to lose so that they can enjoy the "sexual pleasure of being overwhelmed"[74] by Fate, the sublimated father figure; (c) **defensive pseudo-superior gamblers** are latent homosexual men who gamble only with other men in an unconscious attempt to deny their feminine inclinations by asserting their dominance over other masculine figures; (d) **gamblers motivated by unconscious guilt**, those described by Freud, gamble to punish themselves for their incestuous masturbatory fantasies and unresolved Oedipal conflicts; and (e) the **gambler without excitement** represents the imaginary ideal of cool, detached, self-assurance to which all gamblers aspire. Although gamblers of this type do not exist in reality, some veteran gamblers are able to effect such an appearance, at least outwardly. Bergler initially included among gamblers of this type "some frigid hysterical women, who seem to treat gambling as they treat men, coldly and spongingly."[75] He later categorized all female gamblers as classical types, exemplified by the orally fixated psychic masochist who is still seeking omnipotence by denying reality and rebelling against the unconscious image of a sadistically cruel and unjust mother.[76] Bergler's earlier characterization of female gamblers has been labeled "the most notoriously sexist"[77] of all views. While it is indeed neither a flattering nor accurate description, it can clearly be considered no more sexist than his equally unflattering and questionable descriptions of male gamblers.

Ralph Greenson: Sublimated Sexuality

Although many psychoanalysts disagreed as to the ultimate motivation for gambling–particularly whether it represents a fixation at the oral, anal, Oedipal, or some other stage of libidinal development–others found something of value in all previous psychoanalytic theories and attributed gambling to a combination of all the psychodynamic influences that had ever been proposed. Among the first to do so was Ralph Greenson[78] who took cues from all of his predecessors in his assessment of the problem when he attributed the popularity of gambling to the universally felt need to discharge an entire array of id impulses. Gambling, he felt, has the unique ability to satisfy not just one or two, but *all* pregenital libidinal drives including oral, anal, Oedipal, masturbatory, aggressive, masochistic, and homosexual tendencies.

Like Bergler, Greenson also distinguished normal from abnormal gambling. In doing so, however, he described three types of gamblers on the basis of their particular motivations: "normal" gamblers are those who gamble for entertainment and who can stop whenever they wish; "professional" gamblers are those who have chosen gambling as a livelihood; and "neurotic" gamblers are those who are motivated by unconscious needs and who are not able to stop of their own volition.[79] Although the primary reasons for gambling may vary from one person to another, Greenson felt that the same motivations are present to different degrees in all gamblers. To Greenson, gambling clearly represented a denial of reality, a regressive "infantile longing for omnipotence,"[80] and a means of gratifying one's repressed libidinal desires. His classification and other conclusions were based on the case histories of only five male psychiatric patients who also happened to be gamblers.

Like Freud and his other predecessors, Greenson interpreted the observable behavior of active gamblers as a form of sublimated sexuality, or a personality regression to the phallic stage of development. He observed that

> The first striking characteristic is the atmosphere of excitement. This is visible in the tremor and sweating of the players, and in their motor restlessness. It is audible in the noise and in the hushed silences. There is a rhythm of tension–discharge, which is constantly repeated. At the beginning of play it is quiet, gradually there is a crescendo of excitement until a peak is reached, and finally there is a period of quiet. The excitement, the rhythm, the tension–discharge, and the final quiet bear an obvious similarity to sexual excitement.[81]

Greenson saw additional "evidence" of the purported relationship between gambling and sex in the fact that the expression "coming" is used in reference to rolling the dice in craps as well as to an orgasm. He found further confirmation of this association in the fact that the tension experienced while gambling is pleasurable and the participants feel "spent" at the end of a game.[82] (Greenson's comparison of gambling to masturbation was quoted above, in the discussion of Freud's ideas.)

Due to the obvious influence of Von Hattingberg and Simmel, Greenson construed the vocabulary and behaviors that are commonly associated with gambling as confirmation of the notion that it also epitomizes an anal regression. He noted that although the vocabulary of gamblers is profane and aggressive, it is more often anal and scatological than sexual in nature. According to Greenson, evidence for these ideas is apparent in the language of active gamblers who refer to their stakes as "the pot," to winning to "cleaning up," to a winner to someone who has "fallen into a barrel of shit," and to dice games as "craps."[83] "Anal-sadistic derivatives," he continued, "are also seen in the extremes of neatness and sloppiness of dress, in the sorting and piling of chips, and the expelling of gas" which, as a means of assuring good luck, "is accepted as part of the poker ritual."[84] He went so far as to compare losing, which gamblers commonly refer to as being "cleaned out," to an "anal orgasm."[85]

Additional observations of participants engaged in any form of gambling offer similar "proof" of the immature personality development of those involved. Thus, the fact that many gambling games and situations are segregated by gender so that members of the opposite sex are excluded highlights the gambler's phallic and homosexual tendencies:

> The fellow gamblers are cohorts in homosexual activities. Gambling with other men was equivalent, in the unconscious, to comparing penises with other men; winning meant having the largest penis or being the most potent. Excitement together often represented masturbation together. In passive homosexual men who love the type of man they would like to have been, contact with strong men in a game had the significance of gaining additional manhood. Unconscious homosexuality is demonstrated by the neurotic gambler in his sparse or Don Juan type of sexual life.[86]

Greenson also adopted Bergler's ideas on the oral nature of gambling. The oral narcissism of all gamblers is readily apparent in such observable behaviors as eating, drinking, and smoking which are always heavier during gambling than at any other time. Greenson saw further evidence of orally regressive tendencies in the wishful thinking and archaic and childish thought processes that so many gamblers entertain. The superstitious behaviors, magical thinking, and "hunch" betting that are so common among them are indicative of the yearnings for the omnipotence (oral gratification) that they enjoyed in infancy. He reiterated Bergler's original observation that while engaging in them, the gambler's infantile fantasies of omnipotence are replaced by the certainty of his omnipotence.[87] As a later colleague put it, gamblers convince themselves that "I need to win, therefore I will win."[88]

Gambling also reveals a strong Oedipal component in the gambler's regressive personality. Since the gambler equates luck with omnipotence he gambles to convince himself of this. But because he is also plagued by severe self-doubts and anxieties, he requires constant confirmation of his favored status. Therefore, like Fenichel, Bergler, and others, Greenson felt that gambling also represents an oracular appeal to Luck or Fate who, by allowing the gambler to win, is expected to provide both the assurance of the oral omnipotence he is so desperately seeking and acceptance of his forbidden Oedipal desires. However, while most of his predecessors saw Fate or Luck as only a father or a mother surrogate, Greenson believed that it could represent either the mother or the father depending on which emotional conflict happens to be salient at any particular moment. According to Greenson, "It is the powerful, omnipotent, protecting figure that can kill, castrate, abandon, or love."[89] Others have interpreted Greenson's notion of Luck as follows: "It may represent the father, who is being challenged and tested or sought after for acceptance and protection or cowered before in submissiveness. It may also represent the mother who is fickle and powerful and who is being wooed."[90] Thus, the gambler's appeals to Luck or Fate reveal his need for the approval and indulgence of both his oral and Oedipal desires.

For Greenson, the widespread popularity of gambling is explained by three fundamental facts: all individuals retain at least some pregenital instincts, society inhibits their free expression, but gambling can serve to satisfy them indirectly. Although these motivations affect all gamblers, they are most apparent in the neurotic gambler who presents a "caricature" of the other types:

> The neurotic gambler is unable to stop gambling because he cannot bear the feeling of abandonment and depression when he loses; nor can he bear the excitement of winning. In both cases, unresolved tensions require that he continue the game. The feelings aroused by winning are so interwoven with guilt feelings that full satisfaction is impossible and the frustrated wishes return again and again, seeking satisfaction.[91]

The need to lose, of course, represents the gambler's need for punishment to allay the guilt feelings that plague him: "Losing, i.e. being beaten, is eroticized, and becomes an appropriate vehicle for masochistic fantasies."[92] Monetary loss is far preferable to castration at the hands of the father or to the loss of a mother's love and the withholding of her breast. Greenson concluded that the only adequate treatment for the disease of neurotic gambling is psychoanalysis. Even then, however, the prognosis will not be favorable since there are generally legal and financial difficulties and, since the illness is so similar to the addictions and perversions, relapses will be inevitable.

2

PSYCHOANALYTIC THEORY: LATER VIEWS

D. W. Bolen and W. H. Boyd: Dissention and a Break with Tradition

Darrell W. Bolen and William H. Boyd were among the first psychiatrists to dispute the orthodox psychoanalytic interpretations of their predecessors. However, their break with tradition came only with time and a great deal of first-hand experience. Initially, during their medical residency at a Los Angeles neuropsychiatric institute where they worked with a number of pathological gamblers, they uncritically accepted their mentors' pronouncements on the psychodynamic causes of pathological gambling. In their first collaborative publication, which was essentially a review of the existing literature, Bolen and Boyd[1] therefore reiterated point by point the litany of the psychoanalytic doctrines they had digested, many of which they claimed to have encountered in their own patients. Thus,

1. they invoked the popular psychoanalytic analogy in which the act of gambling is symbolically equated with the act of sex;

2. they agreed with Bergler that pathological gamblers do not play for money, but for excitement;

3. they agreed that the thrill of gambling stems from the uncertainty over whether the gambler's daring challenges to fate will be rewarded or punished;

4. like Greenson and others they felt that the very language of gambling–making a "killing," "murdering" one's opponent, and getting "nailed" – constitutes concrete evidence of the unconscious aggression it releases;

5. they saw additional evidence of its aggressive nature in the beliefs and customs of some non-Western tribal peoples in which gambling symbolized a life-and-death conflict between two opposing supernatural forces and losers were sometimes dispatched in sacrificial rituals;

6. evidence of all gamblers' latent homosexuality is evident in their "antifeminine vocabulary" since "queens are referred to as 'whores'"[2] and in anthropological reports in which the gambling activities of certain non-Western tribal peoples are

sometimes accompanied by profanity, ribaldry, and playful genital grabbing during which the women are segregated from the men;

7. they claimed to have encountered Bergler's regression to infantile omnipotence in a patient who reported feeling "omnipotent, all-powerful, and like a king"[3] gambling;

8. they echoed the ideas of Stekel and Greenson by maintaining that gambling represents the sublimated expression of a broad array of pregenital id impulses rather than a personality fixation at just one particular stage;

9. they interpreted the behaviors that accompany gambling–smoking, drinking, eating, neatness, sloppiness, flatulence–as evidence of the gambler's poorly repressed oral, anal, and anal-sadistic impulses;

10. the unconscious pregenital derivation of the passion for gambling is also evident in the guilt with which the gambler regards his winnings: it is "hot money" that "burns a hole" in their pockets and is quickly and foolishly spent, given away, or, more frequently, lost through further gambling;

11. they commented on the irrational magical thinking, unrealistic optimism, and reliance on superstition and lucky charms that are so common among inveterate gamblers and compared them to the beliefs and behaviors of primitive sorcerers whose gambling was also accompanied by elaborate dances, ceremonial performances, and use of ritual paraphernalia; and

12. like Stekel, they felt that these observations constituted further proof of the "primitive, paleological, archaic, 'omnipotent,' 'precausal,' cognitive processes"[4] that underlie all forms of gambling.

In essence, Bolen and Boyd initially saw gambling as a guilt-laden activity which has the ability to satisfy a variety of unconscious aggressive libidinal drives. At the same time that these drives are gratified the intense guilt that arises from their satisfaction–guilt for which the gambler desires and expects punishment–is also alleviated by the gambling losses he inevitably suffers. They pointed out that consistent monetary losses are guaranteed by the inescapable odds ratios of various games, predetermined house takes, and cheating that are intrinsic to gambling. The punishment that all pathological gamblers seek is therefore assured by the "mathematical machinery" inherent in gambling.[5]

Despite their conventional psychoanalytic orientation, however, Bolen and Boyd were able to make several original observations of their own. Unlike most of their predecessors, they distinguished compulsive gamblers from normal gamblers on the basis of their overt behaviors and covert motivations or "intrapsychic phenomena."[6] Normal gamblers, they felt, gamble for entertainment, hope to win both consciously and unconsciously, can realistically assess their chances of doing so, and are able to stop when they are ahead. Conversely, pathological gamblers are differentiated by the greater strength of their unconscious infantile libidinal drives, by the greater pleasure that gambling therefore affords them, by their greater reliance on "omnipotent hope and denial,"[7] by the greater magnitude of guilt they feel when winning, by their unconscious desire to lose, and by their inability to stop whether they are winning or losing.

They also observed that gambling can serve an important social function. Although some gamblers are quiet loners, many others find that the gambling environment provides an ideal opportunity to interact and socialize with like-minded friends. Thus, "Horse players are typically gregarious, loquacious, and generous in their exchange of advice and information."[8] The social aspects of gambling are equally apparent in organized group junkets to Las Vegas, family picnics at race tracks, and in dealer-player interactions at the gaming table. Moreover, they added, in tribal situations, primitive gambling always took place in a religious or other institutionalized social setting.

Bolen and Boyd were also among the first treatment specialists to note the familial aspects of pathological gambling, a phenomenon they ascribed more to modeling or social learning than to any other cause. Among nearly all of the patients they treated, at least one parent and many siblings were also social or pathological gamblers, and in most cases the form of gambling preferred by the patient was the same as that of the parent. One patient began gambling as a teenager while attending the racetrack with his father since this was the only time he felt he was able to communicate with him; he felt that his gambling father was now a part of himself. "It may be," the authors therefore suggested, "that identification with the parent who gambles plays a prominent part in the propensity to gamble."[9]

Noting that pathological gambling is commonly associated with other psychiatric disorders, Bolen and Boyd suggested that gambling may serve some additional functions that their predecessors had failed to recognize. They claimed that among some of their own patients "gambling has served to counteract feelings of 'nothingness' or 'emptiness,' replacing these emotions with a euphoric sense of importance, power, and control."[10] Thus, like some of their contemporary colleagues,[11] they added an Adlerian power-seeking element to their analysis (to be discussed elsewhere). Since they observed that many gamblers were also schizophrenic or manic-depressive, they contended that among their more seriously disturbed patients gambling serves to defend more against loss of contact with reality than against unconscious guilt. They anticipated learned helplessness theory (also discussed elsewhere) when they maintained that many of their patients began gambling only after experiencing a highly stressful crisis or traumatic loss such as spousal separation, divorce, the birth of a child, the death of a parent, or failure in business. They therefore concluded that pathological gambling should be regarded as a symptomatic defense against an array of other psychiatric disturbances rather than as a discreet diagnostic entity.

The authors made a further break with the psychoanalytic tradition in their second collaborative publication in which they further elaborated the idea that pathological gambling can serve as an emotional defense mechanism against feelings of depression and helplessness.[12] Like some of their predecessors, they observed that pathological gambling is frequently precipitated or exacerbated by severe life crises and stress situations such as the loss of a loved one through death or divorce. However, they felt that the standard psychoanalytic explanation which attributes gambling to a masochistic need for punishment stemming from an unresolved Oedipal situation, parental death wishes, and the unconscious guilt that these feelings generate, would be totally inappropriate for explaining the cases they had encountered. Boyd and Bolen suggested instead that gambling represents a "manic defensive maneuver" that temporarily makes people forget the loss of their loved ones and other traumas, the ensuing depression that these experiences create, and their own sense of helplessness in the face of these situations. Since depression and despair are temporarily replaced by the euphoria of betting, gambling often represents an attempt to create a false sense of security by denying death itself:

> Death uniquely confronts us with our existential impotence and the attendant feelings of futility and despair. But the painful awareness of one's total inability to alter the appearance and call of the Grim Reaper is unconfronted by the gambler, who resorts to an active and magical means which temptingly provides the illusion of power, mastery, and control in the face of the inevitable. But the illusion is transient, and, hence, the repetitive need to gamble, with eventual addiction.[13]

Furthermore, if the lost loved one was particularly abusive and sadistic, as, for example, many alcoholics can be, the frustration of losing consistently may be reminiscent of the frustrations encountered in the former relationship. The authors therefore felt that gambling can also represent a symbolic attempt to recapture the essence of a lost relationship, even though it may have been a highly dysfunctional one.

They also anticipated family systems theory (to be discussed more completely in another volume). On the basis of their experience with married couples in conjoint therapy, they concluded that

> Analogous to the individual intrapsychic dynamics, gambling in the marital relationship also serves the defensive function of stabilizing a pathological marriage at a level of minimal disequilibrium that is mutually tolerable by the marital partners. It become a mutually unpalatable, perhaps intolerable, but nonetheless essential factor in the marriage which is the nidus for secondary elaboration into a ceaseless, snowballing series of maladaptive maneuvers and collusive interactions.[14]

Finally, although they were initially reluctant to do so, Boyd and Bolen concluded their reformulation of the psychodynamics of gambling by completely rejecting the notion that it is an unconscious substitute for sex. They judged any similarity of the rhythmic repetitive series of emotional excitement, tension, and release to the arousal, foreplay, and climax of masturbation and sexual intercourse to be "superficial" and any explanation based on this assumption to be "too simplistic."[15] One reason for this was perhaps an economic one: too many of their patients had simply discontinued treatment after being told that they gambled only because they unconsciously wanted to masturbate. Another was that, after a period of critical reflection, they concluded that "such libidinal formulations proved to be theoretically inaccurate and unnecessarily reductionistic.[16] After reading a newspaper article in which a psychiatrist had repeated the standard psychoanalytic canons, the members of a local Gamblers Anonymous group responded that they were no different from anyone else in their attitudes toward sex since virtually everyone was a latent or potential homosexual, spouse abuser, compulsive eater and smoker, and child molester. "It was only some months later," Boyd and Bolen concluded, "that we were able to agree with the essential truth in these remarks."[17]

Peter Fuller: Gambling, the Protestant Ethic, Capitalist Economics, and Anality

Peter Fuller[18] did not agree with Greenson and Bolen and Boyd that gambling serves a multiplicity of pregenital libidinal drives: for him it gratifies only one. Nevertheless, Fuller's proposed relationship among gambling, religion, and repressed anality represents one of the most complex psychodynamic analyses ever proposed. His hypothesis, which he formulated to explain both the aversion some people feel toward gambling and the attraction it holds for others, is an amalgam of early anthropological, Freudian psychoanalytic, and Marxist economic thought. Although very similar ideas had been proposed sixty years earlier,[19] Fuller's were much more highly developed.

Fuller began by linking the idea that modern forms of gambling can be traced to the divinatory practices of our earliest ancestors[20] with Freud's[21] notion that the human need for religious expression, like the id impulses, is deeply ingrained in the collective unconscious portion of the human psyche and is therefore instinctive.[22] However, he sharply disagreed with Freud's characterization of gambling as an addiction: "Gambling is not a drug," he insisted, "it is a ritualistic mode of behavior"[23] having close ties to religious observances. With this background Fuller proceeded to draw a comparison between what he considered to be the individual obsessional neurosis of gambling and what Freud considered to be the "universal obsessional neurosis" of religion.[24]

Gambling and Religion

Fuller initially drew attention to the more evident similarities between gambling and religion–Christianity, in particular–by comparing their external trappings. He compared churches with casinos as places of ritual performance, crucifixes with luck charms as fetishes, rosaries with playing cards and prayer books with racing forms as ritual paraphernalia, Lourdes with Las Vegas as pilgrimage sites, God with Fate and Mary with Luck as father and mother deities, and prayers of the faithful with the invocations of gamblers as appeals for supernatural succor. Fuller also pointed out that individual obsessive neuroses and religion both involve frequent ritual performances. He stressed that although those of the obsessive neurotic are individually contrived and privately performed while those of religion are collective, in either case once a ritual has become established it cannot be altered or abandoned.

Fuller then pointed out some of the less obvious but far more important similarities in the psychodynamics underlying religious expression and gambling. Although their respective goals of eternal life and boundless wealth are unattainable, participants in both religion and gambling are firmly convinced that they will attain them. They are equally committed to irrational beliefs in the efficacy of superstitious ritual behaviors, they are greatly alarmed by any deviation from their prescribed rituals, and they are prepared to endure a lifetime of pain and suffering in their attempts to reach these goals. Of greater importance, however, are that both represent reactions to conflict-anxieties generated by deep-seated unconscious impulses and that both are motivated by guilt, specifically that aroused by sinful acts and intolerable wishes: "Guilt surrounding parricide," Fuller insisted, "is at the core of the symbolism of both the Cross and the pack of cards."[25]

Both gambling and religion, Fuller argued, represent appeals for love and approval (in the form of miracles and money) from a supernatural parental figure, and both represent futile attempts to manipulate this parental surrogate. He felt that the believer's attitude toward the surrogate, and his means of influencing it are crucial to the understanding of both behaviors. Because Freud had described religion as a collective expression of unconscious longings for a father figure, Fuller concluded that gambling expresses the homosexual and aggressive tendencies the gambler feels for his own father,[26] a premise that he failed to elaborate. He did acknowledge, however, that due to the strong maternal component in Christianity (i.e., the worship of Mary), these incestuous impulses also can be directed toward the mother. In either event, any unconscious incestuous desires, whether homosexual or heterosexual, that may be associated with gambling are only secondary in importance to its ultimate cause.

Gambling and Capitalism

Despite the close affinities between religion and gambling, both in terms of their primeval origins and present symbolism, gambling has always been strongly opposed by the moralistic defenders of the Protestant/capitalist ethic. Among the reasons–or, more precisely, the rationalizations–for this antagonism, Fuller explained, is that gambling represents a desire for material possessions which is antithetical to the ideals of Christianity. Puritanism has always promoted the ethic of devotion to God, hard work, subservience, and suffering with limited material rewards in this life since the faithful would be amply rewarded in the next. If workers come to believe that the proper means of acquiring wealth can be subverted, they will no longer apply themselves to the hard physical labor required of them. Furthermore, as an unorthodox road to riches, gambling not only detracts from the proper worship of God whose economy leaves nothing to chance, but it also constitutes an unholy appeal to the un-Christian gods of chance, and even to Satan himself.

As a committed psychoanalyst and advocate of socialism, Fuller argued that representatives of the moral order have never repudiated gambling for the superficial reasons they so often give; the Protestant hostility to gambling is actually a reaction formation against an exploitative practice that is little different from capitalism. (A *reaction formation* is a psychological defense mechanism in which an unconscious anxiety-producing feeling or inclination is substituted in consciousness by its exact opposite in order to conceal one's true impulses.) This "exaggerated fear" of gambling stems partly from its closeness to religion and partly from its closeness to capitalism: not only does it have much in common with religious beliefs and practices but it also serves the same end as capitalism, the redistribution of wealth from the hands of the many into the hands of a few. In true psychoanalytic fashion, then, Fuller interpreted the moralists' public condemnation of gambling as proof of the attraction it really holds for them and their need to expiate the strong feelings of guilt that result from this. Thus, as two sides of the same coin, gambling and Christian capitalism, both of which appeal to the same basic personality type, are simply too much alike for Protestant sensibilities. In repudiating it the moralist can also blame gambling for all the social ills which are actually caused by the capitalist's exploitation of the working classes.[27]

Gambling and Anality

Underlying the Protestant reformers' inability to condone gambling (as opposed to Catholics who did not regard it as inherently sinful and did condone it in moderation) is an anal fixation brought about by unresolved conflict, the same condition that motivates gambling. Although Fuller developed this theme to a far greater extent than did his predecessors, the intrapsychic processes that he described are very similar to those said to be involved in the development of the Oedipal situation described by others.

Fuller began his exposition by again citing the ideas of Freud[28] who had earlier taken note of a certain personality type marked by stubbornness, order, neatness, punctuality, acquisitiveness, frugality, and miserliness. As noted previously, Freud, Simmel, and other psychoanalysts had speculated that children derive intense anal-erotic pleasure from the act of defecation. They therefore refuse to evacuate the bowels on command during toilet training preferring instead to retain the feces until it can be forcefully expelled to provide the greatest pleasure. As a consequence they are severely punished, usually with a painful spanking on the buttocks, for defecating at an inappropriate time. However, they are also rewarded with love and approval by compliance with parental wishes.

In the mind of the psychoanalyst, then, all children find themselves torn between their own desires for an explosive pleasure-laden defecation at the cost of inciting parental anger and punishment, and those of their parents for which they will be rewarded by love and approbation at the expense of their anal-erotic gratification. All children are therefore forced to choose between pleasing themselves but displeasing their parents, or of pleasing their parents but denying themselves of physical pleasure. As it is impossible to do both, the harsh, punitive period of toilet training provokes strong feelings of rage and death wishes directed toward the parent who imposes this dilemma and the punishments that invariably accompany either choice.

Failure to resolve the conflicts associated with toilet training results in a fixation at the anal stage of psychosexual development. The strength of the repressed anal-erotic impulses that continue throughout life and the intense guilt feelings they arouse cause anally fixated personalities to seek an acceptable substitute for their infantile inclinations as they grow older. As also noted previously, Freud, Simmel, and others speculated that for these anal retentive individuals the love of money in adulthood is simply a sublimated expression of the love for defecation in childhood, and money itself is the symbolic equivalent of feces. Fuller elaborated these ideas to a far greater extent than any of his predecessors.

According to Fuller, evidence that gambling is symptomatic of unresolved conflicts stemming from the ordeal of toilet training and that money is the universal psychic substitute for feces is plentiful. By way of demonstration he cited Freud's observation of the mythical truth that "the gold that the Devil gives his paramours turns into excrement upon his departure, and the Devil is certainly nothing else than the personification of the repressed unconscious instinctual life."[29] As further confirmation of his hypothesis, Fuller invoked a number of other associations. He cited an apocryphal tale in which a man won a fortune in Monte Carlo after some pigeon droppings fell on his hat as he was making his way to the casino: "News of his success spread, and a craze developed for the reception of a comparable heavenly faecal blessing before commencing play."[30] Like some of his predecessors,[31] Fuller also pointed out that in addition to its very name the dice game "craps" is replete with references to defecation. It employs such scatologically oriented phrases as "come out line," "coming out the hard way," "they're rolling," and throwing a "pass" or a "crap out." Similarly, money in poker is thrown into a "pot" and casino floor managers are called "pit bosses."

Fuller argued, however, that the most conclusive "proof" of his hypothesis lies in the realization, first noted by Emmanuel Moran,[32] that "gambling is playing *with* money, rather *for* money."[33] This, of course, means that gambling, which requires the constant fondling of money, represents a sublimated expression of the infantile desire to play with feces. The masochistic component of gambling is also apparent since loss, which symbolizes compliance with the parents' wishes to give up the feces, results in punishment. Gambling therefore provides clear evidence of a regression to the anal stage of personality development.

Because Fuller assumed anal conflict to be a universal human phenomenon, he did not differentiate between pathological and occasional gambling since he believed that gambling in any degree was always motivated by the same psychodynamic processes. He nevertheless did acknowledge that a few people who appear to be gamblers–cheaters, sports pool players, and lottery players–are motivated more by monetary considerations than by repressed anality. However, he felt that such individuals could not be considered true gamblers since they are not driven by any neurotic compulsions.[34]

A review of the tortuous lines of reasoning that Fuller followed in arguing that sublimated anality was responsible not only for the alliance of Protestantism with capitalism but also for the entire Protestant Reformation (Luther was chronically constipated) is beyond the scope of the present discussion. However, his conclusions in this regard are summed up in the following few lines:

> For Protestants, a virulent reaction-formation against gambling was almost inevitable. By labelling it as the true satanic means of exchange, they could unload and escape their own guilt about the extent and consequences of their liaison with capitalism. The Protestant moralist needs to be able to shriek against gambling, or else the guilt surrounding his own anal displacement may well become intolerable.[35]

In the final analysis, Fuller was convinced that gamblers gamble and that anti-gambling moralists inveigh against gambling for precisely the same reason: they are all anally fixated.

MORE RECENT VIEWS

The alleged relationship between gambling and sex has always been a popular issue. A number of later researchers have reported on their similarities,[36] on the co-occurrence of gambling and sexual addictions,[37] and that some gamblers prefer gambling to sex.[38] Recent clinical research has also reported a relationship between compulsive gambling and major life crises or other stressful situations. For example, many patients are reported to have experienced the loss of a loved one, often the father, mother, or some other close relative, at an early age and before becoming compulsive gamblers.[39]

Some psychoanalytically inclined theorists have once again turned to Freud's original speculations on these phenomena which have long been held to be a guilt reaction to unconscious parental death wishes.[40] For example, the role of Oedipal conflict in compulsive gambling was resurrected in a later review of the Dostoevsky material.[41] Dostoevsky apparently suffered from severe and recurrent attacks of anxiety and/or depression stemming from a preoccupation with his father's death, an event which occurred when the novelist was only eighteen years old. According to his wife, Dostoevsky could only find relief from these attacks when gambling.[42]

Because many of their patients also claim that gambling provides emotional relief, some modern clinicians are still convinced that "the inevitable losing associated with compulsive gambling [may serve] a need to self-punish, a need based on irrational guilt which is perhaps related to their traumatic experiences."[43] Like their predecessors, some continue to regard it as a defense against the depression, anxiety, and guilt that are generated by poorly repressed Oedipal impulses,[44] to attribute it to fixations at the oral and anal stages of psychosexual development,[45] to claim that the eroticized risk inherent in gambling is a substitute for sex,[46] and to suggest that it is a sublimated expression of poorly repressed homosexuality.[47]

Nevertheless, few contemporary psychoanalytic theorists any longer support explanations which maintain that masochistic desires and unconscious needs to lose provide the primary motivation for pathological gambling. It has been pointed out that "pathological gamblers have an early winning phase lasting three to five years. Masochists could not stand to win for that long."[48] The idea that all pathological gamblers are masochists has also been criticized on the grounds that it was probably an artifact of sampling bias: the psychoanalysts who advocated it were probably exposed to only the heaviest losers since winners and moderate losers would be unlikely to seek their services.[49]

Richard Rosenthal: The Psychodynamic Mechanisms of Self-Deception

Nevertheless, at least one modern psychoanalyst still subscribes to the masochistic hypotheses of Freud, Bergler, and others, as well as to Simmel's and Fuller's notions of the anal-erotic and coprophilial components of addiction. According to psychiatrist Richard Rosenthal, some individuals who experience initial success deliberately sabotage their accomplishments. Moreover, "Not only do some pathological gamblers lose from the very beginning, for some a 'big loss' early in their gambling careers is just as significant as a 'big win' may be for others."[50] Rosenthal also feels that "fantasies about the anus as the locus of 'false creativity,' or about the value ascribed to its contents (heroin and marijuana are commonly referred to as 'shit' as a term of approbation) are central to the dynamics of addiction."[51]

Overall, however, Rosenthal was not really concerned with the hypothetical childhood traumas, personality fixations, and other experiences to which many of his earlier colleagues attributed the genesis of pathological gambling. Although he could not entirely escape the influence of his predecessors, he placed greater emphasis on the psychodynamic forces through which gambling was maintained once it had become established and the therapeutic procedures through which it could be treated. He therefore emphasized the various defense mechanisms that pathological gamblers routinely employ and their relevance to treatment and relapse prevention. According to Rosenthal,[52] the gambler's five most important defense mechanisms are omnipotence, splitting, idealization and devaluation, projection, and denial, all of which are closely intertwined. Together they encompass the pathological gamblers system for self-deception, a series of lies, fantasies, illusions, and delusions through which the gambler fools both himself and others.

Omnipotence, the feeling of being all-powerful, is a defense against feelings of helplessness. The sense of omnipotence that all gamblers cultivate is most apparent in their wishful thinking, the conviction that they will win simply because they have to win.

Since this feeling is born of the gambler's desperation, it is strongest when the gambler is experiencing the greatest difficulties. At these times, Rosenthal maintained, gamblers will engage in provocative acts by taking even greater risks merely to test their omnipotence and to prove to themselves that they really are in control of the situation.

Splitting, which refers to self-idealization and self-devaluation, is a defense mechanism akin to compartmentalization. It refers to the gambler's tendency to think of himself as two separate people, one who is all good–a winner–and one who is all bad–a loser. By simultaneously holding these two self-conceptions, gamblers often make entirely contradictory statements without seeming to be aware of the discrepancy. By mentally separating the contradictions in reality that they so often experience, gamblers are able to avoid the conflicts that these discrepancies would otherwise generate. The overidealized self-image of winner contributes to the gambler's sense of omnipotence through the fanciful images of personal strength and power over others that it creates. The power to control others is something all gamblers attempt to realize.

A similar *idealization and devaluation* of others serves as a defense against intimacy. Rosenthal observed that gamblers rarely see the important people in their lives as equals but tend to regard them as either flawless or useless. Their estimation of any person often alternates between these two views. According to Rosenthal, "There is no easier way of keeping another person at a distance than to put them on a pedestal."[53] It would be equally difficult to become intimate with someone who is held in contempt.

The gambler develops and maintains these attitudes by *projecting* his feelings about himself onto others. Moreover, the attitudes he holds of others at any time change according to the feelings he has about himself at that time. Thus, he either identifies with others or feels threatened and harassed by them. When he feels persecuted he sees himself as not only being controlled by others but also as the victim of their unreasonable and exploitative demands–a situation he finds intolerable. Conversely, by fantasizing that he is in control of others the gambler feels as though he is controlling the things about himself that he has projected onto them. The result is a dysfunctional interpersonal relationship.

In splitting, however, some individuals idealize the bad things about themselves and devalue the good. This reversal further complicates relationships with others onto whom they have projected the features they see in themselves. Such individuals are genuinely masochistic in that they idealize their own ruin. They seem to be thinking, "If I can't do anything creative or beneficial for myself, at least I can be destructive, and I can hurt myself far better than anyone else can."[54] Thus, an orientation to problem solving and control that begins with aggressively hostile breath-holding and temper tantrums in infancy, and which develops into addictive and other perverse behaviors in adulthood, may ultimately culminate in the supreme self-destructive act of suicide. Patients of this sort speak of "carrying suicide around in my back pocket"[55] as a way out of any situation. Ideation of this sort enables them to maintain their fantasies of power and control. Others can only maintain the feeling of control over their parents–generally the parent of the same sex–by avoiding success since this would then allow them to feel successful as parents, a situation the gambler is continually striving to prevent. Some patients transfer these feelings onto the therapist thereby insuring that the treatment also fails. "Such patients," Rosenthal felt, "sacrifice their lives for spite."[56]

Denial, perhaps the most primitive of all

defense mechanisms, refers not only to the gambler's habitual lying to others but also to his continued refusal–despite all evidence to the contrary–to admit the reality of his situation even to himself. In the words of one patient, "Whether I'm telling the truth or not doesn't matter. Even when I'm telling the truth I accuse myself of bullshitting. After all, I've lied in the past so I can always bring that up against myself."[57] While lying to others represents another way of avoiding intimacy with them, the simultaneous denial of reality on one hand while retaining some knowledge of it on the other is the key to splitting. Thus the ultimate purpose of lying is not to deceive others so much as it is to deceive one's self. In many cases, Rosenthal insisted, pathological lying precedes the onset of pathological gambling.

Treatment success hinges on therapists' awareness of these defense mechanisms and their importance to the patient. Since deception is so routine for pathological gamblers, many patients will lie to their therapists not only out of habit but also in an effort to control them along with the other important people in their lives. Treatment can therefore be successful only if the therapist knows how to avoid being misled by the patient's system of deception and how to confront the patient about it.

David Newmark: Fate and Power Needs

David Newmark,[58] a modern psychologist with a somewhat Jungian orientation, still subscribes to the idea that gambling represents a symbolic means of appealing to and communing with the gods of fate but adds an Adlerian power-seeking component (discussed below) to his interpretation. In our modern age in which institutionalized religion has little meaning for many people, gambling is sometimes still interpreted as a sacred activity through which the individual is able to establish and maintain a more personal and intimate relationship with the spiritual world:

> Each toss of the dice, each spin of the roulette wheel, and each blackjack hand he is dealt can be seen as a product of a dialogue with the divine. But the knowledge is transitory; the gambler soon needs to test the vagaries of Fate again in order to receive a new, up-to-date, reading on his status.[59]

But Newmark feels that gambling is more than a religion, it is also an escape mechanism. Since it "springs from the irrational ground of the unconscious and is largely symbolic in nature,"[60] many unwarranted meanings can be attached to it. The money which is used in gambling can become a vehicle through which power, security, competence, sexuality, or any other illusional quality the gambler wishes to project onto it can be symbolically displayed. Gambling therefore offers an easy escape from reality that, for some, is preferable to facing the "existential void" they feel in daily life. Instead of learning more appropriate ways of dealing with it, those of us who cannot accept what life has to offer may find that the "spiritual transcendence" we experience through gambling lends order and meaning to a chaotic, incomprehensible world which we feel powerless to control. Thus, Newmark believes, not only do "pathological gamblers struggle in vain to gain an edge against fate" but they also "chase magical dreams at the expense of their psychological development."[61]

CRITIQUE OF PSYCHOANALYTIC THEORY

Despite the preeminence of psychoanalytic theory throughout the first half of the twentieth century, it has since been met with severe criticism and rejection. After reviewing the work of Bergler, one antagonist complained that "His study was based on a group of sixty neurotic patients, most of whom did not consider their gambling harmful until he had convinced them of it through long analysis."[62] After reviewing Freud's analysis, a second critic argued that "Dostoevsky's heavy gambling losses spurred him on to complete *Crime and Punishment*, *The Brothers Karamazov*, and *The Gambler*. Given the analysis and the functional outcome, it seems that for some individuals, gambling might be better viewed as healthy, rather than pathological."[63]

A major criticism of the psychoanalytic approach focuses on its assumption that compulsive gamblers are motivated by an unconscious wish to lose. One critic argued, for example, that those holding such a view often based their sweeping generalizations on only one case history.[64] Another wrote, "The notion that the heavy gambler is motivated by the wish to lose money is certainly a straightforward explanation of why people gamble. However, the intense elation felt and expressed by many gamblers after success is difficult to explain."[65] A third observed that "The person who gets into difficulties demonstrates that winning money at gambling is, especially in the long term, a rarity. Yet, psychologists attempt to explain this behavior by formulations such as 'playing to lose,' as though the rest of those who gamble were all winners."[66] Finally, there is no real evidence to support this contention.

Freud's analogy between masturbation and gambling is also false since guilt arises from masturbation after successful completion of the act whereas it arises from gambling after failure.[67] Moreover, the Freudian view of gambling as a masturbatory activity was based on observations of card players to the exclusion of other kinds of gamblers such as race track bettors who employ an entirely different method and vocabulary. Thus, one critic pointed out that "between, say, the urge to masturbate and the daily playing of horses lies a huge phenomenological reality that remains unexamined in the psychoanalytic literature."[68] A second, himself a psychoanalyst, stated that in his experience with compulsive gamblers he could find no support for the notion that compulsive gambling is a replacement for compulsive masturbation.[69]

Such committed psychoanalysts as Fuller have even attacked Freud's original treatment of gambling as an "addiction" like alcohol or drug dependence. He insisted that this approach is doomed to failure since physiological dependence is not involved in gambling. It is therefore impossible to determine precisely what it is to whch the gambler is supposed to be addicted.[70] A like-minded anonymous critic who penned a column in *The Lancet*, the influential British medical journal, argued that "It is a large step to take from the firm base of pharmacology to the soggy ground of social behaviour. . . . By all means accept compulsive gambling as a legitimate clinical problem, but until gamblers cower from visual hallucinations of predatory dice in darkened rooms during their withdrawal phase, let us keep addiction for pharmacology."[71] (Others have decidedly different ideas which will be discussed in a subsequent volume.)

Fuller also levelled some other legitimate charges at psychoanalytic theory. He first pointed out that masturbation is not negatively sanctioned in all cultures as it is in the West, and that the intense guilt that Freud presumed always to be associated with masturbation, and hence the cause of gambling, is not a universal phenomenon at all. In Japan, for example, masturbation is not condemned and imposes no burden of guilt, yet the Japanese are also avid gamblers. Consequently, guilt over masturbation has nothing to do with gambling in Japan or anywhere else. Moreover, although he was entirely familiar with Bergler's ideas, Fuller also insisted that by placing so strong an emphasis on the Oedipal situation, psychoanalytic theory is incapable of explaining gambling among women.[72] He therefore suggested either that the existing theory be extended or that entirely new theories be developed to account for female gambling.

Furthermore, psychoanalytic theory is too selective. It attempts to explain only the unconscious motivations underlying abnormal or compulsive gambling while ignoring the far more common occurrence of non-compulsive, normative gambling by normal individuals. Consequently, in concentrating only on inner psychodynamic factors, psychoanalytic theory ignores any external social conditions which may be related to gambling and its popularity.[73] Sociologists are particularly critical of psychoanalytic theory for this very reason. They argue, for example, that "given the widespread nature of the behavior, it may not be possible to classify all of the estimated 23 million Americans who bet on something as neurotic. The *neurotic* gambler accounts for only a very negligible few of the total group,"[74] and "To consider all gambling in the light of abnormal psychology thus involves disregarding the majority of gamblers."[75] Thus, "psychoanalysis has neither contributed much to our understanding of gambling nor generated research."[76]

Psychoanalytic theory is unrealistic. According to a modern psychiatrist, "Psychiatric speculation about the compulsive gambler has . . . too frequently been compromised by a predilection for sweeping generalizations based on limited evidence."[77] Most of the generalizations concerning unconscious symbolic meanings, neurotic fixations at a pregenital (oral, anal, or phallic) or even the genital[78] stage of libidinal development, internal conflicts, repressed Oedipal desires, overwhelming feelings of guilt, sexual sublimation, and masochistic needs for punishment which are the alleged motivations for gambling are rarely, if ever, encountered even in clinical situations since most gamblers in treatment do not exhibit these traits. For example, psychoanalysis of thirteen compulsive gambling patients revealed no connection between their gambling and any masturbatory or Oedipal guilt, nor rebellion against reality, in any of them.[79] Likewise, another treatment specialist conceded that, "I have not found it possible to substantiate the claims of those few psychoanalysts who, after treating one or two gamblers, suppose that their addiction represents a wish to kill their fathers and possess their mothers."[80]

In terms of its therapeutic utility, there is no evidence that it is at all effective in the treatment of pathological gambling or any other compulsive or addictive disorder. Moreover, psychoanalysis is very expensive and often requires years to complete. Although Bergler's[81] own figures were not precise, out of about sixty compulsive gamblers who entered treatment with him, he reported success in "curing" some "thirty-odd" patients through psychoanalytic techniques alone. However, he chose to treat only those patients he deemed suitable and rejected all others, the precise number of which is unknown. Moreover, since no follow-up studies were undertaken of the patients he did treat, it is impossible to determine whether their "cure" was permanent or temporary. Despite the lack of any hard evidence to demonstrate this, some reviewers of Bergler's material feel it would be safe to assume that these cures were permanent.[82] However, precisely because of this lack of evidence, others justifiably contend that "There are certainly no grounds for recommending that a gambler who wants to cease betting should enter psychoanalysis."[83] Even committed psychoanalysts who insist that "The only adequate therapy is psychoanalysis" add that "The prognosis is not favorable."[84]

Psychoanalytic theory provides a textbook example of procrustean a priori reasoning. That is, human behavior is illegitimately interpreted according to a preconceived theoretical framework. Irrespective of any individual circumstances, there are no human behaviors–including gambling–which cannot be cast in a psychoanalytic mold if they are interpreted according to its particular frame of reference.[85] In this regard psychiatrist Thomas Szasz severely criticized the psychoanalyst's penchant for symbolic interpretation:

> An immense psychoanalytic superstructure of "symbolism" has been built on the simple, though fundamental, idea of similarity. . . . On closer examination, the entire edifice appears to be nothing but a tedious reiteration of relations of similarity.[86]

> . . . the logical character of so-called Freudian symbols was not recognized for a long time. . . . Thus [an] analysis of hysteria and hypochondriasis . . . consists in showing how this or that symptom or complaint "meant" such and such, because for the patient (and sometimes the analyst) the symptom was an iconic sign of its psychoanalytic "meaning." In . . . papers on symbolism . . . fresh bed linen, for example, "meant" a sexually approachable (clean) woman . . . ; or that a kite might be a symbol of erection . . . , and so forth. . . . It is evident that there is potentially no end to such "symbols."[87]

It is for this very reason that psychoanalysts disagree so frequently on what gambling symbolizes. Are gamblers seeking rewards or punishments? Is gambling indicative of an oral, anal, phallic, or Oedipal fixation? Does the pleasure of gambling derive from masturbatory, eliminatory, or masochistic impulses? If the pleasure is masochistic, does it derive from the loss of money or from an imagined fear of parental punishment? If it stems from fear of parental punishment, does Fate represent an idealized Mother or Father figure? Furthermore, the "symbolic evidence" that is so frequently invoked to confirm the assumption that gambling is a sublimated expression of one's oral, anal, or Oedipal impulses actually constitutes no evidence at all and the absurdity of this kind of reasoning is quite obvious. Does money represent feces or the breast? If money is also a symbol of success, dominance, strength, sexuality, and power, and if gambling really does reveal the unconscious presence of latent homosexual incestuous impulses as Fuller argued, should not money represent the father's penis? If gambling represents repressed Oedipal desires as so many other psychoanalysts have maintained, should not the poker "pot" represent the mother's vagina instead of a toilet? Could not the very name "poker" really signify the gambler's secret wish to "poke her"? Is this why some gamblers prefer the game of "stud" poker with its all-important "hole" cards? Do the "hits" a blackjack player receives (from the dealer/father or dealer/mother) after "splitting" (her thighs?) represent a reward or a punishment? Is "cutting" the cards in any way symbolic of castration anxiety? Could this also explain the horse fancier's preoccupation with mares, studs, and geldings? What might the phrase "coming down the home stretch" really signify?

What about "covering," "royal flush," "full house," and "bingo" with its striking resemblance to *benjo*, the Japanese word for toilet?

Psychoanalysts have always had an uncanny talent for seeing precisely what they expect to see in any human activity. Thus, gambling, like so many other behavioral phenomena, has the extraordinary ability to assume whatever symbolic quality or meaning that any particular psychoanalyst chooses to assign to it. The resulting profusion of explanatory differences and discrepancies within their ranks has led some of their later colleagues to conclude that a firm commitment to any psychoanalytic interpretation is "untenable."[88] They further submit that among the reasons for this general lack of agreement are the "presuppositional commitments" to which they so tenaciously hold, and the "tendency to elaborate the theory of compulsive gambling to one's own particular view."[89]

Psychoanalytic theory also provides a textbook example of post hoc reasoning.[90] The logical fallacy of *post hoc, ergo propter hoc*, which means literally, "after this, therefore because of this," describes arguments which ascribe causation on a temporal basis. The fallacy of this logic is illustrated in the absurd argument that because the rooster crows before the sun rises, it is his crowing that causes the sun to rise. Similarly, psychoanalysts argue that because a person gambles, he must have become orally, anally, or Oedipally fixated in early childhood. Because most of the psychodynamic phenomena that allegedly underlie these conditions are said to exist only at the level of unconsciousness, much of psychoanalytic theory is entirely speculative and cannot be empirically tested, a fact to which even some psychoanalysts themselves have attested.[91] Indeed, none of the numerous psychoanalytic theories that have been proposed has ever been tested or, for that matter, has even been stated as a testable hypothesis.

Psychoanalytic theory is therefore not at all scientific. One valid criticism of this approach is that its proponents have not bothered to test the propositions of their colleagues.[92] The primary reason they have failed to do so is that it is impossible to do so. As noted at the beginning of this section, psychodynamic explanations for human behavior are founded on a number of assumptions. Among them are speculations concerning the presence of racial memories, infantile eroticism, universally felt incestuous impulses, and rage at weaning and toilet training, none of which has ever been conclusively demonstrated or disproven. As a consequence, psychoanalytic theory fails to meet the most important criterion of a true science, the criterion of falsifiability.[93] To meet the standards of modern scientific inquiry one must be able to imagine a set of observable conditions which, if true, would nullify a hypothesis. Thus, it is hypothetically possible to disprove evolutionary theory through empirical observation (for example, if the various fossils that consistently appear in particular geological strata and in particular sequences were instead randomly distributed throughout all strata) but impossible to disprove through any scientific means the existence of supernatural beings or space aliens who allegedly visit the earth in flying saucers. Similarly, no observable set of conditions can be imagined that would disprove the assumptions and conclusions of psychoanalytic theory. In his discussion of Bergler's explanation of compulsive gambling one critic wrote, "Based as it is on an untestable principle, it becomes lost in psychoanalytic mythology, and to my view, has little practical use."[94]

Consequently, the disciples of psychoanalytic thought have accepted its dubious doctrines more on the strength of their own faith and conviction than on any genuine scientific merit. Since any kind of symbolic meaning can be projected onto any kind of situation, arguments–such as that a gambler was once struck by pigeon droppings or that dice players shoot "craps"–that are invoked to demonstrate that money represents feces and that anality is the root cause of gambling are obviously meaningless. These symbolic "proofs" only underscore the obvious conclusion that psychoanalytic explanations are based more on the principles of imitative magic than empirical science. Since "no substantially stronger claim to scientific status can be made for it than for Homer's collected stories from Olympus,"[95] psychoanalytic theory is actually more a religion or pseudoscience than it is a true science.

After completing his extensive review of the gambling literature Derek Cornish[96] concluded that most such discussions of gambling have been far too general in that, with few exceptions, no distinctions were made between moderate and excessive gambling. Therefore, attempts to provide answers to the question of why people gamble have generally been based on three primary assumptions. The first is that all people who gamble form a single group whose members are in some way similar to one another but different from the rest of the population. The second is that all people who gamble are seen as doing the same thing. As a consequence, the idea that different kinds of gambling might offer different rewards and therefore have different motivations was never considered. The third assumption is that motivations and explanations for people's initial gambling choices must be similar to those for habitual gambling. Since only clinical examples of excess have been discussed, gambling of all degrees has generally been attributed to some severe personality disorder. Since all of these assumptions foster the notion that all gamblers are alike irrespective of the type and extent of their gambling, they all serve to encourage explanations which attempt to attribute all forms and degrees of gambling to one or two simple motivations. However, even if such personality disorders were somehow proven to be responsible for some cases of excess, this would still not allow the conclusion that they must also be responsible for every initial decision to gamble or even for continued gambling in moderation.

Rather than the general "person centered" explanations that were offered in the past, Cornish insisted that the motivations for gambling hinge on a number of other important factors which must also be considered. In contrast to the deep-seated long-term psychodynamic forces suggested by others, Cornish insisted that gambling is most often motivated by personal, social, and situational influences that are often of a specific and temporary nature. They would include, for example, the structure of each particular game, the gambler's beliefs concerning each, the availability of gambling opportunities in the community, and the learning that takes place while gambling. As will be seen, theoreticians in other disciplines have explored these possibilities.

In the final analysis, the psychoanalytic approach is merely an elaborate, theoretical house of cards built upon a precarious foundation of untestable premises and assumptions, supported only by convoluted sophistic argumentation. Nevertheless, despite its many criticisms and overall failure, it posed a major challenge to, and shift away from, the moral and deviance models that dominated popular and scientific thought throughout the nineteenth and early twentieth centuries. Although they regarded excessive gambling, alcoholism, drug addiction, and other aberrant behavioral compulsions as mental rather than physical problems, advocates of psychoanalytic theory were still convinced that people afflicted with these and other "neurotic" illnesses would be helped more through medical attention and scientific treatment than through moral condemnation and religious conversion.

3

PERSONALITY THEORY

Personality theory, which represents a somewhat more recent approach to human motivation, maintains that people's attitudes and general behavior patterns are shaped by their individual personalities. Many earlier personality theorists were strongly influenced by the writings of the psychoanalysts. Since psychoanalytic theory maintains that the individual's childhood environment and early learning experiences are responsible for determining the adult personality, its proponents argued that the stabilization of different traits in different people must logically account for the wide range of individual personality variation. Thus, much of personality theory, as a variant of psychoanalytic theory, explained all aberrant behaviors as the product of some overindulgence or traumatic deprivational experience in childhood.[1]

Because so many early personality theorists were also psychotherapists who worked in clinical settings, "normal" drinking or gambling was seldom studied or even considered worthy of study. Most of those who chose to investigate drinking or gambling therefore drew their conclusions largely from populations of subjects whose involvement in these behaviors was considered excessive or addictive.

It must be noted, however, that not all personality theorists were psychoanalysts: some have always maintained that individual personality types are genetically ordained at birth while others have insisted they are due to differences in early learning and socialization experiences. Currently, the idea that different personality types or psychiatric disorders may be a consequence of different genetic factors appears to be gaining in popularity. One reason for this is that many dispositional and behavioral characteristics once regarded as personality traits have now been upgraded to full-blown medical disorders. For example, behavior that was once described as delinquent or criminal is now diagnosed and treated by modern psychiatrists as "antisocial personality disorder." Nevertheless, despite their different approaches to the origin and development of individual differences in temperament and demeanor, all personality theorists agree that once they are established–whether by nature or by nurture–their basic personalities predispose people to behave in certain ways.

Beginning in the 1940s many researchers came to believe that all addictions could be explained as the result of some inherent personality disorder common to all who exhibit addictive behaviors.[2] Psychoanalyst Iago Galdston,[3] for example, noted an apparent association between compulsive gambling and alcohol use and proposed that this combination of addictions was the product of the same psychodynamic motivations and processes. Similar beliefs have also been expressed or implied by more modern researchers to explain the high rates of multiple addictions that have been found in treatment populations.[4]

Most advocates of personality theory maintain that the addictive behavior is not itself the problem; it is merely symptomatic of an underlying personality disorder which may predispose some individuals toward addictive behaviors.[5] For example, one treatment counselor expressed the opinion that addicts "are clearly seen to have inadequate personalities, are low achievers with little self-esteem, usually from difficult home circumstances."[6] He felt that his client's problems were "secondary to his long term social and emotional deprivation."[7] On the basis of this premise it would not be unreasonable to assume that individuals who are born with or who develop this flawed "addictive personality" are those who will sooner or later in life develop a full-blown addiction.[8]

If this were indeed the case, we would merely need to identify which personality trait or traits are responsible for which addiction. In cases of compulsive gambling, some have commented upon the unconscious hostile, aggressive components of the gambler's personality[9] while others have been struck by what they construe to be the gambler's narcissistic[10] or obsessive-compulsive qualities.[11] Those who have observed that many compulsive gamblers become alcoholics, overeaters, or workaholics once they have stopped gambling suggest that this is due to their enduring, lifelong depression or to the traumatic events they have experienced.[12]

Pathological gamblers have therefore been characterized as an undifferentiated group of nearly identical individuals whose personalities were all forged in the same mold. They have been universally described as "flashy," manipulative, and grandiose;[13] as overconfident and impatient as well as grandiose;[14] as "basically competitive, energetic, success-driven, intelligent, and resourceful individuals."[15] However, others have interpreted these traits as merely external behavioral facades that the gambler uses to mask internal feelings of low self-esteem, poor ego development, and a need for approval. Thus, gamblers have also been collectively characterized as people who "have a disregard for social customs and mores, inability to profit from experience, and immature, aggressive, and shallow personalities"[16] and who display "exaggeration, fantasies of unlimited success, exhibitionism, cool indifference or rage in response to criticism, and feelings of emptiness."[17] Since such individuals would, of course, be terrified of any form of intimacy, the physical gratification of gambling has also been said to serve as a substitute for a mature sexual relationship.[18]

POWER NEEDS AND DEPENDENCY CONFLICT

In the past, two of the more popular personality approaches to addiction were **power theory** and **dependency conflict theory**. Like so many other psychological theories, both of these, in essence, explained addictions by reference to feelings of low self-esteem. More specifically, power theory attributed addictive disorders to an inferiority complex while dependency conflict theory ascribed them to an arrested personality development.

Since both approaches were derived from psychoanalytic theory, both are highly male-oriented. This orientation has been justified on the grounds that, because far more men than women have sought treatment for compulsive gambling, there are far fewer female than male compulsive gamblers. This observation has, in turn, been explained as a consequence of the different status needs of men and women: whereas women are believed to find personal contentment and fulfillment in the role of wife and mother through the acts of childbearing and child rearing, men can gain a sense of achievement only in the role of provider through the realization of independence and the acquisition of wealth and possessions. Those who are otherwise unsuccessful in obtaining the accoutrements of material success that mark them as men of consequence may seek to acquire them through gambling.[19] However, the potential tangible rewards of gambling are less important to most personality theorists than are the intangible emotional rewards it is believed to provide.

Both theories were also based on the premise that gambling, like alcohol and other drugs, can also induce feelings of self-importance and a sense of power or control in one's own life which are believed to compensate for the gambler's poor self-image. These positive aspects of gambling are, of course, more apparent when a gambler is winning. When this occurs the gambler's sensations of control and self-esteem are thought to be so gratifying that he will continue to play or return to gambling as soon as possible in order to maintain these feelings. Conversely, the negative, stressful aspects of gambling, which are especially acute when losses are heavy, can induce feelings of unimportance and low self-esteem. Consequently, losing also causes the compulsive gambler to intensify his playing not only in an attempt to recoup his losses, but also in an effort to regain his positive self-image. Gambling behavior is therefore believed to be motivated not only by the "action" of the play which the gambler finds pleasurable in itself, but also by winning, or just the anticipation of winning, which brings with it a feeling of enhanced self-worth.[20] Whether winning or losing, then, the pathological gambler cannot escape the drive to gamble in order to elevate a poor self-image.

Power theory evolved from the "individual psychology" of Alfred Adler.[21] Unlike Freud and others who attributed human motivation to unconscious infantile sexual desires, Adler believed that human behavior is motivated by the unconscious needs for self-esteem, achievement, and power (masculine traits) in an effort to counteract the feelings of inferiority, dependence, and weakness (feminine traits) that are universally experienced in childhood. In his initial formulation Adler believed that all personal inadequacies were associated with the penis which, like themselves, young boys see as small and inferior in comparison with their father. The negative self-image that these feelings of inferiority produce can persist into adulthood where they are dealt with in a number of ways, some of which can be highly maladaptive. In the words of a prominent psychiatrist who attributes pathological gambling to low self-esteem, "Some drugs create feelings of exhilaration or euphoria. Gambling produces a sense of power."[22] More precisely, "A gambler has to demonstrate his virility by showing himself and the world that he can take chances, whereas if he were really bold and strong, he would not have to set out to prove it";[23] "The inveterate gambler . . . can never really prove his manhood until he is completely 'potent,' which to him means winning every time, or at least winning more than he loses!"[24] Other authorities paradoxically contend that it is not the possibility of winning that attracts the gambler, but the highly ritualized structure of the game itself: the inflexible rules to which all players must adhere "let gamblers feel, at least for the duration of the game, that they are the masters of their fates."[25]

The related **dependency conflict theory** grew out of the work of Whiting and Child[26] who attributed this psychological disorder to unresolved unconscious needs for parental support and dependence that also persist into adulthood. Since independence, like power and material success, is thought to be a far greater concern for men than for women, a man's neurotic needs for continued dependence will clash with society's demands for adult independence to produce high levels of psychic stress and turmoil. These feelings may also be dealt with in potentially maladaptive ways.

According to these approaches, if one's power or dependency needs remain unresolved, the resultant feelings of inadequacy, anxiety, and low self-esteem will often be artificially alleviated through the use of alcohol, drugs, or behaviors that provide an illusion of self-confidence, independence, control, and power. This can lead to addiction if the strength of the underlying inferiority complex and the maladaptive life-style it engenders are great enough.

Consequently, just as drunkenness and alcoholism have often been attributed to unresolved, unconscious dependency conflicts[27] and power concerns,[28] so has gambling.[29] For example, some modern therapists believe that slot machine addiction can be traced to dependency conflicts originating in childhood.[30] Their conclusion is based on the observation that the fathers of many pathological gamblers are weak, alcoholic, or gamblers themselves. They contend that because the father was not available to these gamblers in childhood, they developed an early symbiotic or overly dependent relationship with the mother which they are later unable to overcome. Thus, in adulthood, although they yearn for symbiotic relationships with others, they also fear them. Slot machines offer the perfect solution which the gambler is unable to resist. According to this view, "compulsive gambling is an attempt at self-healing or a strategy of conflict-solving: the slot machine as an inanimate object offers a temporary symbiosis with clear limitations, because gambling will come to a guaranteed end, either when all . . . money is lost, or when the place closes at night."[31] In essence, these theoreticians maintain that by playing slot machines instead of getting married, the neurotic gambler is able to indulge his dependency needs without having to make a permanent commitment.

It is believed that with the proper guidance (generally one form or another of psychoanalysis), the patient will "work through" his power concerns, dependency conflicts, feelings of low self-esteem, and other personal inadequacies and eventually come to realize that he is not really an inferior person. According to one treatment specialist,

> He needs to be treated as the lonely child in need of comforting that he is, and told that he is important, not for his gambling habit, but for himself in his own right. Gradually he needs to learn through improved life experiences that gambling is unnecessary for his self-esteem, that it actually lowers rather than raises his status in the eyes of others and serves for him no constructive purpose.[32]

At this point, it is assumed, the patient will no longer feel the need to "prove" his power, independence, and self-worth through gambling (or drinking or drug use) and will abandon this maladaptive life-style. Nevertheless, even with this kind of long-term treatment, the chances that it will be successful have been characterized only as "slim."[33]

CRITIQUE OF PERSONALITY THEORY

The Search for an Identifying Trait

Unfortunately, personality theory is exceptionally difficult to prove since it cannot be supported by empirical evidence. In attempts to do so, countless gamblers have been administered myriad questionnaires, intelligence, and other personality tests such as the Wechsler Adult Intelligence Scale (WAIS), the Shipley-Hartford Test, the Minnesota Multiphasic Personality Inventory (MMPI), the California Personality Inventory (CPI), the Edwards Personal Reference Schedule, the Millon Clinical Multiaxial Inventory (MCMI), the Edwards Personal Preference Scale (EPPS), the Eysenck Personality Inventory or Questionnaire (EPI/EPQ), the Personal Orientation Inventory (POI), the Schedule for Affective Disorders and Schizophrenia (SADS), and various locus of control tests. Locus of control tests measure the degree to which individuals believe that their lives are controlled by their own decisions and actions (an internal locus of control orientation) or by such factors as luck, fate, chance, or any other supernatural influence (an external locus of control orientation).[34]

While many premorbid social environmental influences and personality correlates of pathological gambling have been suggested, few psychometric test results are complementary and some, in fact, are clearly contradictory. Thus, tests of gamblers have revealed such diverse and often discrepant social correlates and personality traits as: immaturity, narcissism, absence of narcissism, proneness to denial and fantasy, dishonesty, impulsivity, absence of impulsivity, the need for immediate gratification, the inability to learn from experience, a tendency to blame others for personal failings, hostility, rebelliousness, low frustration tolerance, high boredom proneness, normal boredom proneness, high energy levels, emotional explosiveness, aggressiveness, passive-aggressiveness, passivity, exhibitionism, avoidance, family instability, antisociability, alienation, gregariousness, high extroversion, normal extroversion, low extroversion, high interpersonal sensitivity, normal interpersonal sensitivity, nonconformity, stress, high anxiety levels, normal anxiety levels, high depression levels, absence of depression, hypomania, hypermania, psychopathic and sociopathic disorders, obsessive-compulsive disorders, absence of obsessive-compulsive disorders, self-defeating tendencies, absence of self-defeating tendencies, manipulativeness, paranoia, absence of paranoia, schizophrenia, absence of schizophrenia, perfectionism, internal locus of control orientation, external locus of control orientation, above normal intelligence, normal intelligence, below normal intelligence, low achievement motivation, normal achievement motivation, high achievement motivation, weak ego strength, dependence, autonomy, dominance, submissiveness, proneness to alcohol and other abuse, proneness to alcohol abuse without other drug abuse, and no more proneness to drug abuse than anyone else (see Appendix A).

Some specialists have attributed these discrepancies to differences in the gambling preferences (i.e., cards, machines, casino, racetrack, etc.) of the various subject groups tested[35] or to the fact that there are different subgroups of pathological gamblers.[36] Others suggest that the findings of most tests are meaningless since they were obtained solely from gamblers in treatment. In the absence of comparative data from the general population it is not known whether regular nonpathological gamblers have similar or entirely different personality profiles.[37]

Apart from the diversity of these findings, personality tests and profiles of pathological gamblers have created additional problems. Some characteristics such as obsessive-compulsiveness, hypomania or high energy level, impulsivity, low stress and frustration tolerance, insecurity, inadequacy, poor judgment, anxiety, psychopathic deviance, and depression in particular are frequently associated with pathological gambling.[38] However, a study comparing the personality characteristics of thirty-two pathological gamblers with thirty-eight controls found that while the gamblers were significantly more depressed, they were not any more anxious, obsessive-compulsive, or interpersonally sensitive than nonaddicts.[39] In fact, nearly every personality study of pathological gamblers has reported a significant correlation between gambling and depression and every study using the MMPI reports that gamblers score significantly higher than others on the psychopathic deviation scale.[40] However, the nature of the relationship between gambling and these traits is not necessarily causal. For example, in the early 1970s treatment specialist Emmanuel Moran addressed the "common misconception"[41] that all troubled gamblers are psychopaths. In his own study of the personality profiles of 50 pathological gamblers, he found not only that just one-quarter of his sample could justifiably be considered psychopaths, but also that this condition was totally unrelated to their gambling.[42]

It has been frequently pointed out[43] that even if the relationship between pathological gambling and certain personality disorders or mood states were causal, we would still be left facing a classic "chicken and egg" dilemma:[44] do anxiety, depression, and antisocial tendencies cause pathological gambling or does pathological gambling induce anxiety, depression, and antisocial behavior? Or, since a number of studies of pathological gamblers have found these traits to be premorbid in some cases but not in others,[45] could it be a question of individual psychological or physiological differences? Or, since so little is actually known about the cause(s) of pathological gambling, is it possible that both conditions stem from a larger personality disorder that has not yet been identified or even recognized?[46]

Although these questions will be taken up again in discussing the medical model, a number of studies designed to test these propositions have found no evidence that these or other personality factors are in any way involved in either low, medium, persistent, heavy, or pathological gambling.[47] Thus, the author of one literature review felt that "At present it is preferable to assume that excessive gamblers are a heterogeneous group of people; evidence does not permit their excess to be attributed to a specific weakness, predisposition or type of personality."[48] The authors of another also felt that "Psychological tests of pathological gamblers have failed to establish homogenous 'ideal types.'"[49] The authors of a third felt that despite some consistencies in research, "it would perhaps be premature, though it has often been done, to characterize the pathological gambler as possessing a particular personality type. None of the consistencies have lead to predictive identification of pathological gamblers, nor to specific recommendations for therapeutic mode."[50] Finally, the author of an extensive review of the pertinent literature was forced to conclude not only that "no one test has yielded consistent significant differences between gamblers and nongamblers,"[51] but also that "a personality profile distinguishing pathological gamblers from merely social gamblers has not been discovered."[52]

Conversely, the idea of a typical "preaddictive personality disorder" which was popular in the 1950s has been seriously challenged by the findings of studies suggesting that addictive behaviors are the cause, rather than the effect, of the emotional, social, and family difficulties that many addicts experience.[53] One posttreatment follow-up study of sixty-three pathological gamblers found that the state (chronic) anxiety, trait (situational) anxiety, neuroticism, psychoticism, depression, anger, and tension scores of currently abstinent and controlled gamblers were substantially lower than those of subjects who had relapsed into uncontrolled gambling. Before treatment all subjects had shown psychopathological levels of these traits. Some treatment specialists report that while all patients are clinically depressed when they are admitted, "they seem to show the symptomology of true advanced endogenous depression no more often than any randomly selected population."[54] Another study of fourteen depressed pathological gamblers found that in most cases uncontrolled gambling and its adverse effects preceded the onset of depression. Its authors therefore concluded that the depression the subjects experienced was a consequence of their gambling rather than its cause.[55] This impression is supported by a survey of 500 members of Gamblers Anonymous which found that while many respondents reported symptoms of severe depression, anxiety, psychosomatic, and other emotional difficulties during the worst phase of their gambling period, relatively few felt that they still required counseling for these conditions after a period of abstinence. Moreover, their stated need for treatment decreased with the length of their abstinence.[56] Abstinent and controlled gamblers also report greater social, financial, sexual, and marital functioning than uncontrolled gamblers.[57]

Perhaps one of the most serious defects of personality research in pathological gambling is one of sampling bias. One of the most fundamental assumptions of many personality theorists is that if dysphoric or unpleasant mood states such as anxiety or depression play any role in motivating normal gambling, they should be of even greater importance in the genesis of abnormal or pathological gambling. However, this proposition has rarely been tested since, as one critic pointed out, all personality data have been derived from members of Gamblers Anonymous (GA) and other treatment populations to the exclusion of the general population.[58] Although most members of treatment populations are white, middle-class, middle-aged males, epidemiological prevalence studies indicate that there are far more females, ethnic minorities, those in lower income groups, and younger adults in the general population who are probable pathological gamblers than are found in any treatment population. For example, population surveys have found that at least one-third of those identified as probable pathological gamblers are women whereas GA and treatment populations, from which most personality data have been derived, are typically 98 percent white males.[59] Consequently, women, ethnic minorities, the less affluent, and those under thirty-five years of age and the elderly have consistently been grossly underrepresented in all personality profile studies of the "typical" pathological gambler. This led the critic to question,

> I wonder whether the "big ego," "high IQ," and other traits seemingly characteristic of compulsive gamblers . . . are traits of those in the general population or just of those currently in treatment. The "big ego" and "high IQ" may be traits of middle class white males.[60]

Although this concern is entirely valid, it has generated relatively little research. One notable exception is found in a study that was undertaken specifically to examine the purported relationship between gambling and depression in a random telephone survey of 400 nonaddicted adults in the general population of Omaha, Nebraska.[61] In addition to questions on demographic variables and the frequencies, if any, of participation in various kinds of gambling, the researchers also administered a standard depression questionnaire to each respondent. Contrary to the expectations of many personality theorists, the data failed to reveal any association between gambling and depression in this general population sample. However, the authors judiciously pointed out that their findings cannot be read as a contradiction of any studies reporting a relationship between depression and pathological gambling.

Finally, in direct contrast to the popular notion that all gamblers suffer from one or more psychological or personality defects, some studies have concluded that gamblers, in fact, tend to be *better adjusted* psychologically and have *healthier* personalities than nongamblers. One early investigation into the overall personality adjustment of regular female poker players who gambled an average of 18.5 hours a week concluded that "the women used in this study are significantly better adjusted, on the average, than are the female adults of the general population."[62] These findings were attributed to the fact that they gambled to combat boredom rather than for money. Similar findings were reported in a study of male university students which compared the personality traits of avid gamblers to those of nongamblers. On the basis of psychoanalytic theory, regular gamblers were expected to be insecure, socially irresponsible, dominant, feminine, and unhappy. Personality test results revealed that gamblers were slightly less socially responsible and more dominant than nongamblers but more secure, more masculine, and equally happy.[63] A later study found that a sample of racetrack bettors scored lower on tests of hostility, family difficulties, anxiety, and the experiencing of internal sensation than a control group composed of graduate students in psychology. The study also showed a positive correlation between the number of hours spent gambling per week and such variables as tenseness, rebelliousness, dominance, and education. The gamblers also reported feelings of excitement, power, confidence, and of being in control.[64] Similar findings were reported in a study that compared heavy, light, and nongamblers.[65] Since this study also found that among heavy gamblers, the number of years of gambling correlated negatively with anxiety and depression, its authors concluded that "For the Heavy Gamblers gambling seems to be a healthy activity."[66] Consequently, "The assumptions that gamblers who seek help are mentally disordered or have a personality that predisposes them to gamble heavily have not been substantiated."[67] It must be remembered, however, that the subjects of these studies were identified only by such terms as heavy, regular, light, and nongamblers; none were diagnosed or otherwise identified as compulsive or pathological gamblers.

Not only has there been little support for the notion of a premorbid addictive personality to date, but it seems that people of any given personality type are no more prone to addiction than is anyone else.[68] It is also becoming widely recognized that pathological gamblers, like alcoholics and other substance abusers, vary widely in terms of intelligence and personality traits.[69] Thus, it has been concluded that

> Gambling, in one form or another, is likely to attract all levels and classes of people as it becomes more widely available. . . . There is as yet no convincing evidence that pathological gamblers as a population are brighter than, or qualitatively different in terms of personality from, non-gamblers or

those with different addictions.[70]

Trait Constellations

Since no single personality trait which predisposes a person to compulsive gambling has ever been isolated, it has been proposed that certain groups or constellations of traits may be responsible. On the basis of their clinical experience, for example, some researchers have described several different types of gamblers each with a different personality profile. One of the first to attempt such a categorization, for example, was Beverly Lowenfeld[71] who, in trying to discover whether pathological gamblers could be included among those having a basic "addictive personality," compared the MMPI scores of 100 pathological gamblers to those of 100 alcoholics receiving treatment for their respective addictions. Although no major personality differences emerged between these two groups, Lowenfeld reported that the scores of gamblers were higher than those of the alcoholics on several MMPI subscales.[72] The most common categorization in both groups was the "sociopathic personality, antisocial" subtype which included those who scored high on the Psychopathic Deviate and Mania subscales. The next most common subtype was the "paranoid personality," represented by those who scored high on the Paranoid, Psychasthenia, Depression, and Psychopathic subscales. A final subtype, those scoring high on the Depression, Psychasthenia, Psychopathic Deviate, and Hysteria subscales, was designated as the "anxiety reaction in a passive-dependent personality."

Another scheme was devised by Alida Glen[73] whose findings were based on the MMPI scores of forty pathological gamblers in treatment. The most common type was represented by a group of anxiety-ridden gamblers who scored high on the Depression, Psychasthenia, and Schizophrenia subscales of the MMPI. Those in this category, which Glen referred to as "the unemployed teacher" subtype, were described as being plagued by severe feelings of inferiority, inadequacy, hypersensitivity, anxiety, and depression. The next most common subtype consisted of those who had high Depression, Psychopathic Deviate, and Psychasthenia scores. They were referred to as "the salesman" since they demonstrated anxiety, hostility, and immaturity along with the aggressiveness and superficial extroversion typical of salesmen. The third most common subtype was the "sociopathic personality" which included those with high Psychopathic Deviate and Mania subscale scores who were characterized by an inability to live by the rules of society, poor work habits, failed marriages, frequent delinquency and criminality, and an inability to learn from past experience. Those in Glen's final subtype, "the bookkeeper," were typically employed in clerical positions. Scoring high only on the Psychopathic Deviate subscale, they were described as unstable, impulsive, insecure, dependent, and demanding individuals who were given to frequent fits of anger and drunkenness.

On the basis of the personality traits exhibited by the pathological gamblers they encountered, Richard McCormick and Julian Taber[74] described three personality profiles or "prototypes," each of which was illustrated by the case history of a particular gambler. The first personality prototype was demonstrated by an individual with a history of severe chronic depression, severe life trauma, substance abuse, high socialization, and obsessive-compulsive tendencies. Since his "high socialization" resulted from early institutionalization instead of a secure home life, this individual failed in treatment. The second described an individual with moderate situational depression with associated anxiety, periodic alcohol abuse, low socialization, high compulsivity, and only minimal life trauma. Since his socialization was low he never internalized any values of his own, had a poorly developed self-identity, and suffered from acute dependency and borderline personality disorder. Although he benefitted from treatment in the short term, his long-term success was questionable, especially since he dropped out of the program. The third example was represented by an individual who, since childhood, had been pushed to succeed. He exhibited low socialization marked by extreme hostility, low depression, high compulsivity and narcissism, no history of substance abuse, and only minimal lifetime trauma. His treatment outcome was not described. The authors used these examples to stress that "heavy loading on any individual dimension does not seem to be a necessary condition for the development of pathological gambling"[75] and that the hypothesized single unique "compulsive" or "addictive personality" does not exist.

Studies designed to test the trait constellation proposition were undertaken some time ago. They found either no indication of such personality trait constellations,[76] or the components of the particular trait constellation that was predicted were either the opposite of those expected or were not statistically significant.[77] Similar ideas were also explored in attempts to isolate the personality trait clusters of alcoholics[78] but here, too, the expected results failed to materialize.[79] One of the most recent attempts to test the existence of an addictive personality investigated the tendency for people to become addicted to a wide variety of behaviors and substances including gambling, video games, chocolate, sweets, caffeine, nicotine, alcohol, and other drugs. Finding only a weak tendency for addiction across this broad range of behaviors, the researchers concluded that "there is little basis for the assumption of a general tendency to become addicted, a conclusion which casts doubt on the derivative notion of an addictive personality."[80]

Nevertheless, even if a specific personality trait or constellation of traits were found to be unequivocally associated with gambling or other forms of addiction, its mere identification would still tell us very little about the ultimate cause of gambling. As one critic[81] cogently observed, personality traits describe a person's general behavior patterns which are exhibited in a variety of situations. The mere identification of a trait such as the need for achievement, for example, offers little in the way of an explanation since we still do not know how that trait originated in the first place. Moreover, explanations that are based on the presence of a particular personality trait are perilously circular: "This person gambles because they are risk-oriented; we know they are risk-oriented because they gamble."[82] If explanations related to personality traits are to have any value at all, their existence and magnitude must be established independently of the behavior they purport to explain. Even then, however, we would still not know why a particular trait or group of traits should prompt gambling as opposed to any other form of behavior.

In short, the many attempts to isolate the personality traits or trait constellations that may be responsible for addictive behaviors, including pathological gambling, have so far failed. This lack of any solid evidence has led some addiction researchers to conclude that "The main argument for an addictive tendency comes from theories of addiction, rather than the demonstration of an empirical relation."[83] Others feel that "the alcoholic personality is no longer a viable concept."[84] Similarly, some attempts to identify the personality traits of pathological gamblers have led to the conclusions that "all personality patterns may be found among compulsive gamblers"[85] and that "the only generalization that seems to hold is that they all gamble, and that their gambling causes them significant problems."[86] Thus, some gambling researchers feel that, "as with much of the psychometric literature on persons with alcoholism, the utility and value of such studies remain doubtful."[87]

Despite the lack of any supportive evidence, belief in the existence of an addictive personality is still strong and enduring, and the quest for those personality traits most strongly associated with addictive disorders persists to the present day. This search continues not only in studies of the basic personality traits of drug addicts and compulsive gamblers but also in studies of the possible relationships between various neuropsychological/neurobiological deficits and addiction. Thus, the co-occurrence of alcoholism with attention-deficit hyperactivity disorder,[88] affective disorders,[89] and antisocial personality disorder[90] are currently receiving a great deal of attention. Similarly, rates of comorbidity of pathological gambling with affective disorder, attention-deficit hyperactivity disorder, antisocial personality disorder, impulsivity, obsessive-compulsive disorder, panic disorder, schizophrenia, alcoholism, drug addiction, and environmental stresses and traumas are also being investigated.[91]

Much of this research is being undertaken to determine whether these are premorbid traits which increase the risk of addiction or postmorbid traits which develop as a consequence of an addiction. By and large, the search for causal factors of these sorts has so far been disappointing. For example, a number of studies have suggested a strong relationship between crime and pathological gambling but the direction of causality remained unclear: was one a consequence of the other or did gambling and criminality both result from a basic antisocial personality structure? A study designed to answer this question found that in a sample of 109 pathological gamblers, many of whom had committed crimes, the incidence of Antisocial Personality Disorder was only 14.6 percent.[92] Its authors therefore concluded that antisocial features are more often the consequences of pathological gambling than they are its antecedents and contended that "The need to maintain the gambling addiction and not the desire for personal economic gain appears the principle motivation for criminal behavior."[93] Similar results were obtained in a later study of 306 pathological gamblers of whom only 15 percent met the criteria for Antisocial Personality Disorder. Since the majority of the sample had committed gambling-related criminal offenses, the authors were forced to conclude that among pathological gamblers "offenses are not related to a general propensity to engage in criminal behaviours or part of an antisocial personality spectrum but rather emerge in response to gambling induced difficulties."[94] Moreover, none of the females in this sample were diagnosed with Antisocial Personality Disorder. In most cases, therefore, the egg comes before the chicken since gambling problems typically precede any criminal offenses; in those relatively few cases in which pathological gambling and antisocial personality appear together, the two conditions would seem to exist independently of one another. However, the investigation of a number of other personality and behavioral factors begins to blur the line between the purely environmental and purely biological approaches to addiction since some psychiatric disorders may be inherited. For example, since the question of neurological deficits is perhaps more a matter of nature than of nurture, it will receive further treatment in a later volume.

Furthermore, a number of researchers

who favor a multicausal explanation suggest that personality may constitute just one of a number of equally important predisposing factors, that not all pathological gamblers need necessarily have the same personality type, and that different personalities may be attracted to different forms of gambling.[95] It is generally agreed, however, that if personality does indeed play a role in the addictions, a great deal of work remains to be accomplished before its role is understood.[96]

Part II

BEHAVIORAL PSYCHOLOGY

The Role of Rewards, Punishments, and Associational Learning

4

LEARNING OR REINFORCEMENT THEORY

LEARNING THEORY VERSUS PSYCHOANALYTIC THEORY

Learning or reinforcement theory is nearly the antithesis of psychoanalytic theory. Although its roots have been traced to Aristotle, behavioral psychology underwent its most serious development the 1950s, primarily as a reaction to psychoanalytic theory and its inability to explain human motivation in general and addiction in particular.[1] The two approaches are similar only in that they ascribe pathological gambling and other addictions to psychological rather than physiological mechanisms. They are entirely different in a number of other important respects.

Whereas psychoanalytic and personality theories place many of the causes of human behavior within the individual psyche irrespective of any present environmental influences, learning theory locates their source outside the individual but always within his or her immediate environment. Learning theory is therefore far less concerned with unconscious past memories of early childhood than it is with the ways in which organisms learn to respond to the immediate social and physical situations they encounter at any age. For these reasons the methods and conclusions of learning theory, unlike those of psychoanalysis, are thought to apply equally to males and females of all animal species.

Furthermore, whereas psychoanalysts, personality theorists, and advocates of the medical model are more interested in understanding compulsive or pathological gambling among the mentally ill, learning theorists are more interested in exploring the motivations for involvement among normal or "social" gamblers. By extension, they believe, the same factors that ordinarily motivate normal gambling can also account for heavy gambling. In fact, many psychologists are convinced that there is no such thing as "compulsive" or "pathological" gambling. Instead, they acknowledge only the existence of different degrees of gambling involvement–occasional, regular, persistent, and excessive. They maintain that excessive gambling, which others refer to as "compulsive" or "pathological," is no different qualitatively from any other kind of gambling: it merely represents that point along the quantitative continuum of lighter to heavier involvement at which people regularly experience impaired control, become so deeply involved that they begin to encounter financial and legal problems, and seek professional help for these problems. Since this point varies so greatly from individual to individual, it is impossible to distinguish excessive gamblers from recreational gamblers on any other basis.[2] According to one such psychologist,

> compulsive gamblers are not a race apart. . . . The potential for gambling, in one form or another, is to be found in every man. If we are to understand the gambler we must try and see what he has in common with other men. Only then shall we grasp how and where he parts company.[3]

As will be demonstrated in a subsequent volume, many prominent sociologists are also among those who refuse to recognize the validity of any medically defined gambling disorder.

Finally, whereas psychoanalytic formulations of human behavior are based on insight, inference, speculation, and deductive reasoning–the methods of philosophy and theology–those of learning theory hinge upon observation, measurement, experimentation, and inductive reasoning–the methods of empirical science. Due to its scientific approach, learning theory and its behavioral treatment methods are among the most popular approaches to be found within the psychological community.

Behavioral psychologists acknowledge two basic types of learning, Skinnerian or operant conditioning and Pavlovian or classical conditioning, both of which are believed to be instrumental in maintaining repetitive patterns of behavior. According to behaviorism, all learning occurs as a result of the associations an organism makes between events that occur in its immediate environment and its reactions to those events. For this reason, when they speak of behavioral excesses, advocates of learning theory prefer to avoid such terms as "addictive disorders" or "diseases" which have a strong medical connotation. Instead, they prefer to speak of "addictive behaviors,"[4] "addictive-like preoccupations,"[5] "behavioral" or "nonchemical addictions,"[6] "addictive lifestyles,"[7] "appetitive behaviour problems,"[8] or of "impaired control"[9] which suggest that they are learning problems.

Included among the addictive behaviors are such compulsions as drug and alcohol dependence, pathological gambling, overeating or obesity, bulimia, anorexia nervosa, and hypersexuality.[10] Learning theorists believe that all such compulsive behaviors represent "acquired habit patterns."[11] Interestingly, although nicotine is one of the most highly addictive substances known, some list tobacco smoking among these habits[12] while others do not.[13] Some authorities include all obsessive-compulsive disorders including the compulsion to be in love,[14] compulsive spending,[15] pyromania, kleptomania,[16] nymphomania, hypochondria, addiction to needless surgery, overeating, confessing to crimes that one has not committed,[17] trichotillomania or habitual hair pulling, facial tics, and even Tourette syndrome,[18] which is known to be a neurological disorder.

OPERANT CONDITIONING

The operant or instrumental conditioning model was developed by behaviorist B. F. Skinner.[19] The basic premises of this approach are that a habitual voluntary (as opposed to an autonomic or reflexive) behavioral response to any stimulus is learned, and that any learned response can also be unlearned. Learned behavioral responses can be extinguished through punishment or, somewhat more slowly, by a discontinuance of the positive reinforcer. Thus, laboratory animals that are motivated by hunger and thirst can quickly learn or be "conditioned" to peck at a button, press a bar, or pull a lever if they receive the reward of bird seed, food pellets, or a dose of sugared water for doing so. They will continue to press the bar as long as they continue to receive the anticipated reward since this behavior–the conditioned response–is positively reinforced. However, they will quit pressing the bar if they receive a punishment such as an electric shock when they do so or if they consistently fail to receive the anticipated reward.

Learning theorists believe the concept of reinforcement to be especially useful in explaining gambling behavior since they assume that people gamble to win money. Most gamblers do, in fact, express a desire for money and entertainment or excitement as their main reasons for gambling.[20] According to this approach, skillful or lucky gambling will be reinforced by the reward of winning money while careless or unlucky gambling should be extinguished by the punishment of losing it. In cases of occasional or normal recreational gambling, this is generally what happens.[21] In cases of heavy, persistent or pathological gambling, however, extinction of the betting response through monetary loss does not occur. A number of explanations for this phenomenon have been proposed.

Schedules of Reinforcement

Laboratory animals can be conditioned to perform a particular action even when it is not rewarded after each trial. Thus, a conditioned response that is consistently rewarded after every three trials, for example, will be learned as readily as one that is rewarded after each trial. Such patterns are referred to as *fixed-interval* (FI) schedules of reinforcement since the reward always occurs on a regular basis. However, conditioned responses that are learned under FI schedules of reinforcement are rapidly extinguished when the subject learns that the behavioral sequence no longer produces the expected reward. A conditioned response can also be maintained when reinforcement is presented on an irregular basis, sometimes after only a few trials and sometimes after many. Interestingly, experimental psychologists have discovered that the strength and persistence of a conditioned response such as a bar press will be greatest if it is rewarded on a randomly intermittent basis, as long as the average number of rewards remains fairly constant. Behaviorists refer to this pattern of reinforcement as a *variable-ratio* (VR) schedule.[22]

Variable-Ratio Schedules

As is the case with other conditioned behaviors, the strongest and most compelling reward sequence for shaping and maintaining gambling behavior is also the variable-ratio schedule. According to the Skinner[23] and others,[24] variable-ratio schedule is the basis for *all* gambling systems. Although the average monetary payout ratio may be fixed, reinforcement in such patterns always occurs in a random and unpredictable manner so that the gambler can never be sure when the next reward will occur nor how great it will be. Most gambling ventures therefore involve not only variable-ratio but also variable-magnitude schedules of reinforcement. Under these circumstances, whether a gambler's last bet or play was won or lost, the next could always be a winner, and possibly a big winner. This fact is well-known and exploited by professional gamblers and those in the gaming industry. By creating a sense of false hope and anticipation, slot machine[24] owners gain an even greater advantage from the "near miss"[26] or "near win"[27] phenomenon which may be as instrumental in conditioning persistence as actually winning:

> By paying off very generously–the jackpot–for "three bars," the device eventually makes two bars plus any other figure strongly reinforcing. "Almost hitting the jack pot" increases the probability that the individual will play the machine, although this reinforcer costs the owner of the device nothing.[28]

Altering the Variable-Ratio Schedule

Professional gamblers have the advantage of being able to alter a reinforcement schedule during a game by allowing their opponents to win more frequently at the beginning of a game but continually less frequently as the game progresses:

> The professional gambler "leads his victim on" by building a favorable history of reinforcement. He begins with a low mean ratio under which reinforcement occurs so frequently that the victim wins. The mean ratio is then increased, either slowly or rapidly depending upon how long the gambler plans to work with a particular victim. This is precisely the way in which the behavior of a pigeon or rat is brought under the control of a variable-ratio schedule. A mean ratio can be reached at which reinforcements occur so rarely that the pigeon or rat spends more energy in operating the device than he receives from the reinforcement with food, while the human subject steadily loses money. All three subjects, however, continue to play.[29]

In his laboratory experiments, Skinner found that he could stretch the reinforcement schedule of pigeons to the point that they would literally peck themselves to exhaustion and death in anticipation of a reward of bird seed. Likewise, as the professional or dishonest gambler steadily "stretches" the mean reinforcement ratio, "the victim continues to play during a very long period without reinforcement"[30] since he has also been conditioned to anticipate that the next play might bring the long-awaited reward.

Persistence and the Structural Characteristics of Gambling Games

Although people may be motivated to gamble initially by the prospect of winning money, the question arises as to why so many continue to gamble when they are clearly losing. Many behaviorists attribute heavy, persistent, or pathological gambling directly to the uncertainty factor which is built into variable-ratio, variable-magnitude schedules of reinforcement[31] since "It is characteristic of intermittent reinforcement that behavior may be sustained over long periods with very little return."[32] Early tests of this hypothesis involved the use of modified slot machines in two-part experiments intended to determine which types of reinforcement produced the longest extinction periods and, hence, generated the greatest gambling persistence.[33] All participants received an initial training period during which different groups of subjects were exposed to different schedules of reinforcement. This was followed by an extinction period during which nothing was won. These tests found that the longest extinction periods were preceded by training periods of fewer wins and of larger wins. In essence, these experiments found that persistence increases as reinforcement ratios decrease and reward levels increase. These facts are well known and consistently applied by commercial gaming interests.

Reinforcement intervals and payout sizes represent only two of the structural characteristics of gambling activities that may encourage persistence. Other important features of various gambling activities that are influential in the acquisition, maintenance, and escalation of gambling behavior have also been described.[34] Included among them are:

Frequency of Opportunities for Gambling

This feature can be increased by providing readier access to gambling activities and by decreasing the time it takes between bets. For example, the first has been achieved through the legalization of licensed off-track betting offices and other gambling opportunities such as pull tabs, lottery ticket sales, fruit machines, video lottery games, and other electronic gambling games in public places; the second has been realized through the widespread replacement of mechanical gambling machines with their faster electronic counterparts. Betting frequencies are maximized in continuous forms of gambling such as roulette, blackjack, and slot machines which involve a rapid succession of many plays per session as opposed to discontinuous forms such as lottery drawings which require longer periods between the time a stake is made and its outcome is known. The significance of this feature lies in the fact that the faster the "action," the less time players have to think about their cumulative losses.

Payout Interval

The length of time between placing a bet and receiving one's winnings can also contribute to persistence. This is particularly evident at gaming tables and slot machines where instant winnings can be instantly replayed. By eliminating the street bookie legalized betting shops have also reduced both the time needed to learn of an outcome and the time required to collect on a winning bet. Moreover, prompt payouts not only reinforce the persistence of the winners, but they also serve as vicarious reinforcements that encourage potential players to begin betting and induce bettors who have not yet won to chase their previous losses. Since this feature promotes the recirculation of winnings into new bets and attracts new money it is especially important for generating and maintaining a steady flow of cash into the game.

Ranges of Odds and Stakes

The variety of risks that are available in most forms of gambling appeal to a broader range of potential gamblers since they enable participants to control the rates at which their activities proceed. Initial risks of relatively small amounts of money allow novices the opportunity to develop a sense of familiarity and skill with gambling activities that are new to them. Once they feel secure in their knowledge of the most appropriate times for increasing their stakes and making longer-odds bets they will be inclined to gamble for longer periods.

Degree of Personal Involvement; Exercise of Skill

One's physical presence at a gambling venue coupled with active involvement in its activities and choosing among a number of betting alternatives is also believed to reinforce repeated and riskier betting. For example, although craps is a game of chance it is exceptionally popular because it has the highest degree of player involvement of all casino games: the players not only select and place their bets from a wide variety of options but they also throw the dice. Racetrack betting combines a high degree of player involvement with the need for experience and skill. Whether one plays at the track or in an off-track betting office, racing forms provide information that is deemed essential to all serious handicappers. The ability to read and carefully weigh all the published facts before betting provides horse players a strong feeling of involvement and enhances the perception of control over their betting choices. Visiting the track in person as opposed to betting through a bookie or betting office affords closer access to the horses, their owners and trainers, and other track personnel through which they can increase their store of "inside information" about the possible outcome of a race.[35] The greater feelings of foresight, control, and confidence in one's selections that this knowledge inspires can cause optimistic bettors to overestimate their chances for success and adjust their bets accordingly. Even in such games as roulette, which requires no skill and minimal player involvement, the illusion of skill and control have also been found to exert a strong influence over one's betting behavior (see the following section on Cognitive-Behavioral Psychology). Likewise, buttons offering various player options with which British and German slot machines are equipped provide only illusory control that nevertheless serve to prolong playing sessions.[36]

Probabilities of Winning and Payout/Takeout Ratios

The objective mathematically calculable chances for winning and the potential payout ratios–which in commercial gambling situations always favor the house–are discussed more completely in the following section. Although these facts are known to commercial gambling interests, the true odds of winning often are not known to their customers since gambling promoters generally are very careful to avoid publicizing this information. Any lack of specific information about the house advantage and takeout ratios of various gambling games would clearly prevent a gambler from making optimal (from his point of view) betting decisions.

Other Characteristics

Additional structural characteristics of gambling can also influence the frequency and amount of one's bets. One is the degree to which betting is associated with other activities such as sporting events when the excitement, enthusiasm, and favoritism with which people view important athletic spectacles may cause them to forego their usual prudence in betting. Another involves the use of chips, tokens, small stakes, or small denomination coins in place of currency or larger monetary units which also minimizes the perception of many gamblers that any "real" money is being risked. A third characteristic is represented by the built-in mechanical features of slot machines which are constructed so that the left reel is the first to stop spinning, the center reel the second, and the right reel the last. The left reel also has the largest number of winning symbols, the center reel has fewer, and the right has the fewest. This construction design is specifically intended to keep gamblers playing longer by exploiting the "near win" or "false hope" phenomenon since one or two winning symbols are likely to appear before the end of the sequence. In a study intended to test the effects of this design some subjects played standard slot machines while others played machines which were modified so that the symbol frequencies were reversed. Those who were exposed to potential winning symbol combinations early in the sequence played significantly longer than those who played the machines on which they appeared later.[37] Additional situational and psychological variables that can also influence one's betting behavior, such as the erroneous beliefs that are fostered by certain forms of gambling, are discussed in the following section.

Each form of gambling has its own particular blend of characteristics that encourage extended play. In lotteries, for example, the low frequency of drawings, lack of any actual skill requirements, high takeout rates, exceptionally low probabilities of winning, relative lack of substantial reinforcements, and extended payout intervals are offset by their low stake requirements, low awareness of cumulative losses, exceptionally high primary prizes, and a range of secondary prizes.[38] Because casino owners, racetrack managers, and slot machine manufacturers are also well aware of all these characteristics, their table games, racing events, and gambling machines are finely tuned to maximize player persistence and, hence, their own profit margins.

CLASSICAL CONDITIONING

The basic premise of the Pavlovian or classical conditioning model is that a reflexive response to one stimulus can be unintentionally elicited by an unrelated stimulus if the two stimuli are presented together often enough. The early twentieth-century Russian experimental psychologist Ivan Pavlov[39] observed that whenever his laboratory animals were presented with food (the unconditioned stimulus) they would begin to salivate (produce the reflexive unconditioned response). When feeding was regularly paired with the sound of an audio stimulus such as a bell, buzzer, or metronome (the conditioned stimulus) the animals would begin to salivate (produce a conditioned response) as soon as they heard this sound. This happened even when feeding was delayed since the paired audio stimulus had become an environmental cue that the animals had involuntarily learned to associate with feeding. Thereafter, whenever they heard the appropriate sound they would begin to salivate in anticipation of the food they expected to receive, and this response was reinforced by the food they were given soon afterward. Thus, one stimulus can produce the *expectation* of another stimulus as well as the behavioral response that it elicits.

Classical Conditioning and Cue Exposure

It has been argued that whether addictive behaviors are intended to induce positive emotional states or to reduce negative ones, they eventually come to be strongly associated with a variety of situational cues. It has long been held, for example, that the eating response of compulsive overeaters is more often triggered by such external cues as the time of day, the smell of certain foods, or the sight of a bakery than it is by the internal sensation of hunger.[40] Similarly, the social or environmental setting itself is often thought to provide a stimulus for drinking, drug use, or gambling, and whenever addicted individuals find themselves in such situations they will be likely to respond in accordance with their previous experiences or earlier conditioning.[41]

Adherents of this approach believe that habitual behaviors are maintained not only by external stimulus cues, but also by the misinterpretation and inappropriate discrimination of certain internally-felt cues. For example, compulsive overeaters are believed to confuse their sensations of autonomic arousal with "hunger"[42] and respond accordingly. Likewise, substance abusers are believed to misconstrue any change in the internal levels of autonomic arousal they feel as craving, anxiety, tension, or boredom.[43] Ingestion of food or a chemical substance serves to restore autonomic equilibrium, thereby reinforcing these responses. Mislabeled autonomic sensations are also held to be partially responsible for habitual gambling. Such external stimuli as the croupier's call, the spinning of a gaming wheel, the sound or sight of chips and coins, the shuffling of cards, or track announcements can induce internal states of arousal and excitement or tension and anxiety which further reinforce the gambling response.[44] This response can also intensify with experience: "Once [slot machine] players reach a level of weekly and more frequent sessions, the onset of a 'new' session comes to be predictably associated with cues such as the club environment and large cash sums."[45] It has also been reported that just thinking about gambling elicits the conditioned response: "During the period of anticipation, there is also a "rush," usually characterized by sweaty palms, rapid heart beat, and nausea."[46]

Arousal theorists, who are discussed in the following chapter, therefore feel that the repetitive autonomic stimulation that invariably accompanies gambling "is likely to have a powerful classical or Pavlovian conditioning effect . . . and may contribute significantly to the development of gambling addiction."[47] Perhaps one of the most compelling first-hand descriptions of the influence that such associational cues can have is found in a passage in Dostoevsky's *The Gambler:*

> . . . with what a tremor, with what thrill at my heart, I hear the croupier's cry: . . . . With what avidity I look at the gambling table on which louis d'or, friedrichs d'or, and thalers lie scattered: on the piles of gold when they are scattered from the croupier's shovel like glowing embers, or at the piles of silver a yard high that lie round the wheel. Even on my way to the gambling hall, as soon as I hear, two rooms away, the clink of scattered money I almost go into convulsions.[48]

Some behaviorists argue that even such characteristic features as tolerance to an addictive substance or behavior, the withdrawal symptoms that accompany its cessation, and the reinstatement effect or relapse (resumption of an addictive behavior at peak levels even after years of abstinence) are primarily a consequence of Pavlovian conditioning.[49] Although this position is more difficult to maintain in the explanation of chemical addictions whose causes and consequences may be more physiologically based, some specialists feel it is far more easily maintained in cases of nonchemical addictions such as gambling in which no chemical substances are ingested.[50]

Behavior Completion Mechanisms

Although the primary ways in which the Pavlovian or classical conditioning model have been applied to gambling and other addictive behaviors will be the focus of subsequent chapters, one variant of this approach warrants discussion here as it involves a blend of Skinnerian and Pavlovian ideas. According to this hypothesis, which combines classical conditioning with the tension-reduction hypothesis, compulsive gambling involves "behavior completion mechanisms" in which certain behavioral sequences which have been established by repetition are activated by the proper situational cues.[51] Subjective feelings of tension, anxiety, or depression may also work in conjunction with behavior completion mechanisms to reinforce gambling behavior. In theory, then, exposure to gambling or a strong gambling-related cue generates a drive to gamble, and once this drive sequence has been initiated any attempt to interrupt it will arouse heightened states of tension and anxiety which can only be alleviated by completion of that sequence–by gambling.

The therapeutic technique known as imaginal desensitization is based on the

Behavior Completion Mechanism hypothesis. Both the hypothesis and the treatment method were tested with two groups of pathological gamblers seeking treatment.[52] The subjects of the experimental group were first asked to envision themselves entering into gambling situations and to describe the typically arousing sequence of events leading to gambling. However, before they were able to describe completion of the act, they were instructed to imagine themselves leaving the situation without actually having gambled but still feeling relaxed. The success of this group was compared to a similar group of subjects who were treated with the conventional aversive technique of electric shock. Both groups received fourteen treatments in five days. Results of follow-up studies conducted one month and one year later showed significantly greater improvement marked by reduced gambling activities, urges, and anxiety levels among those who had been treated with imaginal desensitization. The researchers interpreted their findings as support for the behavior completion mechanism hypothesis. But this hypothesis appears to have been challenged by a later study in which exposure to gambling cues followed by a delay in access to expected gambling opportunities failed to elicit an emotional response in heavy gamblers.[53] Its authors acknowledged, however, that heavy gamblers are not necessarily compulsive or pathological gamblers. Nevertheless, other clinicians have claimed limited success in treating two cases of clinically diagnosed pathological gambling with the related cue-exposure, response prevention method that also interrupts the gambler's stimulus-response sequence.[54]

CRITIQUE OF REINFORCEMENT THEORY

Opposing Views

Conditioning or reinforcement theorists assume that the intermittent monetary rewards of gambling serve to reinforce persistence despite the large losses it may entail. Some critics therefore challenge Skinnerian explanations for compulsive gambling on the grounds that they do not reflect reality. Psychoanalyst Peter Fuller, who championed the idea that both the attraction and the aversion to gambling were manifestations of an underlying anal fixation, was particularly antagonistic to learning theory:

> Simple conditioning theories just will not work. When a man becomes a gambler, and persists in gambling despite repeated losses, he flies in the face of behavioural learning theory. He is like a rat who keeps returning to the pot for food, even after it has been conditioned long enough to learn that all it will get from that particular source is an electric shock. And, irritatingly for those who wish to equate human behaviour precisely with that of rodents, no such rats exist.[55]

Others contend that since most of the experimental research on the effects of different schedules of reinforcement has been conducted with laboratory animals, their findings may not apply to humans. Cognitive psychologists feel that people's conscious but erroneous thought processes and beliefs are more important than reinforcement schedules in fostering persistence. Thus, following their research on "hindsight bias" (described in the next chapter), an attributional phenomenon that affects the betting decisions of many gamblers, two cognitive theorists came to this conclusion:

> Unlike the lower organisms often studied by behavioral theorists, people have thoughts about the implications of each trial. Certain trials are considered more informative than others and thus have a greater impact on subsequent behavior. . . . People generally attach more diagnostic significance to successful outcomes than unsuccessful outcomes, even when the outcomes are randomly determined. This bias in the evaluation of success and failure only serves to increase the "resistance to extinction" that is produced by the intermittent reinforcement found in all gambling endeavors. The effect of such bias is to produce an impression of one's previous performance that is more favorable than the objective record would indicate. Thus, the . . . cognitive interpretation of gamblers' perseverance goes beyond earlier behavioral formulations by demonstrating how people's biases serve to produce greater persistence than that which is due to simple resistance to extinction.[56]

The results of studies designed to compare the response persistence rates of humans and animals to different schedules of reinforcement are mixed. Some studies have concluded that humans behave exactly as their animal counterparts while others have found no behavioral similarities.[57] It has also been argued that while laboratory rats may be readily conditioned to pull levers when this behavior is intermittently reinforced with the reward of food pellets or sugared water, these animals are not subjected to the same continuous schedule of punishments as slot machine players. Animals pressing bars, pushing buttons, and pulling levers in Skinner boxes generally end up with a net gain; humans pulling the handles of slot machines generally end up with a net loss. Since longer play means greater punishment, the strength of the lever-pulling response among humans should decrease over time just as it does in laboratory animals, but this does not occur among regular slot machine players. Likewise, in theory, placing a winning bet on red in the game of roulette should reinforce further betting on red while a losing bet should weaken this response.[58] Again, this does not happen in practice since it has been shown that roulette players are actually more likely to bet on the color that has just lost.[59] Finally, operant conditioning cannot begin to explain the persistence of lottery gambling among those who have never won a prize since the lack of a reward should steadily diminish the strength of the playing response.[60]

Perhaps one of the strongest criticisms of the reinforcement theory is that, with its emphasis on the strength of external environmental influences, it dismisses the possibility of internal individual differences of either a psychological or biological nature. Consequently, still others theorists feel that although such forms of gambling as lotteries might be explained by reference to behavioral responses to potential monetary rewards, Skinnerian learning theory is unable to account for variations of behavior in other forms of gambling, specifically, why some people become persistent, heavy, or addicted gamblers while others do not although they may have been exposed to the same stimuli.[61] Neither are variable-ratio schedules of reinforcement able to explain compulsive gambling in those who have sustained severe losses or relapse, the resumption of excessive gambling, by those who have maintained prolonged periods of abstinence during which "the chain of reinforcement is broken."[62] It has therefore been argued that if compulsive gambling is due solely to the "uncanny power" of intermittent reinforcement, then "given enough exposure to gambling situations we would all become compulsive gamblers."[63] As this is obviously not the case, these criticisms are quite valid.

The conclusion of most critics is that the development of persistent and pathological gambling must also involve something other than purely monetary considerations and variable reinforcement schedules. These are most often thought to be altered emotional and physiological states or cognitive factors (expectations of reward) resulting from Pavlovian or classical conditioning.[64] In the words of a sociologist who prefers a more humanistic approach:

> A behavioural theory says nothing about the ways in which the events of the game are cognized by the players. It forces one into an assumption that the rationale for playing is one based upon an arithmetic calculus of wins and losses, as these are defined in the formal definition of the game. . . . It does not allow one to explore the possibility that the "game," for the participants is something qualitatively different from the "game" as analyzed by scientific discourse.[65]

A Defensive Response

In defending reinforcement theory against some of these criticisms, behavioral psychologist Michael Frank[66] maintained that if punishment is to extinguish any behavior it must meet certain minimal criteria. In the first place, the punishment must be as intense as possible and in the second place it must be introduced at maximum strength rather than increased gradually. Skinner himself insisted that "The ultimate loss . . . does not offset the effect of the schedule."[67] Second, gamblers rarely stake all their assets on one wager but extend their losses over a gambling session. This means that each loss, including the first, is well below the maximum intensity. Third, to lead to behavioral extinction the frequency of punishment should be as high as possible. This does not occur in gambling since gamblers also win, sometimes nearly as often as they lose. Fourth, punishment cannot become a signal for reward. Since many gamblers believe that each loss enhances their chances for winning on the next try (see the Gambler's Fallacy below) gamblers often regard loss as a cue for impending reward. Fifth, punishment for a particular behavior should not motivate that behavior. Gamblers who "chase," or try to win back their losses by throwing good money after bad, are not only motivated to continue precisely by the punishments they have already received, but each loss actually increases the drive to get even. Sixth, if a response is not punished, then the frequency of reward must gradually be reduced if a behavior is to become extinguished. The overall rate of reward for most casino games is not reduced but remains fixed at a certain percentage. Finally, to extinguish any behavior an alternative response that can produce a reward equal to or greater than the potentially punishing response must be available. Since investing is also a form of gambling, opportunities to win (or earn) more than one bets (or invests) do not exist outside of gambling. The only realistic alternative to gambling and losing or breaking even is simply not to gamble. However, many gamblers who believe that their rewards and punishments are determined by luck or fate–which they also believe can be manipulated and controlled–rather than the laws of probability do not perceive this as an option.

Scientific Tests of Reinforcement Theory

Many of the experiments that were designed to test reinforcement theory have been criticized on methodological grounds, often as being unrealistic.[68] Most have taken place in the safety of a university laboratory during which the test subjects risked none of their own money (either no real money was used or that which was used was provided by the experimenters) and had unlimited access to the playing tokens. Moreover, the potential payoffs rarely resemble those of real gambling situations. Inconsistency in the selection of test subjects is another major concern since some researchers distinguish between normal and compulsive or pathological gamblers while others categorize test subjects according to their frequency of gambling. In fact, unlike serious casino gamblers who have ready access to a wide range of gaming options, the subjects of many laboratory experiments are often university students who do not ordinarily gamble and who have only a limited choice of gambling games. A study which compared the physiological and behavioral responses of students to those of regular casino gamblers as they gambled in an artificial laboratory setting reported no significant differences between the two groups.[69] However, differences in the heart rates, expectations of winning, and betting behaviors of the gamblers were dramatic and highly significant when they were taken from the laboratory and placed in a real casino. Thus, some researchers feel that

> Laboratory experiments set a priori constraints on how the task or problem should be represented and often require instruction that may be too complex . . . , ambiguous, or even contradictory. . . . Whereas in laboratory settings the subject has to identify the representation intended by the experiments; in real-life situations the experimenter is trying to discover the subjects' representations.
>
> Another issue often raised in the context of decision and judgement research concerns subjects' motivation. In particular, where gambling is concerned, there is no substitute for the excitement and arousal that are involved in real-life situations.[70]

It has therefore been argued that "studies conducted with students in simulated gambling environments for bogus money, small prizes, or course credit, will yield nothing of relevance to the real gambling of genuine gamblers in their natural environments"[71] and that "It can no longer be assumed that the psychological determinants of gambling may be generalized to the real world."[72]

More recently, psychologist Mark Dickerson and his colleagues have undertaken a series of real world tests of reinforcement theory by investigating the behavior of regular slot machine players in Australian gambling casinos. Whereas one study found that even heavy slot machine gamblers will quit playing in the absence of any big wins,[73] a second verified the strong association between gambling persistence and the variable-ratio reinforcement schedule.[74] Other researchers have found that the timing of the reward is also critical to gambling persistence since the sooner a reward is delivered after a response, the stronger that response will become. This means that the immediate payoffs of slot machines also result in more persistent gambling. Conversely, any delays in the delivery time of the reward will weaken the response and lead to lower rates of play.

However, Dickerson felt that the factors responsible for heavy or persistent gambling may be different from those that are responsible for the initiation of new gambling sessions since the reinforcement schedules of slot machines are influential only after play begins. Consequently, he did not believe that "schedule-controlled" rates of gambling inevitably lead to impaired control or pathological gambling since the expected progression from low to high frequency gambling has not been observed. In fact, the majority of low-, medium-, and high-frequency players report that their level of play has remained the same for a year or more. Dickerson therefore repeatedly stressed that "there is no necessary progression from low to higher frequencies" since "the stereotypical learnt patterns of play *driven* by the machine payout characteristics do not necessarily result in higher and higher levels of involvement."[75] "Furthermore," he concluded, "contrary to Skinner's assumption, *consistent* impaired control is unlikely to arise from the learnt patterns of play alone."[76]

In essence, his research findings suggest that persistent gambling is not necessarily the same as pathological or problem gambling. However, since frequency of play corresponds directly to the reported frequency of impaired control, he did feel that payout schedules and learning per se are important and perhaps even essential to its development.[77] He also felt that such *external* influences as machine characteristics must be distinguished from such *internal* psychological factors as prior emotional and mood states that also appear to be involved. But, as will soon become apparent, there is also considerable controversy over precisely which mood states are thought to be most responsible.

5

NEED-STATES AND DRIVE-REDUCTION

GAMBLING AS A FORM OF PLAY

Some psychological theorists believe that gambling satisfies certain fundamental human drive–or need–states among which is a need for play or recreation. This approach was developed from ideas originating in the social as well as behavioral sciences. Clemens France, an early twentieth-century psychologist, suggested that since play is an instinctive drive stemming from the ancient past and buried deeply in the collective unconscious, any attempts to prohibit gambling are destined to fail.[1]

In the 1950s play theorist Johan Huizinga described play as "a free activity standing quite consciously outside 'ordinary' life as being 'not serious,' but at the same time absorbing the player intensely and utterly."[2] He added that play is "a voluntary activity or occupation executed within certain fixed limits of time and place, according to rules freely accepted but absolutely binding, having its aim in itself and accompanied by a feeling of tension, joy and consciousness that is quite 'different' from 'ordinary life.'"[3] Although all of these facets of play apply to gambling, Huizinga felt that gambling "is an activity connected with no material interest, and no profit can be gained by it."[4] He nevertheless believed that play is "a contest *for* something or a representation *of* something,"[5] ideas that are reflected in the writings of many gambling theorists. Because he saw elements of play in philosophy, the arts, law, war, literature, art, music, and many other hallmarks of cultured society, Huizinga also suggested that the "play instinct" was an important phylogenetic adaptation which propelled our ancestors along the road to civilization. He felt that leisure cultivated the spirit of play while hard work stifled it. This meant that leisure rather than hard work had been responsible for mankind's loftiest achievements. He argued that insurance, business contracts, and other financial arrangements all developed out of the gambles our forebears took on the outcomes of trading voyages, pilgrimages, and other unpredictable events.

A decade later Roger Caillois[6] rejected the notion that modern games and other forms of play are merely modern vestigial survivals of ancient "instinctive" cultural traditions or, as later writers saw them, as substitutes or learning exercises for real life. Like Huizinga, he acknowledged that play itself produces nothing of value. However, unlike his predecessor, Caillois insisted that it can, and often does, result in the exchange of value. He therefore corrected Huizinga's oversight by expanding the definition of play to include all forms of gambling. In addition to its unproductive nature he also described play as an activity that is free rather than compulsory, separate and distinct from ordinary life, governed by rules, and removed from reality or "make-believe."

According to Caillois, play falls into four basic categories which often overlap or shade into one another. *Agôn* refers to competitive games involving skill and strategy (billiards, chess, athletic events, etc.); *alea*, to games of chance (dice, roulette, lotteries, etc.). Caillois maintained that despite their obvious differences, *agôn* and *alea* are similar in that they both create for players "conditions of pure equality which are denied them in real life."[7] *Mimicry* describes situations in which people assume the personality of others through simulation, illusion, pretense, or disguise (acting, playing pirate or soldier, role-playing, etc.); *ilinx* refers to the pursuit of vertigo through activities that induce sensations of lightheadedness, dizziness, euphoria, and panic, or which otherwise alter one's state of normal reality (rapid spinning, falling, speed, carnival rides, etc.). Illicit drug use and other mood-altering experiences would also fall into this category. Caillois emphasized that, with the exception of professional players (actors, athletes, etc.), when one's involvement in any recreational pastime begins to exceed normative standards and dominate one's thoughts it is no longer play, but a pathology: "What used to be a pleasure becomes an obsession. What was an escape becomes an obligation, and what was a pastime is now a passion, compulsion, and source of anxiety."[8] Thus, any form of play can become addictive.

Ideas similar to those of Caillois are apparent in various theories of gambling. Because the first two categories of play, *agôn* and *alea*, include all gambling games, a number of theorists regard gambling chiefly as a form of adult play.[9]

In his detailed ethnographic description of racetrack life, Marvin Scott[10] described the racing game as one of strategy in which winning involves the acquisition and manipulation of crucial information. The players include not only the regular and occasional grandstand bettors but also the horse owners, trainers, jockeys, betting window employees, and other "backstage" actors whose livelihoods depend on racing. To enhance their chances of winning these players try to obtain or conceal reliable information from one another at the same time that they try to disseminate misinformation that is intended to cause their opponents to lose. Many resort to connivance, guile, and deception to insure their success. Despite his characterization of racing as a "game," Scott made it clear that the serious players are motivated by their purely utilitarian interest in money. Those who see it as a form of recreation are the "occasionals" who visit the track only periodically. According to Scott, "The regulars *expect* to profit from their daily visits; the occasionals *hope* to profit. For the regulars, the race track is a way of life; for the occasionals, a form of recreation."[11] Unlike Scott, however, other play theorists hold decidedly different ideas about the motivations for gambling.

Many advocates of play theory consider play itself as a need or drive that must be satisfied or reduced. Some feel that our reliance on gambling to reduce this drive is learned in childhood through such games as marbles, sports card flipping, and card playing in which the stakes are something other than money.[12] Mimicry allows one to abandon, at least temporarily, one's real self and assume the persona of another while vertigo represents "the attempt to momentarily destroy stability of perception and inflict a kind of voluptuous panic upon an otherwise lucid mind."[13] Mimicry is central to sociological small group interactional theories of gambling while vertigo, which some researchers believe is a major component of slot machine gambling,[14] is central to arousal theories. Since gambling affords amusement, enjoyment, a challenge, a form of escape from reality and the routine of daily living, and can furnish thrills and excitement, it is thought to serve as a psychological drive-reduction mechanism that satisfies certain fundamental human needs, one of which is the need for recreation or play.[15] Thus, some social scientists who advocate play theory have argued that games have value simply because they are fun, not because they serve any utilitarian purpose. In gambling, this value is referred to as "action," which includes both excitement and escape.[16]

Research into the subjectively reported motivations for gambling appear to support this hypothesis. Investigations of slot machine players who were members of private clubs in Australia found that 55 percent of the men and 65 percent of the women surveyed gave "amusement" as their primary reason for playing while only 35 percent indicated that they did so for money.[17] Nearly half (48%) of the subjects of a second survey gave "entertainment" as their principle reason for playing.[18] Likewise, when a sample of regular blackjack players at casinos in Scotland were asked their reasons for gambling 50 percent said they did so for "enjoyment or excitement" and only 8.5 percent claimed to do so "to win money"; 33 percent gambled "to be sociable" and another 8.5 percent "to pass the time."[19]

THE TENSION-REDUCTION HYPOTHESIS: GAMBLING AS AN EMOTIONAL CRUTCH

Other approaches based on Skinnerian learning theory were initially formulated by specialists in chemical dependency to explain alcoholism and drug dependence. In these cases reinforcement of the behavior in question is believed to be negative, resulting from the reduction of a drive which is experienced as a "state of tension arising from an unsatisfied need."[20] Negative reinforcement is not the same as punishment although the two are often confused: in the language of reinforcement theory, punishment refers to an aversive stimulus that is uncomfortable, noxious, or in some other way unpleasant; negative reinforcement refers to the outcome of any act that successfully removes or reduces the strength of an aversive stimulus. An example would be the act of taking aspirin or some other analgesic to relieve sensations of pain. Since negative reinforcement has a beneficial outcome (pain reduction) the act will tend to be strengthened or repeated with greater frequency in response to the aversive stimulus.

Many learning theorists and other students of addiction believe that drinking and drug use are negatively reinforcing because they relieve conditions of emotional tension, anxiety, and/or depression.[21] According to the general paradigm of the behaviorist camp, when such unpleasant feelings as anxiety or stress provide an aversive stimulus, the response of drinking or drug use is immediately and powerfully reinforced by the reward of tension-reduction.[22]

For this reason many behaviorists regard the excessive use of alcohol and other drugs as an "acquired drive" or "bad habit" which the individual learns as a coping mechanism in attempting to diminish the intensity of disappointment, depression, stress, anxiety, guilt, and other unpleasant emotional conditions.[23] In such cases the addictive behavior is negatively reinforced by the use of alcohol and drugs since they serve to relieve or reduce the intensity of an unwanted dysphoric mood state and replace it with a pleasurably gratifying one. Thus, the reinforcement of drinking and drug use can be both negatively and then positively reinforcing since they first reduce an aversive mood state, then produce a pleasurable one. The high rate of recidivism among treated alcoholics and drug addicts is said to result from incomplete extinction of their previously reinforced drug-seeking behavior.

Similarly, since gambling is also believed to act as an analgesic by providing emotional relief or escape from an unpleasant or insecure world, it is also seen as an acquired drive or bad habit. Because tension-reduction has long been a core assumption of many psychological and biological theories of human behavior,[24] it is not surprising that the tension-reducing or relaxation effect of gambling was first noted by a number of earlier psychoanalytic theorists.[25] Many later learning theorists have incorporated anxiety, tension, stress-, guilt-, and depression-reducing elements into their explanations for pathological gambling, as well.[26] Indeed, a study of 19 pathological gamblers who had received prior treatment reported that half (47%) named negative mood states as the primary cause of their relapse.[27]

A number of studies have empirically tested this proposition. One of the first to do so reported that 38, or fully 76 percent, of a sample of fifty patients admitted to a pathological gambling treatment program were also diagnosed as having major depressive disorder.[28] In the words of one prominent treatment specialist, "Gambling caters to our need for immediate relief and gratification";[29] "it can be used to regulate affect, arousal, or self-esteem."[30] He suggested that the expansion of legalized gambling throughout the United States in recent years may be a collective reaction to such generalized pan-societal stressors as "the break-up of the nuclear family, the loss of familiar and established values, the threats of destruction to society and to our planet, uncertainty about our economic futures, and . . . uncertainty about our role as a nation."[31] When people are overwhelmed with feelings of helplessness and uncertainty about life they find a ready solution to their problems in gambling, he maintained, since it gives them a feeling of omnipotence by providing the illusion that they have the ability to control the uncontrollable.[32] Likewise, some argue that "The attraction of gambling is not risk but certainty; it is an escape into order."[33]

Because dysphoric mood states prior to gambling have been associated with increased persistence among habitual or high-frequency gamblers,[34] pathological gambling is believed to develop when gambling becomes the preferred means of offsetting the chronic dysthymia induced by stress, loneliness, anxiety, or trauma. One specialist feels that many gambling addicts "are searching for instant fun or an immediate resolution of stress."[35] Another concluded that the root cause of a client's slot machine addiction was "his inability to communicate or mix socially, hence the need to play the machines to avoid feeling foolish and to dissipate feelings of loneliness."[36]

The clients' own statements often serve to confirm these interpretations. For example, a clinical study involving eleven excessive gamblers receiving clinical treatment reported that eight or 73% indicated that they gambled out of loneliness or a "need to develop a social network."[37] A patient who gambled to relieve stress added, "Eventually I want to phase it out but at the moment I would rather spend one pound on gambling than have the frustration and tension; I have to relieve the need. It stops the need."[38] According to one treatment specialist, "Many excessive gamblers do report that after a spell of heavy gambling with considerable losses they feel as though a burden is gone and that tension is relieved."[39] Others wrote that "Gambling did seem to act as an antidepressant activity for many subjects who reported periods when their overall mood was very depressed except when gambling."[40] Still others reported that a number of their patients claimed that "gambling is my opiate, my escape and comfort."[41] Thus, those who seek escape in gambling are said to use it as an "'anesthetic' which 'hypnotizes.'"[42] Evidence supporting the idea that gambling provides a means of escape or dissociation was provided by a recent study of gambling among adolescents. Among those most heavily involved in gambling 67.7 percent claimed that it made them lose track of time, 61.5 percent that it made them feel like a different person, 53.8 percent that it made them feel as though they were in a trance, 41.5 percent that it made them feel as though they were outside of themselves, and 13.8 percent claimed that they had experienced blackouts while gambling.[43]

If environmental stress is the ultimate cause of habitual gambling, then elimination of the stressor is sometimes believed to be the simplest way of eliminating the problem. Thus, the symptoms of problem gambling described in two brief case histories of adolescent fruit machine addiction were reported to have disappeared when the subjects were removed from their previously original distressful, tension-filled home environments at the recommendation of the author. He concluded that in both cases "the excessive fruit machine gambling was a secondary problem caused by the underlying main problem of feeling out of control in the family environment. By addressing the primary problem, the secondary symptoms disappeared."[44]

It must be emphasized, however, that not all studies support the stress-reduction hypothesis. A series of general population surveys in Germany revealed that only one-quarter (26 percent) of intensive slot machine players (those who played five hours or more per week) claimed that their gambling was stress-related. The researchers therefore concluded that "Subjective stress connected to gambling is an important but not exclusive criterion."[45]

Co-addiction

As noted in the introductory chapter, studies of co-addiction among hospitalized patients and members of self-help groups have confirmed that psychoactive substance abuse and dependence are often associated with problem and pathological gambling.[46] Whereas personality theorists attribute co-addiction to the presence of similar internal personality factors, learning theorists attribute it to the presence of similar external environmental influences. In either case addictive behaviors are all believed to serve as an emotional crutch which enables the addict to make it through another grueling day. Thus, it has been frequently suggested that drinking, drug use, overeating, gambling, and other "patterns of self-indulgence"[47] are all variants of a common maladaptive coping strategy for the alleviation of chronic stress or anxiety. Because these behavioral excesses frequently accompany or substitute for one another, they are often thought of as "functional equivalents."[48] Some addiction specialists maintain that "Drugs or the euphoria of gambling then come to serve multiple purposes. . . . They are used to numb consciousness."[49] It is also believed that the very settings in which gambling and drug use occur together can foster co-addiction:

> Free drinks are served in casinos; card games are invariably teamed up with drinking; there are bars at the race track; furthermore, the local bookie often works out of the neighborhood pub. When the alcoholic who is 'on the wagon' gambles, the tension of gambling combined with the depression of losing and consequent lowered self-esteem gives further reason for loss of sobriety. Amphetamines and cocaine are used by gamblers to stay awake and at some games, the lines of coke are snorted between hands. The resulting atmosphere is so fast-paced that non-users have a difficult time keeping track of the game. Heroin and cocaine abusers who gamble often 'hustle' at gambling games in order to finance their drugs. Conversely, compulsive gamblers who also use drugs frequently deal drugs to finance their gambling.[50]

Some specialists combine personality and learning theories to explain these phenomena. According to one, "This lifelong persistent state of either hypo- or hyper-arousal is believed to predispose the individual to respond only to a rather narrow 'window' of stress-reducing, but potentially addictive substances or experiences."[51] To explain the reciprocity between pathological gambling and drug addiction mentioned above, others have suggested the possibility that "the problem gambler comes to use gambling as a means of escape or for elevation of self-esteem instead of using alcohol or drugs. Once this occurs, there is the chance that the gambling will accelerate and produce problems which will precipitate a return to drinking and drug using."[52]

Records of telephone calls to compulsive gambling hotlines across the United States suggest that the incidence of co-addiction is increasing. In 1988 only 4 percent of the callers reported that they also had a problem with alcohol. This rate increased to 6 percent the following year and to 11 percent by 1990. Concurrent drug problems, though less common, may also be on the rise. Fewer than one percent of the callers reported drug abuse problems in 1988 and 1989 but this figure grew to 5 percent in 1990.[53] Nevertheless, despite the many studies that have investigated and reported on gambling and alcohol or other drug co-addictions, a surprisingly large number of chemical dependency treatment providers appear to be unaware of their existence.[54]

AROUSAL AND SENSATION-SEEKING

In contrast to the drive-reduction hypotheses are closely related arguments that gambling, acting as a stimulant or euphoriant, is rewarded precisely by the subjectively perceived emotions and autonomic sensations it *creates* rather than abates. Thus, individuals who feel bored, experience sensations of hypoarousal, and have a relatively high need for stimulation will drink, use drugs, gamble, seek novel sexual experiences, and the like in an effort to relieve these conditions by inducing affective states of arousal, exhilaration, and euphoria. A number of early writers noted that the "passion" for gambling is motivated not only by avarice, but also by the excitement it affords,[55] an observation that was not lost to many later authorities.

In his psychoanalytic explanation Bergler[56] had attributed the pleasure or "thrill" of gambling to the "pleasurable-painful tension" and anxiety it produces. The "cycle of effects" that always accompanies gambling has been described as follows: "The cycle begins with the decision or bet and is followed by a psychic crescendo of anxiety, dread, and anticipation with subsequent release into joy or disappointment depending on the outcome of the wager."[57] Without the emotional stresses generated by this uncertainty, Bergler concluded, gambling would not be pleasurable. As previously noted, some of his colleagues went so far as to compare the tension and excitement generated and released by gambling to a sexual experience.[58]

More recent theoreticians have adopted the ideas that many human activities are motivated by the pleasure-,[59] arousal-,[60] or sensation-seeking[61] principle. Thus, although they have abandoned the orthodox psychoanalytic perspective, many contemporary researchers still feel that gambling, like a high-speed roller coaster ride, is motivated primarily, or at least in part, by the intense thrill, excitement, and emotional arousal or "action" it provides.[62]

For example, psychologist Michael Walker[63] saw excessive gambling as a learned habit comparable to hypersexuality, the excessive use of chocolate, or any other hedonistic indulgence which is motivated and reinforced by the pleasure it gives. For this reason he recommended that the definition of addiction be broadened to include behaviors other than drug dependence, a behavior Walker believed to have a physiological basis. Excessive gambling should therefore be regarded as just one of many possible addictions that could be defined as a persistent behavior pattern involving:

1. a desire or need to continue the activity which places it outside voluntary control;
2. a tendency to increase the frequency or amount of the activity over time;
3. psychological dependence on the pleasurable effects of the activity;
4. a detrimental effect on the individual and society.[64]

Walker felt that his proposed definition of addiction had several distinct advantages over others, particularly that of the medical model which will be discussed in another volume. In the first place, it eliminates the need to distinguish between physical or psychological dependence. In the second place, it allows determination of whether the behavior is beyond voluntary control to be made by the individual rather than by any external agency or criteria. Third, by making it clear that the behavior is maintained by the pleasure it yields, this definition automatically excludes persistent behaviors such as compulsions that are not pleasurable but that are maintained for fear of the perceived negative consequences that would ensue if they were overlooked. Fourth, it emphasizes that the behavior is a threat to the welfare of both the individual and society. In essence, Walker held the consequences of any behavior to be more important than its causes in determining whether or not it should be considered "addictive." In fact, he felt that "the overwhelming desire to engage in the activity to the detriment of self and society"[65] constituted one of the most important themes running through a wide variety of such behaviors.

However, Walker's insistence that to be considered "addictive" a behavior must be harmful to *both* the individual *and* society would automatically exclude many addicts who did not meet this criterion, particularly those in the early stages of addiction. For example, some alcoholics can exist for years as "maintenance drinkers" who hold steady jobs, support their families, pay all their bills on time, and never operate motor vehicles under the influence of alcohol nor pose any other kind of threat to the general public. Some people smoke only in the privacy of their own homes and in designated smoking areas thereby endangering no one but themselves, and usually doing so only after years of heavy smoking. Likewise, not all heroin addicts find it necessary to steal or endanger the safety of others to support their addiction. So, too, can many excessive gamblers go for extended periods before experiencing the harmful effects of their behavior. While all such individuals have clearly lost voluntary control of their behavior they would not qualify as "addicts" under Walker's definition until their actions cause some definite harm to themselves *and* others. Thus, not even smokers and alcoholics who may have died as a direct result of their addiction but harmed no one else in the process could be considered addicts. Nor could those whose smoking, drinking, or crack cocaine use throughout pregnancy results in the birth of a developmentally disabled child qualify as addicts until their behavior causes them some medical or financial problems of their own.

Erving Goffman: The "Action" Hypothesis

Many of Caillois's ideas are present in the work of sociologist Erving Goffman. In his well-known essay on "action" Goffman used the term in reference to high-risk "activities that are consequential, problematic, and undertaken for what is felt to be their own sake."[66] He derived the term from its use in gambling, which he then used as metaphor for many of life's experiences including such diverse pursuits as mountain climbing, bull fighting, and almost all new endeavors. These, he maintained, are all fateful activities that are socially defined as ones an individual is under no obligation to continue to pursue once he has started to do so. No extraneous factors compel him to face fate in the first place; no extraneous ends provide expedient reasons for his continued participation. His activity is defined as an end itself, sought out, embraced, and utterly his own. . . . It is here that the individual releases himself to the passing moment, wagering his future estate on what transpires precariously in the seconds to come. At such moments a special affective state is likely to be aroused, emerging transformed into excitement.[67]

"The distinctive property of games and contests," he insisted, "is that once the bet has been made, the outcome is determined and payoff awarded *all in the same breath of experience.*"[68] Thus, the action of gambling is much faster than that for other arousing or exhilarating experiences and many people themselves report that the main reason they place a bet is for the fun and excitement exhilaration it provides.[69] However, others have pointed out that Goffman's "action" hypothesis contains a contradiction that makes it difficult to test. Since he assumed that most people are oriented toward risk, he predicted that those in potentially hazardous occupations (steeplejacks, miners, etc.) would also tend to be heavy gamblers since their risk orientation is obvious. However, those in less dangerous occupations, such as accountants and sales clerks, should also tend to be heavy gamblers since they are denied risk in their daily lives.[70]

According to the sensation-seeking hypothesis, gambling is reinforced more by arousal than anything else since it serves to relieve an unwanted affective state such as boredom or hypomania and replace it with a desired affective state such as arousal, exhilaration, or even euphoria. Some argue that this is the case even for habitual slot machine players who Skinner felt were motivated only by a desire for money:

> . . . putting one's winnings back into the machines seems in no way to diminish the pleasure gained from jackpots. The day is counted not in how much is taken home, but in how many jackpots were won and the amount of play that one was able to sustain on the amount of money invested. In other words, as for the adventurer, it is the action that counts.[71]

Play, Sensation, Existentialism, and Self-Esteem

Since the stimulation afforded by gambling is sometimes seen as an indispensable component of play, it has understandably been linked to Caillois's play theory. But some psychological play theorists are convinced that another dimension–a purely psychological one–is also involved. It has been argued that people are motivated by strong needs to confirm their existence and affirm their worth as human beings, and that these goals are realized through the effects they have on their world. Failure to make a difference results in displeasurable feelings of disappointment, anger, sorrow, and low self-esteem. However, success results in feelings of pride and worthiness, the thrilling rush of excitement and euphoria, and similar pleasurable "peak experiences." Advocates of this approach believe that play–and gambling in particular–is able to meet these deeper psychological needs precisely through the physiological arousal and uncertainty it produces:

> the central motive behind gambling and all play activities is the need to confirm our existence and the need to experience the play pleasure that is integral to the confirmation of existence. We confirm our existence when we produce effects in our world and receive sensory and cognitive stimulation from the production of those effects.[72]

In the words of a popular writer on gambling, "action proves we are fully alive."[73] While arousal confirms our existence, the risk-taking involved in gambling enhances our feelings of self-worth.[74] In essence, this version of play theory suggests that we gamble not only because it makes us feel good, but also because it makes us feel good about ourselves.

Optimal Arousal and Addiction

It is often held that if hypoarousal or sensation-seeking motivate "normal" gambling then they are likely to be a major factor in the genesis of pathological gambling, as well.[75] As noted previously, the first empirical test of this idea found that over three-quarters (76%) of a group of fifty pathological gamblers receiving treatment had major depressive disorder. The study also found that well over one-third (38%) were also diagnosed with hypomanic disorder while one-quarter (26%) had both hypomanic and major depressive disorders.[76] A slightly later study of 25 members of Gamblers Anonymous found high rates of major (72%) and recurrent (52%) depressive episodes in addition to an unusually high incidence of panic disorder (20%).[77]

Pathological gambling and other addictive behaviors are therefore believed to represent an ongoing attempt to maintain one's ideal level of stimulation. The "optimal level of arousal" variant of sensation-seeking theory assumes that all human beings have their own ideal level of autonomic or cortical arousal at which their hedonic tone and performance are maximized and which they try to sustain in a variety of ways.[78] This optimal level would be defined by a point at the top of an inverted "U-shaped" curve below which they are understimulated, and beyond which they are overstimulated. Since gambling and other stimulating activities heighten arousal, they would be sought when one's level of arousal is low but avoided when it is high. A further assumption is that this point would be higher for high sensation-seekers than for low sensation-seekers. High sensation-seekers would therefore be predisposed to attempt to attain and sustain their particular optimal level of arousal through gambling, drug use, or some other stimulating and potentially addictive behavior that they find rewarding. Consequently, those most likely to become persistent or pathological gamblers and/or drug addicts would be high sensation-seekers who experience chronic states of depression, boredom, or hypomania which gambling or drug use serves to alleviate.[79] Some arousal theorists therefore see the drive to manipulate and maintain one's ideal hedonic state as the "core of the addictive process."[80] For this reason advocates of the medical model have begun to investigate the possibility that both pathological gambling and chemical dependency can be traced to chronic hedonic need-states imposed by genetically determined neurochemical imbalances in the central nervous system. This issue will be discussed in greater detail in a subsequent volume of this series.

Mark Dickerson: The Dual-Reinforcement Hypothesis

Arousal theorists such as Mark Dickerson,[81] argued that fixed-interval (FI) reinforcement schedules, such as occurs during off-course betting, are perhaps even more important than variable-ratio (VR) schedules in shaping gambling behavior. Skinner, it will be recalled, maintained that since the primary reinforcement of gambling derives from the intermittent presentation of tangible rewards (i.e., chips, tokens, or money), it will occur sporadically and only after an unknown number of trials. In contrast, Dickerson, whose ideas were developed during an extensive investigation of the patrons of Britain's off-course betting offices, maintained that people gamble for the thrill it affords rather than for the money it may yield. He therefore felt that the anticipation and excitement that accompany the uncertainty of risk are more highly reinforcing than an occasional win. Thus, the hedonic rewards that accompany off-course betting are contingent not on winning but on the act of betting. Consequently, they are experienced regularly, every time a bet is placed, even before a race is run and, hence, entirely irrespective of its outcome.

Since every trial is rewarded with emotional stimulation, Dickerson maintained that the betting response is reinforced on a fixed-interval schedule. Moreover, the higher the frequency of betting, the larger the amounts bet, and the closer a bet is placed to the starting time of a race or the spin of a roulette wheel (the "late betting" phenomenon), the greater will be the intensity of arousal and, hence, of the true reward for gambling. He then reasoned that if arousal is, indeed, the principal reason for gambling, and if the build-up of the anticipation and excitement that accompanies betting is, in fact, more important than the satisfaction of winning, then the greatest rewards of gambling will accrue to the most frequent and persistent gamblers.

In time, however, gamblers become habituated to the level of arousal they once felt and must increase their betting levels to continue to experience the level of thrill and excitement needed to maintain their optimal hedonic state.[82] As their involvement escalates they also come into closer personal contact with the core group of heavy bettors who begin to exert social pressures for even heavier betting. Both influences–tolerance to the emotionally arousing effects of betting and social learning or peer pressure–eventually lead to progressively larger losses and "chasing." Dickerson therefore concluded that by encouraging more frequent and higher stakes betting, the FI reinforcement sequence that is characteristic of off-course betting serves to encourage or "train" participants to increase their involvement until they become excessive or compulsive gamblers.

Despite his emphasis on the importance of regularly timed betting, Dickerson clearly did not mean to deprecate the significance of winning. On the contrary, he not only assigned it primary importance in the initial stages of a gambling career but also maintained that it augments the reinforcement of betting even in its later stages when the need for optimal hedonic stimulation is salient. He therefore felt that arousal may constitute just one of the causative factors in the development of problem gambling. Dickerson encountered the "late betting" phenomenon when he found that high frequency bettors were far more likely than low frequency bettors to wait until the last two minutes before the start of a race to place their bets. He proposed that both the enhanced tension and excitement of last-minute betting prior to a race and the prospect of a large monetary reward afterward, may be of equal importance in the development of problem gambling. Thus, both the FI schedule of late betting and the variable-ratio schedule of winning act in concert to reinforce persistence:

> . . . evidence was found to support the hypothesis that fixed interval (FI with clock) schedules, as well as variable ratio (VR) schedules, act in conjunction in the betting shop environment. Customers who stay for longer periods in this environment are trained to bet more frequently and to use higher stakes. As training progresses, the betting response of a customer comes more and more predictably elicited by the stimulus changes that occur just before the start of a race. This is associated with the increased likelihood that the customer will report losing control until he reaches a point when he may describe being unable to stop betting.[83]

However, some gamblers never reach this level of involvement despite years of regular participation. In attempting to account for this phenomenon, Dickerson explained that most people are able to escape this trap through their pursuit of other precluding interests since the beginning of their gambling careers. Thus, he suggested, compulsive gambling results as much from the effects of operant conditioning as it does from the lack of counterbalancing influences in one's personal life.

R. I. F. Brown: Variable-Ratio Emotional Reinforcement

In contrast to Dickerson, arousal theorists such as R. I. F. Brown believed that gambling can be better explained by closer adherence to the principles of conventional Skinnerian theory. Like Dickerson, Brown felt that gambling is reinforced more by emotional than monetary rewards but like Skinner he also felt that reinforcement is strongest if it is presented on a variable-ratio schedule. Since not every gambling experience has the desired result (winning), Brown felt that persistence results directly from the inconsistency of gambling in successfully manipulating one's optimal hedonic state. Thus, just as Skinner insisted that the gambling response is strengthened by randomly presented *monetary* rewards, Brown argued that gambling is reinforced by a variable schedule of *emotional* rewards:

> The very unreliability *of the chosen method of manipulation*, superior though it is to the relatively amateur chaos of the normally conducted search for high positive hedonic tone, gives rise to an intermittent schedule of reinforcement and so makes for great resistance to extinction and tendency to ready reinstatement, not just in gambling, as is well known, but in *all* addictions by their central nature.[84]

Brown[85] also suggested that irregular reinforcement would not only serve to exacerbate the need for stimulation, but it would continue to do so even after the "reinforcement chain" had been interrupted by a long time interval.

Arousal Under Any Circumstances

However, relatively few arousal theorists express any concern over which particular schedule of reinforcement might be responsible for pathological gambling: ever since Bergler's time most have been satisfied only with the understanding that the quest for stimulation rather than money is the ultimate cause. One specialist asserted, for example, that "Gamblers seek out the excitement or *action* in gambling, and all else is irrelevant."[86] Another, referring to excitement as the "gambler's drug," contended that since excitement is all that matters, winning and losing are relatively inconsequential: money is necessary only because it provides access to the game; winning is desirable only because it sustains the action. Because the euphoria that gambling provides is so fleeting, the experience must be repeated frequently.[87] A third felt that for the pathological gambler losing can be just as exciting as winning:

> The thrill and excitement are so pleasurable that they are virtually addicting. There is also a thrill in the expectation of the consequences when one loses. Being in jeopardy from creditors, some of whom are bent on doing the gambler physical harm, intensifies the excitement. It is this charged-up feeling, a mixture of super confidence, enthusiasm, fear, and guilt, that seems to drive the patient toward the gambling table.[88]

Others claimed that "Gambling by problem gamblers is never really a money-oriented activity, although money is a visible passport to gambling action. Gambling seems to be a way of feeling good, at least temporarily, and money is only a vehicle. The gambler's fear is not of losing money but of being unable to gamble."[89] A fifth maintained that "What these gamblers do verbalize is a sense of frequent boredom–a strong enduring need for almost constant excitement and stimulation. . . . Gambling satiates the need-state for these pathological gamblers."[90] Yet another insisted that "if pathological gamblers become addicted to anything, it may be to their own arousal."[91]

Compelling evidence for this approach is found in the descriptions of those who know from their own first-hand experiences what gambling "action" feels like. Again, Dostoevsky provides an excellent example of the emotions that drive the compulsive gambler:

> And then–what a strange sensation!–I remember distinctly how all of a sudden a terrible craving for risk took possession of me, now quite apart from any vanity. It may be that, in passing through so many sensations, the soul does not become sated but is only stimulated by them and will ask for more and ever stronger sensations until utterly exhausted. And I am not lying as I say that if the rules of the game had allowed me to bet fifty thousand at once, I'd certainly have done so.[92]

Similar sentiments were also expressed very

clearly in the response of an habitué of Britain's off-track betting shops who was asked to explain why he and other compulsive gamblers feel the need to gamble:

> You ask me why I gamble and I tell you, it's the thrill. I know the game is crooked and that I haven't a chance, but when I've put my money on a horse and hear its name on the speaker, my heart stands still. I know I'm alive. You might have your last few bob riding on the horse, you know if you lose you've even lost your pastime, it's the excitement, the thrill that gets you every time.[93]

More recently, a study of female pathological gamblers found that many women made the same claim when they said they gambled for the "action" or excitement it arouses:

> I'd need one number, the adrenalin would pick up. I'd get all numb, hoping and praying the number would be called. [Hope B.–talking about bingo.]
>
> I was a maniac at the casino . . . My adrenalin starts to go. Meaning, I start gettin' high, start gettin' nervous, looking forward, rushing compulsively. Ah, going up to the first table where I could get a spot right in the middle so I would have enough room to place my bets wherever I felt hot on a number. [Sue M.–a roulette player].[94]

However, as Bergler and other psychoanalysts had suggested decades earlier, it is important to recognize that the verbal explanations people give for their conduct are very often rationalizations which do not necessarily reflect their true motivations.[95] Other treatment specialists have found that when they are asked, many compulsive gamblers have no idea why they gamble.[96]

Finally, some researchers believe that individual differences in the need for stimulation, as measured by Zuckerman's Sensation Seeking Scale (SSS)[97] and other psychometric instruments, are biologically based rather than learned personality phenomena.[98] Since a complete "sensation-seeking" or "arousal" approach to pathological gambling and other addictive behaviors involves biological factors, specific models will be discussed in a later volume of this series.

R. I. F. Brown: The Bi-Phasic Effects of Indulgence

Some specialists believe that gambling has the remarkable ability to reduce even entirely different drives at the same time. It has been said, for example, that "gambling can induce a stimulating, tranquilizing, or pain-relieving response; often a gambler will report all three occurring simultaneously."[99] In a later effort to reconcile the seemingly contradictory tension-reduction and sensation-seeking explanations, behavioral psychologist R. I. F. Brown,[100] in comparing gambling to the use of alcohol and other drugs, referred to the well-known bi-phasic effects of these substances. For example, alcohol is a depressant yet many drinkers use it as a stimulant. Brown explained this paradox by citing studies which found that a drinker's subjective arousal and mood states increase as long as the blood alcohol concentration (BAC) is rising but begin to diminish as the drug is metabolized and the BAC decreases. After a certain period the negative effects can become so great on the downward leg of the BAC curve that the subject's mood and arousal levels actually become more depressed than they were initially, a phenomenon which Brown refers to as the "rebound effect" but which others call withdrawal. Other alcohol studies, which Brown did not cite, found that the effects of alcohol are also dose-related or dependent on the amount consumed: in both human and animal subjects low doses act as a stimulant while higher doses act as a depressant.[101] Thus, a study of the effects of alcohol on risk-taking behavior among non-addicted subjects found that willingness to gamble increases with small doses of alcohol but deceases with larger doses.[102]

Brown contended that all drugs, including prescription medications and nicotine, act in the same way. To illustrate his point he cited studies concluding that light smokers combat fatigue and depression by using tobacco to enhance alertness and arousal while heavy smokers combat stress and anxiety by using it to diminish arousal. He also noted that many experienced social drinkers, alcoholics, and smokers practice titration to maintain a fairly constant level of arousal. That is, they time their doses to sustain the positive effects of the drug during the course of the day or evening and to delay the rebound effect for as long as possible. When it does appear the drinker (or smoker), overtaken by the cumulation of the drug's negative effects, avoids feeling them by going to sleep. Brown argued that certain potentially addictive or compulsive behavioral activities, such as overeating and excessive gambling, have the same bi-phasic effects as alcohol and other chemical substances and are therefore also used and abused for purposes of arousal regulation and mood management–or mismanagement.

Like other behavior theorists, Brown maintains that all addictions are learned behavioral responses. At the core of the addictive process is the desire to manipulate and sustain positive "hedonic tone" or emotional happiness. However, due to their biphasic effects, the methods that most people employ to manage their moods–drinking, eating, gambling, drug use, etc.–inevitably result in a rebound of the negative emotional state which is then magnified. Alleviation of the negative affective state, or of the withdrawal symptoms, requires another dose of the drug or repetition of the activity that precipitated it. Thus, persistent use of mood-altering substances and behaviors, and the rebound effects that invariably ensue, ultimately give rise to an intermittent schedule of reinforcement that serves to prevent extinction thereby maintaining the addictive cycle. As discussed above, for example, one study reported that both regular but non-pathological gamblers and pathological gamblers experienced sensations of arousal while gambling but sensations of depression when they stopped. The author therefore concluded that although they occur at different times, both mood states serve to reinforce gambling persistence.[103]

According to Brown[104] the key features of any addiction are similar to those described by the Alcohol Dependence Syndrome[105] and American Psychiatric Association's[106] diagnostic criteria (as medical approaches they will be discussed more completely in a later volume). Although antagonistic to the medical model, Brown employed its vocabulary: his scheme includes 1) *salience*, or preoccupation with the addictive behavior; 2) *conflict* between addicts and significant others and within the addicts themselves over their excessive behavior; 3) *loss of control*, which Brown feels is the *apparent* inability to limit the extent of one's indulgence and which he believes can be explained by salience and the need for relief; 4) *relief*, a coping strategy in which addicts temporarily avoid feeling the rebound effects (withdrawal symptoms) of their addictive behaviors by taking maintenance doses or repeating the addictive behavior (with the consequence of actually increasing salience); 5) *tolerance* to the initial effects of a drug or behavior develops thereby necessitating greater indulgence to achieve the desired end; 6) *withdrawals* or distressful sensations with physical symptoms when the addictive behavior is discontinued; and 7) *relapse and reinstatement* of the addictive behavior to previously high levels even after long periods of abstinence.

Brown maintained that his newer model of addiction differs from reversal theory (which will be detailed in a subsequent volume) since cognitive and social factors also may be involved. Although discussions of cognitive factors are generally restricted to erroneous beliefs and expectancies surrounding gambling behavior (discussed below), Brown's scheme leaves room for the influence of such sociologically determined cognitions as hopelessness and anomie. While some people may resort to addictive behaviors when their long-term goals to achieve "hedonic tone" or happiness are interrupted or thwarted by the vicissitudes of life, others, due to the life situation into which they are born, may be unable to envision even the remotest possibility that any long-term plans, goals, and endeavors will ever be rewarded. Individuals finding themselves in these circumstances are more likely to seek immediate gratification of their need for emotional happiness in the pursuit of addictive behaviors, especially where these alternatives are readily available. In the absence of hope, all long-term, goal-directed behaviors and other emotional management skills these individuals may once have practiced are lost and, as the alternative behavior assumes greater salience, they become "locked into or enslaved in their particular addictive activity and life style."[107]

TESTING THE AROUSAL AND SENSATION-SEEKING HYPOTHESES

A purely behavioral arousal model would postulate that gambling, like drugs or sex, is positively reinforced by the pleasurable sensations it produces. However, since this explanation also involves the possibility of fundamental individual differences in the need for hedonic stimulation, it incorporates elements of personality theory and has certain implications for the medical model. Nevertheless, it can be seen that the sensation-seeking hypothesis actually involves two distinct propositions. The first, the "arousal" hypotheses, is that gambling generates emotional excitement that some gamblers have compared to the "high" they feel from using certain drugs. The second, the actual "sensation-seeking" hypothesis, is that boredom or hypoarousal–the drive for stimulation and excitement–motivates gambling behavior because it is pleasurable. A number of studies have been undertaken to test both propositions.

Is Arousal a Factor?

Tests of the first proposition, the "arousal" hypothesis, have yielded mixed results. In these tests both subjective reports of arousal and objective measures of heart rate increases have been investigated. His studies of young fruit machine players in the United Kingdom have convinced psychologist Mark Griffiths that "some form of arousal is a major, if not the major, reinforcer for regular gambling."[108] On the basis of his interviews with eight young British fruit machine addicts, Griffiths reported that

> the group unanimously stated they experience a "high" while playing which they claimed was physiological (as opposed to psychological) because they could feel their heartbeats getting faster and faster. This was especially noticeable to the players when they were winning or "near winning," i.e., a visual display showing two winning symbols and a third losing one.[109]

Although these subjects were unable to describe the specific nature of the "high," two members of the group compared the feeling to sex. Moreover, they claimed that the gambling high was better than that of alcohol and other soft drugs because it was felt immediately rather than after a period of time. Some reported feeling a "secondary high" merely by watching others play when they had no money of their own. Whereas a number of researchers, including Griffiths,[110] have concluded that gamblers play with money rather than for it, in this case money and its risk appeared to be of considerable importance in generating arousal since none of the group would want to play a fruit machine at home that gave free plays on demand.[111]

Griffiths[112] also investigated the role of arousal in a questionnaire that he administered to a group of 50 young fruit machine players, nine (18%) of whom met the current medical criteria of the *Diagnostic and Statiscal Manual of Mental Disorders* (DSM-III-R) for pathological gambling. They were first asked to describe their mood before, during, and after play. Most (60%) claimed to be in a "good mood" prior to playing although some said they were "fed up" (14%) or in a "bad mood" (4%). As they played, 44 percent claimed to feel excitement, 38 percent did not want to stop, and 10 percent admitted they were unable to stop. After gambling their moods tended to deteriorate: those who claimed to be in a "good mood" fell to 38 percent, the number of "bad mood" feelings increased to 18 percent, and 28 percent felt "fed up." Despite their heightened dysphoria, 40 percent wanted to continue playing. Comparing the responses of the pathological gamblers to the rest of the group, Griffiths found significant differences between them: 11 percent of the pathological gamblers but only 2 percent of the others felt excitement before playing while 100 percent of the pathological gamblers and only 32 percent of the others experienced excitement during play. As was expected, significantly more pathological gamblers responded positively to questions based on the diagnostic criteria for pathological gambling. For example, when they were asked "Do you need to gamble more to get more excited," only a few (10%) of the nonpathological gamblers but over half (56%) of the pathological gamblers responded positively.

Griffiths[113] later replicated this study of the subjective mood states of young fruit machine players. For this study, however, his sample of 60 subjects comprised three distinct groups: nonregular gamblers (50%), regular but nonpathological gamblers (32%), and pathological gamblers (18%). Finding that both the regular and pathological gamblers became significantly more excited while gambling than the nonregular gamblers, he concluded that his findings offered further confirmation of the idea that excitement reinforces both regular and pathological gambling. However, he also found that both the regular nonpathological and the pathological gamblers were significantly more likely than the nonregular gamblers to experience depression or bad moods afterward. Griffiths therefore suggested that both regular and pathological gambling appear to be maintained at different times by excitement as well as depression. Moreover, since the moods reported by regular nonpathological gamblers were identical to those of the pathological gamblers at both times, Griffiths also concluded that the only difference between these two groups was the degree of their gambling involvement.

A laboratory study of undergraduates who "gambled" for tokens furnished by the experimenters also supported the arousal hypothesis when it was found that increases in the subjects' heart rates not only accompanied the decision-making process under conditions that were perceived as riskier, but also correlated positively with bet sizes.[114] Conversely, a later study in which the same researchers attempted to replicate these findings reported that although their subjects' heart rates did increase under three different conditions of arousal (low, medium, and high), the between-group differences were not statistically significant.[115] Similar results were reported by a third study in which the mean heart rate increases of students and regular casino blackjack players rose only 4 and 7 beats per minute, respectively, and also failed to reach statistical significance when they were tested in a realistic appearing but nonetheless artificial laboratory situation. However, when the regular gamblers were retested in an actual casino (where students were excluded for "ethical reasons") their heart rates rose a highly significant average of 24 beats per minute with that of some subjects increasing as much as 58 beats per minute.[116] This led to the conclusions that

> (1) gambling is very exciting, (2) some form of arousal or excitement is a major, and possibly the major, reinforcer of gambling behaviour for regular gamblers, and (3) individual differences in sensation seeking are involved with gambling behaviour, probably as one of a number of determinants.[117]

These findings were replicated in a later laboratory study of low- and high-frequency slot machine gamblers that found that while the heart rates of both groups increased as they played, those of the high-frequency group were significantly higher (13.5 vs. 9.1 beats per minute).[118] The arousal hypothesis is also supported by studies that found significant increases in the heart rates and subjectively reported arousal levels of regular gamblers at off-track betting establishments.[119]

Such field studies suggest not only that objectively measured and subjectively reported levels of arousal appear to be consistently associated with at least some forms of gambling, but also that the results of similar investigations conducted in artificial laboratory settings may not be valid. Although a number of other studies appear to confirm that gambling increases the arousal levels of heavy gamblers and pathological gamblers in treatment,[120] other studies dispute these findings. For example, one reported that the arousal levels of both occasional and heavy slot machine gamblers also showed only insignificant increases.[121] A second which compared the heart rates of regular and occasional gamblers in a natural setting also failed to support the hypothesis that the former would become more aroused than the latter.[122] A third compared the blood pressure readings of young British pathological and non-pathological fruit machine players as they gambled in their natural amusement arcade environment. The researchers found that the readings of the pathological players were consistently lower than those of the nonpathological players before, during, and after play.[123] A fourth study compared the heart rates of low-frequency gamblers, high-frequency gamblers, and "chasers" at British off-course betting offices. While the heart rates of all subjects showed significant variations during the event, no significant differences between the groups were observed.[124]

However, most studies of autonomic arousal have been challenged by the findings of a more complex investigation that compared skin conductance and brain wave activity along with heart rates of three groups of slot machine players.[125] On the basis of the behavioral approach to gambling and arousal, the researchers predicted that when they were exposed to gambling-related cues low-frequency social gamblers should exhibit the lowest levels of arousal, high-frequency social gamblers should exhibit greater arousal, and problem gamblers should show the highest levels. Although the heart rates of all three groups increased during the arousal phase of the experiment no significant differences emerged since these increases were nearly equivalent. Likewise, no significant differences in brain wave activity materialized between the three groups. Measures of skin conductance were also similar between the two social gambling groups but were significantly higher among the problem gamblers. Since no significant differences on any measure emerged between the two groups of social gamblers, and only one measure distinguished the problem gamblers, the researchers concluded that conditioning models by themselves would be unable to account for these findings. They also warned that all future studies should be more comprehensive since investigations of only a single measure of arousal will be likely to produce biased results and, hence, erroneous conclusions concerning the role of arousal in gambling behavior. Most importantly, however, since their experimental subjects were only exposed to gambling-related cues and without actually gambling, the researchers found that gamblers can become aroused by certain stimuli even in the absence of gambling behavior. They also found that not all gambling-related cues may be generally relevant to all gamblers but that some cues may be personally relevant only to some gamblers. They therefore stressed the need to study the relationship between arousal and individual cognitive factors and their role in the development of problem gambling, a topic which will be the focus of the following chapters.

A further dilemma lies in the fact that many regular gamblers neither show nor feel any emotion once a gambling session has been initiated. Although some excitement may be experienced in anticipation or at the beginning of a gambling session, it has not been demonstrated that this arousal is maintained throughout the session.[126] In fact, one study has demonstrated that arousal actually *decreases* during play.[127] Another study which found that greater risk-taking and higher stakes betting were preceded more often by high than by low levels of arousal would also appear to contradict the arousal hypothesis and support the tension-reduction view.[128] Finally, the first study to report a high rate of hypomanic disorder among hospitalized pathological gamblers also concluded that these patients "had periods in which their mood was elevated or irritable; this could not reasonably be explained by the act of gambling itself"[129] since they were denied the opportunity to gamble during the treatment period.

Is Sensation-Seeking a Factor?

Although many gamblers report that they gamble for pleasure and excitement as well as for money,[130] tests of the second proposition–that a sensation-seeking drive motivates gambling and other activities involving risk–are also inconsistent and therefore inconclusive. Only two percent of those surveyed during the study of slot machine gambling at a private club in Australia gave "excitement" as their primary reason for gambling. More commonly expressed reasons were entertainment (48%), to win a small amount of money (40%), to win a major payout (18%), to be sociable (16%), to alleviate boredom (10%), and to forget their troubles (6%).[131] A similar study of 144 betting shop gamblers also found that relatively few gave "excitement" (6%) or "something to do" (6%) as their primary reasons for betting; most claimed to gamble for money (63%) or entertainment (22%).[132] Likewise, most of the adolescents queried in a postal survey claimed that their primary attraction to fruit machine gambling was the prospect of winning money (63.2%) while relatively few claimed to do so for excitement (10.2%) or to escape depression (15.8%) or boredom (15.8%).[133] However, a somewhat later study of adolescent gamblers found that nearly all of the heaviest gamblers indicated that they gambled for enjoyment (92.3%) and excitement (92.3%) while relatively few claimed that they did so to escape their problems (20%), to alleviate depression (10.8%), to relax (10.9%), or to escape feelings of loneliness (4.6%).[134]

Personality studies employing standard psychometric instruments to test the betting choices of nonpathological gamblers in laboratory settings have provided some support for the second proposition, the "sensation-seeking" hypothesis. The most widely used of these instruments is Zuckerman's Sensation-Seeking Scale or SSS,[135] a 40-item self-report questionnaire with four subscales: TAS or Thrill and Adventure Seeking; ES or Experience Seeking; Dis or Disinhibition; and BS or Boredom Susceptibility. Two studies tested the hypothesis that individual differences in people's needs for stimulation, as determined by their sensation-seeking scores, should correspond with their preferences for risk, as determined by their wagering preferences. The first involved a series of tests that correlated the SSS scores of 252 undergraduates with their risk-taking behavior as determined by their betting choices among color, suit, denomination, or different combinations of these variables during thirty consecutive draws of a single card from an ordinary playing deck. The probabilities of winning therefore ranged from 1:2 to 1:52.[136] The second was a more elaborate study that tested a sample of 168 mostly female students in a variety of gambling situations including cards, dice, roulette, and the probabilities of selecting balls of a particular color from urns. All of these situations also included a range of winning probabilities.[137] Both studies found that subjects with higher needs for emotional stimulation tended to prefer riskier bets having lower probabilities of winning but higher potential payoffs, while those with lower scores preferred less risky bets.

On the other hand, psychological studies of the sensation-seeking scores of problem gamblers in clinical and other therapeutic settings have shown mixed, but mostly nonsupportive, results. One such study found that problem and pathological gamblers had significantly higher sensation-seeking scores than social gamblers or controls.[138] The findings of a second study, in which pathological gamblers gave positive responses to a series of three questions related to risk-taking at work, were guardedly interpreted as suggesting "selective" sensation-seeking.[139] Nevertheless, its authors recognized that risk-taking per se is not necessarily equivalent to sensation-seeking. However, this study and a large number of others in which the SSS was used failed to support the sensation-seeking hypothesis when no significant differences were found between the sensation-seeking or boredom scores of either recreational or pathological gamblers and controls[140] or between those of uncontrolled and controlled gamblers.[141] One particularly interesting study used two different clinical assessment instruments to compare measures of boredom between groups of pathological gamblers and controls. Analysis showed the gamblers' scores to be significantly higher on the Farmer and Sundberg Boredom Proneness Scale[142] but not on the Boredom Susceptibility Subcale of Zuckerman's Sensation Seeking Scale. Surprisingly, the small and insignificant correlation that appeared between the Boredom Proneness and Boredom Susceptibility scores of the pathological gamblers was in the *negative* direction.[143] A final study of 298 cocaine abusers, 15 percent of whom were also pathological gamblers, found no significant differences between the sensation-seeking scores of these two groups.[144]

Zuckerman and his colleagues, authors

and champions of the "optimal level of arousal" explanation, were ultimately forced to abandon this model of addiction when their research findings did not conform to their theoretical predictions. Specifically, it turned out that high sensation-seekers did not feel or perform better when they were administered hallucinogens and stimulants ("uppers") nor did low sensation-seekers when they were given opiates and tranquilizers ("downers") as the theory predicted. They also found that high sensation-seekers enjoyed both conditions more than low sensation-seekers and that the performance of both highs and lows improved under the influence of stimulants.[145] The "optimal level of arousal" approach was also refuted by a study that contradicted its prediction that risks will be avoided when arousal is high. This study found that when the arousal levels of three groups of subjects were manipulated to produce low, moderate, and high levels of arousal, respectively, those who were the most highly aroused took the greatest gambling risks.[146]

Results of physiological studies of the "sensation-seeking" hypothesis, are also mixed. A study which did find that high frequency slot machine players became more aroused while gambling than low frequency players also found that the two groups showed no differences in heart rates while resting or when they were shown a slot machine.[147] Thus, while this study provided some support for the first part of the sensation-seeking hypothesis–that gambling generates higher levels of arousal in high frequency gamblers–it provided no support for the second part–that high frequency gamblers experience hypoarousal and therefore gamble to relieve this condition. In fact, some studies have found that the sensation-seeking scores and arousal experiences of heavy recreational and pathological gamblers were actually significantly *lower* than those of the general population.[148]

The results of these studies have led to several different interpretations. Some researchers suggest that while sensation-seeking may not directly influence the initial decision to gamble, it may influence the degree of involvement or persistence once gambling has begun.[149] Others have concluded that "what evidence there is suggests that arousal does not have an important role in causing gamblers to persist through long sessions."[150] Still others suggest that sensation-seeking may be a factor in some forms of gambling such as casino games and illegal betting but not in others such as slot machine playing.[151]

Any of the methodological problems that are inherent in many studies may account for these inconsistencies. Some critics have suggested that part of the problem may lie in the various psychometric instruments that have been used. That is, different questionnaires that were designed to assess the same personality dimension–such as susceptibility or proneness to boredom–may actually be measuring two distinct and unrelated dimensions.[152] Other critics point to the research design of the investigators. For example, because the authors of one study[153] failed to control for age, the subjects comprising their control group of nongamblers were younger than the gamblers in their experimental group. The fact that sensation-seeking scores tend to diminish significantly with age may therefore account for the lack of any difference between the sensation-seeking scores of these two groups.[154] Likewise, sensation-seeking scores between males and females also show a significant difference,[155] another factor that is rarely controlled for in psychometric research.

The investigators' interpretations of their findings may also be responsible for the lack of agreement. More specifically, it is altogether possible that gambling actually *does* meet the needs of sensation-seekers. That is, if the need or drive for arousal does motivate gambling, and if gambling does serve to reduce this drive, then the sensation-seeking scores of those who are successfully reducing this drive through gambling should be lower than those who are not. Thus, we would expect the relationship between gambling behavior and sensation-seeking to present a "U-shaped" curve with nongamblers scoring low on sensation-seeking, moderate gamblers scoring higher, and heavy gamblers scoring lower. On the other hand, however, this could also mean that the gambling behaviors of heavy gamblers determines their sensation-seeking score rather than the reverse, thereby refuting the sensation-seeking hypothesis.[156]

Another possible explanation for these inconsistencies is that gamblers' sensation-seeking scores may be related to the sizes and timing of their bets rather than to the frequency or persistence of their gambling. One study did find a positive correlation between the sensation-seeking scores and bet sizes of casino gamblers.[157] However, its authors prudently pointed out that the association they observed between high stakes betting and the arousal levels of high sensation-seekers does not constitute proof of a causal relationship.[158] It must also be pointed out that just as a simple correlation between betting size and arousal does not constitute proof that gamblers consciously (or unconsciously) bet more in a deliberate effort to arouse their emotions, neither do correlations between late racetrack betting or frequency of betting and increased arousal[159] constitute proof that gamblers deliberately delay betting or bet more rapidly only to arouse their emotions. Such correlations merely present another "chicken and egg" dilemma: just as gambling might generate heightened levels of arousal, so might heightened arousal generate more intense gambling. Previous gambling losses could generate considerable negative affect which could in turn lead to raised stakes or faster betting by gamblers who are "chasing" or trying to get even.

Furthermore, not all studies have verified the betting practices that have been interpreted as confirmation of the sensation-seeking hypothesis. A study of the reported "late betting" and "increased betting" phenomena among off-track bettors was conducted specifically to test the hypothesis that FI (fixed-interval) schedules of reinforcement "train" gamblers to conform to certain styles of betting by intensifying their emotional arousal.[160] As in earlier studies of off-course betting behavior, the subjects were actual bettors in a U.K. (Glasgow) betting shop. However, since previous studies had failed to distinguish between the betting practices of experienced and novice bettors, the subjects of this study were divided into "regular" or "high frequency" gamblers and "occasional" or "low frequency" gamblers. If the "late betting" hypothesis were valid then a significant difference should appear between the times bets are placed by "trained" regulars, who should tend to be last-minute bettors, and "untrained" novice and occasional bettors whose betting should cover a broader time range relative to the start of a race. If the "increased betting" hypothesis were correct, then regulars should also bet more than novices. The study found that although experienced bettors did show a tendency to place their bets close to the start of a race, they did not do so consistently enough to support the "late betting" hypothesis. Furthermore, since novice bettors also placed most of their bets near the start of a race, the two groups exhibited no significant differences in the timing of their bets. The study also found no significant differences between the amounts bet by members of the two groups. Since their betting practices were so similar, the FI schedule "arousal" hypotheses was rejected.

Dickerson's explanation for the "late betting phenomenon" as purely a function of FI reinforcement schedules has therefore been challenged by those who feel that other factors may be involved. It could easily result from mere indecision about which horse to play, and this indecision alone could generate considerable negative affect as the post time for a race quickly approaches. On the other hand, this could also be a rational betting strategy which allows gamblers who closely watch for any last-minute changes on the "tote" board to gain greater odds advantages.[161] Finally, since the subjects of all field studies reporting the late betting phenomenon were nonpathological gamblers, their findings reveal nothing concrete about the motivations of pathological gamblers.[162]

Taken together, these inconsistent and often contradictory findings suggest that pathological gambling, like alcoholism, may not be a unitary phenomenon. That is, since neither all people nor all forms of gambling are the same, it is entirely possible that different people respond differently to different forms of gambling and that, as a consequence, different kinds of gamblers gamble for different reasons. Many researchers therefore feel that pathological gambling and alcoholism may represent broad, generic addictive disorders having several distinct subtypes, each with its own etiology.[163] For example, low sensation-seekers might prefer such types of gambling as slot machines and off-course betting which generate relatively little arousal while high sensation-seekers might prefer more exciting and action-producing games such as racetrack and casino gambling or they might be attracted to many different forms of gambling.[164] It has also been suggested that horse race addicts may gamble to reduce boredom while slot machine addicts gamble to reduce anxiety and stress.[165] Studies of female pathological gamblers which lend some empirical support to this hypothesis have reported that different women gamble for different reasons: "escape seekers" gamble to avoid unpleasant domestic situations or other personal problems while "action seekers" gamble for the excitement it provides.[166] A University of Minnesota study of pathological gamblers reported that "escapist" gambling was more common among females who tended to prefer slot machines while "thrill seeking" was more common among males who preferred gaming tables.[167] However, other tests of this hypothesis failed to find any psychological test score differences between slot machine addicts and horse race addicts.[168]

Finally, these inconsistent and contradictory findings have led at least one theorist to conclude that the arousal hypothesis has received far more attention than it merits.[169] Despite the number of arousal studies that have been undertaken, few, if any, have monitored levels of arousal throughout an entire gambling session. Consequently, the only conclusions we can draw are highly generalized ones claiming, for example, that excitement is greatest at the beginning of slot machine play or that it increases near the end of a race. He therefore feels that future researchers would be better advised to concentrate on gamblers' beliefs and thought processes (see the following chapters on Cognitive-Behavioral Psychology).

CRITIQUE OF NEED-STATE OR DRIVE-REDUCTION MODELS

According to the play, tension-reduction, sensation-seeking, and dual-effect hypotheses, it is not merely a potential monetary payoff, but an immediate emotional payoff that reinforces persistent gambling behavior which, in turn, can develop into pathological gambling. In the words of one drive-reduction theorist who was apparently familiar with the thoughts of Moran[170] and Fuller[171] on the subject, "Money loses its economic value since the gambler plays *with* money, not *for* it."[172] These approaches, which are not restricted to pathological gambling, explain all addictions as a continued need to ameliorate negative affective or emotional states or as a purely hedonistic quest for the positive state of euphoria that such behaviors provide.[173] It has therefore been said that "People do not become addicted to drugs or mood-altering experiences as such, but rather to the satiation, arousal, or fantasy experiences that can be achieved through them."[174] In response to such claims psychoanalyst Peter Fuller wrote, "The whole theory comes perilously close to collapse when it has to be argued that an internal reward is preferable to such a tangible external stimulus as money"[175] while the underlying psychological processes are ignored. Some researchers have therefore concluded that emotional and monetary concerns are equally important motivational factors since problem gamblers are more likely than nonproblem gamblers to continue while losing when they are already experiencing negative mood states or when they are already in debt.[176]

Psychiatrist Thomas Szasz questioned the validity of the entire concept of psychological tension-reduction by pointing out that the idea was taken directly from a model of physical energy discharge. More specifically, the tension-reduction model was originally formulated by physical scientists who used it to describe and predict the release of hydraulic pressure. Because it seemed to provide such a good descriptive analogy, it was adopted by members of the psychotherapeutic community who molded it to their purposes:

> The notion that neurotic symptoms "discharge tension" is based on the physical model of energy-discharge. According to this scheme, psychological functioning is conceived on the model of a hydraulic system. . . . A column of water, representing potential energy, is dammed up behind a barrier and seeks release. It may be discharged along a number of different pathways: (1) Along the route mapped out for it–that is, normally, in speech or appropriate overt behavior; (2) Along an alternate route, which represents a "misuse" of the apparatus (e.g., leakage from the hydraulic system, perhaps at the sides of the dam, not via the sluices provided). Dammed-up tension is discharged via "conversion" into "bodily symptoms." This is "conversion hysteria." (3) Along still other channels (e.g., leakage at other points in the system), leading to bodily disease. This is "vegetative" or "organ neurosis."[177]

If the psychological model of tension-reduction is merely a reified concept, the validity of the entire hypothesis may indeed be questionable. Valid or not, however, the tension-reduction hypothesis remains a very popular concept in the psychotherapeutic community and one that has generated considerable research.

As discussed previously, psychometric studies of the relationship between negative affective states and gambling behavior are mixed. Although many researchers maintain that such dysphoric states as anxiety, stress, and depression are frequently or consistently associated with gambling and problem gambling,[178] another feels that "There are few observations that a session of gambling may be calming or anaesthetising."[179] Studies which found negative emotional states to be associated with longer playing sessions and the initiation of new gambling sessions among problem and high-frequency nonproblem slot machine gamblers when they are losing have concluded that such states are highly significant determinants of persistence and impaired control among problem gamblers, many of whom acknowledge that they gamble "to forget troubles."[180] However, these studies also found that emotional dysphoria is actually likely to *inhibit* gambling behavior or *decrease* the length of a gambling session among low-frequency gamblers.[181] Neither state (situational and transitional) nor trait (stable and enduring) anxiety levels were found to be high in a sample of pathological gamblers seeking treatment.[182] This approach was also seriously challenged by a study of former fruit machine addicts which found that gambling tended to exacerbate or create rather than relieve negative emotional states.[183]

The tension-reduction hypothesis finds some support in studies of the subjectively felt motivations of habitual and pathological gamblers but little or no support in those of low-frequency and nonpathological gamblers. Although the subjects of most pathological gambling research have been men, one study investigated the motivations of female pathological gamblers who claimed to be addicted to video poker machines. According to some of these women the machines provided a means of escaping from loneliness or from an abusive spouse.[184] A University of Minnesota study of 40 (15 female; 25 male) pathological gamblers in an outpatient treatment program reported that many subjects claimed to gamble in "an attempt to change mood states, especially boredom or depression; an escape; or to obtain relief from physical pain. . . . Some reported discomfort in social situations and found gambling to be anxiolytic by nature of its isolation from others."[185] Interestingly, the female subjects of this study tended to prefer the social isolation of slot machine gambling while most of the men preferred the more gregarious game of blackjack. However, a survey of the subjectively ascribed motivations for playing slot machines expressed by a nonclinical population, the members of one of Australia's private gambling clubs, found that only six percent of the respondents admitted that they play "to forget one's troubles" while nearly half (48%) claimed to play purely for entertainment.[186] Likewise, a questionnaire survey of another non-clinical group, patrons of Australian betting shops, reported that scarcely any (1%) of the 144 respondents gambled to forget their troubles while most claimed a desire for money (63%) or entertainment (22%) as their primary reason for gambling.[187] A more recent study of 817 adolescent high school students also found that nearly all claimed to gamble for enjoyment, excitement, and for the chance to make money while relatively few indicated that they gambled to escape their problems, to relax, or to alleviate depression.[188]

In the absence of further inquiry and analysis some researchers question whether these self-reported explanations represent a rationale or a culturally sanctioned rationalization for gambling.[189] It must also be stressed that the high rates of co-addiction which have been reported–and which have been presumed as evidence of the tension- and anxiety-reducing effects of addictive behaviors–could be interpreted as support for a medical model of addiction as readily as they could for the tension-reduction model. However, one critic feels that an entirely different approach is necessary: "The kind of tension reduction theories of reinforcement, once so unsatisfactorily prevalent in alcohol studies, are untenable in gambling where the effects of the activity have been more often reported as tension-heightening."[190]

Many of the psychological studies designed to test drive-reduction hypotheses merely report an association–generally a statistically significant correlation–between an addictive or potentially addictive behavior and the presence or absence of certain emotions, affective disorders, or personality traits, as determined by a particular questionnaire. Thus, different people may engage in these behaviors for entirely different reasons. For example, although college students tend to use alcohol more for sensation-seeking than for anxiety reduction,[191] it is important to remember that groups of young, carefree, exuberant carousers are not the same as groups of older, care-worn alcoholics. While the latter may drink, at least in part, to relieve stress, the former may drink because youth alone creates the need for stimulation. Some gambling researchers have therefore postulated the existence of different subtypes of gamblers: those subsumed under Subtype A gamble to reduce depression while those in Subtype B gamble to reduce boredom.[192] Others, building on this scheme, have added a third subtype consisting of those who gamble to relieve both conditions simultaneously.[193]

As noted in a previous section, since most studies of this nature are retrospective in that their subjects are pathological gamblers in treatment who are being tested after the fact, they beg the "chicken and egg" question. That is, do some pre-existing emotional needs or personality traits cause people to gamble excessively, or does persistent gambling, with its resultant heavy losses and big wins, generate the emotional and personality profiles that these studies measure? The same question applies to, and has been asked of, all other addictions, as well: which comes first, the negative emotion or the behavior? Or, in the language of behavioral psychology, which is the stimulus and which is the response? Another critic noted the faulty reasoning inherent in these need-state models. Different gamblers have different needs–for money, for status and prestige, for relief from depression, for solitude, for companionship, for escape from personal problems, etc.–all of which have been given as their reason for gambling. Viewed from this perspective, the critic concluded, need-state models can be seen to be circular and uninformative.[194]

Some treatment specialists feel that the relationship between gambling and emotion is more complex than the drive-reduction theorists would have us believe. In some cases pathological gambling may, indeed, be caused by negative emotional states. In others, however, negative emotional states may be caused by pathological gambling. It is also possible that while negative emotional states are often associated with pathological gambling, in many cases they may not be causally related in either direction even though they are often thought to be. According to some treatment specialists,

> in our experience, patients frequently state that gambling is the way boredom or emptiness is managed. While this may have some truth, that is, feeling bored or empty may be a trigger for gambling and gambling helps to cope with these feelings, these feelings may bear no relationship in a true etiological way to the gambling. . . . By way of "addictive logic," the gambler in early recovery may think that boredom is the reason for the gambling. While gambling and boredom may now have an important and real relationship to each other which needs to be addressed in treatment, boredom was not truly the cause of the gambling problem. Frequently our patients believe that a particular psychological concern may be responsible for the gambling difficulties. This should not, however, necessarily be taken at face value without further exploration.[195]

Clearly, more research into the influences of tension-reduction and arousal on gambling and other potentially addictive behaviors is required. In any case, the punishments that the addict often experiences–such as the possible humiliation of arrest and incarceration, the loss of friends, employment, family, etc., and the loss of money in the case of gambling–are explained by the claim that the immediate, short-term rewards of tension-reduction or arousal that addictive behaviors provide constitute greater reinforcement than, and more than compensate for, any monetary loss or social censure that may follow.

Part III

COGNITIVE-BEHAVIORAL PSYCHOLOGY

The Role of Expectancy and Belief

6

IRRATIONAL THINKING

Some behaviorists, not entirely dissatisfied with the psychoanalytic approach, have added the important cognitive factors of expectancy and belief to their behavioral explanations for persistent and pathological gambling.[1] A number of these modern psychologists have abandoned the orthodox behavioral approaches of their immediate predecessors who stressed the importance of external environmental influences in favor of those which once again focus on internal psychological factors; others have attempted to blend these two approaches. Cognitive, cognitive-behavioral, or sociocognitive theory therefore represents a return to explanations that emphasize the individual's internal mental processes. However, unlike the earlier psychoanalytic theorists who postulated the existence of unconsciously felt and negatively sanctioned motivations, cognitive psychologists maintain that the individual's motivations derive from thoughts that are entirely conscious and often highly valued.

The basic tenets of cognitive or expectancy theory is probably nowhere better summarized than in the following statement by one of its more ardent advocates: "regular gamblers persist in trying to win money at gambling because they hold a set of false beliefs about the nature of gambling, the likelihood of winning, and their own expertise."[2] As a consequence of these false beliefs, "information about gambling decisions is processed in a consistently biased manner which leads the gambler to make less than optimal choices."[3] Some cognitive theorists go so far as to claim that the behavior of all gamblers is governed by their cognitions.[4]

Like religious, political, and other convictions that are often accepted and internalized without being questioned, beliefs related to gambling can be either culturally instilled or they can be learned and assimilated from exceptional or venerable individuals who are respected, admired, and emulated. Cognitive psychologists examine beliefs that are false though cherished and attempt to help persistent gamblers by creating an awareness of these misconceptions and their consequences. They maintain that the beliefs and expectations of winning that many gamblers entertain often serve to maintain or reinforce their gambling even when they are losing. For example, a gambler may firmly believe that a special system of playing or handicapping must eventually prove to be successful or that he or she somehow "knows" when a machine is about to pay out or when a horse will win. It is well known that a "hunch player" of this sort is the bookie's best friend.

Simply stated, cognitive theorists contend that gambling persistence is fostered by unrealistic or irrational thinking. Advocates of the cognitive approach reason that because the odds in all commercial gambling games always favor the house, "no rational person would gamble if wining money was the only consideration."[5] This means that "either people are not rational or winning money is not the only consideration."[6] Since money is the goal of gambling, they conclude that gamblers–at least those who participate in commercial forms of gambling–cannot be rational.

Many cognitive psychologists feel that while payout rates and cognitive factors both appear to reinforce persistence once play has begun, the initiation of new gambling sessions appears to be largely a matter of the gambler's pre-existing beliefs about his or her chances for winning. In behavioral terminology, events that influence subsequent actions are referred to as "discriminative stimuli" since they discriminate or guide behavior in one direction over another. For laboratory animals the anticipation of reward serves as a discriminatory stimulus for bar-pressing behavior. Likewise, studies of slot machine gamblers have found greater persistence among both high- and low-frequency players who expect a larger payout than those who anticipate a smaller payout.[7] It has therefore been suggested that "it is the machine reinforcement schedule that *drives* the behavior and that the cognitive processes are by-products that provide the player with a verbal *explanation* of the behavior."[8] More often than not the discriminative stimuli or expectations that influence much of people's gambling behavior are founded on faulty logic, on erroneous beliefs in the laws of probability, or on other irrational and often purely superstitious beliefs.[9] A variety of such influences, many of which act simultaneously, are thought to be involved.

Biased Estimates of Probability

A good example of one type of irrational thinking has been reported by psychologists who study the ways in which people's false perceptions influence their beliefs and behaviors related to probability and risk. Since the late 1940s researchers interested in risk-taking behavior have compared the objective, mathematically determined probabilities of particular outcomes to people's subjective estimates of them. This research clearly demonstrates that, irrespective of the objective mathematical probabilities for a particular outcome, people tend to base their betting choices on their own subjectively estimated and frequently erroneous assessments. For example, it has been shown that when mathematical probabilities are very low, as in the prospect of winning a lottery drawing or winning on a long shot at the track, people tend to overestimate their chances, often by making unrealistically large bets; when probabilities are high, as in the prospect of winning on a horse with short odds, they tend to underestimate their chances by betting low.[10] Thus, while the common generalization that "most gamblers over-rate their chances of success and underestimate their likelihood of failure"[11] has validity under some circumstances, the reverse holds true under opposite circumstances.

One series of experiments examined people's choices between two options in which the chances of winning and losing were the same.[12] In the first test, when they were offered a choice between picking a card from a stack of 100 containing 10 winners or drawing from a stack of 10 with only one winner, most subjects drew from the larger stack. Apparently, although the objective probabilities of winning were identical, the subjects developed a biased perception of their chances solely on the basis of the absolute numbers of winning cards available. In a second experiment, the fact that most subjects chose from a stack of 10 cards containing nine winners rather than a stack of 100 cards with 90 winners appeared to be influenced solely by the absolute number of losing cards. A third test involved the choice between a stack of 100 cards with ten winners and a stack of 50 cards with five winners. That the subjects again chose from the stack with the greatest number of winners confirmed that subjective estimates of probability can be highly irrational. As is readily apparent to anyone who has ever witnessed the successful operation of certain carnival midway games, gambling and its persistence are easily fostered when biased estimates of the rube's chances of winning are encouraged.

The Gambler's Fallacy

Many gamblers believe that a particular outcome is likely to occur simply because it has not occurred for some time. They therefore bet as though each previous loss increases their probability of winning on the next play no matter what form of gambling they pursue. While this may be true of such games as mechanical slot machines and pull tabs in which overall payouts and payout rates are predetermined, it is certainly not true of electronic slot machines, coin tossing, race track betting, roulette, craps, or most other casino games in which the outcome of any play is unrelated to any other. Nevertheless, many gamblers rely on this erroneous belief, commonly known as "the gambler's fallacy,"[13] the effect of "negative recency,"[14] or the "Monte Carlo fallacy,"[15] and increase the size of their bet after each loss in the belief that they are "overdue" for a win. The "gambler's fallacy" has also been explained as 1) "the belief that a sequence of events in a random process–say the tossing of a coin–will represent the essential characteristics of the process even when the sequence is short,"[16] 2) the idea that probability or chance is a "self-correcting process in which a deviation in one direction induces a deviation in the opposite direction to restore the balance,"[17] and 3) the treatment of independent events as dependent.[18]

The "gambler's fallacy" is exemplified by gamblers who look for "patterns" or "streaks" and then bet accordingly. For example, many roulette players reason that if red or black has not won recently, then it is also "overdue" and therefore more likely to win on the next play. However, this belief appears to operate in only one direction: while gamblers who have experienced a series of losses often expect to win on the next play, those who have experienced a series of wins rarely expect to lose.[19] In reality, of course, every spin of the wheel, every roll of the dice, and every toss of the coin is an independent event which remains totally unaffected by any previous outcome or series of outcomes, and which has no predictive relevance for any future outcome. Thus, the chances for red or black, odd or even, and heads or tails to appear on *any* play remain the same for *every* play.

More recently, a "Type II" gambler's fallacy has been proposed as a complement to the standard or "Type I" fallacy.[20] A Type I fallacy refers to the conviction that if things have been "running" a certain way they are bound to change, as in the belief that a "black" outcome in roulette is more likely after a series of "red" outcomes has occurred. Conversely, a Type II fallacy refers to the belief that if things are "running" a certain way, they will tend to stay that way. More specifically, it describes the tendency of some gamblers to base their bets on the belief that roulette wheels, for example, are biased in such a way that one or more favored numbers can be expected to occur more frequently than chance would allow. Some gamblers believe that such biases might be caused by variations in temperature or humidity which could affect the wheel's spin or by the bending or wearing down of the metal partitions between its numbered compartments. In truth, although such conditions may indeed occur, they would be so slight as to be undetectable except by a close examination with sophisticated precision tools or an exceptionally large number of trials. Nevertheless, anecdotal tales of "professionals" who have won fortunes merely by watching for such biases and then betting accordingly continue to circulate among gamblers.

Racetrack bettors, lottery players, and other kinds of gamblers are also susceptible to these fallacies. Many track bettors will continue to bet on a particular horse, increasing the size of the bet after each loss, in the erroneous belief that irrespective of its condition the animal is overdue for a win and "owes" them the money that they lost in previous races. Others repeatedly play the favorites and escalate their bets race after race in the belief that each favorite's loss further increases their chances of winning. Some will continue to bet on a "hot jockey" in the belief that he will continue to win while others bet against him in the belief that he is overdue for a loss irrespective of which horse he happens to be riding.[21] Many lottery players make their selections on the basis of their belief in "hot" and "cold" numbers. Some will select numbers that have not been drawn recently since they believe them to be overdue. However, others prefer "hot" numbers that have recently appeared more often than chance should allow in the belief that winning numbers are also more likely to be drawn again in the near future. They avoid "cold" numbers which have not appeared recently in the belief that they are also unlikely to be drawn in the near future.[22] Similarly, sports bettors have also been shown to base their betting strategies on the belief that teams that are on "hot streaks" have better chances of winning than are warranted while those that are on "cold streaks" will probably continue to lose.[23]

Persistence and Chasing

Many gamblers are convinced that persistence is the only logical strategy when they are losing: their only chance of getting ahead or merely breaking even is to continue since they would have *no* chance of doing so if they quit. Of course, any past experience of a big win after plunging–whether their own or someone else's–helps to reinforce this idea, even if it has happened only once. Since the actual probability is that they will continue to lose, persistence leads to even greater losses and more "chasing" in an attempt to get even. According to one researcher, "'Chasing' is essentially a cluster of beliefs and behaviours that lead a person to continue to gamble despite heavy losses, 'because a run of bad luck must end,' 'because a machine owes them money,' 'because it is the only way to get their money back,' etc."[24] Consequently, "Chasing and the illusion of control are two cognitive phenomena that play a central role in persistent gambling on poker [slot] machines."[25]

However, some gamblers and even a few problem gamblers entertain no such beliefs[26] since they know full well that chasing works only in the rarest of cases. Casino owners also know that the longer a gambler occupies a seat at a gaming table or machine, the more money he or she is likely to lose. For example, by applying the laws of probability, it has been calculated that, on average, after 100 plays the very luckiest 10 percent of all roulette players will be only eight monetary units ahead. They will be 12 units behind after 1,000 plays and 400 units behind after 10,000 plays. The unluckiest 10 percent will lose 20 units after 100 plays, 94 units after 1,000 plays, and 654 units after 10,000 plays.[27] This means that a lifetime of even moderate gambling can be expensive.

From the casino's point of view, persistence is indeed the key to success: the longer people can be persuaded to gamble, the greater will be the house profits. For example, 67 percent of all roulette players will be losing after 100 plays, 95 percent will be losing after 1,000 plays, and every player will be losing after 10,000 plays.[28] Similar trends occur in all other commercial games such as craps and blackjack with the exception of successful card counters who are in a definite minority and who, in the eyes of the casino management, are cheaters. This means that several hours of play by a few customers are far more profitable than several minutes of play by many. Longer periods of play by more customers translates into even greater profits.

Casino operators therefore do everything possible to extend every customer's playing time. In the words of the chief executive officer of one of Atlantic City's major casinos, "Our goal is not to get more out of a customer in three hours but to get him to stay for four hours."[29] Inducing their customers to play even five minutes longer than they normally would can increase a casino's annual profits by millions of dollars. To achieve this goal, some casinos are now injecting pleasant smelling odors into their air circulation systems as a subtle inducement for gamblers to spend more time–and money–on the premises. During a weekend experiment with a substance known as Odorant 1, the slot machine take at a large Las Vegas casino was 45 percent higher than usual. According to a Las Vegas casino owner, "It's our duty to extract as much money from the customer as we can. And send them home with a smile on their face."[30] Most casinos now resort to a number of standard psychological tactics: fresh air, wider aisles, better lighting, improved color schemes, back supports on playing stools, machines that accept bills, check-cashing booths, in-house automated teller machines, and free drinks all serve to increase the gamblers' playing ease and encourage their persistence.

Attribution Theory

Attributional approaches to human motivation and behavior attempt to discover why gamblers persist, chase, and succumb to the "gambler's fallacy" and other forms of irrational thinking by investigating the reasons and rationalizations they give for their successes and failures. Attribution theorists therefore study the ways in which people explain or justify certain events to themselves. Research in this area has found that people generally attribute their successes to internal causes or to things that are within their control but ascribe their failures to external causes or to things that are beyond their control. This appears to be the case for many gamblers who interpret their wins as verification of their superior knowledge or sound handicapping skills–proof that their "system" is working–but explain away their losses as "bad luck" rather than any personal shortcomings.

Locus of Control Orientation

One area of particular interest to attribution theorists is the gambler's "attributional style" or "locus of control" orientation, a personality trait that refers to a his or her general outlook on life. Some people appear to have a locus of control orientation that is consistently biased in one direction over the other. Those with a strong *external* locus of control orientation–reported to be common among members of Gamblers Anonymous[31] tend to regard each of life's rewards and punishments as a matter of luck, chance, or divine will lying outside their personal control. Even horse players, who regard handicapping more as a matter of skill than of luck, tend to be more externally or luck-oriented than nongamblers.[32] Conversely, those with a strong *internal* locus of control orientation believe they are the masters of their own destiny and therefore regard the outcomes of events as consequences of their own behavioral choices.[33] Attribution theorists have found that people with a particularly strong internal or external orientation tend to explain many of life's occurrences accordingly, regardless of whether these occurrences are matters of chance or skill.

Studies reporting significantly different preferences for risk between internally and externally oriented individuals suggest that an individual's particular locus of control orientation may make a substantial contribution to his or her gambling behavior and persistence. Although most people exaggerate the importance of their own personal ability or control and underrate the role of luck or chance in gambling situations,[34] internals are more likely to do so than externals. Studies of risk-taking behavior have found that subjects with an internal locus of control orientation prefer games of skill while those with an external orientation prefer games of chance.[35] In situations based solely on chance, those with a high internal locus of control orientation also prefer safer, more probable bets than those with a high external orientation who, being more luck-oriented, prefer riskier "long shots" and make their betting decisions on the basis of "hunches," previous outcomes, and superstitious behaviors rather than on objective probability assessments. Internally oriented lottery players are also more likely to pick their own numbers while those who are externally oriented are more likely to allow a machine to select their numbers. Nevertheless, internally oriented subjects are willing to risk more money than externals when they do play games of chance provided their involvement is active rather than passive and provided they know beforehand what they hope to attain. For example, gamblers bet more on the outcomes of dice and roulette when they know in advance which numbers they want, when they are allowed to throw the dice or the ball themselves rather than passively watch someone else throw them, and when they place their bets before rather than after the throw.[36] These tendencies are all believed to reflect the desire for, and subjective perception of, personal control.

Many researchers therefore believe that almost any kind of active involvement gives gamblers the feeling that they have some degree of personal control even when none really exists. Moreover, as opposed to externals, those with a strong internal locus of control orientation appear to be especially susceptible to the belief that they can somehow control the outcomes of even chance-determined events which cannot be controlled.[37] They are also more likely than externals to be influenced by the reinforcement of an early winning phase or "beginner's luck."[38]

THE ILLUSION OF CONTROL

Causality and Foreknowledge

One of the first tests of these ideas did not involve gambling per se but did involve conditions of uncertainty and chance. This experiment was conducted by Camille Wortman[39] to test the hypothesis that perceptions of control can be induced if two conditions are met: causality and foreknowledge. That is, Wortman predicted that people will feel greater control over an outcome if they are actively involved in bringing it about *and* if they know in advance what they hope to achieve. To do so she arranged to have one of two differently colored marbles drawn from a can to determine which of two prizes–one highly attractive, the other minimally so–that her subjects would win. The subjects, 65 male college students, were divided into three groups: those who knew which color would win which prize and who drew their own marble from the can (foreknowledge and causality), those who knew which color would win which prize but whose marbles were picked by an experimenter (foreknowledge but no causality), and those who did not know which color would win which prize but who were allowed to choose their own marbles (causality but no foreknowledge). Following the experiment each subject was given a questionnaire designed to elicit and measure their perceptions of control. Wortman predicted that the perception of control of those in the dual-condition group would be significantly higher than those in either of the single-condition groups. She also predicted that no significant differences in perceived control would emerge between the two single-condition groups. Although all subjects were specifically told beforehand that their outcomes would be determined entirely by chance, Wortman's data analysis bore out her predictions and supported her hypothesis: those in the foreknowledge and causality group experienced significantly higher perceptions of control than the others while the two single-condition groups did not differ significantly from one another.

On the basis of her findings, Wortman concluded 1) that both causality and foreknowledge are necessary for perceived control and 2) that neither causality nor foreknowledge by itself can have such an effect. Unfortunately, her second conclusion is invalid since there was no basis from which it could be drawn. That is, despite the fact that the two single-condition situations did not differ significantly from one another, there was actually no way to determine whether the influence of either condition would differ significantly from a situation in which *neither* condition was present. The experiment would have been far more meaningful had she also included a fourth subgroup of subjects having neither foreknowledge nor choice. This would have established a baseline, free of the influence of either condition, against which the other subgroups could be compared. This would then have provided a legitimate means of determining the extent, if any, to which either condition by itself can induce a perception of control.[40] If nothing else, however, her study did demonstrate that the more potential control-inducing conditions that are involved in chance-determined events, the greater will be the perception of control. Fortunately, as will be demonstrated below, other researchers did analyze in isolation the conditions they believed to be causative.

Competition, Choice, Familiarity, and Involvement

One of the first tests of attribution theory in actual gambling contexts was conducted by psychologist Ellen J. Langer[41] whose more elaborate experiments provided additional evidence that gamblers can be made to believe they can predict or influence the outcome of purely chance events. Langer referred to this phenomenon as the "illusion of control," an expression that was adopted by many later researchers. She defined an illusion of control as "the expectancy of a personal success probability inappropriately higher than the objective probability would warrant."[42] The purpose of her research was to test the proposition that by encouraging participants in games of chance to think and act as though they were participating in games involving skill, she could induce in them an internal locus of control or "skill orientation" by creating the false impression that they actually could exert some influence over the outcomes.

To test her hypothesis that chance situations which simulate skill situations can establish an illusion of control over the uncontrollable, Langer devised a series of six separate laboratory and real-world field experiments in which subjects were encouraged to act as though the outcomes were determined at least in part by their own decisions and actions. Each situation involved one or more conditions that are generally associated with games of skill. These conditions included competition, choice, stimulus familiarity, response familiarity, and active or passive personal involvement.

The first experiment tested and confirmed Langer's prediction that even in chance-determined events the perception of competition can strengthen the gambler's illusion of control. Each subject in this laboratory experiment was paired with a confederate of the research team. Both the subject and the confederate, who was posing as another subject, were instructed to make a series of bets on who would draw the highest card from a deck. Not only was the illusion of control expected to be increased by the simulation of competition, but also by the personal appearance and bearing of the competitor with whom the subjects were paired. Thus, half the subjects "competed" against an "opponent" who was either fashionably dressed and appeared to be very confident and poised–the "dapper" situation–or against one who was unfashionably dressed and appeared to be awkward, lacking in self-assurance, and very nervous–the "schnook" situation. The subjects, who could bet any denomination between zero and twenty-five cents, were expected to bet more against the anxious and apprehensive "schnook" than against the cool and confident "dapper" opponent. Langer found, in fact, that the average bet size of subjects in the "dapper" situation was significantly lower (11.04 cents) than those in the "schnook" situation (16.25 cents). However, later research of a similar nature failed to replicate these findings when the subjects' perceptions of an opponent had no influence over their betting behavior.[43]

Langer's second experiment produced striking evidence that the condition of choice increases the illusion of control. The subjects of this real-life field experiment were participants in two separate business office lottery drawings in which a one-dollar ticket would win a prize of about $50. Half the participants in each office were allowed to choose their own tickets while the other half were allowed no choice. Before the drawings all participants were asked to name the price at which they would sell their tickets. Those who were permitted to choose their own tickets placed a much higher average value on them ($8.67) than those who had no choice ($1.96).

The third experiment established that the condition of stimulus familiarity enhances the illusion of control. Like the second experiment it involved two similar lottery situations but, since it was also intended to replicate the findings of the second study, it was more complex. To establish conditions of stimulus familiarity and unfamiliarity, the identifying marks on the tickets used for one lottery consisted of ordinary letters of the alphabet while those for the other were identified with printers' symbols which were unfamiliar to the subjects. As in the second study, half of the participants in each lottery were allowed their choice of tickets and half were denied a choice. Thus, the subjects of this experiment comprised four distinct categories: "choice (of ticket) and familiarity (ticket identified by letter)," "choice and unfamiliarity (ticket identified by symbol)," "no choice and familiarity," and "no choice and unfamiliarity." After the tickets were sold, all participants were informed that the promoter was running two simultaneous lotteries and told that 26 tickets had been sold for the lottery in which they were participating but only 21 had been sold for the one in which they were not participating. Using the excuse that he had sold too many tickets for "their" lottery, the promoter then offered each participant the opportunity to exchange his or her present ticket for one in the "other" lottery. Although a participant's objective chances of winning would increase from 1 in 26 to 1 in 22 by doing so, 62 percent of those in the "choice and familiarity" situation (which was expected to create the greatest illusion of control) refused the offer. The refusal rate decreased to 38 percent in both the "choice and unfamiliarity" and "no choice and familiarity" groups while only 15 percent in the "no choice and unfamiliarity" situation (which was expected to generate a minimal illusion of control) elected to keep their original tickets. Interestingly, none of those in either of the "unfamiliar" categories who kept their original tickets gave a reason for doing so. However, a number of those in the "familiarity" categories gave what they considered to be sound reasons for keeping them: five said that the letter on the ticket was the initial of their own last name, one said it was the initial of his wife's first name, one wanted the first letter of the alphabet, and one wanted the last. While none of these factors would have any bearing on the outcome of the drawing, the fact that such irrational thoughts were even expressed demonstrates the extent to which certain conditions can induce a false perception of control.

Langer's fourth experiment employed an "illusion of control apparatus" to verify that familiarity with a particular response as well as active personal involvement induce a stronger illusion of control. The laboratory test subjects were instructed to predict one of three possible outcomes that were randomly produced by the apparatus. These subjects were also tested under one of four experimental conditions: "high familiarity/high involvement," "high familiarity/low involvement," "low familiarity/high involvement," and low familiarity/low involvement." Those in the "high familiarity" condition were allowed to "practice" on the apparatus before they were tested while those in the "low familiarity were denied this opportunity; "high involvement" meant that the subjects themselves operated the apparatus while "low involvement" meant that they could only watch passively as the investigator did so.[44] Following their exposure to the apparatus, all subjects were administered a questionnaire. Its key question, intended to induce a skill orientation, asked them to rate how they thought their performance would compare to that of a chess master after five trials apiece. Those in the "high familiarity/high involvement" situation had the highest average confidence scores, those in the "high familiarity/low involvement" and "low familiarity/high involvement" conditions had intermediate scores, and those in the "low familiarity/low involvement" conditions had the lowest confidence scores.[45] These findings were replicated in a later experiment which also found that gamblers express greater confidence, and hence, succumb to the illusion of control, by betting more when they played with familiar cards than they did when the cards were unfamiliar to them.[46]

Langer's fifth experiment found that even passive involvement in a chance situation will increase a gambler's illusion of control. Her subjects, all participants in a lottery at a local racetrack, were asked to rate their confidence in winning at three different points in time before the drawing. Langer felt that the longer people had to think about an event the more they would do so and the greater their confidence would become. She therefore predicted that their average confidence scores would increase over time. Moreover, since the experiment took place at a racetrack, and since men are more actively involved in horse racing than women, she also predicted that women would have higher average confidence scores than men since they would spend less time thinking about racing and more time thinking about the lottery. As predicted, the subjects' average confidence scores steadily increased over time and those of the women were consistently higher than those of the men.

The sixth and final experiment, which retested the findings of the previous experiment, produced additional evidence that greater passive involvement induces a greater illusion of control. Its subjects were divided into two groups: those in the "low involvement" situation were given all three numbers of a lottery ticket on the day of the purchase while those in the "high involvement" situation were given one number on each of three successive days before the drawing. Those in the "high involvement" situation were therefore forced to think about the lottery on three separate occasions while those in the "low involvement" situation were not. Like the third experiment, each subject was offered the opportunity to exchange his or her original ticket for one in a second lottery offering better chances of winning (1 in 21 vs. 1 in 25). Shortly before the drawing, all subjects were also asked to rate their confidence of winning on a scale of 1 to 10. As Langer predicted, those in the "low involvement" condition were far more likely to want to exchange their tickets in return for a better odds advantage than those in the "high involvement" situation. Likewise, the average confidence scores of those in the "high involvement" situation were significantly higher than those of the "low involvement" group (6.45 and 3.00, respectively). When the scores of only those who chose to keep their original tickets were analyzed separately, the difference between the two involvement groups was even more striking (8.36 and 3.67).

The results of these experiments led Langer to conclude that "the more similar a chance situation is to a skill situation, the more likely it is that people approach the chance situation with a skill orientation."[47] Thus, even in chance situations a gambler's subjective and irrational thought processes appear to be more influential than his or her rational assessment of objective reality. The illusion of control became so strong in some subjects that those who were given an irrelevant choice actually denied themselves the opportunity to make a relevant choice by refusing objectively better odds. Greater degrees of personal involvement and familiarity or "practice" had similar effects.

Langer explained her findings by reference to the psychological theories with which she was familiar. First, she offered an explanation related to play theory when she suggested that people gain enjoyment and satisfaction from the ability to control their environment, and that their satisfaction is greatest when they are made to believe that they can control the uncontrollable. Next she offered a tension-reduction explanation when she proposed that even a semblance of control might allow people to avoid the anxiety that usually comes with the realization that they have no control at all. In the third place, skill and chance come to be closely associated through Pavlovian learning: in the experience of most people, "there appears to be an element of chance in every skill situation and an element of skill in every chance situation."[48] This is particularly true of gamblers who know the best odds combinations for which casino games and which slot machines are set for maximum returns. Finally, she pointed out that they are also associated through Skinnerian learning: "the distinction between skill and chance situations is further complicated by the fact that positive outcomes are most often attributed to the action that preceded them."[49] In fact, she insisted, "This occurs regardless of the actual contingency because in reality most outcomes *are* caused by the immediately preceding act."[50]

Langer then discussed the implications that her findings might have for commercial gambling by pointing out the obvious effect of incorporating skill-related factors into situations of chance. However, she maintained, if these changes were made in such legalized forms of gambling as state lotteries they would have the positive effect of reducing the incidence of such illegal forms as numbers games. She therefore suggested that state lotteries would be more attractive to potential players if they were allowed to choose their own numbers thereby providing them "the opportunity to exert illusory control"[51] just as numbers games do. To increase player participation state lotteries should also offer different types of tickets so that people would be allowed to choose those representing things with which they are most familiar. Reiterating her findings, she concluded with the observation that

> we can say with a fair degree of certainty that when an individual is actually in the situation, the more similar the chance situation is to a skill situation in outcome-independent ways, the greater will be the illusion of control. This illusion may be induced by introducing competition, choice, stimulus or response familiarity, or passive or active involvement in a chance situation. When these factors are present, people are more confident and are more likely to take risks.[52]

Internal Attribution, Winning, and Familiarity

In their attempts to replicate Langer's findings, some later investigators were at first unable to find any evidence of the illusion of control phenomenon.[53] Initially, these nonsupportive findings led experimental psychologist Robert Ladouceur and his research associates to conclude that "These results cast doubt on the value of the illusion of control for explaining the acquisition and maintenance of gambling behavior."[54] They suggested instead that personal control should perhaps be viewed as "a crediting of oneself for successes obtained in a situation of chance without necessarily overestimating one's chances of success."[55] Upon reflection, however, Ladouceur and his colleagues realized that

> A puzzling fact emerged from these studies; although the subjects reported an objective perception of the gambling situation as measured by various pencil-and-paper instruments, an informal discussion with the subjects after the game was over indicated the presence of many irrational and subjective beliefs, which could well be interpreted as the illusion of control.[56]

Primary and Secondary Illusory Control

On the basis of a "two-process model" of personal control that had recently appeared,[57] Ladouceur and his associates[58] then suggested that this "puzzling fact" might be due to the existence of two distinct types of illusory control, one of which Langer's earlier studies failed to investigate. According to this model, *primary illusory control* refers to the belief that through their personal actions, gamblers can directly influence the outcomes of events; *secondary illusory control* refers to the belief that they have the ability to predict these outcomes. Langer's research, they felt, pertained only to the former. Thus, while people may not always succumb to primary illusions of control, they may succumb to secondary illusions of control. Ladouceur and his colleagues therefore suggested that the need for control may be so strong in some people that they are able to enjoy an illusion of control in the belief that, through their own personal attributes or other factors unrelated to chance, they are able to forecast certain events. In essence, they come to believe that they can control their own luck. The researchers also suggested that the frequency of winning might also influence a gambler's illusions of control.

To test their hypotheses the researchers recruited subjects to participate in a series of fifty computerized roulette trials, a game with which they had no prior experience. Before the experiment they were divided into two groups on the basis of whether they believed their outcomes would be determined more by strategy or chance. Each of these groups was then subdivided into two additional groups whose outcomes would be manipulated so that half would win frequently (50 percent of the time) and half infrequently (20 percent of the time). Results verified that those who initially believed that their outcomes could be influenced by their own betting choices–those who had an internal locus of control orientation–demonstrated primary illusory control when a post-test interview revealed that they attributed far more of their outcomes to strategy than to chance. Similarly, those who initially believed their outcomes to be determined by chance–externals–demonstrated a secondary illusory control. This experiment also verified that a greater frequency of wins induced greater perceptions of both forms of control than infrequent wins.

These results not only confirmed Langer's original findings but they also suggested 1) that two forms of illusory control may influence gambling behavior, 2) that these illusions of control are stronger in those with an internal locus of control orientation, and 3) that winning reinforces these illusions. They also generated considerable additional research. A later study in which Ladouceur and his team used a real roulette wheel whose numbers and ball slots could be hidden from view found that subjects risked more money when their bets were placed before the throw than afterward even though the outcome was unknown to them.[59] This finding was attributed to the influence of secondary illusory control since, by placing their bets before the throw, the subjects demonstrated the belief that they could personally control the outcome by predicting the winning number. This study also provided further evidence that active participation enhances illusory control since subjects who threw the ball themselves took greater risks by betting significantly more money than those who only watched. It also confirmed that winning reinforces persistence since the subjects were more strongly motivated to continue after a win than a loss.

A number of other studies also confirmed that the illusion of control is, in fact, stronger in internally oriented subjects who have a greater need for control than in subjects having an external locus of control orientation whose needs for control are correspondingly lower.[60] For example, a recent study of British adolescents found that pathological fruit machine gamblers were more likely to have a strong internal locus of control orientation, to express a skill orientation, and to overestimate their chances of success on unfamiliar machines than nonpathological players. The nonpathological gamblers tended to be less internally oriented, to attribute success to luck rather than skill, and to express more realistic expectations of winning.[61] As will be shown below, later research also verified that the frequency of winning, particularly when it occurs early in a series of trials, also influences the gambler's illusion of control and subsequent gambling behavior. Researchers who were able to replicate Langer's original findings were unable to explain their additional finding that the illusion of control was stronger in subjects who were mildly depressed than in those who were not depressed.[62]

Familiarity and the "Risky Shift"

Ladouceur and his colleagues also verified that greater familiarity with a gambling game fostered greater monetary risk since the bet sizes of all subjects increased as the experiment progressed.[63] When this "risky shift" phenomenon was first reported among blackjack players it was found to be more pronounced among groups of players than in individuals who played alone. The phenomenon was observed in both field and laboratory settings where, under some circumstances, bet sizes were also reported to decrease over time. The authors of these studies therefore attributed these shifts in betting patterns to social influences or the desire of individual players to avoid appearing overly cautious or overly confident by conforming to the changing betting norms of the group.[64] Later studies by Ladouceur and his associates as well as others[65] offered further verification of the "familiarity" or "tolerance" hypothesis that increased experience with gambling results in heavier betting but reported no reductions in bet sizes under any circumstances.

Ladouceur and his research team repeatedly replicated these findings when they observed that although experienced gamblers tended to bet more than occasional or nongamblers at the beginning of a roulette session, the bet sizes of both groups steadily increased over time. In fact, the stakes of the less experienced gamblers escalated so dramatically that after only 30 spins they matched those of their more experienced cohorts. Moreover, the stakes of both experienced and inexperienced gamblers increased irrespective of their win-loss ratio, irrespective of whether they perceived the game to be one of skill or chance, and irrespective of whether they were playing in groups or in isolation. The researchers also found that monetary risk increased not only within a single gambling session, but also between sessions.[66] These findings suggest that the "risky shift" is neither a product of winning, nor of a particular locus of control orientation, nor of purely social influences: it appears instead to be more a product of the familiarity that comes with exposure. The researchers believed that "exposure to gambling is a crucial variable in the acquisition and maintenance of this habit and triggers risk-taking behavior in order to stay 'in the action.'"[67]

BEGINNER'S LUCK: THE "EARLY WIN" HYPOTHESIS

Attribution theorists believe that people's early learning experiences are responsible for their later personality development and related behavior. Many feel that a particular locus of control orientation is largely a matter of operant or Skinnerian learning that is directly contingent upon the presence or absence of reinforcement. They therefore contend that the tendency of gamblers who win to adopt an internal control orientation and those who lose to fault some outside influence is especially likely to develop early in their gambling careers:

> in chance situations where people are, by chance, successful at early trials, it is likely that an attribution to personal causation will be made. On the other hand, in chance sit-

> uations where the outcome is a loss early on, people will attribute the outcome to bad luck or some other external attribution.[68]

However, since attribution theory incorporates strong cognitive elements, its advocates maintain that a gambler's *expectations* of success, which result from an early history of positive reinforcement, can serve as a discriminative stimulus to encourage future gambling sessions. Early winners also would be likely to attribute any losses they may later experience to external causes but, since an internal locus of control orientation has already been established, they also would be likely to believe that their bad fortune could be overcome by persistence and determination. Thus, even when losing, the gambler's established attributional style or locus of control orientation is held responsible for persistence during a current gambling session as well as for the initiation of new gambling sessions.

A number of studies have investigated the influence of previous outcomes on subsequent betting behavior by examining the consequences of losing as well as winning. Although these studies were generally consistent in their findings that those who experienced a series of prior wins tended to increase their stakes, their conclusions on the effects of losing were mixed. Some studies found that gamblers would either decrease or maintain their level of involvement after a series of losses[69] while others found that losers increased their stakes more than winners.[70] One of these found that only those who had experienced equal numbers of wins and losses decreased their stakes.[71] Another found that betting choices were related to age: subjects in both the youngest (age 10) and oldest (undergraduate) categories tended to decrease their bets after losing and increase them after winning while adolescents (age 14) tended to follow the opposite course of action.[72]

Despite the diversity of these findings, they clearly suggest that previous experiences–at least those in the recent past–do influence future betting. However, the interpretation of these results is problematic: are increased stakes indicative of the growing confidence levels that accompany a developing skill orientation, of desperation and chasing, of growing excitement, of familiarity and boredom, or of all of these possibilities under different sets of circumstances? One critic interpreted the different betting patterns of different age groups to mean that some choices are made to maximize playing time while others are made to maximize monetary gain. He therefore suggested "that no simple relationship exists between prior outcomes and subsequent behavior in gambling, but that previous outcomes are evaluated by participants according to their expectations and aims."[73]

Inducing a Skill Orientation in Chance Events

To clarify the findings of their predecessors, these ideas were further explored by Ellen Langer and her colleague Jane Roth.[74] However, instead of focusing on the behavioral effects (subsequent bet sizes) of winning and losing, Langer and Roth focused on the cognitive psychological effects of reinforcement history or past "luck." Specifically, they wanted to determine whether a pattern of early successes would, in fact, induce an internal control or "skill" orientation in their subjects. Langer and Roth felt that

> Since people are motivated to see themselves as causal agents responsible for their successes . . . , they are likely to seize cues in the environment to support this attribution.

> . . . When one expects or wants to see oneself as a causal agent and begins to succeed on a task, one will make internal attributions.[75]

They predicted that an internal attribution should occur even in situations that are determined purely by chance and that "the sequence of outcomes may serve as a cue signaling whether or not a task is controllable and whether or not one has that control."[76]

To test these hypotheses Langer and Roth asked 90 male undergraduates attending Yale University to predict the results of 30 coin tosses, an event that they should perceive as entirely chance-determined. However, the outcomes were not random but were predetermined by the investigators who established three different conditions of 15 "wins" and 15 "losses" each. Those tested in "descending" (early win) condition experienced more initial wins than losses with ten wins appearing in the first fifteen trials and only five in the last fifteen. The situation was reversed for those in the "ascending" (early loss) condition who experienced only five wins in the first half of their series and ten in the last. Those in the "random" condition were accorded an even distribution of wins and losses throughout the series. To assess the influence of active participation two additional conditions were imposed: half the subjects in each condition were to be active participants or "actors" while the other half were to be passive participants or "observers." "Actors" guessed the outcomes of their series of tosses while "observers" merely watched the proceedings as another subject did the guessing. Thus six groups of fifteen subjects each were tested under one of six different conditions. In all cases the coin was tossed and its outcome "read" by a member of the research team who also gave the necessary reinforcement or feedback to the subject. To allay any suspicions that might develop, the subjects were shown the coin every time their response happened to coincide with the scheduled outcome.

The study found, in fact, that early successes would reinforce the development of an illusion of control to a much greater extent than would early failures. Following the coin tosses, all subjects were administered a questionnaire that confirmed the researchers' predictions that those in the "descending" (early win) and "actor" conditions would have the greatest "skill" or internal locus of control orientation while those in the "ascending" (early loss) group would be more externally or chance-oriented. In addition to asking whether the subjects believed their performance was determined by chance or skill, the questionnaire also asked how they thought they might fare in additional trials. A "skill" orientation was indicated if they believed that greater concentration, fewer distractions, or additional practice would improve their performance. According to the researchers,

> Apparently a skill attribution is determined early in a sequence of outcomes. After the attribution is made, outcomes inconsistent with it are not given much weight. An early, fairly consistent pattern of successes leads to a skill attribution, which in turn leads subjects to expect future success.[77]

Langer and Roth were also struck by their finding that, irrespective of the conditions under which they were tested, so many supposedly intelligent and rational subjects as Yale students would perceive such an obviously chance-determined event as skill-determined: more than one-quarter of all subjects felt that their performance would decline with more distractions and nearly half (40%) felt that they would improve with practice. "It appears." they concluded, "that the motivation to see events as controllable is so strong that the introduction of just one cue, a fairly consistent sequence of wins, . . . is enough to induce an illusion of control over the task of coin flipping even in sophisticated subjects."[78]

These findings were later replicated in a similar study in which 66 school children (aged 9 to 11) were also instructed to guess the outcomes of a series of 30 coin tosses.[79] As in the previous experiment the same three "ascending," "descending," and "random" conditions were imposed on three subgroups although the "actor" and "observer" conditions were omitted. Afterward, the children were also administered a questionnaire in which they were asked to evaluate their present performance and to estimate how they might perform in another series of trials. Most of those in the descending (early win) condition thought they did well, while most in the other two conditions thought they did poorly. Likewise, more of those in the descending group thought that with practice they would do better in future trials than those in the other groups. Like Langer and Roth, these researchers interpreted their findings as confirmation of the "early win" hypotheses and suggested that a pattern of early wins would be likely to influence one's future expectations of success. They also ascribed the phenomena they observed to the "skill attribution" or "illusion of control" that an early winning phase instills in people and concluded that "the results of this study provide some interesting support and encouragement for a general attribution theory to explain persistence in gambling behavior in the face of losses."[80] Another study found this phenomenon to be more pronounced among subjects with a high internal locus of control orientation than among those who were externally oriented.[81] However, a third study was unable to verify that betting behavior was influenced by either an early win or an early loss situation.[82]

BIASED EVALUATIONS OF OUTCOMES

Wishful Thinking

Wishful thinking is a foresight bias that causes the betting choices of gamblers to be influenced by their hopes for particular outcomes. This phenomenon, which is believed to be especially prevalent among sports bettors, was the subject of a study by Elisha Babad and Yosi Katz.[83] For this study, which took place in the actual soccer stadia and betting shops or "betting stations" as they are known in Israel, the researchers surveyed 630 nonbetting stadium fans and 350 betting station bettors. They felt that these two different contexts would yield two types of subjects with two distinct motivations: "Stadium spectators pay to enjoy the atmosphere, to watch their team beat the other team, to be subjective and emotionally expressive. Bettors pay in order to win."[84] Unlike the sports stadium where sports fans behave in their typically enthusiastic fashion, the betting station was described as a sober, businesslike place where people behave rationally and displays of emotionalism are discouraged. The intensity of wishful thinking, which they defined as "the link between preferences and expectations,"[85] was measured by comparing the subjects' self-reported degrees of "fanhood" or favoritism, either "diehard," "enthusiastic," or "moderate," with their predictions of the outcomes of various games. Half the subjects were pointedly instructed to try to be as objective as possible.

The researchers expected that wishful thinking would vary according to the intensity of "fanhood" in both groups and that it would be less pervasive among the bettors. Since monetary risk is presumed to be a rational economic activity, they reasoned that those who risked their money by betting on the matches would be more objective, less biased, and therefore more accurate in their forecasts than fans who risked no money.

Contrary to their predictions, Babad and Katz found that all degrees of "fanhood" strongly colored their subjects' predictions and that high degrees of wishful thinking affected the predictions of bettors and non-bettors alike. High levels of wishful thinking bias occurred even among those who were specifically instructed to be objective. Babad and Katz explained these findings by reference to A. W. Kruglanski's "lay theory of epistemology."[86] According to this theory, when people are searching for knowledge they are engaged in a continuous process of analysis and deduction. This process stops when they think they have the knowledge they were seeking. When it stops too early, before all the information necessary to make an impartial judgment has been assimilated, their assessments are distorted and biased. This commonly occurs because "people want to feel that they 'know' even when they are not in full possession of the facts."[87] It is even more likely to occur if the limited knowledge they have assimilated accords with their wishes. Any such overconfidence in predicting outcomes is believed to play a major role in maintaining gambling behavior.[88] Even lottery players, who have an obviously poor understanding of chance and probability, entertain unrealistic levels of optimism regarding their chances of winning.[89]

Near Misses, Flukes, and Hindsight Bias: The Rationalization of Loss

When their predictions turn out to be wrong and gamblers can no longer entertain their delusions of control over chance-determined events, they can resort to other means of distorting the reality of the situation: they may reevaluate their losses to minimize their importance and recast them in a more favorable light. Thus, many gamblers have a tendency to formulate "biased evaluations of outcomes"[90] or "hindsight biases"[91] which allow them to rationalize their losses. Hindsight bias frequently occurs in situations in which losses can be explained away as "flukes" caused by random, uncontrollable external factors rather than failures of the gamblers' own expertise or instincts. Racetrack and sports bettors are especially prone to hindsight bias if their losses are "near misses" or "near wins": they *should* have won and *would* have won if only their horse hadn't stumbled; if only "their" team hadn't fumbled the ball or barely missed scoring during a critical play; if only the officials had called it correctly; if only the star player hadn't been benched because of an unexpected injury, etc. Such cases reinforce both winners' and losers' beliefs in the value of their own knowledge and abilities: losses are always attributed to circumstances outside the gamblers' sphere of influence while wins are seen as evidence of their keen prognostic abilities and handicapping skills.[92]

In his ethnographic account of horse racing, Marvin Scott maintained that racetrack bettors pass through two distinct developmental stages in becoming addicted to playing the horses. The first is mastering the *Racing Form* and learning the intricacies of handicapping. The second, the ability to "rationally cope" with unexpected results, clearly referred to the formulation of biased evaluations of outcomes. For Scott, "rationally coping" with the unexpected meant the player's ability to analyze and explain why his horse lost and why another horse won:

> Reasonable accounts as to why his horse–presumably a fit and ready animal–lost are

easy to come by: the distance of the race was a little too long or a little too short; the condition of the track was slightly off, or too hard; the cinch was too tight or too loose; the horse's shoe was thrown or too tight; his recent workout was too stiff, or not stiff enough; he didn't like the blinker change (on or off); he was pressed too soon on the lead, or wasn't pressed enough; he didn't like the way the jockey rode him; he sulked at the whip; he was carried wide, forced against the rail, bumped, or tripped on the heels of another horse; he was caught flat-footed at the break; his saddle slipped; he got scared by his shadow and tried to jump over it and lost stride; he was shaken by the noise of the crowd. And so on.

Accounting for the loser is easy; explaining why the horse that won–but wasn't bet–was playable is only slightly more involved. . . . the addict finds an interpretation in a contradictory pattern and in this way explains any occurrence. . . . Therefore, a horse won because it was recently raced . . . or not raced in some time . . . ; because it had fast workouts . . . or slow workouts . . . ; because the horse dropped weight . . . or picked up weight . . . . In short, an item–or its opposite–may serve as a warrant to account for the outcome of the race.[93]

By enabling gamblers to view their past losses and wins in the most favorable light, hindsight bias is believed to foster persistence even in the face of loss: it encourages adherence to faulty betting "systems" thereby continuing to reinforce the illusion of control. Biased outcome evaluations are not restricted to sports and racetrack handicappers; they also are known to occur among poker tournament players[94] and other kinds of gamblers.

The "near win" or "near miss" phenomenon applies even to such games of pure chance as slot machine and lottery playing. Skinner's ideas on the reinforcing properties of the near miss in slot machine gambling have already been mentioned. Thus, slot machines and instant lotteries are often "contrived to ensure a higher frequency of near misses than would be expected by chance alone."[95] This induces the players to think that "they are not constantly losing, but constantly nearly winning, i.e. experiencing a psychologically rewarding situation although there is no financial reward."[96] Lotto and numbers games players are also susceptible to the influence of near misses, especially when they have conferred with astrologers, studied books on numerology, or carefully selected their numbers to match the birthdates of family members. In these cases, "the occurrence of a near miss may be taken as an encouraging sign, confirming the player's strategy and raising hopes about future success."[97] The frequent attribution of gambling outcomes to "fixing"–the perception that lotteries, races, bingo games, spins of the roulette wheel, boxing matches, and other contests of skill and events of chance are decided beforehand and known only to a select few–is another popular way to explain away one's failures.

Flukes and Hindsight Bias in Games of Skill

Hindsight bias was first investigated in gambling situations by Thomas Gilovich[98] who initially conducted a three-part study to determine why American sports bettors persist in a behavior that is so infrequently rewarded and so often punished. Specifically he wanted to determine how gamblers' interpretations of their own past successes and failures might influence their subsequent betting behavior. Gilovich emphasized that his research was intended only to explore persistence among already established gamblers and not why people start gambling in the first place. His review of the attribution literature revealed that people in nongambling situations often evaluate the outcomes of important events in consistently biased ways and spend more time thinking about their failures than their successes. Since gamblers should be expected to do likewise, his first study was designed to test several hypotheses: he predicted that gamblers would spend more time and effort pondering their losses than their wins, that the greater attention they paid to losses would make the circumstances surrounding them more memorable, and that the explanations they offered for their losses would serve to rationalize them while those for winning should stress their inevitability.

In his first experiment Gilovich found that after football games which had been decided by such flukes as fumbled balls and bad calls by the officials, neither the winners nor the losers would have altered their bets. Even though the same "flukes" that caused some bettors to lose also caused others to win, all subjects believed they had made the only logical choice in the first place and all would bet on the same team to win in a rematch. He gained this knowledge by having his subjects tape record their thoughts and feelings about the outcomes of games on which they had bet. Analysis of these tapes revealed that while the losers seized upon these random "fluke" events to justify their losses, the winners discounted them as irrelevant since, for them, the outcomes turned out just as they had expected. Consequently, his subjects tended to make "undoing" comments about their losses (remarks that the outcomes should and would have been different were it not for the flukes) and "bolstering" comments about their wins (remarks supporting the outcome in spite of the flukes). However, as he also predicted, they spent much more time re-examining and "undoing" their losses than in "bolstering" their wins. They were also able to recall more about their losses than their wins when they were recontacted several weeks later. Gilovich therefore concluded that "people apparently accept success at face value but carefully scrutinize failure."[99]

His subsequent tests extended these findings by demonstrating the extent to which past flukes can influence the attributions and subsequent behaviors of sports bettors. The second experiment tested the hypothesis that manipulating (i.e., increasing) the salience of a fluke that may have decided the outcome of an earlier event would induce a more strongly biased evaluation of that event and have an even greater subsequent effect. This experiment took the guise of a formal interview during which Gilovich "offhandedly" reminded his subjects of a critical fluke play in a recent championship basketball game on which they had bet. He found that the salience he interjected by reminding them of this play "tended to restore the faith of the losing subjects in their team without decreasing the faith of winning subjects in theirs."[100] His final experiment, which investigated the influence of winning and losing under both fluke and no-fluke outcome conditions, replicated these findings. Gilovich found that the subsequent bet sizes of winners in either condition and losers in the fluke condition who could attribute the outcome to it were significantly larger than their first. He felt that the outcome served to encourage these subjects since they had lost none of their original confidence. However, the subsequent bets of losers in the no-fluke condition–those who were denied the opportunity to blame their losses on any extraneous factors–were significantly smaller than their first. He interpreted this to mean that these subjects lost confidence in their original choices because they had become discouraged by the outcome.

The results of his studies led Gilovich to conclude that sports bettors do not evaluate their past betting choices objectively and that their biases can have a profound influence on their future gambling behavior. Specifically, he felt that persistence in such a costly endeavor was due primarily to the inability of many gamblers to recognize that their betting strategies and rationalizations are indefensible:

> The tendency to accept wins at face value but to transform losses into "near wins" can produce overly optimistic assessments of one's gambling skill and the chances of future success. Spurred on by such inflated expectations, gamblers may continue to engage in unrewarding gambling activities. Thus the tendency to evaluate outcomes in a biased manner can be seen as an important determinant of why people continue to gamble despite persistent losses.[101]

In essence, like so many people in other circumstances, gamblers are unwilling to acknowledge their mistakes and admit that they can be wrong.

Flukes and Hindsight Bias in Games of Chance

Gilovich and a colleague later found that hindsight bias is not restricted to events involving skill since it also occurs in games of chance.[102] To determine whether the same biases that occur in sports betting could also be found in a purely chance-determined game as bingo they conducted a similar study among two groups of bingo players. By introducing an experimental fluke situation into a computerized form of bingo (certain numbers allowed a player to cover two squares instead of one), they were able to establish the same four sets of conditions (win/loss; fluke/no-fluke) that existed in the earlier study. Although their subjects were led to believe that success and failure were randomly determined, the outcomes of each game were actually predetermined. Thus, half the winners and half the losers were exposed to the fluke element while the other half were not. The researchers once again found that manipulation of the fluke situation had a dramatic effect on the subjects' subsequent betting behavior: as in the earlier study, subsequent bets of losers in the no-fluke condition were smaller while those tested under the other three conditions were larger. This finding was again taken as confirmation of the idea that those who cannot blame their losses on external conditions tend to become discouraged and lose their original confidence.

Having demonstrated that gamblers' evaluations of outcomes can be biased in situations involving either skill or chance, Gilovich and his associate then determined that the ultimate cause of this bias involved the illusion of control that many gambling games induce. On the basis of his findings, Gilovich felt that most gambling games possess one or more features that serve to create an illusion of control over the outcome. His own computerized bingo game produced this illusion by allowing the subjects to choose their own card numbers and select which of five keys would generate the random numbers needed to fill them. To test this hypothesis Gilovich added the conditions of "illusion of control" and "no control" to his final experiment. He did so by having the researchers make all such selections for half the subjects, thereby denying them any element of choice. Apart from these additional factors, which produced a total of six possible outcome conditions, this last bingo experiment proceeded exactly as before. The researchers found that the fluke served to increase the confidence of losers in the "no control" situation losers but decrease the confidence of winners to an even greater extent. Nevertheless, these differences were not statistically significant. As predicted, however, they found that in the "illusion of control" situation the fluke manipulation had little effect on the confidence of the winners but a highly significant effect on those who had lost since the subsequent bets of those in the no-fluke condition were much lower.

Earlier investigators had suggested that hindsight bias fosters persistence despite heavy losses because it enables gamblers to continue to justify the erroneous betting strategies or "systems" in which they have come to believe.[103] Like Langer and these researchers, Gilovich and his colleague also concluded on the basis of their own research that persistence in the face of loss can ultimately be traced to the erroneous perception that the outcomes of even chance-determined events somehow lie within the gambler's sphere of influence:

> gamblers' unwarranted optimism about their future success is fueled by a pervasive tendency to evaluate the outcomes of their bets in a biased manner. Successful outcomes are readily accepted at face value, whereas unsuccessful outcomes are carefully scrutinized, explained away, and discounted. As a result of this asymmetry in the evaluation of wins and losses, many gamblers emerge from an objectively bad night of gambling confident of their skill and convinced that their overall strategy just needs a little fine tuning.[104]

The persistence of many gamblers in the face of earlier failures may therefore be a consequence of their "attitudinal inertia," the belief that, for them, "success is just around the corner."[105]

Selective Memory Bias

In addition to flukes, near misses, and perceptions of fixing, is the phenomenon of selective memory bias. This form of outcome bias was reported by Michael Frank[106] who studied underage casino gamblers in New Jersey. Frank found that two-thirds (66 percent) of the subjects who gambled reported that they were either winning or breaking even at the Atlantic City casinos where they played. He insisted, however, that this would be impossible since the built-in house advantage of all casino games insures that far more players will lose than win. Although some of the respondents may have been deliberately lying to the interviewer, Frank offered an alternative explanation. Whereas Gilovich reported that gamblers tend to remember their losses to a greater extent than their wins, Frank thought it more likely that his subjects tended to remember their wins and forget their losses. A very similar kind of selective memory bias been observed among blackjack players in the casinos of Amsterdam who take special notice of outcomes which support their preexisting beliefs about the way the cards are supposed to run and ignore those that do not.[107] This means that a selective memory bias in either direction may help to reinforce persistence despite loss.

ENTRAPMENT

"Entrapment" occurs when gamblers have lost so much that they cannot afford to quit since they have passed the point at which they could safely cut their losses. In essence, gamblers become entrapped when they begin to believe that they are "in too far to quit now." However, it is believed that since the seeds for entrapment are often planted by an early winning phase, the gambler becomes

> hypnotized into thinking that his "system" (whatever it may be, and none of them work for long) actually is valid. All he needs now

> is faith in his "system," he believes, for with faith he can go on to greater triumphs that will impress the world. Gambling becomes a religion, but a blind one.[108]

Losses steadily mount with continued gambling until the gambler feels he has passed the point of no return and must therefore continue to play and even escalate his commitment if he is to recover. Such irrational thinking inevitably leads to increasingly heavier losses and "chasing." Chasing of this nature is especially common among those whose faith in a particular system, even though it has been a consistent failure, blinds them to the reality of their situation: they "know" only that they are "overdue" for a win.

Gamblers can become entrapped in many different kinds of games. One laboratory experiment showed that people can become entrapped and chase their losses even in games in which they can expect to lose.[109] For example, entrapped lottery players frequently select a particular number combination which they play continually, drawing after drawing, in the belief that this combination will eventually win and that every loss brings them one step closer to their goal.[110] However, each loss also strengthens their commitment to this strategy until they dare not stop for fear of losing when the cherished number combination, which they are convinced is sure to come up sometime, does appear. Eventually, some players become so entrapped that they cannot take a vacation unless they arrange to have their lottery tickets bought for them.[111] In terms of their expected return value, casino games with their built-in house advantage are essentially no different. In *The Gambler* Dostoevsky provided the example of a roulette player who became entrapped by the number zero and would bet on nothing else. Slot machine players frequently become entrapped by a machine that refuses to pay even though a jackpot is long "overdue." Similarly, some horse players, for example, bet on a particular horse, losing bet after bet, until it does win. Gamblers who "slavishly follow 'winning systems'"[112] personify entrapment. As one authority explained the situation, "The pathological gambler thus follows an impossible dream, a 'long term fantasy', which he rarely gives up no matter what happens to him."[113]

CHANCE, SKILL, AND IRRATIONAL THINKING

Games of chance are those over which the player has no control while games of skill are those whose outcomes can be influenced, at least in part, by one's choices and actions. Some studies reveal that regular gamblers are more likely to regard gambling as an activity that requires as much skill as luck whether such perceptions are rational or not. A large survey of American gamblers[114] found, for example, that a surprising number of players believe that even such games of pure chance as bingo, slot machines, lotteries, and numbers require at least some skill, and some players are convinced that these games require even *more* skill than luck.

To determine the degree to which irrational thinking and beliefs in one's own skill may influence gambling behavior and persistence, behavioral psychologists Robert Ladouceur, Anne Gaboury, and their associates employed the "thinking aloud" method in a series of studies involving such games of chance as blackjack, roulette, video poker, and slot machines.[115] The subjects of these studies were provided with tape recorders and instructed to verbalize continuously every thought and impression they had while gambling without worrying about censoring their words, justifying them, or completing their sentences. This method had the advantage of doing away with questionnaires and the necessity of interrupting the natural behavior of the gambler. In some of these studies, however, questionnaires designed to elicit information on the subjects' motivations and illusory control were periodically administered during the gambling session. After the session the subjects' verbalizations were transcribed and classified as either rational or irrational.

These studies revealed that from about 70 to more than 85 percent of the players' recorded vocalizations were irrational. Those related to chance were considered to be rational; those referring to causal influences other than chance, including remarks of a superstitious nature, near-misses, groundless attribution, and personal control, were classed as irrational. The researchers found that the subjects employed various strategies to enhance their success, expressed a firm belief in the "gambler's fallacy," and attributed personalized volition to a machine by thinking that it was deliberately thwarting their efforts. Although they attributed their losses to such external factors as bad luck, they attributed their wins to their own actions or skill, even when the exercise of any personal influence was impossible. These studies also have implications for arousal theory since they found that arousal, as measured by increases in heart rate, corresponds to the frequency of irrational thoughts.[116]

While these "thinking aloud" studies were innovative and yielded some very worthwhile results, the authors themselves cautiously admitted, "it is not clear whether the irrational thinking is directly linked with risk-taking behavior."[117] However, they do feel that it is related to the need for and illusion of control since the tendency to voice irrational thoughts is greater among those with stronger perceptions of control.[118] Nevertheless, as discussed previously, the greatest criticism of these studies is that they were conducted in an unrealistic artificial laboratory setting most often with university students and staff who were nonpathological and even nonregular gamblers. In response to this criticism, Ladouceur and his associates conducted a comparative study of video poker players in both laboratory and natural settings. Finding no differences between the responses of gamblers who were tested in either environment, they concluded that "playing videopoker in the laboratory produces cognitive, behavioral, and motivational phenomena which are equivalent to those observed in a natural setting."[119] They therefore contended that, under some circumstances, the results of laboratory studies are just as valid as those of field studies.

LUCK AND SUPERSTITION

The Manipulation of Luck

Other studies of gamblers' cognitive processes have demonstrated that many regard chance, luck, and skill as entirely distinct phenomena.[120] Although chance refers to the occurrence of random events that are described by the laws of probability, luck is thought to be a personal attribute that is predetermined or "caused" and can therefore change or, like Lady Luck or mana, is a personalized animistic force that can "cause" certain outcomes. Thus, a survey of blackjack players in an Amsterdam casino revealed that

> All these players regard luck as a concept that refers to a person, whereas chance refers to the event or the outcome. Some people may be luckier than others, whereas chance is the same for everyone. Neither luck nor chance can be directly affected by people, but one can take certain actions in

> order to take advantage of good luck and avoid bad luck. Chance cannot be exploited in such a manner.[121]

The subjects of this study therefore attributed their successes and failures to the combined influences of luck, skill, and chance in that order.

Many gamblers see luck as occurring in a "wave form" that cannot be predicted but that can be detected: "The art of the game is to catch the crest of the wave, that is the lucky periods. . . . Early detection, that is, the realization that you are in a lucky period, is considered to be part of the skill of the game."[122] Similarly, some roulette players believe in a phenomenon known as the "periodicity of luck" or certain time periods during which red or black numbers will be more likely to win.[123] Comparable beliefs have been reported among slot machine players who believe they can predict when a machine will pay.[124] Belief in the transitory nature of luck is reflected in the gamblers' adage advising that "You ought to make at least one bet every day, otherwise you might be walking around lucky and not even know it."

The fact that gamblers tend to exaggerate their illusion of control or skill over purely random or chance-determined outcomes is often revealed in their betting strategies. For example, dice players often regard craps as a game of skill, much as they do competitive athletic events. A participant observer in numerous noncommercial craps games reported that players tend to bet more money when they throw the dice and less when someone else throws them since they are less confident that the winning number will come out. They also tend to make the same bets as those who give the appearance of having the greatest control and to avoid betting against them. Because they believe that effort can influence the outcome they take their time and concentrate very hard before shooting. They also believe that changing one or both dice can profoundly change their luck.[125]

Slot machine and blackjack players have their own strategies for manipulating luck. Slot machine players often attempt to change their luck by changing machines,[126] blackjack players try to do so by changing playing positions or moving to an entirely new table. Because some blackjack players also believe that the course of their luck is decided once the cards are shuffled, they may also try to change it by making plays they would normally avoid, such as splitting or taking a hit when these options are inadvisable. They do this in the belief that such "sacrifices" will interrupt and alter the predetermined sequence of bad cards they were originally "fated" to be dealt. Conversely, they also believe that inexperienced players can take "too many cards" thereby breaking the predetermined lucky streak of others at the table.[127]

Roulette and dice players often believe that the timing of their bets can somehow improve their chances of winning. Specifically, bets placed before the throw are larger, hence riskier, while those placed after the throw but before the outcome is known are more conservative. Thus, the illusion of control appears to be stronger before the throw than afterward.[128] In reality, of course, the objective mathematical probabilities of winning and losing remain the same no matter when the money is laid down. Interestingly, the smaller the size of their stake, the more likely British sports pool bettors are to impute their wins to luck; the larger the stakes, the more likely they are to attribute their successes to skill.[129] Some researchers hold the view that gambling becomes pathological when the illusion of control itself becomes the sought-after reward of gambling: "*Pathological gambling is basically an addiction to a false state of mind."*[130]

Magical Thinking and Ritual Performance

Many gamblers believe that various superstitious behaviors and ritual performances can also influence their present luck and enhance their ability to win. Although superstitious beliefs are often a product of social learning, many novel ritualistic behaviors arise when they are accidentally paired with a strong reinforcer. Among the earliest and most well-known research in this area is that of behaviorist B. F. Skinner.[131] During his classic studies of stimulus-response conditioning in pigeons, Skinner found that the presentation of a hopper of food would reinforce whatever behavior a pigeon coincidentally happened to be engaged in at the time. Thereafter, it would behave as though there was some causal connection between this behavior and the appearance of the food:

> The conditioning process is usually obvious. The bird happens to be executing some response as the hopper appears; as a result it tends to repeat this response. If the interval before the next presentation is not so great that extinction takes place, a second "contingency" is probable. This strengthens the response still further and subsequent reinforcement becomes more probable. It is true that some responses go unreinforced and some reinforcements appear when the response has not just been made, but the net result is the development of a considerable state of strength.[132]

When reinforcement was continuously random, the pigeons actually conditioned themselves to perform a variety of strange behaviors in their efforts to make the food hopper reappear. Different birds would hop from one foot to the other, bow and scrape, strut, walk three times around the cage in a counterclockwise direction, thrust their heads into the corners of the cage, lift their heads as though they were raising an invisible bar, sway their heads and bodies to and fro, or make incomplete pecking motions at the cage door. Although each particular behavioral response was determined by pure happenstance, once established it persisted even when it was reinforced only occasionally. In some instances the conditioning was so strong that unrewarded behavior was repeated more than 10,000 times before it was extinguished. Skinner described learning of this kind as superstitious, a phenomenon to which human beings are equally susceptible.

It no secret that gamblers are among the most superstitious people in the modern world. This is not surprising when one considers that because winning occurs so randomly in so many forms of gambling, good fortune can become associated with any number of entirely unrelated events. Although one of the most amusing general descriptions of typical gambling magic appeared nearly fifty years ago, it could apply to committed gamblers of any generation:

> In the highly scientific and realistic twentieth century United States, the gambler is among the last practitioners of superstition. He throws spilt salt over his left shoulder, knocks on wood, avoids black cats and goes out of his way to give a beggar money on route to the races or his dice games. He has an old hat, a necktie or a tiepin that brings him good luck, and if bad luck sets in he chases it by walking three times around a chair. He begs, cajoles and pleads with the dice, talking to them more tenderly than he talks to his wife. He can feel in his bones when a slot machine is about to drop a jackpot or when the red is going to come up at roulette, and when the feeling turns out to be wrong he looks at the machine with the

> aggrieved expression of a man deceived by his best friend. He dreams the winning numbers of horses and sees visions of a lottery killing in the license of a taxicab that brushes him at a street corner. No matter how many times he has failed, today is always the day.[133]

One of the earliest and most fascinating scholarly accounts of gambling magic was that of James Henslin[134] who, as a participant observer, studied craps playing among a group of taxi drivers in St. Louis. Although the outcomes of their games were purely random the players were nevertheless firmly convinced that their personal actions had the ability to influence them. The craps shooters employed compulsive magic by "talking to the dice," telling them which numbers to show, and loudly snapping their fingers after throwing them to achieve the desired point. They were careful to throw the dice softly when they wanted low numbers, hard when they wanted high numbers, and to make exaggerated expressions of their own confidence. Confidence was expressed, for example, by announcing the outcome before throwing or by making unusually large or even-money bets on points that are hard to make (4 and 10 are difficult points that usually warrant odd-money bets). Contagious magic, a player's personal spiritual "power" or mana, and his current needs were also believed to influence the dice.

On one occasion the good fortune of a particularly lucky player who was described as a "store-front preacher" was ascribed to his close association with the Bible. Since this artifact was held to be a repository of the mana that was transferred to him, several other players announced that they, too, were going to start reading the Bible to improve their luck. On another occasion his luck was ascribed to the fact that he said he needed the large amount of money he had won to pay his rent which was due the next day: "Oh," said another player, "that's why you won."[135]

Because different players are believed to have different degrees of mana or "power" over the dice, the bets of the others are often influenced by which player happens to be shooting at the time. Smaller amounts are bet against those who are believed to have more mana and larger amounts against those having less. When shooters feel they are losing control over the dice they will sometimes increase the size of their bets after each throw in the belief that this will restore their control and enable them to make their point. Some players believe that "odd money" bets of one dollar plus one cent, for example, will cause a favorable outcome.

Accidentally dropping one or both of the dice is a bad omen that signifies "dropping your luck" and will cause an unfavorable outcome unless the luck is restored by rubbing the dice on the playing surface or on the skin or clothing of a player who is betting against you. It is also a bad omen when a shooter has difficulty making his point as this signifies that the dice are behaving contrary to his wishes. Since they will not give up the point without "something extra," the shooter may try to regain control by bribing them into compliance with the "promise" of a larger bet next time.

Just as a shooter can employ magic to aid his success, his opponents can also use countermagic against him. "Catching the dice" by stopping them while they are still rolling is believed to "break the shooter's control" and cause him to lose on his next throw. This strategy, which is permitted, is believed to be particularly effective when a shooter is on a roll since interrupting the dice also interrupts his momentum which causes him to "get shook" and lose control. Sometimes an opponent will catch the dice and rub them on his own body to "cool them off" before returning them in order to end a successful shooter's "hot streak."

Henslin ascribed the tenacity of his subjects' superstitious thoughts and behaviors in part to the random reinforcement phenomenon described by Skinner and in part to the antithetical anthropological explanations of Bronislaw Malinowski[136] and Alfred Kroeber.[137] As a functionalist, Malinowski felt that magic "functions" to reduce the anxiety and tension that people experience under conditions of uncertainty. As a cultural determinist, Kroeber contended that the origins of any people's magical and religious beliefs can never be known, but once introduced they often become ritualized and therefore continue to be culturally transmitted and inculcated during the socialization process. Henslin argued that unlike Skinner's experimental animals whose superstitious behaviors were learned in isolation, human beings are social animals most of whose behaviors are learned in a social context. Many human behaviors–including their superstitious and ritualistic performances–are therefore imparted by others and shaped or reinforced by their reactions to them.

However, Henslin also argued that because the reduction of tension is rewarding, the principles of Skinner's reinforcement theory accord with those of Malinowski's tension-reduction theory. Moreover, cultural learning also can be reinforced when it is found to be rewarding. Henslin therefore concluded that some superstitious beliefs and behaviors are learned by example and some by happenstance. In either case, such learning will persist if it is occasionally reinforced:

> *Magical behavior arises adventitiously; being reinforced it is informally taught in a social situation and accepted by the members; and being occasionally reinforced on a variable ratio reinforcement schedule, it maintains itself.*[138]

Therefore, like any other superstition, Henslin felt that the magical beliefs and behaviors of the gamblers he observed resulted from three processes: 1) individual learning arising from the temporal association of two otherwise unrelated phenomena, 2) social learning arising from the examples set by others, and 3) the reinforcement of these behaviors through the rewards of social approval and acceptance as well as through their ability to reduce the tensions and anxieties generated by the uncertainty of gambling.

The many published accounts of similar kinds of irrational human behaviors and beliefs can be easily verified by casual observation during a stroll through any commercial gaming establishment. For example, it is not uncommon to see bingo players surround their cards with toy elephants, all with their trunks turned upward, to magically "catch the luck" for them, thereby enhancing their chances of winning. Some bingo players believe they can enhance their chances of winning by sitting near previous winners so that some of their luck will "rub off" onto them. Others "chase luck" by continually changing tables in the hope of finding a "lucky seat." Many wear "lucky" shirts and use special "lucky" daubers until the luck in these objects runs out.[139] Some slot machine gamblers refuse to play a roll of coins unless a particular "heads" and "tails" combination is showing at the ends of the unopened roll. Coin rolls without this proper combination are thought to be "unlucky" and will certainly be lost if played. Some serious players feel it necessary to keep the number of credits in a machine above a particular "essential" level or to hold a certain number of coins in their hand as they play. Many players have a "lucky" machine that they prefer over all others and guard jealously.[140] Avid pull tab players resort to various kinds of "pull tab magic" such as kissing their tickets, rubbing them on certain parts of the body (hair, buttocks, breasts, etc.), or arranging and opening them in "special" ways which they believe will magically produce winners.[141] Vendors of lottery tickets have reported the "lucky machine" and "lucky kiosk" phenomena in which lottery sales at a particular location become much higher than usual for several weeks after a big winner has been purchased from it: avid lottery players come to believe that the ticket machine or sales outlet itself is lucky.[142]

Associations of this kind are also highly likely to occur when a gambler is following certain "rules" for winning. It has been said that "VR [variable-ratio] schedules may reinforce certain strategies all out of proportion to their practical value . . . by the fortuitous juxtaposition of response and reinforcement on a number of occasions."[143] In this way gamblers become even more convinced of the efficacy of such "winning systems" as the gambler's fallacy, playing the longshot in the third race of the day, and the commonly voiced exhortation to "bet big when you're losing."

As the psychoanalysts suggested in their discussions of narcissism and wish-fulfillment fantasies, perhaps the most extreme irrational beliefs and illusions of control are held by gamblers who believe that certain events and outcomes can be controlled solely by their thoughts. Some individuals firmly believe in the existence of "psychic" powers which are available to anyone who can exercise the proper mental discipline. Thus, they believe that the outcome of a coin toss, the roll of the dice, the cut of the cards, the position of the roulette ball, the next bingo number, and the winning lottery numbers are not merely random or chance events, but can be, and often are, influenced by unseen mental forces. Although parapsychologists have been unsuccessful in their attempts to demonstrate the existence of psychokinesis and other psychic phenomena for decades, the conviction that these etherial, otherworldly powers are real and can be mastered is still widespread.[144]

Belief in omens, magical signs, dreams, and other portents that some benevolent, omniscient supernatural power is attempting to communicate the outcome of future events to the gambler is not far removed from wishful thinking. The choices of many racetrack bettors are influenced by the "omens" they encounter in license plates, newspapers, and radio announcements they see or hear on their way to the track; many lotto players select their "lucky numbers" on the basis of astrology, "dream books," telephone numbers, zip codes, computer programs, the birthdates of their loved ones, anniversaries, and other important events in their lives as though this will influence the outcome of the drawing.[145] No less than one-third of a group of lottery winners attributed their good fortune to a "system" involving psychic communiqués and supernatural influences.[146] According to one psychologist, "This belief in the power of thought . . . is what keeps the gambler working at games or investing in lotteries when it is well known that they are constituted so as to give bad returns. Gamblers may be well aware that the large body of gamblers as a whole must lose, but they think that their own special powers may make them, as individuals, win."[147]

Indeed, such ideas are sometimes nurtured by scientific research. For example, one research team, after conducting four years of meticulous on-site study, reported their discovery that the payout percentages in one Las Vegas casino were positively correlated with the lunar cycle and gravitational tidal forces but negatively correlated with the earth's geomagnetic field flux.[148] The clear implication was, of course, that gamblers should time their casino visits accordingly. Irrespective of the pragmatic value of such beliefs and behaviors, they all serve to reinforce and amplify the illusion of control that many gamblers entertain. These kinds of irrational, magical thinking are also believed to be responsible for persistence among troubled gamblers.[149]

Ironically, the players in the gambling arena are not the only ones who resort to magic and superstition: casino owners and managers who take steps to change their own luck are just as susceptible to irrational thinking and the illusion of control as are their customers. Sociologists conducting participant observational research as casino employees have noted that dealers and croupiers who experience their own runs of bad luck and lose too much money to their players are likely to be replaced and may lose their jobs entirely.[150] During an interview for a popular weekly news magazine, the owner of a large Las Vegas casino admitted, "For twenty days in a row my crap pit lost money. After five days I changed the dice manufacturer. After 18 days I bought new tables and burned the old ones. Put new tables in, new dice, new stick, new dealer. All the praying in the world isn't going to change your luck."[151]

7

COGNITIVE-BEHAVIORAL THEORISTS

Cognitive-behavioral (or behavioral-cognitive) theorists believe that purely behavioral explanations of persistent and pathological gambling are inadequate. Such approaches focus only on monetary or emotional rewards while ignoring equally important cognitive and contextual influences that reinforce gambling. They also ignore the punishment of continued loss which, according to the precepts of learning theory, should serve to reinforce quitting.

To overcome these shortcomings, cognitive-behavioral approaches often combine Skinnerian and Pavlovian learning processes with cognitive factors–the gambler's beliefs, thoughts, and assumptions concerning gambling. In general, operant and classical conditioning mechanisms are believed to operate together to maintain gambling persistence. According to this view the two main Skinnerian reinforcers of gambling are the possibility of winning money and the excitement that gambling also provides. As Mark Dickerson[1] suggested, since cash is delivered intermittently (on a variable-ratio schedule with each win) while hedonic arousal or "action" is delivered continuously (on a fixed-interval schedule with each play), gambling persistence may be reinforced by both kinds of reward delivery schedules. If the persistence induced by these Skinnerian reinforcers is long enough, arousal can become identified with winning through classical conditioning. The Pavlovian association of arousal with winning then serves to increase its reinforcement value. Other associated stimulus cues such as certain locations, the sound of coins, chips, cards, wheels, track announcements, croupiers' calls, etc., would, of course, vary with different forms of gambling. The gambler's mood state, the sound of coins hitting a metal tray, or any other conditioned stimulus may then serve to trigger a new gambling episode. Cognitive-behavioral theorists believe that cognitive factors play an important role so that a combination of these Skinnerian and Pavlovian reinforcers with the gambler's irrational beliefs and expectancies contributes to the rapid acquisition and slow extinction of the gambling response.[2] However, most cognitive-behavioral theorists have tended to emphasize the cognitive dimensions of problem gambling.

David Oldman: Chance and Roulette

One of the earliest field studies of the influence of gamblers' cognitions over their betting behavior in a game of chance was undertaken by sociologist David Oldman[3] worked in a casino for several years as a roulette croupier. The experience convinced him that gambling persistence is often maintained by the players' faith in their ability to predict the outcome of plays which, in reality, are impossible to predict. Oldman stressed that roulette is purely a game of chance and the wheel is merely a random number generator. The apparatus and its betting table are constructed to insure not only that the outcome of every spin is an entirely random event, but that they also consistently yield a house advantage of roughly two and one-half percent. Thus, "There is *no* system for 'beating the table,'"[4] and it is impossible for the wheel spinner to determine or even remotely influence the outcome of any play. Nevertheless, the betting strategies of many regular players are influenced by their strong beliefs to the contrary.

Oldman found that the numbers selected and amounts bet by most players are generally determined by two erroneous and contradictory playing theories to which they subscribe. The first of these is the "gambler's fallacy" which causes players to bet that the outcome of future plays will be different from those previous. In the case of roulette, this betting strategy is based on the belief that the longer it has been since the last appearance of a certain color, number, or number combination, the more likely it is to appear in the future. Thus, many players select certain numbers which they play repeatedly in the belief that they are "overdue." The second strategy is based on the belief that the outcome of future plays will be similar to those previous.

One reason many roulette players hold so tenaciously to these theories is that they are also convinced that each play is controlled either intentionally or unintentionally by the wheel spinner who determines where the ball will land. Players who believe that a spinner's influence is unintentional constantly look for changes in the "pattern" of winning numbers. Since this pattern is often perceived as corresponding to the numbers in a certain section of the wheel, these players bet on "the way 'things are running.'"[5] Those who believe that the ball is intentionally controlled also believe that skillful spinners have the ability to select numbers that favor the house. Since they believe that spinners deliberately select numbers and sections of the wheel on which no bets have been placed, flurries of bets are made after the ball has been dropped, many of which are placed on vacant numbers. Even when using this strategy, some players will also continue to bet on their regular numbers. Others will switch from one strategy to the other according to the perceived circumstances.

Here, too, Dostoevsky provides an excellent real-life example of the gambler's conviction that the outcomes of roulette are not entirely random but fall into distinct patterns:

> I came to one conclusion which is, I think, correct: there is in fact, though not a system, some sort of order in the sequence of fortuitous chances–which is, of course, very strange indeed. For instance, it will happen that after twelve straight numbers from the second dozen, the third dozen will finally come up; twice, let's say, it will hit there, then switch to the first dozen. Having fallen on the first dozen only once, it will then return to the second dozen with three or four straight hits, whereupon it is once more the third dozen with two straight numbers, and back to the first dozen for a single time, and again three straight hits in the middle, and so on and on in the same fashion for an hour and a half or two hours. One, three, and two; one, three, and two.[6]

From the point of view of many players, then, roulette is not merely a game of chance but a contest of skill that pits the abilities of the spinner against those of the player. Since spinners are viewed as loyal employees of the house who must try to avoid all paying numbers, it is the task of the players to outwit them. Skillful players are therefore those who are able to perceive and exploit the spinners' patterns and intentions while keeping this awareness from them.[7] These erroneous cognitions are reinforced by some croupiers who deliberately assume an aura of self-confidence and efficiency to foster the notion that their actions will indeed favor the house. This is done to discourage gamblers from playing their tables so that the croupiers might avoid the tedium of counting and stacking large numbers of chips, a laborious task which takes up most of their time at the table. Casino managers also reinforce these beliefs when they unnecessarily replace croupiers at tables where the players are winning.

Arguing against purely economic theories that postulate that people gamble only in hopes of increasing their wealth, Oldman felt that most players consider gambling to be a form of public entertainment. Since this entertainment is provided by the casino, a place of business, player losses are generally looked upon as its entrance fee. Furthermore, most regular players successfully budget their money by restricting their losses to predetermined amounts. Since they seldom exceed these self-imposed limits, Oldman concluded that gamblers vie with the croupier not to garner wealth but to merely minimize the entrance fee. Regular players succeed often enough to keep returning for more entertainment.

Mark Griffiths: Irrationality and Skill Among British Fruit Machine Players

Slot machines in the arcades of the United Kingdom, where they are known as fruit machines, have a number of features and options with which players of standard slot machines in the United States may not be familiar. For example, the displays of modern U.S. slot machines are purely random, electronically generated video images while fruit machines in the United Kingdom have three physically spinning reels each with its own fixed sequence of twenty symbols. The mechanical nature of these machines allows a degree of handicapping, or perhaps merely an illusion of handicapping, that is not available to U.S. players and which enable seasoned players to estimate when any machine is more likely to pay. Furthermore, many fruit machines in the United Kindgom also have "nudge" buttons, that can be used to alter the current position of any reel, and "hold" buttons that can retain the current position of any reel during subsequent plays. When a winning combination appears a "gamble" button allows side bets which can multiply a player's winnings for that play. The possible outcomes of this option, which flash on and off in an apparently random pattern, range from "lose" to multiples of as many as ten-to-one. The most experienced players claim to have a broad knowledge of fruit machine play in general, an intimate knowledge of the idiosyncrasies of specific machines, and playing strategies that they are convinced gives them a distinct advantage over others.[8]

A Questionnaire Survey

Psychologist Mark Griffiths has conducted a series of studies of adolescent fruit machine players in the amusement arcades of Great Britain. One of his earlier studies involved a questionnaire survey of a group of 69 adolescent players, nine of whom were judged to be pathological gamblers.[9] Over one quarter (28%) of his sample indicated that they played "for a challenge," a response which implies a belief that this type of gambling is a matter of skill.[10] When asked specifically whether they thought any skill is involved, only 12 percent responded negatively. Although 40 percent believed that this was a "mostly chance" activity, nearly half (48%) of the sample, including all nine of the pathological gamblers, felt that it required at least some degree of skill. When they were asked to name specific playing skills most of their responses fell into one of nine distinct types. Six of them referred to a general knowledge of playing features, such as the proper use of the buttons, and of the characteristics of individual machines, such as knowing when it is "full of money." Other skills involved quick reflexes and decisions, good hand-eye-coordination, and knowing payout probabilities. One respondent emphasized the value of practice. When asked about their losses, several of them spontaneously added information indicating that their biggest losses were due to such external factors as "bad luck" or a "bad day" while some attributed them to such internal causes as poor concentration. Similar responses were given by a similar group of 19 self-admitted fruit machine addicts.[11]

Griffiths felt that the option buttons and other specialist play features that are unique to British fruit machines serve to "stimulate the illusion of control through personal involvement and familiarity of particular machines"[12] and greatly contribute to the perception that their play involves an element of skill. Not only were perceptions of skill salient in the biased evaluations of loss outcomes and attributions that his subjects expressed, but the pathological gamblers in his sample appeared to have an even greater skill orientation than the others.[13] He interpreted his findings as support for the idea that cognitive factors may be central to gambling persistence. He also pointed out that whether the skill attributed to fruit machine success is "actual" or "perceived" has never been determined and suggested that this question be investigated in future studies. He then took it upon himself to do so.

The "Thinking Aloud Method"

Griffiths next employed the "thinking aloud method" in conjunction with observational records and semi-structured interviews. His goals were to determine whether the element of skill in fruit machine playing is genuine or illusional and to assess the extent to which irrational thinking occurs while gambling. The subjects of one study[14] were 60 university students (44 male; 16 female) who were also observed in the real-life gambling environment of an amusement arcade. Half were regular players and half were nonregular and therefore less experienced players. All subjects were given enough money for 30 plays, but were instructed to try to win enough to achieve a total of 60 plays. Accurate observational records of their gambling behavior, their number of wins and losses, and the amounts they won and lost were kept so that success rates of the experienced players could be compared to those of the inexperienced players. Half the members of each group were also supplied with a portable tape recorder and lapel microphone so that the thoughts they voiced during play could be recorded for analysis. On the basis of the earlier findings of Ladouceur and his colleagues,[15] Griffiths anticipated that regular players, who are thought to entertain stronger illusions of skill and control than occasional players, would exhibit a greater degree of irrational thinking. Following their gambling session, all subjects were administered a questionnaire similar to that used in his earlier study.

Analysis of the observational records revealed that nearly half (14) of the regulars managed to attain the goal of 60 plays while less than one-quarter (7) of the nonregulars did so. Moreover, while the nonregular group experienced a slightly higher average rate of wins than the regulars (7.2 vs. 7.0), the regular players were, in fact, able to achieve more total plays on average than the occasional players (60.9 vs. 51.7). This occurred because they were better able to parlay their smaller winnings into larger ones through use of the "gamble" button. However, because they tended to play faster, they actually spent a little less time playing the machines than the nonregulars (9.2 vs. 9.9 minutes). Finally, more than two-thirds (10) of the regulars who attained 60 plays continued until they had lost everything while less than one-third (2) of the nonregulars did so. However, seven of the regulars quickly became dissatisfied with the machines to which they were originally assigned and left then in order to play others. Some changed machines as many as three times.

Analysis of the tape recordings revealed that regulars voiced more irrational explanations for their losses and tended to attribute their successes to skill rather than luck. In this case, however, vocalizations pertaining to skill did not always turn out to be manifestations of irrational thoughts since the observational data demonstrated that an element of skill is involved. Although irrational thoughts made up only 14 percent of the regular players' vocalizations, this was still over five and one-half times as many as were expressed by the nonregular players whose irrational thoughts comprised 2.5 percent of their utterances. The lack of agreement between the frequencies reported by Ladouceur and his colleagues, who found during their own "thinking aloud" studies that 80 percent of their subjects' verbalizations were irrational, and those of Griffiths has several possible explanations. For example, Ladouceur undertook his study in a laboratory setting while Griffiths conducted his in the field. However, Griffiths therefore felt it more likely that his more "stringent" coding system for types of vocalizations might account for the difference. That is, Griffiths considered all vocalizations made during the gambling session whether they pertained directly to play or not whereas Ladouceur considered only those that pertained directly to play.[16] Thus, the findings of the various "thinking aloud" studies may actually be more in accord with one another than their numerical data alone would suggest.

His interview data again allowed Griffiths to distinguish among several different kinds of irrational thoughts that his subjects expressed. For example, regulars tended to personify or humanize the machine to a greater extent than occasional players, often by cursing, swearing, and talking to it. Although he gave no examples in this study, one of the subjects of his earlier questionnaire study claimed that "each machine has its own personality and you have to master it. You have to relate to it and know what its next move is going to be."[17] As in his earlier questionnaire study, most responses describing specific skills referred to knowledge of specific machines and playing features (i.e., the "nudge," "hold," and "gamble" buttons).

Griffiths's findings not only confirmed that regular players express a higher incidence of irrational thoughts and place more emphasis on skill than do occasional players, but they also demonstrated that skill is, indeed, a factor in playing British slot or fruit machines. Whereas there is no opportunity to develop or exercise any playing skills on standard North American and Australian slot machines, this is not true of those in the United Kingdom. Such fruit machine features as "nudge" and "hold" buttons and mechanical reels with fixed symbol sequences are lacking in their electronic American and Australian counterparts. Thus, when Griffiths asked his subjects whether they thought any skill was involved in playing them, most of the occasional players indicated they thought it was largely a game of chance while the regular players tended to believe that skill was a definite factor. Moreover, most of the occasional players considered themselves to be unskilled while most of the regulars rated their playing skills as above average. Although all subjects began gambling with the same initial stake, the regular players were, in fact, able to win more money and achieve more plays than the occasional players. This finding clearly demonstrates that the element of skill in British slot machine playing cannot be entirely discounted as a product of irrational thinking, but is a very real quality that can be developed through experience. However, Griffiths tempered the significance of this finding when he emphasized that, in his estimation, regular players believe themselves to have greater skill than they actually possess since the only observable difference was that it took them just several more plays to lose an equal amount of money.[18] He interpreted the fact that seven regulars abandoned their assigned machine in favor of one with which they were more familiar as confirmation of Langer's illusion of control through familiarity hypothesis. He interpreted his finding that regulars tend to play until they have lost everything and initiate new sessions fully expecting to lose again as confirmation of the observations of earlier researchers that gamblers play "with" money rather than "for" it.

The Structural Characteristics of Fruit Machines

In addition to variable ratio reinforcement schedules and frequent "near miss" situations which serve as operant reinforcers of gambling behavior, Griffiths[19] believed that fruit machines possess additional built-in structural or physical characteristics that also may serve to encourage persistence. For example, since the first reel of fruit machines has a greater number of winning symbols than the second, which in turn has more than the third, the symbol ratio proportions of these machines produce many "near misses" that serve to extend the gambler's playing time.[20] Some of the others characteristics he listed are found in many other forms of gambling, as well. They include:

1. Multiplier potentials: manipulation of odds on the outcome of one or a series of events. This is achieved by playing high-stakes fruit machines and by playing daily doubles, trifectas, etc., at the racetrack. Progressive slot machines in the United States allow players to risk from one to five coins per play. Printed promotional materials supplied by some U.S. casinos exhort their customers to bet the maximum with such advice as, "Remember, the less you bet, the more you lose when you win."

2. Event frequencies: the time between events is relatively long for racetrack bettors but very short for fruit machine players. Short event frequencies allow little time for financial considerations.

3. Payout intervals: the time between the outcome of an event and receipt of payment for winning. For fruit machine players, positive reinforcement is immediate.

4. Bettor involvement: the degree to which gamblers perceive themselves as being active participants in a gambling game. This perception is encouraged by the "nudge," "hold," and "gamble" buttons which enhance the illusion of control as does being allowed to choose one's own lottery numbers.

5. Perception of skill: the degree to which gamblers believe a game requires skill whether any is actually required or not as in roulette. Again, the fruit machine's play buttons foster this perception.

6. Win probability: the true odds of winning. Fruit machines in the United Kingdom have fixed rates of return ranging from 70 percent to 90 percent. However, the probability of winning money does not appear to be very important to fruit machine players. Like video game players, their primary goal is to play for as long as possible by spending the least amount of money.

7. Payout ratio: the size of the prize compared to the size of stake. The highest possible fruit machine jackpots and lottery prizes are many times larger than the price of a play.

8. Light and sound effects: such sensory stimuli as the machines' flashing lights, music, and other sound effects create an ambience that is conducive to gambling by generating feelings of fun, activity, and excitement. Not only are certain colors associated with particular moods and emotions, but changing patterns can influence such physiological responses as heart and breathing rates that are associated with heightened arousal. Many machines emit a loud buzz or musical refrain after each win. These sounds, augmented by the clatter of coins falling into metal trays, suggest that wins are more common than losses. They also create the impression that the amounts won are much larger than they actually are. As noted previously, some casinos are now experimenting with the release of certain odors in their slot machine areas which will add to these effects.[21]

9. Machine naming: the names of various machines are chosen to elicit certain emotional responses. For example, the name of the first slot machine, "The Liberty Bell," was intended to evoke sentiments of independence and patriotism. Many fruit machine names refer to money ("Cashline"), banks ("Piggy Bank"), skill ("Fruitskill"), the reels ("Reel Money"), etc.

10. Suspension of judgment: tactics which impede a gambler's normal economic value system such as the use of small denomination coins which lead the gambler to believe that little can be lost. In some instances the machine credits or tokens that are won cannot be exchanged for currency thereby forcing the player to put any winnings back into the machine.

11. Intrinsic association: the degree to which betting is associated with other activities. Griffiths felt that this is less applicable to fruit machine gambling than, for example, sports betting.

All of these structural influences can act in concert both to induce the initiation of a gambling session and to prolong a session once it has begun. These machine and other environmental characteristics have the potential to influence gambling behavior irrespective of an individual's psychological or physiological condition. Griffiths felt that a thorough understanding of all such characteristics would permit "psychologically context-specific explanations of gambling behaviour, rather than global explanations such as 'addictive personality.'"[22] This knowledge, if acted upon, might also aid in reducing the potential for addiction.

Michael Walker: Sociocognitive Theory

Irrationality and Skill Among Australian Poker Machine Players

On the basis of the findings of Ladouceur and Griffiths, cognitive psychologist Michael Walker[23] tested the propositions that slot machine gamblers would display more irrational thinking than other types of machine players, that they would prefer a particular machine over all others, and that slot machines would induce more irrational thinking than other kinds of machines in all who played them. Walker therefore conducted a similar study of nine slot machine, eight video poker machine, and nine amusement (nongambling) video game players using the "thinking aloud" method. Unlike Ladouceur, however, Walker took several steps to eliminate all artificiality. Rather than obtain his data in a psychology laboratory, he conducted his study in the arcades of Australia. Although his 26 subjects were university students, he studied only those who were already regular (twice a week) players. Finally, all subjects were required to use their own money.

Walker's findings confirmed all three of his hypotheses. He found that as they played their preferred games, 37.9 percent of all vocalizations made by regular slot machine players were irrational as opposed to 11.8 percent of those of video poker players and only 1.2 percent of those of amusement game players. Examples included such demands as "You owe me!" and such bargains as "You pay me and I'll pay you"; one subject spoke of being able to win by "getting 'in tune' with the machine and visualizing winning combinations."[24] He also found that 80.3 percent of the strategic statements (those related to winning) of slot machine players, 57.6 percent of those of video poker players, and 8.3 percent of those of amusement game players were irrational. Furthermore, the verbalized thoughts of all subjects were recorded while they played games other than those they normally preferred. All three groups expressed more irrational thoughts while playing slot machines than they did while playing the other two kinds of games. However, Walker judiciously insisted that since his findings were purely statistical, they did not demonstrate that irrational thinking *causes* persistent or heavy gambling but that other noncognitive influences such as reinforcement schedules, arousal, prior mood states, and personality factors may also be responsible. Moreover, since his sample included only nine slot machine players, all of whom were university undergraduates, he insisted that his initial findings would require confirmation by more extensive research with a larger and more heterogeneous sample before they could be generalized to all slot machine players.

The Anticipation of Winning

Walker argued that although many factors may be involved to some extent, the primary motivation for gambling is neither arousal, tension reduction, social interaction, nor entertainment: it is money. For him even "problem gambling is about the winning and losing of money and little else."[25] Nevertheless, apart from the economic motive, the sociocognitive approach that he developed[26] is little different from the cognitive explanations of others; it was founded on the premise that persistent gambling is maintained by "irrational thinking" and the other cognitive processes outlined in the previous chapter. More accurately, then, since excessive gamblers tend to lose more than they win, their behavior is motivated and reinforced more by the expectation of winning than by any actual returns. In Walker's own words:

> heavy gamblers believe that they can "beat the system" and make money. They believe that through logic or special insight they have an advantage over other gamblers. They believe that there is more opportunity to use skill or special knowledge in picking the outcome than there is in fact. They discount losses as being caused by factors beyond their control but count wins as evidence that their system or special knowledge is working. Thus despite losing large sums of money, the gambler can continue gambling with the firm expectation that shortly the gambling investment will begin to pay, the losses will be erased, and a small fortune will be acquired.[27]

In reality, the very essence of commercial gaming dictates that "anyone who gambles should expect to lose"[28]–anyone except the house, that is. Walker pointed out that "the casino is not a gambler . . . because it is betting on a certainty: the casino arranges its games so that it has an edge."[29] The built-in odds advantages of all casino games insure that the house will never pay out more than it takes in. Walker therefore insisted that "Gambling would not be popular if gamblers engaged in a rational appraisal of the activity."[30] Casino owners realize, of course, that few gamblers do so.

While Walker clearly did not invent the cognitive approach he did gather together the many observations and ideas of his predecessors and colleagues and integrate them into a unified theory focusing on the groundless beliefs that foster gambling. While he held the principles of cognitive psychology to be of primary importance, he also incorporated some aspects of psychoanalytic, behavioral, and social learning theory into his own explanation.

Occasional vs. Regular Gamblers

In developing his theory Walker found it necessary to distinguish the occasional gambler, for whom gambling is an amusing novelty, from the regular gambler, who regards gambling as a challenge. According to sociocognitive theory, the two have markedly different attitudes toward gambling losses: the money lost by an occasional gambler is merely "written off as part of the entertainment" while that lost by a seriously committed gambler is "considered as a temporary setback which must be made good."[31] Thus, the occasional gambler gambles for entertainment while the regular gambler gambles for money. Walker acknowledged that there are exceptions to this generalization since many lotto and lottery players who avoid or only occasionally participate in other kinds of gambling are also motivated to make a great deal of money with a minimal investment. He also acknowledged that psychoanalytic and learning factors, such as early childhood traumas or the excitement that gambling provides, may also be involved, at least in part. Nevertheless, he considered his observations on the incentive of money to be generally valid. Furthermore, occasional gamblers do not chase their losses whereas committed gamblers avidly do so.

Despite his distinction between occasional and regular gamblers, Walker remained convinced that, as far as sociocognitive theory is concerned, the difference is not qualitative and cautioned against categorization. He steadfastly held to the position that different degrees of gambling do not represent different kinds of gamblers but merely different points along the single continuum of lesser to greater involvement. Inveighing against the medical model of pathological gambling, he argued that the use of various labels (e.g., social, problem, escapist, excitement, pathological, etc.) to distinguish different degrees of gambling involvement has led some treatment specialists to believe that different types of gamblers actually exist. Implicit in such typologies is the notion that moderate gamblers are psychologically normal while compulsive gamblers are inherently maladjusted. In turn, this idea has led to the formulation of various diagnostic criteria designed to differentiate the "healthy" from the "sick" gambler who can only be "cured" through abstinence. In contrast, sociocognitive theory maintains that certain social and cognitive processes can lead anyone to increase his or her gambling involvement, even to the point at which problems develop.[32]

The Challenge of Gambling

Walker felt that gambling presents a challenge which different people meet in different ways. Occasional gamblers who experience more losses than wins often find the challenge of gambling too great and never progress beyond their initial low level of involvement or even quit gambling altogether. Conversely, serious gamblers often find gambling a challenge that they are unable to resist. Walker compared the challenge of gambling to those of mountain climbing or marathon running, for example, since all of these endeavors require talent, resourcefulness, commitment, and persistence. The difference with gambling, however, is that it also offers potential financial rewards. Following an initial gambling success, some individuals come to believe that while others may lose, they are among the chosen few who possess the special knowledge, insights, skills, and luck that it takes to win and make money at gambling. Thus, committed gamblers may gamble either to "beat the system" or to make money. In either case, since money constitutes the only mark of success, money is the object of the endeavor.

The Regular Gambler's Set of Core Beliefs

Precisely what does induce people to climb the ladder of gambling involvement? According to Walker, three core beliefs are responsible. These are the beliefs that 1) persistence, knowledge, and skill can enable a gambler to make money, 2) unlike others who often fail, the gambler has the unique ability to win, and 3) persistence will ultimately be rewarded.[33] Although gambling continually tests and challenges the individual's core beliefs, the serious gambler denies or alters any contrary evidence which might contradict them.

Not all of these beliefs are altogether baseless since others have shown that it is indeed possible to make money through gambling. A few famous professional gamblers have won large amounts of money on the basis of their knowledge, skill, and persistence and multimillion-dollar lottery winners are frequently publicized. A gambler's awareness of the successes of others and the perception that these successes can be duplicated through imitation represent the social learning aspect of sociocognitive theory. However, these facts alone are not enough to induce everyone to increase their involvement: a committed gambler must also have unbridled faith in the superiority of his or her own techniques and talents.

Faith in one's abilities is often confirmed by an early winning experience, which a number of researchers believe to be very important in the development of pathological gambling. An early big win or winning phase is generally held to be responsible for generating the narcissistic feelings that many psychoanalysts and treatment specialists have noted among their patients. However, some gamblers develop and maintain these same narcissistic beliefs in the absence of an initial winning experience. Walker contended that the strong motivations of some gamblers derive precisely from the challenge of early losses which they are then driven to overcome. Even after losing large amounts they remain convinced that their losses are temporary and persistence is the key, especially when they feel they have an intellectual advantage:

> Clearly if you have an edge, then you must persist until the profits have accrued. No matter that ten thousand dollars have been lost: it would be foolish to stop when success is guaranteed in return for perseverance. Losses must be expected and victory will never be won with a weak will.[34]

In reality, of course, one's previous experience or "luck" in gambling, whether good or bad, has no bearing on any future outcomes. Nevertheless, the belief in one's ability to win appears to be a decisive factor in the development of greater involvement, and the stronger this belief, the greater the involvement.

Irrational Thinking

Apart from narcissism and the belief in luck, other irrational beliefs that many gamblers hold include overestimation of their chances for winning, the illusion that they can somehow control the outcomes of games of chance, biased evaluations of the outcome when they lose, and entrapment. Walker illustrated these points by citing examples of lottery players. Although someone must win a lottery, many players are completely unaware of the astronomical odds against their winning–odds that are typically one in hundreds of thousands or even tens of millions for the largest prizes. Moreover, many players believe they can increase their chances of winning by purchasing tickets only from a particular "lucky" vendor. Walker cited many other examples including earlier research which found that raffle players prefer to choose their own tickets rather than allow the vendor to do so since they also believe this will enhance their chances of winning.[35] The illusion of control is even greater in lotto and keno in which the players can personally choose their own "lucky" numbers such as the birthdates of family members. In reality, of course, no method of choice has an advantage over any other.

Although no losing ticket is worth any more than any other losing ticket, "near misses" also serve to reinforce superstitious and persistent lottery playing just as Skinner[36] found they would among slot machine gamblers. "Almost winning" a multimillion-dollar lotto drawing seems to convince many players that they have a better than average chance of winning in the future. As noted above, similar kinds of irrational thought and illusions of control have also been reported for slot machine, video poker, roulette, and blackjack players.[37] In reality, lotteries, raffles, standard slot machines, and roulette are games of chance, not of skill. Despite the illusion of control they provide, superstition and persistence have no influence at all over purely random events since at every lottery drawing or spin of the roulette wheel all numbers have equal chances of winning–and losing. "Near misses" in racetrack betting may have an even greater influence on persistence than lotteries. Betting on a "close second" whose failure to win could be easily rationalized would be almost as reinforcing as choosing the winner since this outcome would also serve to validate one's method of picking horses.

Problem Gambling as Entrapment

Cognitive theorists tend to regard problem gambling as merely an extension of normal gambling since it is thought to be driven by the same irrational thought processes. However, different cognitions are thought to be more influential in fostering different kinds of gambling. Thus, biased evaluations of outcomes would tend to encourage persistence in games of skill while entrapment would be more likely to impel persistence in games of chance. As previously noted, entrapment refers to an increasing commitment to a strategy or decision-making system that has already failed but to which the gambler tenaciously holds in an attempt to get even. Lotto, keno, and roulette provide excellent examples of games which invite entrapment. Nevertheless, Walker felt,

> All gambling is entrapping, provided that you believe that, with persistence, you will win. Regular horse players are heavily entrapped by their methods and their systems. Blackjack players are entrapped by basic strategy and the lure of counting. Slot machine players know how to avoid the "hungry" machines. Lotto players have magical insight into winning combinations. All that is necessary is persistence. But persistence produces losses which increase the importance of remaining in the game until those losses are recouped. The greater the losses the greater the entrapment.[38]

According to sociocognitive theory, then, problem gambling does not arise from gambling per se, but from consistent losses and the large debts that accrue from them. The money that is lost therefore constitutes the root of the problem. Even in the face of the heaviest losses, problem gamblers remain committed to their core beliefs. They are sure that the inevitable big win is just around the corner and that they must persevere if they are not to miss out on it when their luck changes. Thus, it has been said that, "The individual who gambles to excess denies facts, replacing them with unrealistic beliefs about having fate on his or her side."[39] But perseverance requires money that they are forced to obtain in any way they can, often by borrowing indiscriminately. For any gambler so religiously committed to his or her beliefs, quitting while losing is unthinkable since they "know" their winning system cannot possibly fail.[40]

Walker listed several behavioral changes that occur as a losing streak continues, many of which have been reported by others. At first the entrapped gambler will escalate the size of each bet in the belief that the recent run of bad luck must end soon and the system which worked so well in the past will work again in the future. With continuing losses and mounting debts the gambler becomes increasingly more depressed. Gamblers also become more withdrawn and secretive as they attempt to hide the extent of their losses from their spouses and other family members. Keeping them in ignorance is imperative because if they knew the true state of affairs they would only try to force the gambler to quit, making it impossible to get even. Moreover, unsuccessful gamblers would then have to admit their failures to themselves. Secrecy goes hand in hand with increased lying and deceit about where and how gamblers spend their time and their money. Gamblers also become more irritated and angry at anything that might interfere with their objectives. Finally, they begin to make reckless financial transactions to obtain the money they need to gamble. They go through their savings, mortgage their homes, borrow from any source, and may even begin to steal. Owing to the strength of his conviction that all gamblers are motivated solely by the prospect of making money, Walker insisted that it is not gambling that is responsible for such problems as depression and the breakup of relationships: these and all other problems associated with gambling are traceable only to the debt that it causes rather than to the act of gambling itself.[41]

Although many of these behavioral changes have been noted by advocates of the medical model, Walker explained them in terms of cognitive psychology as a direct result of the irrational beliefs embraced by so many serious gamblers. Consequently, sociocognitive theory does not recognize problem gamblers as sick, addicted, compulsive, or pathological since their gambling is entirely rational in light of their erroneous cognitive orientation: "There is no pathology, only the damage caused by financial loss. There is no addiction, only false beliefs and irrational thinking."[42] Walker felt that "pathological" or "compulsive" gambling is more a matter of timing than of degree since no matter how heavily some people gamble, they never adopt these labels until their losses and debt levels have forced them to seek outside help. Moreover, he argued, "The treatment agency, whether it is Gamblers Anonymous or a gambling clinic, is motivated to apply the label because the gambling disease is their *raison d'etre.* The psychiatrist can then set about curing the compulsion or excising the pathology."[43]

At one point, however, Walker appeared to have softened his hard partisan stance with the qualification that his scheme should not be misinterpreted to mean that there is no such thing as pathological addictive gambling since he was concerned primarily with the degree of involvement in gambling as opposed to its ultimate cause.[44] This could be taken to suggest that sociocognitive theory does not purport to explain the clinical entity of compulsive or pathological gambling, but only persistence by heavy but noncompulsive normal gamblers. However, Walker did not make this concession in any of his other writings nor did he ever temper his antagonism toward the medical model. He maintained that no matter how forceful a person's urge to gamble may be, a professional gambler will never be branded a pathological gambler as long as he wins more money than he loses. Likewise, regular lottery players who cannot rest or think about anything else until they have played their lucky numbers will never be classified as pathological gamblers since their gambling will never cause them any financial problems.

Overview

In summary, Walker's sociocognitive approach maintains that persistent heavy gambling, serious losses, and "chasing" are not caused by unconscious desires and guilt feelings, personality disorders, reinforcement schedules, or the need to increase or decrease emotional arousal: they are caused by irrational, wishful thinking and the strength of people's faith in their false beliefs. Specifically, gambling behavior is thought to be reinforced by narcissistic beliefs in one's own intellectual superiority or luck, by overestimating one's chances for winning, by the gambler's illusion that he or she can somehow control the outcome of purely random events, by biased evaluations of the outcomes of past events, and by beliefs in the efficacy of failed gambling systems.

Walker therefore contended that there is no need to distinguish between the heavy but "normal" gambler and the "compulsive" or "pathological" gambler since there is no qualitative difference between them. The only difference he saw was that "the former is still out there hanging on with the resources necessary to continue while the latter has no resources left and thus no opportunity to continue."[45] He also insisted that irrational beliefs in themselves do not constitute a motivation for gambling. Although they strongly influence the direction that gambling will take they do not generate gambling behavior. Like Skinner, Walker was convinced that the primary motivation of all gamblers is the lust for money. But "Why," he asked, "does the heavy gambler continue despite the massive losses? Because he believes he will win in the long run."[46]

Mark Dickerson: A Union of Behavioral and Cognitive Principles

Not all modern psychologists have entirely rejected the principles of learning theory in favor of those of the cognitive approach: some have blended the principles of each. One such psychologist is Mark Dickerson[47] who, after conducting research in each of these areas, came to the conclusion that behavioral and cognitive factors both contribute to persistence and impaired control. He insisted, however, that the relative influence of each varies from one form of gambling to another.

Dickerson challenged the assumption that the same factors are responsible for persistence and impaired control in all forms of gambling by contrasting the situational and psychological variables that are specific to each. In the first place, he noted, some forms of gambling are "discontinuous" while others are "continuous." Discontinuous forms, such as lottery drawings and raffles, are distinguished by the considerable delay between the time of a stake and its outcome. "Continuous" forms, such as racetrack betting, slot or poker machine playing, blackjack, and poker, provide the opportunity for many rapidly repeated cycles of bets, plays, and outcomes during the course of a single gambling session. As observed in a previous chapter, other game-related situational or structural variables that vary from one form of gambling to another include the relative degrees of skill and chance that are involved, the duration of each play, the timing between sequential plays, reinforcement schedules, variability of odds and bet sizes, and the presence or absence of external gambling-related stimuli. Psychological variables include subjective perceptions of the degrees of skill and excitement associated with different forms of gambling, prior mood state, need for arousal, and the nature of the relationship between the gambler and his or her opponent, whether it is a machine, a bookie, a dealer or croupier, or another poker player. According to Dickerson, each of these dimensions has a significant influence over the gambler's persistence and self-control.

Dickerson, largely on the basis of his own research since few studies have been completed in this area, felt that our present knowledge of the game-related psychological and situational differences between slot machine playing and racetrack betting could sufficiently illustrate this point. Both are obviously continuous forms of gambling but they are quite different in other aspects. For example, slot machines require no skill while successful racetrack betting is commonly thought to require a great deal of skill. Thus, the beliefs that slot machine players hold concerning the importance of skill are far weaker than those of racetrack handicappers. This means, Dickerson argued, "that if the weakly-held beliefs of poker-machine players contribute to the development of persistence when losing, then in [racetrack] betting, beliefs about skill may make a more significant impact on control."[48] Likewise, poor information processing will have relatively little bearing on the average slot machine player but may have a profound influence on the persistence, control, and debt level of the unsuccessful racetrack bettor. In this case, additional questions are raised: has the handicapper never learned any information processing skills or is the lack of control purely a matter of the reinforcement schedule inherent in racetrack betting? Finally, excitement, which has little influence over slot machine players who experience relatively little arousal, appears to be integral to both on- and off-track betting and may also provide a strong reinforcement for continued betting which may lead to loss of control and chasing in these situations.

Dickerson felt that these simple examples illustrate the fallacy of assuming that the same psychological models and principles can be called upon to explain impaired control in all forms of gambling and cases of excess.[49] To do so, he concluded, "is not only naive but runs the risk of not fully exploiting the significant differences between different forms to develop a far richer and informative vein of research."[50]

R. I. F. Brown: Social Learning or Modeling Theory

Social learning theory is a product of social psychology that also blends the tenets of cognitive psychology with those of behaviorism to explain certain human behaviors. It is also related somewhat to social interactional theory, a sociological approach that will be discussed in greater detail in a subsequent volume. Social learning, which is also known as imitative learning, vicarious learning, or modeling, describes the process through which people acquire certain behaviors by following the examples and standards of others who are looked upon as role models. For children these role models would include parents, siblings, peers, and any other influential people in their lives. The acquisition of language by children is one of the most obvious examples of social learning. It is also apparent in the frequent use of chewing tobacco by youthful baseball enthusiasts who do so in emulation of their major league heroes and in the use of psychoactive drugs by aspiring musicians whose idols also use these substances.

Social learning theory differs from operant and classical conditioning theory in two important ways. The first is that specific behaviors are believed to be acquired through observation alone in the absence of any direct reinforcements or punishments. Some addiction specialists[51] therefore stress the primacy of cognitive processes over all other influences in their discussion of social learning theory. This idea found strong support in a study which found that preschool children who were exposed to a peer group that played a risk-taking game and won would themselves take more risks to win a highly valued prize. Conversely, those in a control group who were exposed to a peer group that won nothing took fewer risks. The researchers concluded that "modeling can enhance risk-taking/gambling-like behavior in young children."[52] However, other authorities feel that the social and other environmental contexts in which modeling occurs are perhaps even more influential than cognitive factors in motivating these behaviors. This is because social learning theory also postulates a reciprocal rather than a unilateral relationship between these behaviors and the environments in which they take place, a second major theoretical difference. According to Albert Bandura, one of the principal architects of social learning theory, "By their action, people play an active role in producing the reinforcing contingencies that impinge upon them. . . . Behavior partly creates the environment, and the environment influences the behavior in a reciprocal fashion."[53] In other words, Bandura argued that human behavior is neither compelled by internal psychodynamic forces nor is it merely the pawn of external environmental forces. Instead, the individual and the environment act upon one another in concert: not only can human behavior be modified by environmental changes, but a particular environment can be changed by a modification of people's behavior, as witnessed by the fact that cigarette smoking is no longer widely held to be fashionable as it once was. A number of addiction specialists have found social learning theory to be especially useful in explaining psychoactive drug use, chemical dependency, and relapse as well as its prevention after treatment.[54]

Although some researchers believe that social learning theory can provide an adequate explanation for all addictive behaviors in general,[55] R. I. F. Brown[56] observed that it has rarely been called upon to explain gambling in particular. He therefore developed a hypothetical social learning model of gambling. Brown suggested that such a theory would see gambling as beginning with imitation learning or modeling, "perhaps copying a hero figure in adolescence, but more commonly learning from one's social peers."[57] Indeed, one psychoanalyst found that in most, if not all, of his compulsive gambling cases, "There was a romanticized, male gambling figure in the patient's early life."[58] Cognitive psychologist Michael Walker defined social learning somewhat more broadly as a phenomenon in which one's initial involvement in gambling is learned and vicariously reinforced through the observation of the gambling experiences of others.[59] He also pointed out that most social learning takes place in the context of the family or primary reference group and that most of the things a novice gambler learns–how to play a game, how to collect winnings, any social and other rules of etiquette that apply, and proper behavior including how to win or lose gracefully–are generally a matter of social learning.[60] Psychologist Mark Griffiths[61] suggested that the significant gender differences which have been observed and reported in studies of all age groups are due to social learning since gambling allows males to exhibit courage, independence, and bravery–traits that are socially defined as "masculine."

Dostoevsky provided an excellent example of social learning when he juxtaposed the gambling comportment of wealthy European aristocrats with that of their children. In Doestoevsky's time–as in our own–a cardinal rule of the privileged classes was that, win or lose, no concern and very little emotion must ever be openly expressed:

> Our General walked up to the table solidly and with dignity. An attendant rushed to offer him a chair, but he didn't notice him, spent a long time taking out his wallet, then an equally long time producing three hundred francs in gold, put them on black, and won. He did not pick up his winnings, but left them on the table. Black came out again. He let it ride again, and when it was red the next time around he had lost twelve hundred francs at one stroke. He walked away with a smile, keeping his composure. I am positive that he was sick at heart, and if the bet had been two or three times higher he

> would not have remained so cool but would have betrayed his excitement. However, I was present when a Frenchman won, and then lost, as much as thirty thousand francs gaily and without getting in the least excited. A true gentleman doesn't get excited even when he loses his entire fortune. Money must be so much below a gentleman's dignity as to be hardly worth bothering about.[62]

Through the example of their elders, children of this class learn to behave in the prescribed manner:

> I have seen many a mother push forward her innocent and elegant daughter, a lass of fifteen or sixteen, give her a few gold coins, and teach her how to play. The young girl would win or lose, invariably with a smile, then leave the table very well pleased.[63]

The influence of one's early exposure to gambling–often through parental examples–on the development of pathological gambling in later life was noted some time ago[64] and some modern researchers still believe that it constitutes one of the most important causes. In Spain, for example, pathological gambling generally refers to slot machine addiction. Slot machines can be found in many different kinds of public establishments including bars, restaurants, and hotels. Their use by parents during family outings is believed to present one of the greatest risks to children and adolescents who have not yet learned financial responsibility. Although gambling is illegal for children and adolescents, the law is seldom enforced. According to one group of researchers, it is traditional in Spain for whole families to go to bars and restaurants together and to feel that such laws are made to be broken. Because parents want their children to enjoy the same diversions they do and because the proprietors of these establishments do not want to upset their customers, the authorities generally turn a blind eye to underage gambling. As a result,

> Different factors seem to be contributing to the development of addiction in the underage group. The first is the modeling effect. Given the frequency with which Spanish families visit bars and cafeterias, the fact that the parents gamble on the machines creates an especially powerful behaviour-modeling effect. On the other hand social acceptance of gambling leads to the fact that one often sees parents show their children which buttons to press on the slot machines or even give them coins to gamble with.[65]

Support for the idea that juvenile and adolescent gambling behavior can be traced to social learning processes was provided by a study of 477 Montreal school children nine to 14 years of age.[66] The investigators found that 81 percent had gambled at least once in their lives and that 52 percent were weekly gamblers. While many (75%) of those who gambled did so with friends, even more (81%) gambled with family members: 40 percent gambled with their parents, 53 percent with siblings, and 46 percent with other relatives (grandparents, aunts, uncles). Relatively few (18%) gambled alone or with strangers (8%). Although some children gambled in school, the most common location for these activities was in the homes of their parents and friends. Consequently, only 20 percent of these children expressed any fear that they might be caught gambling by their parents or some other authority figure. Some of these children already seemed to be experiencing some gambling problems: 19 percent had borrowed money in order to gamble, 27 percent indicated that they gambled more than they would like to, and 10 percent felt that their gambling was excessive. The researchers concluded that "parents and peers play a monumental role in the acquisition and maintenance of this behavior"[67] since they communicate the idea that gambling is an acceptable social activity having no potentially adverse consequences.

Brown felt that once the fundamentals were learned, the extent of one's gambling would be then strongly influenced by various factors in that person's social environment including occupation and finances, friends or relatives and their habits, one's own leisure pursuits, and the availability of gambling opportunities. If gambling grows beyond a recreational activity and becomes a requirement for the relief of emotional dysphoria, then the gambler's life will take a course similar to that described by Henry Lesieur in *The Chase*:[68] gambling will lead to losses which will lead to increased gambling, chasing, the development of strategies to obtain more gambling money, and a series of life crises leading to even more gambling and heavier losses. Brown also added a Pavlovian element to his explanation: as gambling increases it becomes more strongly associated with various environmental cues which, when encountered, will trigger the gambling response.

More recently psychiatrist Richard Rosenthal[69] has attributed the development of pathological gambling to a combination of psychodynamic, learned helplessness, and social learning factors. These include: 1) an intolerable state of emotional dysphoria and a sense of low self esteem, often accompanied by guilt, brought about by the lack of love and acceptance in childhood, 2) feelings of omnipotence marked by irrational beliefs and the illusion of control, and 3) exposure to gambling in an environment–often a home environment–in which it was highly valued. Rosenthal felt that "Compulsive gambling seems to run in families"[70] since, as children, gamblers were often introduced to the activity by a parent. Frequently, he maintained, the family poker game provided the only setting in which the pathological gambler had ever experienced any feelings of acceptance, either as an adult or as a family member, by the parent. Sometimes, however, a gambler's early winning phase in games away from home provided the badly needed status, esteem, and recognition from others that was lacking in the home. In Rosenthal's view either environment would foster the development of pathological gambling since, he insisted, "I have never seen a pathological gambler who did not have significant problems in self-esteem prior to the onset of his or her gambling."[71]

In essence, social learning theory represents an amalgam of behavioral, cognitive, and even some sociological principles. Social learning, modeling, or imitation may very well account for the initiation of smoking, drinking, gambling, and other potentially harmful behaviors in many cases. Once the behavior is initiated, persistence is thought to be maintained primarily in the beliefs and expectations that the behavior will bring with it certain social and, in the case of gambling, perhaps even monetary rewards. While perhaps, as Brown observed, no strictly social learning theory of gambling may ever have been proposed, a number of approaches have certainly come close. One of these was Michael Walker's sociocognitive theory which has already been discussed. Others are the play theory of James Smith and Vicki Abt and the social interactional theory of John Rosecrance and others whose ideas will be explored in a subsequent volume.

Glenn Walters: Gambling Lifestyle Theory

Glenn Walters,[72] who contended that pathological gambling is a consciously chosen life-style, added several new cognitive dimensions to his Gambling Lifestyle

Theory. In formulating this approach Walters, a psychologist at a federal correctional institution, attempted to synthesize the elements of learning theory, social learning theory, existential philosophy, and cognitive-interactional theory. As noted, the major tenet of social learning or modeling theory is that children learn many behaviors by imitating the adults in their lives while the major contributions of learning theory are variable-ratio reinforcement schedules and Pavlovian or associational conditioning. According to existential philosophy, the principles of which are similar to those of psychoanalytic theory, the gambling life-style is further motivated by low self-esteem, especially in the form of fears and anxieties related to feelings of insecurity, inadequacy, and powerlessness.

Walters also distinguished between current-contextual conditions and historical-developmental conditions that can act either as risk factors for or as protective factors against the development of a gambling life-style. The former would include such factors as family and peer pressures while the latter would include one's genetic endowment and basic personality type. He stressed that risk for the development of a gambling life-style is determined more by an individual's perceptions of these conditions than by the conditions themselves. Ordinarily, for example, a stable home life would serve a protective function while associating with gambling peers would constitute a risk factor. However, a stable home environment in which immoderate gambling is positively sanctioned could constitute a risk factor for children who model their behavior after parents who openly gamble. None of these environmental influences directly determine a person's behavior, but they do help to channel it by expanding or limiting one's awareness of the number of behavioral options that are available.

Cognitive Factors

Gambling not only makes people feel better by decreasing their existential fears and insecurities, but it also leads to a distortion of their perceptions of self. The cognitive factors that reinforce the maintenance of a gambling life-style choice are the most novel ingredients of Walters's theory. Walters insisted that these cognitive patterns do not represent relatively permanent personality traits, but temporary thought processes that constantly change with different situations. These elements, which come into play once the gambling life-style is firmly established, serve to excuse, rationalize, and justify the gambler's behavior despite its adverse consequences. Many of the cognitions that Walters suggests can be seen to function as psychological defense mechanisms that aid in the gambler's denial of any problem.

Mollification refers to efforts to minimize the seriousness of one's involvement in the gambling life-style. A gambler might argue, for example, that bingo and other forms of charitable gambling are harmless because the money goes to a good cause or that they gamble merely to relieve stress or boredom. Walters[73] cited the example of a man who justified going to the racetrack as a good way to meet clients.

Cutoff refers to the attempt to distance one's self from the reality of the consequences that would normally deter further gambling. Some might use alcohol or other drugs to nullify the impact of such deterrents as an angry spouse or unpaid bills; others might reason that they've already lost so much that a little more won't make any difference. The phrase most commonly employed to express this attitude, according to Walters, is "fuck it."[74]

Entitlement refers to the conviction of many pathological gamblers that they are different from other people and therefore warrant special treatment. For example, embezzlement might be justified on the grounds that it isn't really stealing since they intend to pay the money back. Walters also claims that the idea that pathological gambling is an uncontrollable disease (as Gamblers Anonymous maintains), is another example of entitlement since it gives gamblers permission to think that they are powerless to control their "addiction." It is therefore the means by which they give themselves permission to gamble.

Power orientation refers to the need of many gamblers to feel "in control" in order to have a positive self-image. When they are losing this feeling evaporates and their sense of self-worth is threatened. In an effort to eliminate their feelings of powerlessness, many gamblers attempt to gain control over other people and other situations.

Sentimentality refers to the ploy of doing good things for others so that they can disavow the consequences of their life-style and maintain a positive self-image. By giving to charities or lavishing their spouses and others with money or expensive gifts, for example, they are able to preserve and project an image of themselves as good people who do nice things for others.

Superoptimism refers to the belief that gamblers can escape the consequences of their behavior indefinitely. It originates in the initial successes they often have in surviving various gambling-related crises. They may reinforce this notion by obsessively learning as much as possible about their preferential form of gambling and perhaps developing an "infallible" system for winning. Chasing one's losses is one of the more common results of superoptimism.

Cognitive indolence refers to the gamblers' tendency to look for short cuts in solving their problems and attaining their goals. Rather than assessing their plans in a realistic and rational fashion, they seek out and take the seemingly quickest and easiest route to success. Unfortunately, this is often the most dangerous choice since it results in very poor money management which sets the stage for imminent failure.

Discontinuity refers to the ability of many gamblers to compartmentalize their lives and act as two entirely different people. On one hand they may act as respectable and honorable pillars of the community; on the other hand they may also be resorting to criminal activities to support their gambling habit. Inconsistent or uncharacteristic behavior is a key indicator of discontinuity.

Behavioral Styles

According to Walters, the gambling lifestyle is characterized by four behavioral styles. The combination of a gambler's cognitions, personal conditions or risk factors for gambling (i.e., genetics, personality and other psychological factors, family, friends, finances, etc.), and personal choices will determine the degree to which any of these behavioral styles will be adopted.

Pseudoresponsibility describes to the pretense of responsibility that many gamblers are able to maintain. They do so, for example, by holding steady jobs, paying most of their bills, and avoiding arrest. These external appearances are false, however, since in reality they are unable to meet the emotional needs of their families, friends, and other important people in their lives. Walters contrasted this behavioral style with the complete irresponsibility of the criminal lifestyle. Like the drug addict, however, the gambler's ability to maintain a pseudoresponsible behavioral style diminishes as the gambling problem becomes more severe. He suggested that the reason drug abuse, crime, and gambling occur together so often is because they are overlapping life-styles. Consequently, as a person's commitment to any of these life-styles increases, so does the probability that he will fall into one or both of the others.

Self-ascension characterizes those who seek altered senses of identity and consciousness that committed gamblers achieve through the rapid and dramatic emotional shifts they continually experience. According to Walters, rapid mood swings from despair at losing to elation at winning and back again are responsible for the gambler's growing reliance on and deepening commitment to gambling to solve all of life's problems.

Hypercompetitiveness refers to those who need to crush their opponents whether they are other card players, bookies, dealers, croupiers, slot machines, or video games. According to Walters, the intense feelings of power, domination, and satisfaction that winning induces provide the "action" that gamblers crave. For gamblers, the "rush" of winning is similar to the high that drug addicts feel and the excitement that criminals experience when committing and getting away with crimes.

Social rule breaking/bending/twisting is typical of those whose commitment to gambling overrides all other commitments and obligations. Gambling has become so important to them that they will do anything it takes to be able to gamble even if it means suspending normative rules of social conduct. Experts at lying and deception, they personify the quintessential self-serving con artist.

Stages of Gambling Involvement

According to Walters, the individual who has chosen a gambling life-style typically passes through four consecutive stages of gambling involvement:

The *pre-life-style stage* of involvement is characterized by occasional gambling motivated by such psychological, social, or physical influences as curiosity, peer pressure, and/or sensation-seeking, as well as a belief that gambling can provide amusement. At this stage gambling is one of many possible diversions that offer entertainment and excitement. Most individuals either stop gambling, learn to gamble in a moderate and controlled manner, or advance to the next stage of involvement.

The *early stage* of gambling involvement is marked by the growing preoccupation with gambling that accompanies an increasing commitment to the gambling life-style. According to Walters, this stage can be precipitated either by an early big win, by a devastating loss or "bad beat," or by a series of big wins and "bad beats."

The *advanced stage* is characterized by a complete commitment to gambling, a nearly total preoccupation with gambling, and gambling that is out of control. The gambler's thoughts and cognitions focus only on the positive and immediately gratifying aspects of gambling such as the "high" to the exclusion of any that are negative or rational such as monetary losses.

The *burnout/maturity stage* represents the point at which the strength of the gambler's commitment to the gambling lifestyle begins to diminish. Walters believed that with age and the concomitant accumulation of negative experiences, all impulse-disorder life-styles–including drug abuse, criminality, and gambling–eventually begin to alter in conformance with the behavioral norms of greater society. Thus occurs because the behavior no longer provides the thrill it once did and, as a result, the individual begins to mature psychologically and to regard his preoccupation with gambling and past gambling activities with disgust and remorse. Walters compared this stage to the well-known "mid-life crisis" phenomenon faced by many middle-aged people when they begin to reassess their career and other life choices. This stage can sometimes be hastened by intervention and maintained through such measures as stress management training, the substitution of other pastimes for gambling, and the avoidance of gambling-related cues, gambling peers, and gambling opportunities.

CRITIQUE OF COGNITIVE-BEHAVIORAL THEORY

Tests of the influence of gamblers' cognitions on their gambling behaviors have yielded mixed results. One investigation found that frequent and problem gamblers did report beliefs in luck and the efficacy of chasing as important reasons for gambling.[75] Another found that while most casino gamblers expected to win at least somewhat more money than they would lose, the heaviest and most committed high-frequency gamblers consistently expected to win far greater amounts and held the strongest beliefs in their ability to win.[76] As previously noted, the failure of some researchers to replicate Langer's findings on the "illusion of control" was explained by her failure to distinguish between primary (direct) and secondary (predictive) illusory control. However, other researchers have questioned the utility of the entire "locus of control" concept in explaining the initiation and perpetuation of gambling sessions. Some investigators have found that while individual differences in people's needs for, and illusions of, control may influence gambling behavior once they are engaged in it, "a desire to control events is not what drives people to begin or maintain excessive levels of gambling"[77] since excessive gamblers (GA members) tend to have an external locus of control orientation. Others contend that differences in locus of control orientation are determined more by culturally instilled class and gender role expectations than by individual personality factors.[78] Still others have been unable to find any significant relationship between the locus of control scores of treated pathological gamblers and their likelihood of relapse.[79] Likewise, the "gambler's fallacy" has been demonstrated in some studies but not in others. Some have found that expectations of winning and bet sizes both tend to increase after each loss until a win occurred.[80] This phenomenon was also observed in a study which found that most roulette players, when playing only red or black, would bet on black if red had just won and on red if black had just won.[81] However, the "gambler's fallacy" failed to materialize in an experiment which found that students tended to increase the size of their bets after winning and decrease them after losing.[82]

Michael Walker[83] found that in comparison with occasional and regular off-track bettors, heavy gamblers thought they were better able to predict the outcome of the next race, thought they were more skillful handicappers, changed their selection at the last minute to gain the best odds advantage, and chased their losses to a greater extent. He interpreted these results as strong support for his sociocognitive theory. However, several other studies of gamblers' subjective thoughts and feelings concerning their likelihood of winning failed to support the cognitive or "expectancy" hypothesis.[84] Even Walker himself, champion of the sociocognitive approach, admitted that "the data available on poker [slot] machine playing does not fit the cognitive explanation at all well."[85]

The high frequency of irrational thoughts that have been reported in studies using the "thinking aloud" method probably should not be taken too literally since people who express irrational thoughts do not necessarily take them literally themselves. For example, just because some players may talk to a slot machine and beg it to pay or curse it when it fails to pay does not mean that they actually believe the machine is animated by a consciousness of its own and is therefore capable of choosing whether or not to act on these supplications and admonishments as some researchers imply. Many such utterances are probably intended to be far more symbolic or figurative than literal; even atheists call out the names of deities in their cursing and swearing. Nevertheless, since the beliefs, expectancies, and biases that are held by so many gamblers show promise in providing at least a partial explanation of gambling persistence and chasing despite even heavy losses, cognitive theory should continue to generate considerable research in the future. However, since cognitive explanations also raise the "chicken and egg" question, it will be important to determine whether these erroneous beliefs represent a rationale or a rationalization for gambling.

Some of the arguments that cognitive theorists have invoked to counter opposing viewpoints are themselves clear illustrations of irrational thinking. For example, some psychologists maintain that adoption of the term "pathological" to describe one's gambling is not a question of degree, but of timing. However, the argument that people who gamble heavily and regularly are not "pathological" gamblers until they have lost enough money and encountered sufficient social or legal problems to force them to enter a treatment program that designates them as such is unrealistic. The clear implication of this argument is that people in these circumstances readily adopt these labels only as a psychological defense mechanism, to avoid feeling any responsibility for the adverse consequences of their previous behavior. This argument is every bit as questionable as maintaining that habitual, chronically intoxicated heavy drinkers cannot be considered "alcoholics" until they enter a treatment program that designates them as such, that habitual smokers are not really nicotine "addicts" until they are hospitalized for lung cancer or emphysema, or that drug dealers, serial rapists, professional killers, and mob bosses become "criminals" only after being tried and convicted by a legal system that designates them as such. Can the behavior of those who have gambled away their family's life savings, embezzled from their employers, or resorted to armed robbery to obtain gambling money be considered nonpathological just because they have not yet joined GA? Can those who choose suicide before seeking help be considered "normal" gamblers just because they never entered a treatment program? Obviously, the behavior exhibited by many heavy gamblers can be considered problematic or "pathological" long before they seek help.

The accusation that use of the terms "compulsion" and "disease" in reference to problem gambling constitutes the *raison d'etre* of those who favor the medical model violates a cardinal rule of logic. Any criticism that is levelled against the value of people themselves rather than against the value of the ideas they hold represents the logical fallacy of *argumentum ad hominem*. Examples of *ad hominem* (literally, "to the man") attacks are particularly evident in the statements of ideological partisan politicians and religious zealots when they attempt to disparage the words and ideas of their opponents: "Well, naturally he'd say something like that, he's a liberal / conservative / Catholic / Protestant / Moslem / Jew / atheist!" Obviously, any attempt to discredit a message by attempting to discredit the messenger is fallacious since the character of the person carrying the message has no relevance to the validity of the message itself. However, the use of such arguments in this context are actually not at all surprising since debates over whether addictive gambling, drinking, and drug use are "diseases" or "learned behavioral responses" are currently highly charged political issues in the field of addiction studies. Those in the other camp might be just as likely to attempt the same ploy (and perhaps some already have): "Well, naturally he'd say that, he's a behaviorist! Convincing others that addictive behaviors are learned is his *raison d'etre* because then he can proceed to make a very comfortable living by claiming to be able to turn compulsive gamblers into normal gamblers and alcoholics into normal drinkers." Here, too, of course, the argument would still have no relevance to the issue at hand. Arguments and indictments that those who adhere to one theory or another are merely mercenaries who are trying to justify their own existence are fruitless, senseless, and entirely unwarranted. Although they may be useful to the extent that they might disclose something of the motivations of the *theorist* who voices them, they do nothing to further our understanding of the motivations of the *addict*, the question with which we are actually concerned.

Finally, as a prison psychologist, Glenn Walters admitted that his Gambling Lifestyle Theory was based on a "small, biased sample of incarcerated males"[86] and conceded that the burnout/maturity stage was the most controversial feature of his theory. Unlike the medical or disease model which maintains that pathological gambling, alcoholism, and other drug addictions are permanent and immutable disorders, Walters contended that these are temporary and mutable conditions. Allowing that there may, indeed, be gamblers who do not reach the final burnout and maturity stage, however, he acknowledged that his theory would require much more empirical study before it could be accepted and generalized to all problem gamblers. Nevertheless, his additional cognitive factors–many of which can be seen as rationalizations for continued gambling–constitute an original contribution to our understanding of gambling behavior.

8

CONCLUDING SUMMARY

This volume has reviewed the most influential psychodynamic and psychological theories that have been advanced to explain why people gamble and continue to do so even when they consistently lose more than they win. Psychodynamic explanations include psychoanalytic and personality theories: the former explain excessive gambling as a consequence of some deep-seated emotional trauma while the latter explain them as a consequence of one's basic personality type. Psychological explanations include behavioral or learning theories and cognitive or cognitive-behavioral theories: the former explain all degrees of gambling as learned response patterns which are reinforced through intermittent monetary and/or emotional rewards; the latter explain gambling persistence as a consequence of the irrational beliefs gamblers have about gambling and their ability to win.

Psychoanalytic Approaches to Gambling

Psychoanalytic theories are based on a number of untestable, therefore, undemonstrable and indefensible assumptions, all of which have been incorporated into various explanations for compulsive gambling. Included among them are the suppositions that 1) a great deal of human mental activity is subliminal, taking place at the level of unconsciousness, 2) much of our behavior is instinctive, impelled by the subliminal motivations housed in a universally shared "collective unconscious" which retains all the biologically inherited baser instincts and "racial memories" of our earliest human ancestors, 3) the libidinous or sexual drives and Oedipal impulses contained in the collective unconscious are experienced even in infancy, 4) all human beings pass through the same psychosexual stages of personality development (oral, anal, phallic, and genital) as they mature and that the guilt feelings experienced when these libidinous desires appear in childhood are sometimes intense enough to cause personality fixations at these stages which are responsible for various neuroses in adulthood, 5) all humans are born inherently bisexual and become either hetero- or homosexual as a consequence of the environment influences they experience during the maturation process, and 6) the phenomenon of sublimation, the substitution of more acceptable behaviors such as drinking and gambling, for others that are unconsciously desired but which are so socially and/or morally unacceptable, such as the fulfillment of one's Oedipal desires, that cannot be overtly expressed.

These assumptions are readily apparent in the writings of all psychoanalytic theorists who have attempted to explain the motivations underlying gambling:

- Hans Von Hattingberg felt that compulsive gambling represented a quest for parental love, a substitute for unrestricted defecation that was so pleasurable in infancy, and a masochistic need for punishment.

- Ernst Simmel agreed that gambling represented an anal fixation but added that it also represented unresolved dependency needs and a masochistic need for self-punishment as well as a sadistic need to punish others.

- Wilhelm Stekel saw compulsive gambling as the love of play and a regressive escape from the harsh reality of adulthood into an fantasy world of childhood. For him gambling was a substitute for latent sadistic homosexual love that serves both to reduce tension and to incite arousal.

- Sigmund Freud explained compulsive gambling as fixation at the phallic stage of psychosexual development that serves both as a substitute for masturbation and as a punishment for guilt over the incestuous Oedipal fantasies and parricidal death wishes that accompany this proscribed activity.

- Otto Fenichel also explained gambling as a sublimated masturbatory activity resulting from a fixation at the phallic stage. However, he added the idea that Fate, a universal father figure, represents an oracle through which the gambler hopes to determine whether his unconscious incestuous fantasies will be realized or punished.

- Edmund Bergler saw compulsive gambling as an attempt to regain infantile omnipotence as well as an expression of "psychic masochism" or self-punishment for the guilt the gambler feels over the rage and hatred he directed toward his parents, especially during the weaning but also during the toilet training processes. Thus, for Bergler, compulsive gambling resulted from a fixation primarily at the oral, but also at the anal stage of psychosexual development.

- For Ralph Greenson, compulsive gambling incorporated elements from all stages of psychosexual development. Fate, he reasoned, repesented both a mother and a father figure.

- Darrell Bolen and William Boyd, who originally accepted the ideas of their predecessors, eventually broke with the orthodox psychoanalytic tradition when they noted the familial aspects of gambling, recognized that it can serve social as well as psychological needs, and suggested that it can provide an emotional defense against other psychiatric problems. Their observations led them to reject the idea that gambling is an unconscious substitute for sex.

- Peter Fuller, who incorporated anthropological and Marxist theories into his explanation, traced the origin of gambling to the shamanic divinatory rituals of our ancestors. He felt that the need for religious expression, like other unconscious pregenital drives, was also instinctive and that both gambling and religious expression are motivated by guilt over parricidal impulses. The Protestant establishment objects to gambling not because it is inherently immoral, but as a reaction against the strong appeal that gambling, which is only superficially different from capitalism, secretly has for them. Capitalists, antigambling moralists, and compulsive gamblers are all anally fixated.

- Richard Rosenthal, a contemporary psychoanalyst, attributed the origin of pathological gambling to an anal fixation. However, it is maintained by an array of emotional defense mechanisms which buttress the gambler's illusions and fantasies about gambling and enable him to deceive himself and others.

- David Newmark saw gambling not only as a religious means of divining fate, but also as an escape mechanism that removes the gambler from the reality of daily life by providing him with the illusion of any positive personal quality (power, control, self-confidence, etc.) that he chooses to project onto it.

Psychoanalytic theory has been criticized on numerous grounds. It is unscientific since the assumptions on which it is based are untestable and therefore invalid. The conclusions of many psychoanalytic theorists are based on only a small number of case histories rendering them ungeneralizable to the general population. There is no real evidence to support the contention that gambling is a substitute for masturbation and its accompanying Oedipal sexual fantasies or that gamblers are masochists who unconsciously wish to lose to expiate their guilt feelings. Neither is there any concrete evidence to support the idea that the personality of compulsive gamblers is arrested at any stage of development: the "symbolic evidence" that is cited as proof of any such fixation is not only illusory but it is also open to a multitude of interpretations. Such male-oriented explanations are unable to account for gambling among women. With their focus on abnormal gambling psychoanalytic explanations also are unable to account for the far more common occurrence of normative gambling. With their focus on internal psychodynamic mechanisms they ignore any external social and other environmental factors that may influence gambling behavior. Finally, as a treatment method, psychoanalysis is time-consuming, expensive, and ineffective.

Personality and Gambling

Personality theory assumes that individual behavior is a consequence of one's basic personality type. Most early personality theorists, strongly influenced by psychoanalytic theory, agreed that all aberrant behaviors are a consequence of one's childhood experiences and were generally thought to involve either some overindulgence or severe deprivational trauma. However, others were convinced that every person's basic personality is genetically determined at birth and persists throughout life irrespective of their experiences. In either case, personality theorists insisted that maladaptive behaviors are the direct consequence of a basic personality defect. Pathological gamblers and drug addicts are therefore characterized as a homogeneous group of individuals all sharing the same personality structure. The goal of personality research was therefore to identify which personality traits or trait clusters are responsible for these behvaiors.

Two of the most popular approaches to addictive behaviors are power theory and dependency conflict theory, both of which trace the maladaptive behavior to feelings of low self-esteem. Power theory attributes all addictive disorders to an inferiority complex caused by a lack of achievement, material wealth, and control over one's own life. When the gambler is winning these feelings are replaced by illusions of success, power, and self-worth which he attempts to perpetuate through continued gambling. When he is losing, the heightened sensations of inferiority and powerlessness he now feels cause him to intensify his gambling not only to recoup his losses but also to regain the sense of mastery and power he craves.

Dependency conflict theory traces addictive behaviors to an arrested personality development resulting from unresolved needs for parental support and dependence. In adulthood these immature dependency needs clash with society's demands for autonomy and independence. This unconscious emotional conflict produces high levels of stess and anxiety that can be temporarily relieved by gambling, alcohol, and other drugs. These behaviors become maladaptive when the addict's relationship with them are preferred to mature interpersonal relationships.

Like psychoanalytic theory, personality theory has been criticized on the grounds that it lacks the support of empirical evidence. Although countless pathological gamblers and other addicts have been administered countless psychometric tests, no single personality type or profile has emerged that is unique to them or which can distinguish them from anyone else. In fact, few psychometric test results are complementary and many are contradictory. Although they often reveal that the gambler is anxious or depressed, they are unable to determine whether these conditions are a cause or a consequence of gambling. Some studies have concluded that gamblers are, in fact, emotionally healthier and better adjusted than nongamblers. Finally, personality research also suffers from sampling bias since the subjects of most of these tests were recruited not from the general population but from Gamblers Anonymous and other treatment populations whose members were mostly white, middle-class, middle-aged, affluent males. Thus, females and those from other age, income, and ethnic groups are grossly underrepresented.

Behavioral Psychological Approaches to Gambling

Learning or reinforcement theory is similar to psychoanalytic theory in that both approaches ascribe gambling to environmental influences. However, unlike psychoanalytic theorists who see compulsive gambling as a consequence of a personality fixation stemming from some unconscious emotional trauma experienced in infancy or early childhood, learning theorists see excessive gambling as a consciously learned habitual response to immediate external stimuli that can appear at any stage of life. Furthermore, psychoanalytic theorists see a qualitative difference between compulsive and normal gamblers while learning theorists do not: the former see compulsive gamblers as mentally ill or neurotic while the latter see excessive gambling merely as that point along a continuum of gambling involvement at which heavy gamblers begin to encounter financial and social problems. Finally, psychoanalytic theory is based on inference, speculation, and deductive reasoning–the methods of philosophy–while learning theory is based on observation, measurement, experimentation, and inductive reasoning–the methods of empirical science.

The two basic types of learning that are responsible for repetitive behavior patterns are Skinnerian or operant conditioning and Pavlovian or classical conditioning. The basic premise of the former is that a habitual voluntary response to any stimulus represents a learned behavior and anything that is learned can be unlearned. Repetitive behaviors are reinforced by the rewards that are experienced as a result of these behaviors. In the case of gambling these rewards can be monetary, emotional, or both. Rewards that occur on a regular basis, for example, after every three trials, are said to occur on a fixed-interval or FI schedule of reinforcement. Those that are presented randomly and unpredictably are said to occur on variable-ratio or VR schedules. Conditioned responses that are learned under FI schedules can become extinguished rapidly after the reward is discontinued while those that are learned under VR schedules persist for much longer periods after the reward is withheld.

According to behavioral psychologist B. F. Skinner, excessive gamblers are victims of the VR schedules of reinforcement which are inherent in all games of chance. He noted that professional gamblers often condition their opponents by allowing them to win more frequently at the beginning of a game but gradually "stretch" the reward schedule so that the opponents continually win less frequently. Other manipulatable factors that can reinforce gambling persistence are the size of the potential reward, the availability of gambling opportunities, a range of odds and stakes, the degree of skill involved, probabilities of winning, takeout and payout ratios, the time between bets, and the time between a win and payout.

The structural characteristics of specific gambling games can also encourage persistence. Included among them are the degree to which betting is associated with other activities such as sporting events, the use of chips or tokens in place of real money, certain mechanical features such as the ratio of winning to losing symbols on the various reels of a slot machine, and whether the game involves continuous or discontinuous betting. Continuous forms such as slot machines and blackjack involve a rapid succession of plays per gambling session while discontinuous forms such as lotteries and raffle drawings require much longer periods between the time a bet is made and its outcome is known.

The basic premise of the classical or Pavlovian conditioning model is that an involuntary reflexive response to a specific stimulus can be elicited by an environmental cue that is regularly presented in association with that stimulus. Thus, after pairing an audio stimulus with the presentation of food, behavioral psychologist I. P. Pavlov was able to elicit the salivation response in dogs merely by the presentation of the audio stimulus which the animals had involuntarily learned to associate with feeding. He therefore found that one stimulus can produce the expectation of a second stimulus as well as the behavioral response that the latter elicits. Adherents of this approach feel that new gambling sessions can be initiated by external environmental cues that the gambler has learned to associate with the rewards of gambling. Thus, the croupier's call, the sight or sound of chips or coins, the spinning of a gaming wheel, or the shuffling of cards can induce states of arousal, excitement, tension, or anxiety that can reinforce the gambling response and perhaps even contribute to the onset of addiction.

Some behavioral theories of gambling are based on Skinnerian principles, others are based on Pavlovian principles, and still others explain it as a combination of both influences. A number of behavioral psychologists have offered their own variants of reinforcement theory to explain the ways in which persistent gambling is fostered.

Need-state theories explain gambling as a response to certain physical and emotional drives or needs which are satisfied by the gambling response. These aversive emotional need-states may be either instinctive or learned. One instinctive drive is thought to be the need for recreation or play. Gambling is an adult form of play that offers amusement, enjoyment, a challenge, a form of escape from the reality of a routine daily existence. The "action" of gambling describes both the enjoyable excitement it generates and the escape from reality it provides. When our involvement in gambling and the fantasy world it creates begin to dominate our thoughts it can no longer be considered play but an obsession or pathology.

Behaviorists who advocate the tension-reduction model maintain that gambling and other addictive behaviors reduce an emotional drive that is experienced as stress, anxiety, and/or depression. Since gambling, alcohol, and other drugs serve as analgesics which act to reduce these unpleasant emotional states and replace them with enjoyable ones, persistence is thought to be negatively reinforced by the reward of tension- or anxiety-reduction they provide. Thus, excessive drinking, drug use, and gambling, which some theorists believe to be "functional equivalents" since they often accompany or substitute for one another, are said to be "acquired drives" or "bad habits" that are learned as coping mechanisms. The high rates of recidivism among alcoholics, drug addicts, and compulsive gamblers is believed to result from the incomplete extinction of their preferred coping response. Some research studies supports tension-reduction theory while others do not.

Proponents of the sensation-seeking or arousal approach feel that addictive behaviors are reinforced by the pleasurable mood states they induce. Those who are chronically bored and in need of stimulation will therefore seek out ways to experience higher levels of excitement and exhilaration. Those most likely to become addicts are those who have the highest needs for arousal. Pathological gambling and other addictions are therefore seen as forms of self-medication through which the addict attempts to maintain an optimal level of emotional arousal.

Mark Dickerson proposed a dual-reinforcement hypotheses when he suggested that persistent racetrack betting is reinforced in two ways. The emotional reward or "action" is not derived from winning but from betting, and the closer a bet is placed to the start of a race, the greater will be the level of excitement it generates. Because every race is regularly timed and every bet is equally exciting, the reward of emotional arousal is delivered on a FI reinforcement schedule. The reward of money, which occurs intermittently since not every bet is a winner, is delivered on a VR reinforcement schedule.

R. I. F. Brown also felt that gambling is reinforced more by the emotional rewards it provides than by monetary rewards but argued that these, too, occur on a VR schedule since the ability of gambling to maintain a constant hedonic state is unreliable. Inconsistent emotional reinforcement not only exacerbates the need for stimulation, but also accounts for reinstatement of addictive behaviors after the "reinforcement chain" of rewards has been broken.

In a later attempt to reconcile the tension-reduction and sensation-seeking explanations, Brown also claimed that gambling, like alcohol and other drugs, has bi-phasic effects since it can act as both a stimulant and a tranquilizer and is therefore used to satisfy both needs either simultaneously or consecutively. Like other addicts, gamblers experience arousal while they are engaged in their addictive behavior and become depressed when they stop. He explained withdrawal symptoms as a rebound of the negative emotional state they attempt to reduce through gambling, drinking, or drug use and which they alleviate by repeating whichever behavioral response they have learned. Thus, addictive behaviors serve not only to induce pleasant emotional states but also to relieve unpleasant ones. According to Brown, these effects are also delivered on a VR schedule of reinforcement.

Few arousal theorists are concerned with particular schedules of reinforcement but contend that the "action" of gambling, no matter how regularly or irregularly it is experienced, is the key to persistence. Thus, some feel that winning and losing are unimportant except for the role they play in sustaining "action." Others feel that losing actually contributes to the "action" since some gamblers experience a thrill in anticipating and dealing with the potentially harmful consequences of loss.

Skinnerian reinforcement theory with its emphasis on operant conditioning has been criticized for a number of shortcomings. Its advocates maintain that the intermittent monetary rewards presented to gamblers reinforce persistence. However, its critics argue that because the subjects studied by behavioral psychologists are usually laboratory animals, their findings cannot be generalized to humans whose thought processes are far more complex. Moreover, laboratory animals who are conditioned to pull levers or peck at buttons to receive a reward of food are not subjected to the continuous schedule of losses that are sustained by regular casino gamblers and slot machine players, for example. Consequently, this approach has also been criticized on the grounds that it does not reflect the reality of gambling since consistent losses should extinguish the gambling response. However, this does not occur among compulsive gamblers. Laboratory experiments using human subjects also have been criticized as unrealistic since the experimental design and potential payoff do not resemble real gambling situations: they usually involve college students who may be occasional or even nongamblers rather than regular gamblers, the subjects do not risk any of their own money, and the researchers do not distinguish recreational from problem gamblers.

The operant conditioning model has several other weaknesses, as well. It cannot explain persistence among lottery players who have never won nor the resumption of excessive gambling after long periods of abstinence when the "chain of reinforcement" has been broken. Reinforcement theory also is unable to explain why some people become heavy or excessive gamblers while others do not even though they have been exposed to the same schedule of reinforcement. Opponents of reinforcement theory argue that if compulsive gambling is indeed the result of intermittent reinforcement then everyone who has ever gambled should be a compulsive gambler. These critics contend that excessive or compulsive gambling must therefore involve factors other than monetary rewards and intermittent schedules of reinforcement. They suggest instead that it is not the actual reward or the reinforcement sequence that furthers persistence among humans, but their ability to hope for and anticipate a reward as well as the altered emotional and physical states that gambling produces.

The arousal or sensation-seeking model, which maintains that excessive gambling is reinforced by emotional rather than monetary rewards, actually involves two distinct propositions. The first, the arousal hypothesis, is that gambling generates emotional excitement. The second, the sensation-seeking hypothesis, is that gambling is motivated by boredom or hypoarousal. Tests of the first proposition have yielded mixed results. While many heavy gamblers claim the subjective experience of a "high" while gambling, others claim to feel no emotional changes. Moreover, objective measures of such autonomic responses as heart rate, blood pressure, brain wave activity, and skin conductance of test subjects do not consistently support these claims: some studies have found significant increases in these physiological activities after the start of a gambling session, some found insignificant increases, some found no differences, some found that an initial increase was not maintained throughout the session, and some reported that the autonomic responses of their subjects actually decreased when they started gambling. Tests of the second proposition, that the need for arousal motivates gambling, are also inconsistent and inconclusive: only very small percentages of test subjects claim to gamble for excitement and most studies involving the use of psychometric instruments designed to measure levels of boredom and the need for stimulation in their subjects have yielded mixed but mostly nonsupportive results. Studies of the "late betting" phenomenon, which is believed to generate even higher levels of excitement, also failed to support this hypothesis.

Despite the lack of empirical evidence to support the sensation-seeking hypotheses, its advocates are reluctant to reject it. Instead they suggest that individual differences may be involved: different people respond differently to different forms of gambling and will therefore gravitate toward those forms that are more suited to their individual emotional needs. Thus low sensation-seekers may prefer slot machines to reduce anxiety and stress while high sensation-seekers may prefer racetrack betting or casino games to reduce boredom. Recent studies have distinguished between "escape seekers" who gamble to avoid unpleasant situations and "action seekers" who gamble for excitement. There may also be gender differences in these motivations since escape seeking was reported to be more common among women who gamble while action seeking was more common among men.

The tension-reduction hypothesis has also been criticized as untenable. One critic argued that the idea is merely a reified concept based on a model of energy discharge employed in the physical sciences and is therefore invalid when it is adapted for use in the behavioral sciences. Other critics have argued that few empirical studies have actually shown gambling to have a tranquilizing effect. Instead, some studies have found that negative emotional states are, in fact, exacerbated rather than relieved by gambling and that they therefore serve to decrease the duration of gambling sessions and inhibit the initiation of new ones. Likewise, while some studies have found that escape is often given as a subjective reason for gambling, far more have found that most frequent self-reported motivations are money and entertainment.

Other critics of need-state models also raise the "chicken and egg" question since studies supporting them generally report only an association between gambling and certain emotional states. They are incapable of determining whether these associations are causal or, if they are, the direction of causality. That is, are pre-existing dysphoric mood states the cause of excessive gambling or do they develop as a consequence of it? Clearly, additional research will be required to resolve this question and other issues related to the ways in which excessive gambling is reinforced.

Cognitive-Behavioral Approaches to Gambling

Cognitive-behavioral psychologists feel that gambling persistence is a consequence of the unrealistic thoughts and irrational beliefs that gamblers have about the nature of gambling and their ability to win. Excessive gamblers can be influenced by a variety of irrational beliefs and thought processes, many of which are often held simultaneously.

Gamblers frequently base their betting choices on biased judgments, one example of which is their tendency to make biased estimates of probabilities. Studies have demonstrated that instead of basing their decisions on the objective, mathematically determined probabilities of winning, gamblers frequently overestimate their chances of success. This is particularly evident among regular lottery players and long-shot bettors whose chances of winning are extremely poor. They are also inclined to make biased evaluations of outcomes on the basis of their desires. Irrational overconfidence of this sort is especially common among sports enthusiasts who tend to bet on their personally favorite athletes or teams rather than on those that are actually most likely to win. Research has verified that sports fans are more likely to bet according to their hopes and wishes rather than to any other criteria.

Gamblers who are committed to particular betting systems often resort to a form of denial referred to as hindsight bias which enables them to rationalize their losses by making biased evaluations of the outcomes of past events. Thus, rather than admit that their system is flawed and they really cannot control chance outcomes, they recast their losses in a more favorable light. Such hindsight biases commonly occur in situations in which losses can be explained away as flukes caused by random, uncontrollable, external events rather to any deficiency in their own skill or expertise at picking winners. It is therefore common to hear gamblers explain their losses through such statements as the track was wet and the horse stumbled, the player missed the winning catch because the wind shifted, the officials made the wrong call, the fight was fixed, etc. Losers see flukes as the most important determinants of events and seize upon them to justify their losses while winners discount them as irrelevant since the outcome was precisely what they had predicted in the first place.

Selective memory bias refers to the similar tendency of gamblers to remember their past wins and forget their past losses. This form of denial allows them to minimize the extent of their involvement and the consequences of their gambling.

Near misses or near wins that occur when the gambler's horse loses by a nose or a favored team loses by only a few points, for example, are especially likely to result in biased evaluations. Biases of this sort encourage persistence not only by allowing gamblers to avoid taking any responsibility for their own mistakes, but also by reinforcing the illusion that the superiority of their system, their skills, and their knowledge will continue to enable them to control and predict future events. The near miss phenomenon also encourages persistence among slot machine and lottery players since "almost winning" further reinforces these behaviors. For this reason slot machines and instant lotteries are often designed to yield higher percentages of near misses than would occur if their outcomes were truly random. Because flukes can turn losses into near wins, and because near wins validate the gambler's betting system, biased evaluations are seen as important factors in justifying erroneous betting strategies and encouraging persistence despite heavy losses.

The "gambler's fallacy" refers to the belief that past outcomes are predictive of future outcomes. Many gamblers look for patterns or streaks and then bet accordingly. It is therefore common to see gamblers increase the size of their bets after each loss in the belief that every successive loss increases their chance of winning on the next play. In reality, the odds of heads or tails, red or black, odd or even, etc., remain the same for every trial irrespective of all previous outcomes. However, many gamblers are just as susceptible to the converse belief that a series of past outcomes is likely to continue.

Thus, some will bet only on "hot" lottery numbers, horses, or jockeys because they expect them to continue to win while others will bet against them solely on the basis of the belief that they are overdue for a loss.

Attribution theorists examine the reasons and rationalizations that gamblers give for their successes and failures. Their studies have found that gamblers often attribute their successes to some internal quality such as superior skill or knowledge but attribute their failures to external factors such as bad luck, chance, or divine intervention which are beyond their control. Those with an external locus of control orientation are more likely to ascribe their successes and failures to these uncontrollable factors while those with an internal locus of control orientation are more likely to ascribe them to their own behavioral choices. Attribution theorists have found that people with an external locus of control orientation tend to prefer games of chance while those with an internal locus of control orientation prefer games of skill.

Initial cognitive-behavioral research revealed that the acquisition and maintenance of gambling behavior can be encouraged by inducing an illusion of control over purely chance outcomes. It is well known to commercial gambling interests that any kind of active involvement by their patrons, such as choosing their own keno and roulette numbers or personally throwing the dice, fosters the belief that they can enhance their chances of winning by having at least some degree of control over an outcome which is, in fact, uncontrollable. Many games of pure chance therefore incorporate elements that are designed to inspire a simulated skill orientation. More recent research has revealed the existence of two kinds of illusory control: primary illusory control refers to the belief that gamblers, through their personal actions, can influence outcomes directly; secondary illusory control refers to the belief that they can predict future outcomes. The former is stronger in test subjects having an internal locus of control orientation while the latter is stronger in those with an external locus of control orientation.

The risky shift phenomenon refers to the fact that familiarity with a particular gambling game encourages persistence and greater risk. Thus, the longer gamblers participate in a particular form of gambling, the larger their bets become irrespective of their locus of control orientation or of how much they may win or lose in the process. The risky shift phenomenon is especially apparent in group situations but solitary gamblers also exhibit dramatic increases in bet sizes over relatively short periods of time. Moreover, bet sizes increase not only during individual gambling sessions but also between them.

The early win hypothesis attributes excessive gambling to an early history of positive reinforcement and the belief that this initial good fortune will continue. Thus, gamblers who have experienced a series of wins or a single exceptionally large win early in their gambling careers become convinced that the losses they experience later are only temporary and can be overcome through persistence. Although this hypothesis failed to find conclusive support in the initial studies that were designed to test it, it found strong support in later studies.

Persistence and chasing are often seen as the only logical solutions when gamblers are losing. Because they would have no chance of recouping their losses and possibly winning if they quit, they see continued betting as their only chance of breaking even. They therefore chase their losses, often increasing the size of their bets, in an effort to recover. In reality, however, since the odds always favor the house, the most probable outcome of chasing one's past losses is continued loss.

Casino managers know this and therefore do all that they can to extend every customer's playing time.

Entrapment is a common cause of persistence and chasing. This occurs when gamblers have lost so much that they feel they have passed the point of no return and cannot afford to quit. Gamblers can become entrapped in many ways: instead of cutting their losses by quitting, lottery and roulette players will continue to play the same numbers again and again, racetrack bettors will continue to bet on a particular horse or jockey, and slot machine players will keep playing a particular machine in the belief that it must eventually yield a jackpot.

Gamblers are commonly convinced that luck is a personal attribute that can be predicted and manipulated. Many believe that luck is a cyclically recurring phenomenon and that they will therefore experience periods during which they are luckier than others. One goal is to discover when their lucky periods are beginning so that they can bet accordingly. Dice and horse players often make the same bets as other gamblers who they believe are currently in one of their own lucky periods. Other goals involve a more direct manipulation of luck. For example, craps shooters often bet more when they are throwing the dice in the belief that through their personal touch they can inspire them to fall according to their wishes. Many gamblers believe that they can change their luck merely by changing dice, cards, tables, or machines.

Because they believe that luck can be manipulated, many gamblers engage in magical thinking and a wide variety of superstitious behaviors to increase their chances of winning. When they happen to win, the particular extraneous behavior they happened to be engaged in immediately prior to winning, or a particular item of clothing they were wearing, or an object they were holding at the time also becomes associated with winning. Thus, gamblers often perform specific ritualistic behaviors such as touching their noses or talking to the dice, the cards, or the machine either to bring good luck or banish bad luck before betting; they often have lucky ties, hats, socks, jewelry, or other good luck charms they wear religiously while gambling; they often rely on omens derived from license plates, radio reports, and birthdates in picking lottery numbers or horses. Such classical or Pavlovian conditioning is particularly likely to occur when reinforcement is random. Many gamblers are equally convinced that the outcomes of purely chance events can be influenced through the intervention of supernatural powers or entities which they are constantly trying to manipulate for their own personal benefit.

Cognitive-Behavioral Theorists

Cognitive-behavioral theorists often combine Skinnerian and Pavlovian learning processes with cognitive factors. The two primary Skinnerian reinforcers of gambling are monetary rewards and emotional arousal. The Pavlovian association of excitement with winning also serves to reinforce gambling behavior. The sound of coins hitting a metal tray, the croupier's call, track announcements, the sight of a spinning wheel, neatly piled chips, etc., then serve to induce the excitement that triggers a new gambling session. These learned associations, prior mood states, and the erroneous beliefs, thoughts, and assumptions concerning gambling outlined above are all thought to work in concert to contribute to the rapid acquisition and slow extinction of the gambling response.

- David Oldman, a sociologist who worked as a roulette croupier, observed that the betting strategies of most roulette players are based upon the gambler's fallacy. Many also believe that roulette is not really a game of chance since they are convinced that the outcome of each play can be controlled by the wheel spinner. They therefore employ betting strategies intended to overcome this perceived influence. Oldman felt that since most regulars regard gambling as a form of entertainment for which they pay with their losses, their primary objective is not so much to win money but to outwit the spinner and minimize the cost of playing.

- Mark Griffiths, a psychologist who studied adolescent fruit or slot machine players in the United Kingdom, found that both cognitive factors and the built-in structural characteristics of these machines work together to induce new gambling sessions and prolong existing ones. Griffiths felt that the ultimate goal of most players was to prolong their playing time rather than to win money.

- According to Michael Walker's sociocognitive theory, money rather than arousal, tension-reduction, or entertainment is the primary motivation for gambling. Persistent and excessive gambling are maintained by the irrational beliefs related to the gambler's expectations of winning rather than any monetary rewards that may actually be received. In addition to the standard cognitive factors that encourage persistence, Walker added an element of social learning theory. He suggested that persistence is also reinforced by the gambler's awareness of the successes of others whose large winnings have been publicized and the belief that these successes can be duplicated through imitation. The ultimate cause of gambling problems is not the act of gambling itself, but the losses and debt levels that can result from it.

- Mark Dickerson combined learning theory with cognitive theory to explain persistence and impaired control. However, rather than calling upon the same motivational principles to explain all forms of gambling, he suggested that different forms of gambling are likely to have different motivations. Thus, the principles of reinforcement theory may be more appropriate in accounting for slot machine gambling while those of cognitive theory may be more applicable to racetrack betting.

- R. I. F. Brown combined the principles of social learning theory, reinforcement theory, and cognitive theory to explain persistence. Social learning or modeling describes the process through which people acquire certain behaviors through the imitation of others, either their peers or those they regard as role models they are attempting to emulate. Brown felt that once the fundamentals of gambling were learned in this way, persistence would then be influenced by various environmental and cognitive factors that become associated with gambling.

- Glenn Walters, a psychologist at a correctional institution, combined elements of learning theory, social learning theory, cognitive theory, and existential philosophy to argue that pathological gambling is a consciously chosen life-style that gamblers adopt to combat feelings of anxiety, insecurity, low self-esteem, and powerlessness. Not only does gambling make one feel better, but it also leads to a distorted self-image that minimizes the extent of their involvement and the consequences of their behavior.

Tests of cognitive-behavioral theory have yielded mixed results since the idea that irrational beliefs and locus of control orientations strongly influence gambling behavior is supported by some studies but not by others. Nevertheless, since cognitive theory shows a great deal of promise in providing at least a partial explanation for excessive or pathological gambling, it should continue to generate considerable research. The grounds upon which some learning and cognitive theorists condemn theoretical explanations that do not accord with their own are often invalid or amount to little more than personal *ad hominem* attacks.

As much as some behavioral scientists would like us to believe that they alone hold the key to our understanding of gambling and its motivations, and as much as some of them would like to disavow the ideas of others, the contributions of those in other disciplines cannot be so readily dismissed without a thorough examination of all facets of their theories and the evidence they have marshalled to support them. Employing their own designs and methods, specialists in the social and medical sciences have conducted an enormous amount of research that has also contributed greatly to our knowledge and understanding of this complex phenomenon. Their achievements and explanations will be the focus of other volumes in this series.

Appendix A

SUMMARY OF FINDINGS IN PSYCHOMETRIC RESEARCH

Evidence for the following psychometric characteristics was reported by the authors listed below each.

Achievement Motivation (Need for Achievement), High
Moravec and Munley 1983
Custer, Meeland, and Krug 1984

Achievement Motivation, Low or Absent
Taber, Russo, Adkins, and McCormick 1986

Aggression
Dell, Ruzicka, and Palisi 1981
Kusyszyn and Rutter 1985
McCormick 1993

Passive-Aggression, High
Lowenfeld 1979
Glen 1979
Graham and Lowenfeld 1986

Passive-Aggression, Low or Absent
Specker, Carlson, Edmonson, Johnson, and Marcotte 1996

Agoraphobia
Linden, Pope, and Jonas 1986
Bland, Newman, Orn, and Stebelsky 1993

Alienation, Social
Roston 1965
Bolen, Caldwell, and Boyd 1975
Ciarrocchi, Kirschner, and Fallik 1991

Antisocial Personality Disorder/Sociopathy

Lowenfeld 1979
Glen 1979
Custer, Meeland, and Krug 1984
Graham and Lowenfeld 1986
Bland, Newman, Orn, and Stebelsky 1993
Kroeber 1992
Steel and Blaszczynski 1996
Blaszczynski, Steel, and McConaghy 1997
Steel and Blaszczynski 1998
Black and Moyer 1998

Anxiety, High

Glen 1979
Lowenfeld 1979
Blaszczynski, Buhrich, and McConaghy 1985
Blaszczynski, Wilson, and McConaghy 1986
Lorenz and Yaffee 1986
Linden, Pope, and Jonas 1986
Graham and Lowenfeld 1986
Taber, McCormick, and Ramirez 1987
Galski 1987
Martinez-Pina, Guirao de Parga, Fuste i Vallverdu, Planas, et al. 1991
Ciarrocchi, Kirschner, and Fallik 1991
Bland, Newman, Orn, and Stebelsky 1993
Bergh and Külhorn 1994
Steel and Blaszczynski 1996
Specker, Carlson, Edmonson, Johnson, and Marcotte 1996
Blaszczynski and Steel 1998

Anxiety, Low or Absent

Conrad 1978
Kusyszyn and Rutter 1985
Ladouceur and Mayrand 1986
Raviv 1993
Vitaro, Ladouceur, and Bujold 1996

Autonomy

Moravec and Munley 1983

Avoidance

Taber, McCormick, and Ramirez 1987
McCormick, Taber, and Kruedelbach 1989
Specker, Carlson, Edmonson, Johnson, and Marcotte 1996
Black and Moyer 1998

Bipolar Disorder/Manic-Depression

McCormick, Russo, Ramirez, and Taber 1984
Linden, Pope, and Jonas 1986
Lesieur and Blume 1990
Kroeber 1992

Boredom/Aversive Unipolar Resting State

Blaszczynski, McConaghy, and Frankova 1990
Martinez-Pina, Guirao de Parga, Fuste i Vallverdu, Planas, et al. 1991
Carroll and Huxley 1994
Steel and Blaszczynski 1996

Borderline Personality

Blaszczynski and Steel 1998

Co-Addiction with Substance Abuse, High

Greenson 1948
Galdston 1951
Tyndel 1963
Harris 1964
Adler, J. 1966
Haberman 1969
Moran 1970a
Moran 1970b
Glen 1979
Miller, P. 1980
Dell, Ruzicka and Palisi 1981
Ramirez, McCormick, Russo, and Taber 1983
McCormick, Russo, Ramirez, and Taber 1984
Robins, Helzer, Weissman, Orvaschel et al. 1984
Adkins, Rugle, and Taber 1985
Blaszczynski, Buhrich, and McConaghy 1985
Custer and Milt 1985
Marty, Zoppa, and Lesieur 1985
Orford 1985
Peele 1985
Blaszczynski, Wilson, and McConaghy 1986
Linden, Pope, and Jonas 1986
Graham and Lowenfeld 1986
Lesieur, Blume and Zoppa 1986
Taber, Russo, Adkins, and McCormick 1986
Lesieur and Klein 1987
Blume and Lesieur 1987
Ciarrocchi 1987
Galski 1987
Kagan 1987

Taber, McCormick, and Ramirez 1987
Lesieur 1988a
Lesieur 1988b
Blaszczynski and McConaghy 1989a
Ciarrocchi and Richardson 1989
McCormick, Taber, and Kruedelbach 1989
Coyle and Kinney 1990
Lesieur and Blume 1990
Ciarrocchi, Kirschner, and Fallik 1991
Elia and Jacobs 1991
Lesieur and Blume 1991
Lesieur and Rosenthal 1991
Martinez-Pina, Guirao de Parga, Fuste i Vallverdu, Planas, et al. 1991
Ibàñez, Mercadé, Aymami Sanromà, and Cordero 1992
Kroeber 1992
Steinberg, Kosten, and Rounsaville 1992
Schwarz and Lindner 1992
Gambino, Fitzgerald, Shaffer, Renner, and Courtnage 1993
Templer, Kaiser, and Siscoe 1993
McCormick 1993
Bland, Newman, Orn, and Stebelsky 1993
Lesieur 1993
Yafee, Lorenz, and Politzer 1993
Bergh and Külhorn 1994
Feigelman, Kleinman, Lesieur, Millman, and Lesser 1995
Spunt, Lesieur, Hunt, and Cahill 1995
Daghestani, Elenz, and Crayton 1996
Miller and Westermeyer 1996
Roy, Smelsen, and Lindeken 1996
Shepherd 1996
Specker, Carlson, Edmonson, Johnson, and Marcotte 1996
Spunt, Lesieur, Liberty, and Hunt 1996
Feigelman, Wallisch, and Lesieur 1998
Gupta and Derevensky 1998
Black and Moyer 1998
Spunt, Dupont, Lesieur, Liberty, and Hunt 1998
Vitaro, Ferland, Jacques, and Ladouceur 1998

Co-Addiction with Substance Abuse, Low or Absent
Briggs, Goodin, and Nelson 1996

Competitiveness
Hraba and Lee 1995

Defensiveness
Galski 1987

Depression/Dysthymia

Greenson 1948
Niederland 1967
Moran 1969
Moran 1970a
Livingston 1974a
Bolen, Caldwell, and Boyd 1975
Custer and Custer 1978
Glen 1979
Lowenfeld 1979
Lorenz 1981
Moravec and Munly 1983
Custer, Meeland, and Krug 1984
McCormick, Russo, Ramirez, and Taber 1984
Lyons 1985
Zimmerman, Meeland, and Krug 1985
Blaszczynski, Buhrich, and McConaghy 1985
Blaszczynski, Wilson, and McConaghy 1986
Lorenz and Yaffee 1986
Linden, Pope, and Jonas 1986
Graham and Lowenfeld 1986
Blaszczynski and McConaghy 1987
Galski 1987
Taber, McCormick, and Ramirez 1987
McCormick and Taber 1988
Blaszczynski and McConaghy 1988
Roy, Custer, Lorenz, and Linnoila 1988
Blaszczynski and McConaghy 1989a
Ciarrocchi and Richardson 1989
Blaszczynski, McConaghy, and Frankova 1990
Lesieur and Blume 1990
Martinez-Pina, Guirao de Parga, Fuste i Vallverdu, Planas, et al. 1991
Ciarrocchi, Kirschner, and Fallik 1991
Kroeber 1992
Raviv 1993
Rugle and Melamed 1993
Taber 1993
Templer, Kaiser, and Siscoe 1993
Bland, Newman, Orn, and Stebelsky 1993
Bergh and Külhorn 1994
Lumley and Roby 1995
Steel and Blaszczynski 1996
Specker, Carlson, Edmonson, Johnson, and Marcotte 1996
Becoña, Del Carmen Lorenzo, and Fuentes 1996
Gupta and Derevensky 1998
Blaszczynski and Steel 1998

Depression and Anxiety (Negative Affectivity)
Tyndel 1963
Bolen and Boyd 1968
Glen 1979
Graham and Lowenfeld 1986
Blaszczynski and McConaghy 1989a
Lyons 1985
Ciarrocchi, Kirschner, and Fallik 1991
McCormick 1993
Törne and Konstanty 1992

Depression, Low or Absent
Tepperman 1977
Dell, Ruzicka and Palisi 1981
Kusyszyn and Rutter 1985
Ladouceur and Mayrand 1986
Ciarroicchi 1987
Steinberg, Kosten, and Rounseville 1992
Thorson, Powell, and Hilt 1994

Dominance
Morris 1957
Moravec and Munley 1983

Egocentric
Hraba and Lee 1995

Ego Strength, Weak
Taber, Russo, Adkins, and McCormick 1986
Taber, McCormick, and Ramirez 1987

Exhibition Needs, High
Cameron and Myers 1966
Livingston 1974a
Moravec and Munley 1983

Extroversion, High
Seager 1970
Graham and Lowenfeld 1986
Malkin and Syme 1986
Kagan 1987
Roy, De Jong, and Linnoila 1989

Extroversion, Low or Absent
Moran 1970c
Koller 1972

Glen 1979
McConaghy, Armstrong, Blaszczynski, and Allcock 1983
Blaszczinski, Wilson, and McConaghy 1986
Roy, Custer, Lorenz, and Linnoila 1989
Carlton and Manowitz 1994

Family Instability/Dysfunction
Lorenz 1981
Lorenz and Yaffee 1986
Martinez-Pina, Guirao de Parga, Fuste i Vallverdu, Planas, et al. 1991

Fear
Galski 1987

Femininity, Low
Morris 1957

Gregariousness
Dell, Ruzicka and Palisi 1981

Happiness, High
Morris 1957

Happiness, Normal
Gupta and Derevensky 1998

Histrionic
Blaszczynski and Steel 1998

Hostility
Lindner 1950
Roston 1965
Graham and Lowenfeld 1986
Glen 1987
Roy, Custer, Lorenz, and Linnoila 1989

Hypersensitivity
Glen 1987

Hypomania
McCormick, Russo, Ramirez, and Taber 1984
Templer, Kaiser, and Siscoe 1993
Bland, Newman, Orn, and Stebelsky 1993

Hysteria
Lowenfeld 1979

Impulsivity/Attention Deficit Hyperactivity Disorder (ADHD)
Bolen, Caldwell, and Boyd 1975
Glen 1979
Zimmerman, Meeland, and Krug 1985
Goldstein, Manowitz, Nora, Swartzburg, and Carlton 1985
Graham and Lowenfeld 1986
Carlton and Goldstein 1987
Carlton and Manowitz 1987
Carlton, Manowitz, McBride, Nora, et al. 1987
Goldstein and Carlton 1988
Hraba, Mok, and Huff 1990
Ciarrocchi, Kirschner, and Fallik 1991
Gonzalez-Ibanez, Mercade, Ayman, Saldana, and Vallejo-Ruiloba 1991
Carlton and Manowitz 1992
McCormick 1993
Rugle and Melamed 1993
Templer, Kaiser, and Siscoe 1993
Carlton and Manowitz 1994
Castellani and Rugle 1995
Hraba and Lee 1995
Steel and Blaszczynski 1996
Blaszczynski and Steel 1998
Blaszczynski, Steel, and McConaghy 1997
Vitaro, Arseneault, and Tremblay 1997
Vitaro, Ferland, Jacques, and Ladouceur 1998
Black and Moyer 1998

Impulsivity, Low or Absent
Swyhart 1976
Allcock and Grace 1988

Immaturity
Glen 1979
Taber 1993
Livingston 1974b
Graham and Lowenfeld 1986

Inferiority, Inadequacy, Rejection, Low Self-Esteem
Glen 1979
Custer 1984
Rosenthal 1985
Graham and Lowenfeld 1986
Martinez-Pina, Guirao de Parga, Fuste i Vallverdu, Planas, et al. 1991
Kroeber 1992
Volberg, Reitzes, and Boles 1997

Inferiority, Inadequacy, Low Self-Esteem, Absent
Gupta and Derevensky 1998

Intelligence/IQ, Average
Bolen, Caldwell, and Boyd 1975
Custer and Custer 1978
Moravec and Munley 1983

Intelligence/IQ, Above Average
Reagan 1987
Detterman and Spry 1988

Intelligence/IQ, Below Average
Martinez-Pina, Guirao de Parga, Fuste i Vallverdu, Planas, et al. 1991
Templer, Kaiser, and Siscoe 1993

Intelligence not Related to Gambling Success
Ceci and Liker 1986
Ceci and Liker 1987
Liker and Ceci 1987

Interpersonal Sensitivity, High
Boyd and Bolen 1970
Jacobs 1982
McCormick, Russo, Ramirez and Taber 1984
McCormick, Taber, Kruedelbach, and Russo 1987

Interpersonal Sensitivity, Normal
Raviv 1993

Locus of Control Orientation, High External
Kusyszyn and Rubenstein 1985
Hong and Chiu 1988
Moran 1970c
Devinney 1979
Kweitel and Felicity 1998

Locus of Control Orientation, High Internal
McCormick and Taber 1988
McCormick, Taber, and Kruedelbach 1989
Carroll and Huxley 1994
Browne and Brown 1994

Locus of Control Orientation, No Significant Differences
Kusyszyn and Rutter 1985
Ladouceur and Mayrand 1986

Malkin and Syme 1986
Conrad 1978

Narcissism
Livingston 1974a
Greenberg 1980
Dell, Ruzicka and Palisi
Rosenthal 1985
Taber, Russo, Adkins, and McCormick 1986
Galski 1987
Martinez-Pina, Guirao de Parga, Fuste i Vallverdu, Planas, et al. 1991
Kroeber 1992
Blaszczynski and Steel 1998

Narcissism, Absent
Specker, Carlson, Edmonson, Johnson, and Marcotte 1996

Hypersensitivity
Taber, McCormick, and Ramirez 1987
Galski 1987
Lowenfeld 1979
Galski 1987
Bland, Newman, Orn, and Stebelsky 1993

Obsessive-Compulsive Disorder
Roston 1965
Glen 1979
Linden, Pope, and Jonas 1986
Bland, Newman, Orn, and Stebelsky 1993
Black and Moyer 1998

Obsessive-Compulsive Disorder, Absent
Raviv 1993
Specker, Carlson, Edmonson, Johnson, and Marcotte 1996

Occupational Instability
Martinez-Pina, Guirao de Parga, Fuste i Vallverdu, Planas, et al. 1991

Panic Disorder
Linden, Pope, and Jonas 1986
Bland, Newman, Orn, and Stebelsky 1993
Specker, Carlson, Edmonson, Johnson, and Marcotte 1996

Paranoia
Lowenfeld 1979
Graham and Lowenfeld 1986

Templer, Kaiser, and Siscoe 1993
Kroeber 1992
Black and Moyer 1998

Paranoia, Absent
Specker, Carlson, Edmonson, Johnson, and Marcotte 1996

Post Traumatic Stress Disorder
Taber, McCormick, and Ramirez 1987

Psychasthenia
Lowenfeld 1979
Glen 1979
Galski 1987
Templer, Kaiser, and Siscoe 1993

Psychopathy/Sociopathy
Roston 1965
Bolen, Caldwell, and Boyd 1975
Glen 1979
Lowenfeld 1979
Moravec and Munley 1983
Graham and Lowenfeld 1986
Hickey, Haertzen, and Henningfield 1986
Galski 1987
Blaszczynski and McConaghy 1988
Blaszczynski, McConaghy, and Frankova 1989
Templer, Kaiser, and Siscoe 1993

Psychoticism and/or Neuroticism (Anxiety and Depression)
Moran 1970c
Steel and Blaszczynski 1996
Blaszczynski, Buhrich, and McConaghy 1985
Blaszczynski, Wilson, and McConaghy 1986
Roy, Custer, Lorenz, and Linnoila 1989
Carroll and Huxley 1994

Schizophrenic/Schizoid
Glen 1979
Graham and Lowenfeld 1986
Galski 1987
Lesieur and Blume 1990
Templer, Kaiser, and Siscoe 1993
Kroeber 1992
Black and Moyer 1998

Schizophrenia/Schizoid, Absent
Bland, Newman, Orn, and Stebelsky 1993
Specker, Carlson, Edmonson, Johnson, and Marcotte 1996

Security, High
Morris 1957

Self-Defeating Personality Disorder, No Significant Differences
Raviv 1993

Sensation-Seeking/Boredom Proneness, High
Steel and Blaszczynski 1996
Kuley and Jacobs 1988
Gupta and Derevensky 1998

Sensation-Seeking/Boredom Proneness, Low to Normal/No Significant Differences
Anderson and Brown 1984
Lyons 1985
Blaszczynski, Wilson and McConaghy 1986
Ladouceur and Mayrand 1986
Dickerson, Hinchy, and Fabre 1987
Blaszczynski, McConaghy, and Frankova 1990
Blaszczynski, McConaghy, and Frankova 1991a
Dickerson, Walker, Legg England, and Hinchy 1990
Dickerson, Cunningham, Legg England, and Hinchey 1991
Allcock and Grace 1988
Martinez-Pina, Guirao de Parga, Fuste i Vallverdu, Planas, et al. 1991
Gonzalez-Ibanez, Mercade, Ayman, Saldana, and Vallejo-Ruiloba 1991
Coventry and Brown 1993
Dickerson 1993a
Raviv 1993
Castellani and Rugle 1995

Social Responsibility, High
Morris 1957

Appendix B

SUMMARY OF ETIOLOGICAL THEORIES OF GAMBLING

Psychodynamic Approaches

Psychoanalytic Theory. Any inclination for gambling is symptomatic of a personality fixation at an early stage of psychosexual development.

Personality Theory. Gambling is a manifestation of a particular basic personality type. Earlier personality theorists assumed that environmental factors determined the individual's basic personality; more recent theorists, focusing on neurochemical and other physiological imbalances, have begun to explore biological differences.

Power Theory. A personality theory which assumes that gambling is motivated by low self-esteem and the need for achievement.

Dependency Conflict Theory. A personality theory which assumes that gambling is motivated by unconscious needs for independence.

Behavioral Psychological Approaches

Learning or Reinforcement Theory. All behaviors represent learned responses to various environmental stimuli; addictions are habits that have been acquired through repeated reinforcement of those behaviors.

The Continuous Form Model. Continuous forms of gambling such as casino and machine gaming which involve rapidly repeated cycles of bets, outcomes, and rebets will be more addicting that noncontinuous forms such as lotteries in which the outcome does not immediately follow the bet.

The Skinnerian or Operant Conditioning Model. All behavioral responses that are rewarded will be reinforced; those that are no longer rewarded or are punished will be extinguished.

The Pavlovian or Classical Conditioning Model. Associational learning through which a reflexive response to one cue or stimulus can be unintentionally elicited by an unrelated stimulus. The gambling response can be elicited by certain cues that are often associated with it such as a croupier's call or track announcements.

Drive-Reduction or Need-State Theories. Gambling reduces the intensity of certain drives or needs.

Play Theory. Gamblers do not gamble for money, they gamble for fun. Some theorists see play as an instinctive drive or basic survival need while others see it as learned. In either case, the drive is met by gambling. Others see gambling as a socialization mechanism through which cultural values are transmitted and reinforced to successive generations.

The Tension-Reduction, Dysphoria-Reduction, or Escape Hypothesis. Gambling reduces or relieves unpleasant hedonic or emotional states.

The Arousal or Sensation-Seeking Hypothesis. Gambling is motivated by the intense thrill and excitement or "action" it provides.

The Dual-Effect Hypothesis. Addictive behaviors can simultaneously reduce tension and increase arousal.

The Dual-Reinforcement Hypothesis. Gambling is reinforced by the emotional reward of "action," which is delivered on a fixed-interval schedule with each wager, *and* by monetary rewards which are delivered on a variable-ratio schedule with each win.

Behavior Completion Mechanism Theory. A combination of the tension-reduction and classical conditioning models. Exposure to a strong gambling-related cue stimulates a drive to gamble; any interruption of the sequence of behaviors that usually follow will produce a state of heightened tension and anxiety which can be relieved only by gambling.

Cognitive Approaches. Gamblers persist even when they are losing because of the erroneous beliefs about winning and rationalizations of loss they maintain.

Attribution Theory. Investigates the reasons and rationalizations gamblers give for their successes and failures. Those who ascribe the outcomes of events to such agencies as luck or fate are externally oriented; those who ascribe outcomes to their own skill are internally oriented.

The Illusion of Control Hypothesis. Gamblers become more confident and will take greater risks when they are led to believe that their own actions and choices can influence the outcome of chance-related events.

The "Big Win" or "Early Win" Hypothesis. Gamblers who win large amounts or smaller amounts consistently early in their careers will attribute their success to their own personal talents which leads them to expect similar success in the future. Such an orientation will serve to encourage persistence when they are losing as well as the initiation of new gambling sessions.

The Superstition Hypothesis. Gamblers persist because of their conviction that luck can be influenced through magical thinking and ritualistic performances.

Social Learning or Modeling. People acquire certain behaviors by imitating those they admire and regard as role models.

Frustration Theory. Persistence derives from frustration over the failure to achieve a seemingly attainable goal.

Social Science Approaches

Social Structural Models. Gambling is in one way or another related to social class.

Leisure Class or Affluence Theory. As a form of conspicuous consumption, gambling represents a visible status symbol among members of the upper classes.

Deviance Theory. Gambling, which is controlled by a vast criminal network, is one of many immoral and antisocial behaviors typical of the unprincipled lower classes.

Structural-Functional Models. Gambling serves some positive social purpose, usually tension-reduction and/or the promotion of social solidarity.

Alienation/Decision-Making Theory. Gambling allows members of the powerless working classes to make at least some of their own decisions and exercise at least some degree of control over their own lives.

Anomie, Deprivation, or Status Inequality Theory. Gambling offers an alternative means of social and economic advancement for members of the impoverished lower classes.

Rural-Urban Residence/Community Size Hypothesis. Gambling will be relatively more prevalent in urban areas and cities and less so in rural areas and smaller towns.

The Religion Hypothesis. Those who subscribe to the Protestant ethic and attend religious services on a regular basis will be less likely to gamble than those who do not. Protestants will therefore be less likely to gamble than either Catholics or Jews. The religion hypothesis was also used to explain the community size hypothesis since the Protestant ethic is presumed to be stronger in smaller rural towns and weaker in larger urban areas.

The Ethnic Minority or Ethnicity Hypothesis. Ethnic minorities will be more likely to gamble and develop gambling problems than those in the predominant ethnic group.

Economic Theories. People risk something of value to acquire something of greater value.

Value-Maximizational or Utility Theory. Gamblers are rational decision makers who assume only those risks that have the lowest potential cost and the highest probability of reward.

The Regressivity Hypothesis. Gambling taxes and losses are disproportionately higher among low-income groups who can least afford it.

Consumption Theory. Gambling is a consumer service that must be purchased. Akin to play theory, consumption theory maintains that the true reward of gambling lies in the enjoyment and satisfaction it offers the customer. Because gamblers who frequent commercial gaming establishments expect to lose, their losses represent the cost of this amusement. The gambler's goal is to minimize this cost.

Marxian Theory. Gambling is just another means through which the bourgeois ruling class continues to exploit the proletarian masses.

Small Group Theory. Gambling provides an arena for role playing in which gamblers can act out their wish-fulfillment fantasies by assuming other identities through which they can exhibit idealized behavioral and personality traits. The primary goal of gambling is not to accrue money, but "character" and prestige.

Interactional Theory. The gambling venue constitutes a social world. As gamblers become increasingly committed to gambling, their social life increasingly centers around their gambling associates. Gamblers persist despite the losses they incur for the reward of social interaction with others who share this commitment.

Transactional or Family Systems Theory. Gambling is caused by strained, dysfunctional family relationships.

Transactional Script Theory. Gamblers persist despite their losses to fulfill negative parental expectations. They want to lose because in early childhood they adopted the "life script" of loser as a result of their parents' harsh criticism of their failures and repeated predictions that they would grow up to be losers.

Family Systems Theory. Gambling is a result rather than a cause of family discord. Gamblers and their significant others are playing different roles in a maladaptive social interactional game which they find rewarding.

"On Tilt" Theories. Problem gambling is a transient, often short-term condition brought about by unexpected and devastating losses which induce a state of emotional disequilibrium. This temporary loss of normal emotional control leads to poor judgment, irrational betting, and even greater losses. Since the condition is temporary it is therefore correctable. The period of uncontrolled betting ceases with the return of normal emotional control.

Chasing. Problem gambling is a long-term condition brought about by the need to keep gambling in order to get even for all past losses. As gamblers chase their previous losses, they escalate the size and frequency of their bets, often betting and losing money slated for other purposes and borrowing or stealing to continue gambling. The more they gamble, the more they lose, and the more money they need to pay old debts and continue to chase in the futile quest to get even.

Statistically-Based Models

Quantitative studies, which are generally based on questionnaire data, look for associations between gambling and various sociodemographic, environmental, and other behavioral variables. Statistically significant correlations are assumed to be causal.

The Status Frustration/Hope/Aspiration Hypothesis. Closely related to anomie or status inequality theory, the status frustration hypothesis posits that gambling is motivated not by greed but by dissatisfaction with one's present socioeconomic status and hope for a better future. It will be most prevalent among those who are in the upper levels of a given social class and hope to move up to the next higher social class.

The Subcultural Hypothesis. Gambling or its avoidance is largely determined by the family, subcultural, or cultural values that people have internalized. In cultural contexts in which gambling is highly valued, it will be motivated by the need to "fit in" with one's primary reference group.

The Life Cycle Hypothesis. Owing to their diminishing needs for stimulation, the older people become the less likely they are to gamble.

Continuity Theory. Related to the life cycle hypothesis, this approach suggests that a person's attitudes toward gambling are internalized in youth and maintained for life. Decreases in age-related gambling reflect a "cohort-effect" with older generations gambling less because they internalized the antigambling sentiments that were prevalent in their youth and younger generations gambling more because antigambling sanctions and sentiments have steadily weakened over time.

The Age of Majority Hypothesis. Predicts that rates of gambling among adolescents will show rapid and dramatic increases when they reach the legal gambling age.

The Home Centeredness Hypothesis. Predicts that "conjugal role sharing," or the extent to which husbands actively participate in such domestic activities as daily housework and shopping along with their wives, will be inversely related to gambling.

The Work Centered Leisure Hypothesis. Predicts that gambling should be least prevalent among those whose free time activities such as studying at home are most closely related to their work.

The Parental Gambling Hypothesis. Predicts that people's gambling-related attitudes and behaviors will reflect those of their parents. The risk of becoming a pathological gambler is greater for those having at least one parent who was pathological gambler.

The Availability or Availability and Exposure Hypothesis. Predicts that any increase in the sanctioning and availability of gambling will lead to concomitant increases in gambling expenditures, rates of problem gambling, and criminal activities associated with the gambling trade.

The Gender Hypothesis. Predicts that rates of both normative and pathological gambling will be higher among males than females.

The Marital Status Hypothesis. Married people will be less likely to gamble and to develop gambling problems than single, divorced, or widowed people.

The Age of Initiation or "Early Start" Hypothesis. The earlier in life people start to gamble, the more likely they are to develop gambling problems.

The Gateway or Precursor Hypothesis. Heavy video game involvement in childhood acts a "stepping-stone" to addictive machine gaming later in life.

The Risk Factor Model. Those who experience or exhibit a number of risk factors are more likely to become addicted to gambling than those who do not.

The Social Control Hypothesis. Being married is negatively correlated with pathological gambling while being single or widowed is positively correlated. Therefore, the natural inclinations of potential problem gamblers are suppressed in the presence of marriage partners but expressed in their absence.

The Co-Addiction Hypothesis. Those who are addicted to one behavior or chemical substance are more likely than those who are not to become addicted to others.

Medical or Disease Models

Pathological gambling is a medically diagnosable and treatable disorder. It may be either psychological or biological in origin.

Evolutionary Theory. Risk-seeking and the emotional arousal it incites are instinctive needs. They arose from the life-threatening hazards that our pre-human ancestors encountered in their constant struggle for survival. Repeated exposure to situations that provoked the involuntary "fight or flight" reaction eventually established a biological need for such experiences. Today gambling is an intellectual substitute for the physical conflicts and risks our forebears were required to seek out and overcome to meet their survival needs.

Pathological Gambling as a Medical Syndrome (Moran). Pathological gambling is identifiable by a concurrence of one or more of the following phenomena: concern that gambling is excessive, an urge to gamble, loss of control over gambling, disturbances to family functioning. There are several varieties of pathological gambling, each of which has its own motivation.

Compulsive Gambling as a Psychological Illness (Custer). All addictions and the withdrawal symptoms that sometimes accompany them are purely psychological, resulting from the intense pleasure, relief, or escape they provide. Despite their outward demeanor, compulsive gamblers are lonely, anxious, depressed, insecure, and lacking in self-esteem.

The Heritability Hypothesis. The predisposition for pathological gambling is a genetically determined trait and therefore transmissible from parent to offspring.

Multicausal Theories

Pathological gambling and other addictions are caused by a variety of influences, including both hereditary biological and environmental learning factors.

The Sensation-Seeking or Arousal Hypothesis. Potential addicts are born with a greater than normal biological need for excitement which they learn to satisfy through such stimulating behaviors as drug use and gambling.

Opponent-Process Theory. Like sky divers, pathological gamblers do not become addicted to the initial unpleasant emotions that their behavior arouses, but to the highly enjoyable opposite emotional reactions that automatically ensue to diminish or counteract them.

Reversal Theory. People who are stressed or anxious gamble to relax; those who are bored gamble for excitement. Their motivations for gambling can undergo rapid reversals during the course of a gambling session. Pathological gambling develops when anxiety itself becomes a powerful internal associational cue that further stimulates the gambling response.

The Addictive Personality Syndrome. Some people are born either overaroused or underaroused, both of which they find unpleasant and will attempt to alleviate. Those who feel rejected, inferior, and have low self-esteem will, under certain environmental circumstances, resort to gambling and other addictive behaviors as a means of escaping into a make-believe world of wish-fulfillment fantasy.

A Parsimonious Need-State Model. There are two fundamental types of pathological gamblers, who can be motivated by either biological or psychological influences: the chronically depressed who gamble to relieve this condition and the chronically understimulated who gamble for excitement. The temporary relief that gambling provides is followed by an even stronger rebound need-state which the gambler again attempts to relieve through further gambling.

Learned Helplessness Theory. Addiction is a direct consequence of chronic negative affect (low self-esteem, depression, guilt, anxiety, etc.) which, in turn, is a direct consequence of self-blame which, in turn, is a direct consequence of a learned internal locus of control orientation which, in turn, is a direct consequence of one's past life experiences and traumas. Learned helplessness, which also takes such forms as post-traumatic-stress syndrome or "shell shock," affects only those who are genetically predisposed for it.

The Synoptic Model. Rather than immoral, deviant, or sick, gambling is a normal social activity. As a form of entertainment, it is motivated either by internal psychological factors, external social factors, or the particular structure of a game and the challenge it offers. Nonconventional or excessive gambling results from the individual's inability to follow the rules and conventions of normative gambling.

NOTES

SERIES INTRODUCTION

1. Lesieur 1990; 1992; cf. Lorenz and Politzer 1990.
2. Lesieur 1988c.
3. see Ladouceur, Boisvert, Pépin, Loranger, and Sylvain 1994 and Lesieur 1990 for more detailed discussions.
4. e.g., Shaffer 1989, p. 1; Tarter and Schneider 1976, pp. 80–82.
5. cited by Wagner 1972, p. i.
6. Aristotle 1953, p. 98.
7. Hopper 1970, p. 360.
8. quoted by Rosecrance 1988, p. 107.
9. Rosecrance 1988 pp. 96–100.
10. e.g., Blaszczynski, McConaghy, and Frankova 1989; Bolen and Boyd 1968; Brown 1987e; Cressey 1971; Custer and Custer 1978; Lemert 1953; Lesieur 1984; 1979; 1987; 1993; Livingston 1974a; Maurer 1974; Roebuck 1967.
11. Abt, Smith, and Christiansen 1985, p. ix.
12. ibid.
13. for reviews and examples see Bell 1976; Clotfelter and Cook 1989, pp. 47–48; Inglis 1985; Orford and McCartney 1990; Reid 1985; Shaffer and Gambino 1989; Tarter and Schneider 1976.
14. e.g., Abt, Smith, and Christiansen 1985; Caldwell 1985a, p. 18; Campbell 1976; Kusyszyn 1976; 1984; 1990; Rosecrance 1986a; 1988; Smith and Abt 1984.
15. Abt, Smith, and Christiansen 1985, p. 136.
16. e.g., Blaszczynski, Buhrich, and McConaghy 1985; Brown 1987a; 1990; 1993; Coventry and Brown 1993, p. 543; Custer and Milt 1985, p. 28; Dickerson 1977a; 1984; 1987; 1989; Ferrioli and Ciminero 1981; Gaboury and Ladouceur 1993; Galdston 1960, p. 555; Jacobs 1986; Koller 1972; Kusyszyn 1972; Leary and Dickerson 1985; Larkin and Griffiths 1998; Lesieur and Rosenthal 1991; Lester 1979, p. 106; Marks 1990; Miller 1980; Moran 1970a; 1970b; Orford 1985; Rosenthal 1993; Shaffer 1989, p. 7; 1996; 1997; Shaffer, Stein, Gambino, and Cummings 1989, p. xv; Thorson, Powell, and Hilt 1994; Tyndel 1963; Victor 1981, p. 280.
17. American Psychiatric Association 1980; 1987; 1994.
18. World Health Organization 1991; 1992.
19. cf. Fisher 1993a, p. 413.
20. Brown 1993, p. 265.
21. Dickerson 1991, p. 317.
22. e.g., Custer and Milt 1985; Jacobs 1986.
23. McConaghy 1980.
24. Orford 1985.
25. Glasser 1976.
26. Brown 1993, p. 251.
27. Becker and Murphy 1988, p. 676; Peele and Brodsky 1975; Wittman, Fuller, and Taber 1988.
28. Goddard 1993, p. 48.
29. Goodman 1990, p. 1403; Herman 1967, p. 103; Livingston 1974a, p. 3; Marks 1990, p. 1391; Shaffer 1989, pp. 12, 28; 1996; 1997.
30. Shaffer 1989.
31. Shaffer 1989, p. 6, note 3.
32. Walker 1985.
33. Cornish 1978; Dickerson 1989; Kroeber 1992; Orford 1985; Orford and McCartney 1990; Walker 1992c, p. 151.
34. Büringer and Konstanty 1992; Törne and

Konstanty 1992.
35. McCormack 1994.
36. Oldman 1978.
37. Dickerson 1984; 1985; 1989.
38. Burglass 1989, p. 206.
39. Gilovich and Douglas 1986, p. 229.
40. Shaffer, Hall, and Vander Bilt 1997.
41. Atlas and Peterson 1990; Browne 1989; Dickerson 1989, p. 158; Rosecrance 1986b; 1988, p. 117; Walker 1992c, p. 151.
42. Rosenthal 1989, pp. 118–119.
43. Abt, Smith, and Christiansen 1985.
44. Rosenthal 1989, p. 120.
45. Custer and Milt 1985, p. 25.
46. Rosenthal 1989, p. 120.
47. Walker 1985.
48. Greene 1982; Walker 1992c.
49. Büringer and Konstanty 1992.
50. Dickerson 1984; 1985.
51. Miller, P. 1980, p. 268.
52. Custer and Custer 1978.
53. e.g., Kallick, Suits, Dielman, and Hybels 1976; 1979; Volberg and Steadman 1988.
54. Haberman 1969, p. 164.
55. Leiseur and Heineman 1988.
56. Lesieur, Blume, and Zoppa 1986.
57. McCormick 1993, p. 333.
58. Elia and Jacobs 1991.
59. Lesieur and Rosenthal 1991, p. 18.
60. Feigelman, Kleinman, Lesieur, Millman, and Lesser 1995.
61. Spunt, Lesieur, Hunt, and Cahill 1995.
62. Spunt, Lesieur, Liberty, and Hunt 1996.
63. Shepherd 1996.
64. Daghestani, Elenz, and Crayton 1996.
65. Miller and Westermeyer 1996.
66. McCormick, Russo, Ramirez, and Taber 1984.
67. Lesieur 1988a.
68. Yaffee, Lorenz, and Politzer 1993.
69. Lesieur 1988a.
70. Lesieur 1993, p. 501.
71. Linden, Pope, and Jonas 1986; Lesieur 1988b.
72. Lesieur 1988b.
73. Ramirez, McCormick, Russo, and Taber 1983.
74. McCormick, Russo, Ramirez, and Taber 1984.
75. Adkins, Rugle, and Taber 1985.
76. Ciarrocchi and Richardson 1989.
77. Lesieur and Klein 1985.
78. Ciarrocchi, Kirshner, and Fallik 1991.
79. Schwarz and Lindner 1992.
80. Bland, Newman, Orn, and Stebelsky 1993.
81. Steinberg, Kosten, and Rounsaville 1992.
82. Gambino, Fitzgerald, Shaffer, Renner, and Courtnage 1993.
83. Specker, Carlson, Edmonson, Johnson, and Marcotte 1996.
84. e.g., Bergh and Külhorn 1994; Blaszczynski and McConaghy 1989a; Blaszczynski, Buhrich, and McConaghy 1985; Blume 1994; Blume and Lesieur 1987; Ciarrocchi 1987; Coyle and Kinney 1990, p. 35; Custer and Milt 1985; Feigelman, Wallisch, and Lesieur 1998; Feigelman, Kleinman, Lesieur, Millman, and Lesser 1995; Galdston 1951; Graham and Lowenfeld 1986; Greenson 1948; Harris 1964; Ibàñez, Mercadé, Aymami Sanromà, and Cordero 1992; Kagan 1987; Lesieur and Blume 1990; 1991; McCormick, Taber, and Kruedelbach 1989; Marty, Zoppa, and Lesieur 1985; McCormick 1993; Martinez-Pina, Guirao de Parga, Fuste i Vallverdu, Planas, Mateo, and Auguado 1991; Miller and Westermeyer 1996; Moran 1970a; 1970b; Orford 1985; Peele 1985; Robins, Helzer, Weissman, Orvaschel, Gruenberg, Burke, and Regier 1984; Roy, Smelsen, and Lindeken 1996; Shepherd 1996; Spunt, Dupont, Lesieur, Liberty, and Hunt 1998; Spunt, Lesieur, Hunt, and Cahill 1995; Spunt, Lesieur, Liberty, and Hunt 1996; Taber, McCormick, and Ramirez 1987; Taber, Russo, Adkins, and McCormick 1986; Templer, Kaiser, and Siscoe 1993; Tyndel 1963; Vitaro, Ferland, Jacques, and Ladouceur 1998.
85. Briggs, Goodin, and Nelson 1996.
86. Becoña 1993.
87. Kroeber 1992, pp. 86–87.
88. Rosenthal 1992, p. 76.
89. Lesieur 1993, p. 511.
90. Custer and Custer 1978.
91. Miller, P. 1980, p. 267.
92. Ciarrocchi 1987, p. 25.

93. Moran 1970d, p. 67.
94. Lesieur 1989, p. 231; Lesieur, Blume, and Zoppa 1986, p. 33.
95. Ciarrocchi and Richardson 1989, p. 63.
96. Rosenthal 1970.
97. e.g., Madsen 1974; Sexias, Omenn, Burk, and Eggelston 1972.
98. Saunders and Wookey 1980, p. 1.
99. Brown 1987b.
100. Freud 1950 [1928]; see also Abraham 1960; Bergler 1936; 1943; 1958; Rado 1926; Rosenthal 1987; Simmel 1920.
101. Skinner 1974; see also Dickerson 1979; 1984; Knapp 1976.
102. e.g., Dickerson 1991; 1993a; Dickerson and Adcock 1987; Gaboury and Ladouceur 1988; 1989; Ladouceur and Gaboury 1988; Griffiths 1990a; 1990d; 1993d; Ladouceur and Gaboury 1988; Ladouceur, Gaboury, Dumont, and Rochette 1988; Walker 1985; 1988; 1992a; 1992b; 1992c; 1992d.
103. e.g., Devereux 1949; Goffman 1967; 1969.
104. e.g., Moran 1970a; Newman 1972; Zola 1963.
105. e.g., Carlton and Goldstein 1987; Carlton and Manowitz 1987.
106. e.g., Carlton and Goldstein 1987; Jacobs 1986; 1988; 1989a; McCormick 1987; Roy, Adinoff, Roehrich, Lamparski, Custer, Lorenz, Barbaccia, Guidotti, Costa, and Linnoila 1988.
107. e.g., Kallick, Suits, Dielman, and Hybels 1976; 1979; Volberg 1993; 1994; Volberg and Steadman 1988; 1989.
108. e.g., Blaszczynski and McConaghy 1987; Ciarrocchi and Richardson 1989; Hraba, Mok, and Huff 1990; Specker, Carlson, Edmonson, Johnson, and Marcotte 1996.
109. e.g., Downes, Davies, David, and Stone 1976; Newman 1972; Price 1972; Roberts and Sutton-Smith 1966; Tec 1964.
110. Lesieur 1993; Mark and Lesieur 1992; Specker, Carlson, Edmonson, Johnson, and Marcotte 1996; Rosenthal 1987, p. 42; Strachan and Custer 1993.
111. France 1902, p. 380.
112. Dickerson 1984, p. 39.
113. Laundergan, Schaefer, Eckhoff, and Pirie 1990, pp. 15–16, 41; Legarda, Babio, and Abreu 1992, p. 769; Lesieur 1988b; Lesieur and Blume 1991; Sommers 1988, p. 484; Volberg and Steadman 1988; 1989.
114. Strachan and Custer 1993, p. 235.

Chapter 1
PSYCHOANALYTIC THEORY: EARLY VIEWS

1. Freud 1938; 1943 [1920]; 1949; 1950 [1928]; 1954.
2. Fink 1961, p. 252.
3. Cofer and Appley 1964, p. 601.
4. Freud 1913.
5. Ferenczi 1952 [1914], p. 319.
6. e.g., Freud 1905, pp. 181–182; Lolli 1961, p. 213; Menninger 1938, p. 181; Rado 1933.
7. Bergler 1949, p. 446; Fenichel 1945, p. 379.
8. Devereux, G. 1947, p. 530; 1961, pp. 529–530, 544.
9. Von Hattingberg 1914.
10. Rosenthal 1987, pp. 42–43.
11. see also reviews by Lesieur and Rosenthal 1991; Rabow, Comess, Donovan, and Hollos 1984.
12. Freud 1959 [1908].
13. e.g., Fachinelli 1974 [1965]; Fenichel 1945; Ferenczi 1952 [1914]; Fuller 1974; Simmel 1920; 1948.
14. Rosenthal 1987.
15. Simmel 1920; 1948.
16. Simmel 1948, p. 20.
17. cf. Fuller 1974.
18. Bacon 1974; Bacon, Berry, and Child 1965.
19. Stekel 1929.
20. ibid., p. 236.
21. ibid., p. 234.
22. ibid., p. 241.
23. ibid.
24. ibid.
25. ibid., p. 239.
26. ibid., p. 238.
27. ibid.
28. ibid., p. 240.
29. ibid., p. 239.
30. From *The Gambler* (p. 31), by Fyodor Dostoevsky, translated by V. Terra, 1972

[1866], Chicago: University of Chicago Press. Copyright 1973 by the University of Chicago Press. Reprinted with permission.
31. e.g., Bergler 1943; Fenichel 1945; Galdston 1951; 1960; Greenson 1948; Lindner 1950; Matussek 1953; Reik 1940.
32. Greenson 1948, pp. 112–113; Laforgue 1930, p. 318.
33. Lindner 1950, p. 107.
34. From *The Gambler* (p. 170), by Fyodor Dostoevsky, translated by V. Terras, 1972 [1866], Chicago: University of Chicago Press. Copyright 1973 by the University of Chicago Press. Reprinted with permission.
35. Stekel 1929, p. 241.
36. Greenson 1948, p. 121.
37. Greenberg 1980, p. 3279.
38. Stekel 1929, p. 241; cf. Galdston 1960; Greenson 1948, p. 121.
39. Stekl 1929, p. 237.
40. cf. Bolen and Boyd 1968, pp. 621–622.
41. Freud 1954 [1897], pp. 238–239.
42. e.g., Salzman 1981, p. 341.
43. Freud 1950 [1928].
44. Freud 1950 [1928], p. 238.
45. ibid.
46. ibid., pp. 240–241.
47. Bolen and Boyd 1968, p. 621; cf. Boyd and Bolen 1970, p. 88.
48. Fuller 1974, p. 23.
49. ibid., p. 105, note 20.
50. Lindner 1950, p. 107.
51. Greenson 1948, p. 119.
52. Freud 1950 [1928], p. 242.
53. Fenichel 1945.
54. cf. Maze 1987, p. 209; Moran 1970d, p. 60.
55. cf. LaForgue 1930; Lindner 1950.
56. Rosenthal 1986, p. 108.
57. Fenichel 1945, pp. 372–373; cf. Reik 1940, pp. 170–171.
58. Lindner 1950, p. 106; cf. Greenson 1948, p. 118.
59. Reik 1940, p. 171.
60. Fuller 1974, pp. 6–7.
61. Galdston 1960; Greenson 1948.
62. Matussek 1953.
63. Galdston 1951.
64. Bergler 1943, p. 379 emphasis in original; cf. Galdston 1960.
65. Bergler 1943, pp. 380–382; 1949, pp. 255–258; 1958.
66. Bergler 1936; 1943; 1958.
67. cf. Olmstead 1962.
68. cf. Ferenczi 1952.
69. Menninger 1938, pp. 160–184.
70. Maze 1987, p. 210.
71. Lesieur and Rosenthal 1991, p. 27.
72. cf. Bolen and Boyd 1968, p. 622; Greenson 1948.
73. Bergler 1943, pp. 390–392; 1958.
74. ibid., p. 391.
75. ibid., p. 392.
76. Bergler 1958.
77. Mark and Lesieur 1992, p. 553.
78. Greenson 1948.
79. ibid.
80. ibid., p. 118.
81. ibid., p. 112.
82. ibid., p. 113.
83. ibid.
84. ibid., p. 114.
85. ibid., p. 119.
86. ibid., p. 121.
87. ibid., pp. 115–116.
88. Rosenthal 1986, p. 110.
89. Greenson 1948, p. 116.
90. Wolkowitz, Roy, and Doran 1985, pp. 314–325.
91. Greeson 1948, p. 118.
92. ibid., p. 120.

Chapter 2
PSYCHOANALYTIC THEORY: LATER VIEWS

1. Bolen and Boyd 1968.
2. ibid., p. 622.
3. ibid., p. 625.
4. ibid., p. 622.
5. ibid., p. 626.
6. ibid.
7. ibid.
8. ibid., p. 623.
9. ibid., p. 629.
10. ibid., p. 627.
11. e.g., Fink 1961; Harris 1964.

12. Boyd and Bolen 1970.
13. ibid., p. 87.
14. ibid., p. 89.
15. ibid., p. 88.
16. ibid.
17. ibid.
18. Fuller 1974.
19. Ferenczi 1952 [1914].
20. e.g., Tylor 1958 [1871].
21. Freud 1907; 1913.
22. cf. France 1902; Thomas 1901.
23. Fuller 1974, p. 31.
24. Freud 1927, p. 43.
25. Fuller 1974, p. 63.
26. ibid., p. 48.
27. ibid., p. 67.
28. Freud 1959 [1908]; 1917.
29. Freud 1959 [1908], p. 174.
30. Fuller 1974, p. 74.
31. i.e., Simmel 1920; Greenson 1948.
32. Moran 1970a, p. 594.
33. Fuller 1974, p. 73; emphasis in original.
34. ibid., p. 96.
35. ibid., p. 81.
36. Bolen and Boyd 1968; Boyd and Bolen 1970; Steinberg 1990; Wagner 1972.
37. Adkins, Rugle, and Taber 1985.
38. Steinberg 1993; Victor 1981, pp. 276–277.
39. Bolen and Boyd 1968, p. 628; Boyd and Bolen 1970; Ciarrocchi and Richardson 1989, pp. 60, 62; McCormick and Taber 1987, pp. 24–25; Niederland 1967; Rosenthal 1986.
40. Freud 1950 [1928]; Lindner 1950.
41. Herman 1976a.
42. ibid.
43. Taber, McCormick, and Ramirez 1987, p. 78; cf. McCormick, Taber, and Kruedelbach 1989, p. 484.
44. Greenberg 1980; Harris 1964; Tyndel 1963.
45. Geha 1970; Maze 1987; Rabow, Comess, Donovan, and Hollos 1984, p. 199.
46. Wagner 1972.
47. Geha 1970; Rabow, Comess, Donovan, and Hollos 1984, p. 198.
48. Lesieur and Custer 1984, p. 150; cf. Lesieur 1984, pp. 247, 258.
49. Niederland 1967.
50. Lesieur and Rosenthal 1991, p. 27.
51. Rosenthal 1987, p. 44.
52. Rosenthal 1986.
53. ibid., p. 111.
54. ibid., p. 113.
55. ibid.
56. ibid., p. 118.
57. ibid., p. 114.
58. Newmark 1992.
59. ibid., pp. 449–450.
60. ibid., p. 453.
61. ibid.
62. Campbell 1976, p. 218.
63. Frank 1979, p. 72.
64. Allcock 1985, p. 167.
65. Walker 1985, pp. 149–150.
66. Moran 1993, p. 138.
67. Walker 1992c, p. 185.
68. Scott 1968, p. 88.
69. Galdston 1960.
70. Fuller 1974, p. 19.
71. Lancet 1982, p. 434; cf. Walker 1992c, pp. 174–182.
72. Fuller 1974, p. 95; cf. Walker 1992c, p. 185.
73. Graham and Lowenfeld 1986, p. 59; cf. Salzman 1981, p. 339.
74. Li and Smith 1976, p. 190; emphasis in original.
75. Tec 1964, pp. 56–57; cf. Allcock 1985, p. 166; Newman 1972, p. 9.
76. Dickerson 1984, p. 71.
77. Greenberg 1980, p. 3275; cf. Cohen 1970, p. 467.
78. Devereux, G. 1950.
79. Rabow, Comess, Donovan, and Hollos 1984, p. 198.
80. Cohen 1975, p. 268.
81. Bergler 1958.
82. Walker 1992c, p. 208.
83. Dickerson 1984, p. 101; cf. Barker and Miller 1968.
84. Greenson 1948, p. 125
85. Popper 1962, p. 35.
86. Szasz 1961, p. 124.
87. ibid., p. 125.
88. Rabow, Comess, Donovan, and Hollos 1984, p. 199.
89. ibid.
90. Ashton 1979, p. 60.
91. Galdston 1960, p. 553.

92. Rabow, Comess, Donovan, and Hollos 1984, p. 199.
93. Popper 1962, pp. 36–37.
94. Allcock 1985, p. 166.
95. Popper 1962, p. 38.
96. Cornish 1978, pp. 88–90.

Chapter 3
PERSONALITY THEORY

1. e.g., Adler 1927; 1930; Gross and Carpenter 1971; Whiting and Child 1953.
2. e.g., Landis 1945; Lolli 1949; Seliger and Rosenberg 1941.
3. Galdston 1951.
4. e.g., Ciarrocchi and Richardson 1989; Ciarrocchi, Kirschner, and Fallik 1991; Graham and Lowenfield 1986; Kagan 1987; Linden, Pope, and Jonas 1986; Lowenfeld 1979; McCormick, Taber, and Kruedelbach 1989; Taber, McCormick, and Ramirez 1987.
5. e.g., Boyd 1976, p. 371; McCormick, Taber, and Kruedelbach 1989; Ciarrocchi, Kirschner, and Fallik 1991; Roy, Custer, Lorenz, and Linnoila 1989, p. 39; Specker, Carlson, Edmonson, Johnson, and Marcotte 1996, pp. 77–78; Taber, McCormick, and Ramirez 1987.
6. Griffiths 1994, p. 380.
7. ibid.
8. e.g., Fenichel 1945, p. 376.
9. Lindner 1950; Roy, Custer, Lorenz, and Linnoila 1989.
10. Fenichel 1945; Livingston 1974b, p. 51; Rosenthal 1986; 1987; Roston 1961; Taber 1982; Taber, Russo, Adkins, and McCormick 1986.
11. McCormick and Taber 1987, p. 22.
12. ibid.; Taber, McCormick, and Ramirez 1987; McCormick, Taber, and Kruedelbach 1989.
13. Lesieur 1984.
14. Custer and Milt 1985; Greenberg 1980; Livingston 1974b, p. 51.
15. Nora 1989, p. 131; cf. Peck 1986, p. 463.
16. Graham and Lowenfeld 1986, p. 63.
17. Taber, Russo, Adkins, and McCormick 1986, p. 78.
18. ibid.; cf. Bergler 1943; Boyd 1976, p. 375; Fenichel 1945; Galdston 1960.
19. Fink 1961, p. 255.
20. Custer 1984, p. 35; Kusyszyn 1990, pp. 164–168; Moran 1993; Peck 1986, p. 463; Rosenthal 1993.
21. Adler 1917; 1927; 1930; 1969.
22. Rosenthal 1993, p. 144.
23. Fink 1961, p. 255.
24. ibid., p. 254.
25. Abt, Smith, and Christiansen 1985, p. 20.
26. Whiting and Child 1953.
27. e.g., Bacon 1974; Bacon, Berry, and Child 1965; Barry 1976; Blane and Barry 1973; Blane and Chafetz 1971; Myerson 1953.
28. e.g., Boyatzis 1974; Cutter, Boyatzis, and Clancy 1977; McClelland 1977; McClelland and Davis 1972, McClelland, Davis, Kalin, and Wanner 1966; Markowitz 1984; Scoufis and Walker 1982.
29. Aubry 1975; Custer 1984; Fink 1961; Harris 1964; Kusyszyn 1990; Roberts and Sutton-Smith 1966.
30. Haustein and Schürgers 1992.
31. ibid., p. 140.
32. Fink 1961, p. 260.
33. ibid.
34. Rotter 1966; 1975.
35. Blaszczynski, Wilson, and McConaghy 1986, p. 115; Schwarz and Lindner 1992.
36. Glen 1979.
37. Dickerson 1989, p. 159.
38. e.g., Blaszczynski 1996; Blaszczynski and McConaghy 1988; 1989a; Blaszczynski, Wilson, and McConaghy 1986; Bolen, Caldwell, and Boyd 1975; Castellani and Rugle 1995; Ciarrocchi and Richardson 1989; Davis and Brissett 1995; Graham and Lowenfeld 1986; Knapp and Lech 1987; Linden, Pope, and Jonas 1986; Lorenz and Yaffee 1986; Lowenfeld 1979; McCormick 1993; McCormick and Taber 1987; Moravec and Munley 1983; Rugle and Melamed 1993; Taber, McCormick, and Ramirez 1987; Zimmerman, Meeland, and Krug 1985.
39. Raviv 1993.

40. Knapp and Lech 1987, p. 33; Lesieur and Rosenthal 1991, p. 29.
41. Moran 1970d, p. 67.
42. Moran 1970a.
43. Lesieur 1989, pp. 227–228; Blaszczynski and McConaghy 1988, p. 550; Blaszczynski, Buhrich, and McConaghy 1985, p. 317; McCormick, Russo, Ramirez, and Taber 1984; Walker 1992c, p. 94.
44. Lesieur and Rosenthal 1991, p. 29.
45. Custer and Custer 1978; Kroeber 1992; McCormick 1987; McCormick and Taber 1988; McCormick, Taber, and Kruedelbach 1989; McCormick, Russo, Ramirez, and Taber 1984, p. 217; Taber, McCormick, and Ramirez 1987.
46. Murray 1993, p. 798.
47. Allcock and Grace 1988; Atlas and Peterson 1990; Blaszczynski, McConaghy, and Frankova 1991b; Dell, Ruzicka, and Palisi 1981; Dickerson 1984, pp. 32–35, 43; 1991, p. 324; Dickerson, Cunningham, Legg England, and Hinchy 1991; Dickerson, Walker, Legg England, and Hinchy 1990; Kagan 1987; Kusyszyn and Rutter 1985; Ladouceur and Mayrand 1986; Malkin and Syme 1986; Slovic 1962; 1964.
48. Dickerson 1989, p. 159.
49. Blaszczynski and McConaghy 1989b, p. 48.
50. Knapp and Lech 1987, p. 33.
51. Murray 1993, p. 793.
52. ibid., p. 798.
53. Raviv 1993, pp. 18–19.
54. Taber and McCormick 1987, p. 164.
55. Roy, Custer, Lorenz, and Linnoila 1988.
56. Lorenz and Yaffee 1986.
57. ibid.; Blaszczynski and McConaghy 1993.
58. Lesieur 1989.
59. e.g., Volberg 1993; Volberg and Steadman 1988; 1989.
60. Lesieur 1989, p. 226.
61. Thorson, Powell, and Hilt 1994.
62. McGlothlin 1954, p. 147.
63. Morris 1957.
64. Kusyszyn and Kallai 1975.
65. Kusyszyn and Rutter 1985.
66. ibid., p. 62.
67. Dickerson 1984, p. 132.
68. e.g., Cox 1985; Gendreau and Gendreau 1970; Kagan 1987; Lang 1983; Nathan 1988; Sutker and Allain 1988.
69. Dell, Ruzicka, and Palisi 1981; McCormick 1987.
70. McCormick and Taber 1987, pp. 12–13.
71. Lowenfeld 1979.
72. cf. Graham and Lowenfeld 1986.
73. Glen 1979.
74. McCormick and Taber 1987, pp. 28–36.
75. ibid., p. 36.
76. Hunter and Brunner 1928.
77. Morris 1957.
78. e.g., Armstrong 1958, p. 42; Gross and Carpenter 1971; Lisansky 1960; Zwerling 1959.
79. Coopersmith 1964; Lisansky 1967; Witkin, Carp, and Goodenough 1959.
80. Rozin and Stoess 1993, p. 81.
81. Walker 1992c, p. 93.
82. ibid.
83. Rozin and Stoess 1993, p. 82.
84. Cox 1987, p. 63.
85. Dell, Ruzicka, and Palisi 1981, p. 151.
86. McCormick 1987, p. 259.
87. Knapp and Lech 1987, p. 33.
88. Tarter 1990; Tarter, Alterman, and Edwards 1985; Tarter, Hegedus, and Gavaler 1985; Tarter, Kabene, Escallier, Laird, and Jacob 1990.
89. Bedi and Halikas 1985; Schuckit and Monteiro 1988; Weddige and Ostrom 1990.
90. Hesselbrock 1991; Hesselbrock and Hesselbrock 1992; Schuckit 1985.
91. Blaszczynski 1996; Blaszczynski and McConaghy 1994; Blaszczynski, Winter, and McConaghy 1986; Lesieur 1988b; Graham and Lowenfeld 1986; Kagan 1987; Linden, Pope, and Jonas 1986; McCormick and Taber 1987; McCormick, Russo, Ramirez, and Taber 1984; Martinez-Pina, Guirao de Parga, Fuste i Vallverdu, Planas, Mateo, and Auguado 1991; Ramirez, McCormick, Russo, and Taber 1983; Rugle 1996, Rugle and Melamed 1993, Specker, Carlson, Edmonson, Johnson, and Marcotte 1996.
92. Blaszczynski, McConaghy, and Frankova 1989.
93. ibid., p. 138.

94. Blaszczynski and McConaghy 1994, p. 141.
95. Adkins, Kruedelbach, and Toomig 1987; McCormick 1987, pp. 258–259; McCormick and Ramirez 1988; Malkin and Syme 1986.
96. Cox 1987, p. 83; Galski 1987, pp. 130–134.

Chapter 4
LEARNING OR REINFORCEMENT THEORY

1. Shaffer and Schneider 1984, pp. 39–41.
2. e.g., Dickerson 1989; 1991.
3. Cohen 1975, p. 268.
4. e.g., Marlatt and Gordon 1985; Miller, W. 1980; Miller and Hester 1980.
5. Dickerson 1989.
6. Marks 1990.
7. Marlatt 1985a.
8. Orford 1985.
9. Corless and Dickerson 1979; Dickerson 1989; 1991; 1993a; Dickerson, Hinchy, Legg England, Fabre, and Cunningham 1992; Shewan and Brown 1993.
10. Carnes 1983; Marks 1990; Miller 1980; Miller and Hester 1980; Orford 1978; 1985, p. 3.
11. Marlatt 1985b; cf. Peele 1989.
12. Marlatt 1985c; Miller, W. 1980; Miller and Hester 1980; Shiffman, Read, Maltese, Rapkin, and Jarvik 1985.
13. Orford 1985, p. 3.
14. Peele 1989; Peele and Brodsky 1975.
15. Lesieur 1988a.
16. American Psychiatric Association 1980.
17. Jacobs 1989, p. 41.
18. Marks 1990.
19. Skinner 1938; 1953; 1971; 1974.
20. Anderson and Brown 1984, p. 405; Bergler 1958; Blaszczynski and McConaghy 1989a, pp. 344, 345; Wagenaar, Keren, and Pleit-Kuiper 1984.
21. Dickerson, Cunningham, Legg England, and Hinchy 1991.
22. Ferster and Skinner 1957, p. 391.
23. Skinner 1953, pp. 104, 396–397; 1969, p. 119; 1971, p. 35; 1974, p. 60.
24. Frank 1979, pp. 80–81.
25. "Slot machines" or simply "slots" as they are sometimes called in the U.S. are referred to as "poker machines" or "pokies" in Australia and "fruit machines" in the U.K. where they are officially but euphemistically known as "amusement-with-prizes" or AWP machines. In the U.S. these three- or five-wheel "one-armed bandits" are entirely games of chance. In the U.K., however, Sue Fisher (1993) and Mark Griffiths (1990a) provide evidence that successful fruit machine gambling requires certain playing skills and a thorough knowledge of particular machines. "Poker machines" or "video poker" machines in the U.S. are electronic versions of "draw" poker and "blackjack" or "twenty-one" games that entail greater player involvement. Since each play requires choice and decision among a variety of playing options, "video poker" players must have a working knowledge of these card games and some degree of playing skill.
26. Reid 1986.
27. Gilovich 1983.
28. Skinner 1953, p. 397; cf. Gilovich 1983; Reid 1986; Scarne 1975; Strickland and Grote 1967.
29. Skinner 1953, p. 397.
30. Skinner 1969, p. 60.
31. e.g., Edwards, W. 1955; Frank 1979, p. 81; Griffiths 1993b; Knapp 1976; Rachlin 1990; Skinner 1953, p. 104; 1971, p. 35.
32. Skinner 1974, p. 61.
33. Lewis and Duncan 1956; 1957; 1958.
34. Cornish 1978, pp. 166–175.
35. Scott 1968.
36. see Fisher 1993; Griffiths 1993b; Fabian 1995.
37. Strickland and Grote 1967.
38. see also Rogers 1999.
39. Pavlov 1927.
40. Schachter 1971.
41. e.g., Bolles 1972; Brown 1987a, p. 112; Cummings, Gordon, and Marlatt 1980, pp. 292–293; Marlatt 1985c, pp. 139–142; Siegel 1983; 1988; Zinberg 1984.
42. Schachter 1971.
43. Miller, P. 1980.

44. Dickerson 1984.
45. Dickerson 1991, p. 324.
46. Lesieur 1992, p. 44; Lesieur and Blume 1993, p. 93.
47. Anderson and Brown 1984, p. 406; cf. Brown 1986; 1987a, p. 114; 1989, p. 110.
48. Dostoevsky 1914 [1866], pp. 124–125.
49. e.g., Brown 1993; Peele 1985; Siegel 1979; 1983.
50. Brown 1993, p. 255.
51. Blaszczynski and McConaghy 1989a, p. 339; Blaszczynski, Wilson, and McConaghy 1986, p. 116; McConaghy 1980; 1991; McConaghy, Armstrong, Blazczynski, and Allcock 1983.
52. McConaghy, Armstrong, Blaszczynski, and Allcock 1983.
53. Leary and Dickerson 1985, p. 639.
54. Symes and Nicki 1997.
55. Fuller 1974, p. 87.
56. Gilovich and Douglas 1986, pp. 239–240.
57. see Lea, Tarpy, and Webley 1987, pp. 286–288 for a brief review.
58. Walker, 1992c, p. 118.
59. Cohen 1972.
60. Walker 1985, p. 151.
61. Lea, Tarpy, and Webley 1987, pp. 288–289; Walker 1992c, p. 75.
62. Anderson and Brown 1984, p. 402; Blaszczynski, Winter, and McConaghy 1986, p. 5; Brown 1987c, p. 1056; 1988, p. 191; 1989, p. 110; Dickerson 1984, p. 14.
63. Brown 1986, p. 1004; cf. Corless and Dickerson 1989, p. 1535; Dickerson 1984, p. 14; Dickerson, Hinchy, and Fabre 1987, p. 674; Walker 1985, p. 151.
64. Anderson and Brown 1984, pp. 402, 406; Brown 1986, pp. 1004 ff.; 1987b, p. 1057; 1989, p. 110; Cornish 1978; Dickerson 1984, p. 90; 1991, p. 327; Saunders and Wookey 1980, pp. 2, 5; Walker 1985; 1992a, 1992b, 1992c.
65. Oldman 1974, p. 411.
66. Frank 1979, pp. 75–77.
67. Skinner 1969, p. 56.
68. Dickerson 1984, p. 84; 1989, p. 166; Dickerson and Adcock 1987, pp. 4–5; Kusyszyn 1976; Murray 1993, p. 797.
69. Anderson and Brown 1984, p. 405.
70. Kerren and Wagenaar 1985, p. 155.
71. Walker 1992c, p. 12.
72. Dickerson, Hinchy, Schaefer, Whitworth, and Fabre 1988, p. 93; see also Dickerson 1979; Dickerson, Walker, Legg England, and Hinchy 1990; Gilovich and Douglas 1986; Griffiths 1990b; 1990c for criticisms aof laboratory studies.
73. Dickerson, Cunningham, Legg England, and Hinchy 1991.
74. Dickerson, Hinchy, Legg England, Fabre, and Cunningham 1992.
75. Dickerson 1991, pp. 326–327; 1993a, p. 14 emphasis in original.
76. Dickerson 1991, p. 327.
77. Dickerson 1991, p. 327; 1993a, p. 14; Dickerson, Hinchy, Legg England, Fabre, and Cunningham 1992, p. 226.

Chapter 5
NEED-STATES AND DRIVE-REDUCTION

1. France 1902, p. 407.
2. Huizinga 1950, p. 13.
3. ibid., p. 28.
4. ibid., p. 13.
5. ibid., emphasis in original.
6. Caillois 1961.
7. ibid., p. 19.
8. ibid., p. 44.
9. e.g., Herman 1976a, p. 1; 1976b; Kusyszyn 1976; 1978; 1984; 1990; Kusyszyn and Rutter 1985, p. 63; Lester 1979; Smith and Abt 1984.
10. Scott 1968.
11. ibid., p. 81, emphasis in original.
12. Smith and Abt 1984; cf. Griffiths 1989.
13. Caillois 1961, p. 23.
14. Downes, Daviess, David, and Stone 1976, p. 185.
15. e.g., Kusyszyn 1976; 1984.
16. Abt, Smith, and Christiansen 1985, p. 39.
17. Caldwell 1985, p. 265.
18. Dickerson, Bayliss, and Head 1984, cited by Caldwell 1985, p. 265.
19. Anderson and Brown 1984, p. 405.

20. Conger 1951, p. 29.
21. e.g., Chafetz 1970, p. 1976; Dollard and Miller 1950, pp. 185–187; Krystal and Raskin 1970; Ludwig 1972; Marlatt and Gordon 1985; Masserman 1961; Miller, Hersen, Eisler, and Hilsman 1985; Moore 1968; Orford 1985.
22. e.g., Cappell and Herman 1972, pp. 33–34; Shipley 1987.
23. e.g., Armor, Polich, and Stambul 1978; Bandura 1969, p. 533; Cain 1964; Polich, Armor, and Braiker 1981; Sobell, M. 1978; Sobell and Sobell 1977; Volger and Bartz 1982.
24. Cofer and Appley 1964, p. 601.
25. e.g., Fenichel 1945; Greenson 1948; Israeli 1935; Kris 1938.
26. e.g., Blaszczynski and McConahghy 1987; 1988; 1989a; Blaszczynski and Silove 1995; Blaszczynski, Buhrich, and McConaghy 1985, pp. 317–318; Blaszczynski, McConaghy, and Frankova 1990; Blaszczynski, Wilson, and McConaghy 1986; Boyd 1976, p. 372; Corless and Dickerson 1989, p. 1535; Custer and Milt 1985, pp. 36 ff., 124 ff., 236–237; Ferrioli and Cimenero 1981; Galdston 1960; Griffiths 1995; Jacobs 1986; 1988; 1989; Linden, Pope, and Jonas 1986; Livingston 1974b, p. 55; McCormick 1987; McCormick, Taber, and Kruedelbach 1989; McCormick, Russo, Ramirez, and Taber 1984; Moran 1970d; 1993; Rosenthal 1986; 1989, p. 122; Taber, McCormick, and Ramirez 1987; Whitman-Raymond 1988.
27. Cummings, Gordon, and Marlatt 1980, p. 303.
28. McCormick, Russo, Ramirez, and Taber 1984, p. 216.
29. Rosenthal 1993, p. 143.
30. ibid., p. 144.
31. ibid., p. 143.
32. Rosenthal 1986; 1993.
33. Abt, Smith, and Christiansen 1985, p. 122.
34. Corless and Dickerson 1989; Dickerson 1993a, p. 17; Dickerson and Adcock 1987; Zimmerman, Meeland, and Krug 1963.
35. Griffiths 1994, p. 380.
36. ibid.
37. Orford and McCartney 1990, p. 149.
38. ibid., p. 150.
39. Allcock 1985, p. 165.
40. McCormick, Russo, Ramirez, and Taber 1984, p. 217.
41. Shaffer and Gambino 1989, p. 225.
42. Lesieur and Blume 1991, p. 186; Lesieur 1993, p. 505.
43. Gupta and Derevensky 1998, p. 33.
44. Griffiths 1991a, p. 465.
45. Bühringer and Konstanty 1992, p. 37.
46. Substance dependence is differentiated from substance abuse in that the former is equated with addiction or physiological dependence involving loss of control, craving, withdrawl, etc., while the latter, which is considered to be a matter of personal choice, is not. Unfortunately, the fact that these terms are often used indiscriminately and interchangeably leads to confusion in the interpretation of research results.
47. Haberman 1969, p. 157.
48. Adler, J. 1966; Adler and Goleman 1969; Haberman 1969, p. 157.
49. McCormick, Taber, and Kruedelbach 1989, p. 484.
50. Lesieur and Heineman 1988, p. 766.
51. Jacobs 1986, p. 17.
52. Lesieur and Heineman 1988, p. 766.
53. Lorenz 1993, pp. 609–610.
54. Griffiths 1994.
55. e.g., France 1902; Steinmetz 1870, p. 24; Thomas 1901.
56. Bergler 1943, p. 382.
57. Bolen and Boyd 1968, p. 621.
58. ibid.; Greenson 1948, pp. 112–113; Laforgue 1930, p. 318; Lindner 1950, p. 107.
59. Campbell 1973.
60. Berlyne 1967.
61. Zuckerman 1974; 1978; 1979; 1983.
62. Anderson and Brown 1984; Blaszczynski, Wilson, and McConaghy 1986; Brown 1985; 1986; 1987a; 1987c; 1988; 1993; Carlton and Manowitz 1987; Coventry and Brown 1993; Custer 1982; Custer and Milt 1985, pp. 38, 236; Dickerson 1979; 1984; Dickerson and Adcock 1987; Dickerson, Hinchy, and Fabre 1987; Dumont and Ladouceur 1990; Goffman 1969, p. 137; Griffiths 1991b; Kuley and Jacobs 1988;

Kusyszyn 1976; 1984; 1990; Lesieur 1993; Lesieur and Blume 1991, p. 181; Lewis and Duncan 1956; 1957; 1958; McCormick 1987; Martinez 1976; Moody 1985; Moskowitz 1980; Rosenthal 1993; Rule, Nutter, and Fisher 1971; Scarne 1975; Slovic 1964; Spanier 1994; Walker 1989; Wolfgang 1988.

63. Walker 1989.
64. ibid., p. 185.
65. ibid., p. 197.
66. Goffman 1967, p. 185; cf. Zuckerman 1979, p. 10.
67. Goffman 1967, pp. 184–185.
68. ibid., p. 156, emphasis in original.
69. Anderson and Brown 1984, p. 405; Dickerson and Adcock 1987; Kallick, Suits, Dielman, and Hybels 1976, p. 77.
70. Downes, Davies, David, and Stone 1976, pp. 82–83.
71. Campbell 1976, pp. 221–222.
72. Kusyszyn 1990, p. 162.
73. Spanier 1994, p. 168.
74. Kusyszyn 1984.
75. Abt, McGurrin, and Smith 1985; Graham and Lowenfeld 1986; Taber and McCormick 1987, p. 161.
76. McCormick, Russo, Ramirez, and Taber 1984, p. 216.
77. Linden, Pope, and Jonas 1986.
78. Zuckerman 1979; Brown 1986; 1987a.
79. e.g., Anderson and Brown 1984; Brown 1986; Leary and Dickerson 1985.
80. Brown 1987a, p. 117.
81. Dickerson 1977b; 1979; 1984.
82. cf. Lesieur 1992, p. 44.
83. Dickerson 1979, p. 297.
84. Brown 19871a, p. 117, emphasis in original.
85. Brown 1987a, p. 114.
86. Bolen 1976, p. 17, emphasis in original.
87. Boyd 1976, p. 372.
88. Moskowitz 1980, pp. 787–788.
89. Taber and McCormick 1987, p. 161.
90. McCormick 1987, p. 262.
91. Brown 1987a, p. 114; 1988, p. 191.
92. From *The Gambler* (p. 158), by Fyodor Dostoevsky, translated by V. Terras, 1972 [1866], Chicago: University of Chicago Press. Copyright 1973 by the University of Chicago Press. Reprinted with permission.
93. Newman 1972, p. 206.
94. Lesieur and Blume 1991, p. 186.
95. see also King 1990; Smith and Preston 1984.
96. Cohen 1975, p. 268.
97. Zuckerman 1979.
98. Blaszczynski, McConaghy, and Frankova 1990, p. 38.
99. Custer 1984, p. 35; cf. Peck 1986, p. 463.
100. Brown 1993.
101. see e.g., Freed 1978, Pihl and Smith 1983; Tucker, Vuchinich, and Sobell 1982 for reviews.
102. Sjoberg 1969.
103. Griffiths 1995.
104. Brown 1991; 1993.
105. Edwards and Gross 1976.
106. American Psychiatric Association 1987.
107. Brown 1933, p. 264.
108. Griffiths 1991b, p. 355.
109. Griffiths 1990a, p. 36; cf. 1991b; 1993c.
110. Griffiths 1990b.
111. Griffiths 1991b, p. 353.
112. Griffiths 1991b.
113. Griffiths 1995.
114. Rule and Fisher 1970.
115. Rule, Nutter, and Fischer 1971, p. 244.
116. Anderson and Brown 1984.
117. Brown 1987a, pp. 113–114.
118. Leary and Dickerson 1985.
119. Dickerson 1979; 1991, p. 329; 1993a, pp. 17, 20; Dickerson, Hinchy, and Fabre 1987.
120. e.g., Brown 1986, pp. 1001–1002; Carlton and Manowitz 1987; Dickerson and Adcock 1987, pp. 9–10; Kuley and Jacobs 1988; Meyer 1989; Rosenthal and Lesieur 1992; Roy, DeJong, and Linnoila 1989; Roy, Adinoff, Roehrich, Lamparski, Custer, Lorene, Barbaccia, Guidotti, Costa, and Linnoila 1988; Wray and Dickerson 1981.
121. Dickerson, Hinchy, Legg England, Fabre, and Cunningham 1992, p. 245.
122. Coulombe, Ladouceur, Desharnais, and Jobin 1992.
123. Carroll and Huxley 1994.
124. Coventry and Norman 1997.
125. Sharpe, Tarrier, Schotte, and Spence 1995.
126. Walker 1992c, p. 128.

127. Dickerson, Cunningham, Legg England, and Hinchy 1991, p. 537.
128. Rule, Nutter, and Fischer 1971, p. 243.
129. McCormick, Russo, Ramirez, and Taber 1984, p. 217.
130. Anderson and Brown 1984, p. 407; Bergler 1958; Dickerson and Adcock 1987; Dickerson, Hinchy, and Fabre 1987, p. 678; Gupta and Derevensky 1998; Wray and Dickerson 1981.
131. Dickerson, Bayliss, and Head 1984, cited by Caldwell 1985, p. 265.
132. Dickerson, Walker, Legg England, and Hinchy 1990, p. 174.
133. Griffiths 1993c, p. 36.
134. Gupta and Derevensky 1998, p. 33.
135. Zuckerman, Kolin, Price, and Zoob 1964; Zuckerman 1979.
136. Waters and Kirk 1968.
137. Kozlowski 1977.
138. Kuley and Jacobs 1988.
139. Martinez-Pina, Guirao de Parga, Fuste i Vallverdu, Planas, Mateo, and Moreno Auguado 1991, p. 287.
140. Allcock and Grace 1988; Anderson and Brown 1984, p. 404; Blaszczynski, Wilson, and McConaghy 1986; Coventry and Brown 1993, p. 549; Castellani and Rugle 1995; Dickerson 1993a, p. 10; Dickerson, Hinchy, and Fabre 1987; Dickerson, Cunningham, Legg England, and Hinchey 1991; Ladouceur and Mayrand 1986; Lyons 1985; Martinez-Pina, Guirao de Parga, Fuste i Vallverdu, Planas, Mateo, and Moreno Auguado 1991.
141. Blaszczynski, McConaghy, and Frankova 1991b, p. 302.
142. Farmer and Sundberg 1986.
143. Blaszczynski, McConaghy, and Frankova 1990, pp. 38–39.
144. Steinberg, Kosten, and Rounsaville 1992.
145. Carroll, Zuckerman, and Vogel 1982; cf; Carroll and Zuckerman 1977.
146. Rule, Nutter, and Fischer 1971, p. 245.
147. Dickerson and Adcock 1987.
148. Blaszczynski, Wilson, and McConaghy 1986, p. 115; Dickerson, Hinchy, and Fabre 1987, p. 677; Dickerson, Cunningham, Legg England, and Hinchy 1991, p. 536; Dickerson, Walker, Legg England, and Hinchy 1990; Kusyszyn and Kallai 1975.
149. Dickerson, Hinchy, and Fabre 1987.
150. Walker 1992c, p. 128.
151. Dickerson 1991, p. 330.
152. Blaszczynski, McConaghy, and Frankova 1990, p. 41.
153. Anderson and Brown 1984.
154. Kuley and Jacobs 1988.
155. Murray 1993, p. 796.
156. Walker 1992c, p. 96.
157. Anderson and Brown 1984, p. 405.
158. ibid., p. 406.
159. Dickerson 1977b; 1979; 1984.
160. Shewan and Brown 1993.
161. Saunders 1981, pp. 335–336; Saunders and Wookey 1980, p. 5; Shewan and Brown 1993, pp. 123–124.
162. Murray 1993, p. 797.
163. Blaszczynski, Wilson, and McConaghy 1986; Blaszczynski, Winter, and McConaghy 1986; Brown 1987d, p. 228; Coventry and Brown 1993, p. 543; Dickerson 1987; 1989; Dickerson, Hinchy, and Fabre 1987; Jellinek 1960, p. 35 ff.; Moran 1970a; Saunders and Wookey 1980, pp. 1–2.
164. Coventry and Brown 1993, p. 551; Dickerson, Hinchy, and Fabre 1987, p. 678.
165. Blaszczynski, Winter, and McConaghy 1986; Cocco, Sharpe, and Blaszczynski 1995.
166. Lesieur 1988a; 1993; cf. Fink 1961, p. 251; Kroeber 1992, pp. 90–91.
167. Specker, Carlson, Edmonson, Johnson, and Marcotte 1996, pp. 79–80.
168. Blaszczynski and McConaghy 1989a; Blaszczynski and Steel 1998; Blaszczynski, McConaghy, and Frankova 1990.
169. Walker 1992c, p. 240.
170. Moran 1970a, p. 594.
171. Fuller 1974, p. 73.
172. Kusyszyn 1990, p. 163 emphasis in original; cf. Kusyszyn 1976, p. 257; 1984, p. 134.
173. Cofer and Appley 1964, p. 583.
174. Milkman and Sunderwirth 1983, p. 38.
175. Fuller 1974, p. 88.
176. Dickerson 1991, p. 326.
177. Szasz 1961, p. 108.
178. Bolen, Caldwell, and Boyd 1975; Lesieur

and Blume 1991; Lowenfeld 1979; Martinez-Pina, Guirao de Parga, Fuste i Vallverdu, Planas, Mateo, and Moreno Auguado 1991; Rosenthal 1993; Taber, McCormick, and Ramirez 1987.

179. Dickerson 1984, p. 93.
180. Corless and Dickerson 1989, p. 1535; Dickerson 1993a, p. 13; cf. Dickerson 1991, pp. 325, 329.
181. Corless and Dickerson 1989, p. 1535; Dickerson 1991, pp. 324, 329; 1993a, pp. 10, 12, 17; Dickerson and Adcock 1987; Dickerson, Hinchy, Legg England, Fabre, and Cunningham 1992.
182. Blaszczynski, Wilson, and McConaghy 1986, p. 115.
183. Griffiths 1993c, p. 39.
184. Lesieur, Blume, and Zoppa 1986, p. 37.
185. Specker, Carlson, Edmonson, Johnson, and Marcotte 1996, p. 73.
186. Dickerson, Bayliss, and Head 1984, cited by Caldwell 1985, p. 265.
187. Dickerson, Walker, Legg England, and Hinchy 1990, p. 174.
188. Gupta and Derevensky 1998.
189. Walker 1992c, p. 91.
190. Brown 1987a, p. 113.
191. Schwartz, Burkhart, and Green 1978.
192. McCormick 1987.
193. Blaszczynski, McConaghy, and Frankova 1990.
194. Walker 1992c, p. 107.
195. Levy and Feinberg 1991, pp. 45–46.

Chapter 6
IRRATIONAL THINKING

1. e.g., Brown 1993; Dickerson 1991; 1993b; Dickerson and Adcock 1987; Griffiths 1990a; 1993a; Ladouceur 1993; Sharpe and Tarrier 1993; Walker 1992a, 1992b, 1992c; 1992d.
2. Walker 1992d, p. 245.
3. Frank 1993, p. 393.
4. Wagenaar 1988.
5. Walker 1992d, p. 245.
6. ibid., p. 246.
7. Dickerson 1991, p. 325; 1993a, p. 12.
8. Dickerson 1991, p. 328; Dickerson 1993a, p. 15 emphasis in original.
9. Frank 1979, pp. 809–81; Edwards 1955; Moran 1970d; Orford 1985, pp. 176–177; Tonneatto, Blitz-Miller, Calderwood, Dragonetti, and Tsanos 1997; Walker 1985; 1988; 1992a; 1992b; 1992c.
10. Attneave 1953; Griffith 1949; Preston and Baratta 1948; Sprowls 1953.
11. Moran 1970d, p. 64.
12. Cohen 1964, 1975.
13. Anderson and Brown 1984, p. 403; Oldman 1974, p. 417; Orford 1985, p. 177; Rogers 1999, p. 120; Shewan and Brown 1993, p. 124.
14. Allcock 1985, p. 164; Cohen, Boyle, and Schubsachs 1969.
15. Moran 1970d, p. 63.
16. Spanier 1994, p. 152.
17. ibid., p. 153.
18. Scott 1968, p. 119; see also Ladouceur and Dubé 1997.
19. Cohen 1964.
20. Keren and Lewis 1994.
21. Scott 1968, p. 120.
22. Clotfelter and Cook 1989; Rogers 1999, p. 121.
23. Camerer 1989; Paulson 1994; Wood 1992.
24. Dickerson 1989, p. 160.
25. Dickerson 1993a, p. 14.
26. ibid., p. 14.
27. Spanier 1994, p. 150; cf. Wilson 1965, pp. 6–7.
28. Spanier 1994, p. 149.
29. Popkin 1994, p. 48.
30. ibid., p. 49.
31. Burger and Smith 1985.
32. Kusyszyn and Rubenstein 1985, p. 107.
33. Rotter 1954; 1966.
34. e.g., Langer 1975; Wortman 1975; 1976.
35. The related **self-determination theory** makes similar predictions: researchers testing this approach have found that people with self-determined or intrinsic gambling motivations will be drawn to games of skill while those with non-self determined motivations or external regulation, will gravitate toward games of chance (Chantal and

Vallerand 1996; Chantal, Vallerand, and Valliéres 1995).

36. Burger 1991; Burger and Cooper 1979; Ladouceur and Mayrand 1987; Liverant and Scodel 1960; Schneider 1968; 1972; Strickland, Lewicki, and Katz 1966; Wortman 1975.
37. Burger 1986; Burger and Cooper 1979; Burger and Schnerring 1982.
38. Frank 1979, pp. 81–82.
39. Wortman 1975.
40. Since Wortman was testing the influence of only two conditions–foreknowledge and causality–she reasoned that her research design involving the three subgroups she selected would be adequate to demonstrate that both conditions together are required to induce a perception of control. She included the comparative single-condition subgroups only to be able to reject the possibility that one condition might be more influential than the other. Although the results she obtained supported these particular predictions, her decision to have only three subject groups was unfortunate.
41. Langer 1975.
42. ibid., p. 313.
43. Breen and Frank 1993.
44. Langer's "illusion of control" apparatus consisted of an electrically wired box with three separate wavy, meandering copper strips of paths etched into the top surface. Connected to the box was a stylus which would complete a circuit and sound a buzzer when it was placed on the "correct" path. Which of the three paths was "correct" at any given time was determined by a series of switches along one side of the box. These switches could not only activate one path at a time, but they could also activate or deactivate all three at once. An internal motorized switch was also set to complete and interrupt the circuit to all three paths to allow the buzzer to sound for only two seconds out of every ten and prevent it from sounding for the remaining eight seconds even when the stylus was touching correct path. Those in the "high involvement" condition were asked to choose which of the three paths they thought would sound the buzzer, then to pick up the stylus and slowly trace along that path to see if they had chosen correctly. Those in the "low involvement" situation were asked to select the path they thought was "correct" but could not move the stylus. Subjects in the "high familiarity" condition were told that the electrical plug had just broken and needed to be repaired before the experiment could proceed. During the two minutes required to make the "repair" they were invited to familiarize themselves with the apparatus by "practicing" with it. Those in the "low familiarity" condition were denied this opportunity.
45. Actually, two estimates per subject were analyzed. Before initiating the experiment, all subjects were aksed to rate their confidence of success on a scale of 1 (least confident) to 10 (most confident). A single "successful" trial (during which all paths were activated) was followed by a second questionnaire so that the subjects' pre-trial and post-trial confidence levels could be compared. Both ratings produced similar results.
46. Burger 1986.
47. Langer 1975, p. 323.
48. ibid., p. 324.
49. ibid.
50. ibid., emphasis in original.
51. ibid.
52. ibid., p. 327.
53. Ladouceur and Mayrand 1984; 1986; Ladouceur, Mayrand, Dussault, Letarte, and Tremblay 1984; Reid 1986, p. 36.
54. Ladouceur, Mayrand, Dussault, Letarte, and Tremblay 1984, p. 47.
55. ibid, p. 51.
56. Letarte, Ladouceur, and Mayrand 1986, p. 299.
57. Rothbaum, Weitz, and Snyder 1982.
58. Letarte, Ladouceur, and Mayrand 1986.
59. Ladouceur and Mayrand 1987.
60. Burger 1986; 1991; Burger and Cooper 1979; Burger and Schnerring 1982; Burger and Smith 1985.
61. Carroll and Huxley 1994.

62. Dykstra and Dollinger 1990.
63. Letarte, Ladouceur, and Mayrand 1986.
64. Blascovich and Ginsberg 1974; Blascovich, Ginsberg and Howe 1976; Blascovich, Ginsberg and Veach 1975; Blascovich, Veach, and Ginsberg 1973.
65. e.g., Breen and Frank 1993.
66. Ladoceur and Gaboury 1988; Ladouceur and Mayrand 1986; 1987; Ladouceur, Mayrand, and Tourigny 1987; Ladouceur, Tourigny, and Mayrand 1986.
67. Ladouceur and Gaboury 1988, p. 125.
68. Frank and Smith 1989, p. 130.
69. Blascovich, Veach, and Ginsberg 1973; Cohen, Boyle, and Shubachs 1969; Hochauer 1970; Levitz 1973.
70. Greenberg and Weiner 1966; McGlothlin 1956.
71. Greenberg and Weiner 1966.
72. Cohen, Boyle, and Shubachs 1969.
73. Cornish 1978, p. 178.
74. Langer and Roth 1975.
75. ibid., p. 952.
76. ibid.
77. ibid., p. 954.
78. ibid., p. 955.
79. Frank and Smith 1989.
80. ibid., p. 135.
81. Burger 1986.
82. Breen and Frank 1993.
83. Babad and Katz 1991; cf. Babad 1987.
84. ibid., p. 1924.
85. ibid., p. 1922.
86. Kruglanski 1980; Kruglanski and Ajzen 1983.
87. Babad and Katz 1991, p. 1922.
88. e.g., Wood 1992.
89. Rogers 1999, pp. 122–123.
90. Gilovich 1983.
91. Shewan and Brown 1993, p. 124.
92. Gilovich 1983, Gilovich and Douglas 1986; Griffiths 1993a.
93. Scott 1968, pp. 91–92.
94. Corney and Cummings 1992.
95. Reid 1986, p. 32; see also Scarne 1975; Strickland and Grote 1967.
96. Griffiths 1993c, p. 43.
97. Reid 1986, p. 32.
98. Gilovich 1983.
99. ibid., p. 1111.
100. ibid., p. 1119.
101. ibid., p. 1122.
102. Gilovich and Douglas 1986.
103. Kallick, Suits, Dielman, and Hybels 1979, p. 85; Cohen 1972.
104. Gilovich and Douglas 1986, p. 229.
105. Gilovich 1983, p. 1111.
106. Frank 1993.
107. Keren and Wagenaar 1985, p. 154.
108. Fink 1961, p. 255.
109. Brockner, Shaw, and Rubin 1979.
110. Rogers 1999, p. 120.
111. Walker 1992c, p. 66.
112. McCormick and Taber 1987, pp. 20.
113. Fink 1961, p. 255.
114. Kallick, Suits, Dielman, and Hybels 1979, p. 86.
115. Dumont and Ladouceur 1990; Gaboury and Ladouceur 1988; 1989; Ladouceur 1993; Ladouceur and Gaboury 1988; Ladouceur, Gaboury, and Duval 1988; Ladouceur, Gaboury, Dumont, and Rochette 1988; Ladouceur, Gaboury, Bujold, Lachance, and Tremblay 1991.
116. Coulombe, Ladouceur, Desharnais, and Jobin 1992; Ladouceur 1993, p. 335.
117. Ladouceur and Gaboury 1988, p. 122.
118. e.g., Gaboury and Ladouceur 1989.
119. Ladouceur, Gaboury, Bujold, Lachance, and Tremblay 1991, p. 115.
120. Wagenaar 1970; 1988.
121. Keren and Wagenaar 1985, p. 152.
122. ibid.
123. Oldman 1974, pp. 417–418.
124. Dickerson 1993a, p. 15.
125. Henslin 1967; cf. Burger and Cooper 1979; Strickland, Lewicki, and Katz 1966.
126. Griffiths 1990a; 1990d.
127. Keren and Wagenaar 1985.
128. Ladouceur and Mayrand 1986; 1987; Strickland, Lewicki, and Katz 1966.
129. Downes, Davies, David, and Stone 1976, p. 114.
130. Rosenthal 1993, p. 145, emphassis in original.
131. Skinner 1948.
132. ibid., pp. 168–169.
133. Havemann 1952, p. 10.

134. Henslin 1967.
135. ibid., p. 325.
136. Malinowski 1948.
137. Kroeber 1963.
138. Henslin 1967, p. 329; emphasis in original.
139. King 1990.
140. Walker 1992c, pp. 72–73.
141. Aasved and Schaefer 1995, p. 334.
142. Aasved and Schaefer 1992, p. 21; Walker 1992c, p. 139.
143. Cornish 1978, p. 192.
144. see e.g., King 1990.
145. Clotfelter and Cook 1989, pp. 77–82.
146. Kaplan 1978, cited by Kaplan 1988, p. 176.
147. Maze 1987, p. 211.
148. Radin and Rebman 1998.
149. Burger 1991; Dickerson 1993a, p. 15; Gabory and Ladouceur 1988; Walker 1992c, pp. 65–67.
150. Goffman 1967; Oldman 1974.
151. Popkin 1994, p. 49.

Chapter 7
COGNITIVE-BEHAVIORAL THEORISTS

1. Dickerson 1977b; 1979; 1984.
2. Corless and Dickerson 1989, p. 1535; Dickerson 1979; 1984, pp. 90–91; Sharpe and Tarrier 1993; Shewan and Brown 1993, p. 123.
3. Oldman 1974.
4. ibid., p. 415, emphasis in original.
5. ibid., p. 418.
6. From *The Gambler* (p. 31), by Fyodor Dostoevsky, translated by V. Terras, 1972 [1866], Chicago: University of Chicago Press. Copyright 1973 by the University of Chicago Press. Reprinted with permission.
7. cf. Ladouceur and Mayrand 1986; 1987; Letarte, Ladouceur, and Mayrand 1986.
8. Fisher 1993a; 1993b; Griffiths 1990a.
9. Griffiths 1990a.
10. Other reasons included “for fun” (84%); “friends do” (58%); “nothing else to do” (50%); “to win money” (48%); “to meet friends” (30%); they would “miss [it] if not” able to play (20%); “can’t stop” (10%); and “to impress friends” (2%).
11. Griffiths 1993c, p. 38.
12. Griffiths 1990a, p. 40.
13. cf. Griffiths 1990c.
14. Griffiths 1990a.
15. Ladouceur and Gaboury 1988; Ladouceur, Gaboury, Dumont, and Rochette 1988.
16. Walker 1992c, p. 83.
17. Griffiths 1990a, pp. 37–38.
18. Griffiths 1990d, p. 239.
19. Griffiths 1993b.
20. cf. Strickland and Grote 1967.
21. Popkin 1994.
22. Griffiths 1993b, p. 116.
23. Walker 1992d; see also Walker 1992c, pp. 74–75.
24. Walker 1992d, p. 259.
25. ibid., p. 246.
26. Walker 1985; 1988; 1992a; 1992b; 1992c.
27. Walker 1992d, pp. 249–250; see also Walker 1992c, pp. 72–73.
28. Walker 1992c, p. 129.
29. ibid., p. 131.
30. ibid., p. 129.
31. ibid., p. 134.
32. ibid.
33. ibid., p. 136.
34. ibid., p. 138.
35. Langer 1975.
36. Skinner 1953, p. 397.
37. Gaboury and Ladouceur 1988; 1989; Ladouceur and Gaboury 1988; Walker 1992b.
38. Walker 1992c, pp. 146–147.
39. Victor 1981, p. 273.
40. Walker 1992c, p. 29.
41. ibid., p. 241.
42. ibid., p. 150.
43. ibid.
44. ibid., p. 135.
45. Walker 1985, p. 159.
46. Walker 1992a, p. 391.
47. Dickerson 1991; 1993a; Dickerson and Adcock 1987.
48. Dickerson 1991, p. 331.
49. cf. Saunders and Wookey 1980, pp. 1–2.
50. Dickerson 1991, pp. 331–332.
51. e.g., Shaffer and Schneider 1984, p. 46.

52. Kearney and Drabman 1992.
53. Bandura 1977, p. 203.
54. Marlatt and Gordon 1979; 1985; Zinberg 1984.
55. e.g., Orford 1985.
56. Brown 1987d.
57. ibid., p. 227.
58. Rabow, Comess, Donovan, and Hollos 1994, p. 198.
59. Walker 1992c, p. 8.
60. ibid., p. 125.
61. Griffiths 1989, p. 74.
62. From *The Gambler* (pp. 18–19), by Fyodor Dostoevsky, translated by V. Terras, 1972 [1866], Chicago: University of Chicago Press. Copyright 1973 by the University of Chicago Press. Reprinted with permission.
63. From *The Gambler* (p. 18), by Fyodor Dostoevsky, translated by V. Terra, 1972 [1866]. Copyright 1973 by the University of Chicago Press. Reprinted with permission.
64. Livingston 1974b.
65. Becoña, Labrador, Echeburúa, Ochoa, and Vallejo 1995, p. 283.
66. Gupta and Derevensky 1997.
67. ibid., p. 188.
68. Lesieur 1984.
69. Rosenthal 1993.
70. ibid., p. 145.
71. ibid.
72. Walters 1994a; 1994b.
73. Walters 1994b, p. 220.
74. Walters 1994a, p. 168; 1994b, p. 228.
75. Corless and Dickerson 1989, p. 1535.
76. Lowenhar and Boykin 1985.
77. Burger and Smith 1985, p. 151.
78. Hong and Chiu 1988; Zenker and Wolfgang 1982.
79. Johnson, Nora, and Bustos 1992.
80. Leopard 1978; Rule and Fischer 1970.
81. Cohen 1972.
82. Cohen 1970, p. 453.
83. Walker 1988.
84. Dickerson and Adcock 1987; Dickerson, Cunningham, Legg England, and Hinchy 1991, pp. 537, 543; Dickerson, Hinchy, Legg England, Fabre, and Cunningham, 1992, pp. 245–246.
85. Walker 1992b, p. 489; cf. Walker 1988.
86. Walters 1994a, p. 177.

REFERENCES

Aasved, M. J., and Schaefer, J. M. (1992). *Who needs Las Vegas? Gambling and its impacts in a southwestern Minnesota agricultural community.* St. Paul: Minnesota Department of Human Services, Mental Health Division.

Aasved, M. J., and Schaefer, J. M. (1995). "Minnesota Slots": An observational study of pull tab gambling. *Journal of Gambling Studies 11*(3), 311–341.

Abraham, K. (1960). The psychological relation between sexuality and alcoholism. In Bryan, D., and Strachey, A. (Trans). *Selected papers of Karl Abraham.* New York: Basic Books.

Abt, V., Smith, J. F., and Christiansen, E. M. (1985). *The business of risk: Commercial gambling in mainstream America.* Lawrence, KS: University of Kansas Press.

Abt, V., McGurrin, M. C., and Smith, J. F. (1985). Toward a synoptic model of gambling behavior. *Journal of Gambling Behavior 1*(2), 79–88.

Adkins, B., Kreudelbach, N., and Toomig, W. (1987). The relationship of gaming preferences to MMPI personality variables. In Eadington, W. R. (Ed.) *Gambling Research: Proceedings of the Seventh International Conference on Gambling and Risk Taking, Vol. 5.* Reno, Nevada: Bureau of Business and Economic Research, College of Business Administration, University of Nevada.

Adkins, B., Rugle, L., and Taber, J. (1985, November). *A note on sexual addiction among compulsive gamblers.* Paper presented at the First National Conference on Gambling Behavior, National Council on Compulsive Gambling, New York.

Adler, A. (1917). *A study of organ inferiority and its psychical compensation.* New York: Nervous and Mental Diseases Publishing Co.

Adler, A. (1927). *The practice and theory of individual psychology.* New York: Harcourt.

Adler, A. (1930). Individual psychology. In Murchison, C. (Ed.) *Psychologies of 1930.* Worcester, Mass.: Clark University Press.

Adler, A. (1969). *The science of living.* Garden City, NY: Anchor Books.

Adler, J. (1966). Gambling, drugs, and alcohol; A note on functional equivalents. *Issues in Criminality 2*, 111–117.

Adler, N., and Goleman, D. (1969). Gambling and alcoholism: Symptom substitution and functional equivalents. *Quarterly Journal of Studies on Alcohol 30*(3), 733–736.

Allcock, C. (1985). Psychiatry and gambling. In Caldwell, G., Haig, B., Dickerson, M., and Sylvan, L. (Eds.) *Gambling in Australia* (pp. 163–171). Sydney: Croom Helm.

Allcock, C. C., and Grace, D. N. (1988). Pathological gamblers are neither impulsive nor sensation-seekers. *Australia and New Zealand Journal of Psychiatry 22*, 301–311.

American Psychiatric Association (1980). *Diagnostic and statistical manual of mental disorders, third edition (DSM-III).* Washington, D.C.: American Psychiatric Association.

American Psychiatric Association (1987). *Diagnostic and statistical manual of mental disorders, third edition, revised (DSM-III-R).* Washington, D.C.: American Psychiatric Association.

American Psychiatric Association (1994). *Diagnostic and statistical manual of mental disorders, fourth edition (DSM-IV).* Washington, D.C.: American Psychiatric Association.

Anderson, G., and Brown, R. I. F. (1984). Real

and laboratory gambling, sensation seeking, and arousal. *British Journal of Psychology 75*(3), 401–410.

Aristotle. (1953). *The ethics of Aristotle*, Thompson, J. A. K. (Ed. and Trans.) London: Allen and Unwin.

Armor, D. J., Polich, J. M., and Stambul, H. B. (1978). *Alcoholism and treatment.* New York: John Wiley and Sons.

Armstrong, J. D. (1958). The search for the alcoholic personality. *Annals of the American Academy of Political and Social Science 315*, 40–47.

Ashton, N. (1979). Gamblers, disturbed or healthy? In Lester, D. (Ed.) *Gambling today* (pp. 53–70). Springfield, IL: Charles C Thomas.

Atlas, G. D., and Peterson, C. (1990). Explanatory style and gambling: How pessimists respond to losing wagers. *Behaviour Research and Therapy 28*, 523–529.

Attneave, F. (1953). Psychological probability as a function of experienced frequency. *Journal of Experimental Psychology 46*(2), 81–86.

Aubry, W. E. (1975). Altering the gambler's maladaptive life goals. *International Journal of the Addictions 10*(1), 29–33.

Babad, E. (1987). Wishful thinking and objectivity among sports fans. *Social Behaviour 2*, 231–240.

Babad, E., and Katz, Y. (1991). Wishful thinking: Against all odds. *Journal of Applied Social Psychology 21*(23), 1921–1938.

Bacon, M. K. (1974). The dependency-conflict hypothesis and the frequency of drunkenness; Further evidence from a cross-cultural study. *Quarterly Journal of Studies on Alcohol 35*(3), 863–876.

Bacon, M. K., Barry, H., III, and Child, I. L. (1965). A cross-cultural study of drinking. *Quarterly Journal of Studies on Alcohol, Supplement No. 3.*

Bandura, A. (1969). *Principles of behavior modification.* New York: Holt, Reinhart, and Winston.

Bandura, A. (1977). *Social learning theory.* Englewood Cliffs, NJ: Prentice-Hall.

Barker, J. C., and Miller, M. (1968). Aversion therapy for compulsive gambling. *Journal of Nervous and Mental Disease 146*, 285–302.

Barry, H., III (1976). Cross-cultural evidence that dependency conflict motivates drunkenness. In Everett, M. W., Waddell, J. O., and Heath, D. B. (Eds.) *Cross-cultural approaches to the study of alcohol: An interdisciplinary perspective.* The Hague: Mouton.

Becker, G. S., and Murphy, K. V. (1988). A theory of rational addiction. *Journal of Political Economy 96*(4), 675–700.

Becoña, E. (1993). The prevalence of pathological gambling in Galicia (Spain). *Journal of Gambling Studies 9*(4), 353–369.

Becoña, E., Del Carmen Lorenzo, M., Fuentes, M. J. (1996). Pathological gambling and depression. *Psychological Reports 78*(2), 635–640.

Becoña, E., Labrador, F., Echeburúa, E., Ochoa, E., and Vallejo, M. A. (1995). Slot machine gambling in Spain: An important new social problem. *Journal of Gambling Studies 11*(3), 265–286.

Bedi, A., and Halikas, J. A. (1985). Alcoholism and affective disorder. *Alcoholism: Clinical and Experimental Research 9*, 133–134.

Bell, R. C. (1976). Moral views on gambling promulgated by major American religious bodies. In Commission on the review of the national policy toward gambling (Eds.) *Gambling in America*, Appendix 1. Washington, D.C.: U.S. Government Printing Office.

Bergh, C., and Külhorn, E. (1994). Social, psychological and physical consequences of pathological gambling in Sweden. *Journal of Gambling Studies 10*(3), 275–285.

Bergler, E. (1936). On the psychology of the gambler. *American Imago 22*, 404–441.

Bergler, E. (1943). The gambler: a misunderstood neurotic. *Journal of Criminal Psychopathology 4*, 370–393.

Bergler, E. (1949). *The basic neuroses: Oral regression and psychic masochism.* New York: Grune and Stratton.

Bergler, E. (1958). *The psychology of gambling.* New York: International University Press.

Berlyne, D. E. (1967). Arousal and reinforcement. In Levine, D. (Ed.) *Nebraska symposium on motivation* (pp. 1–110). Lincoln, Neb.: University of Nebraska Press.

Black, D. W., and Moyer, T. (1998). Clinical features and psychiatric comorbidity of subjects with pathological gambling behavior. *Psychiatric Services 49*(11), 1434–1439.

Bland, R. C., Newman, S. C., Orn, H., and Stebelsky, G. (1993). Epidemiology of pathological gambling in Edmonton. *Canadian Journal of Psychiatry 38*(2), 108–112.

Blane, H. T., and Barry, H., III (1973). Birth order and alcoholism: A review. *Quarterly Journal of Studies on Alcohol 34*(3), 837–852.

Blane, H. T., and Chafetz, M. E. (1971). Dependency conflict and sex-role identity in drinking delinquents. *Quarterly Journal of Studies on Alcohol 32*(4), 1025–1039.

Blascovich, J., and Ginsburg, G. P. (1974). Emergent norms and choice shifts involving risk. *Sociometry 37*, 205–218.

Blascovich, J., Ginsburg, G. P., and Howe, R. C. (1976). Blackjack, choice shifts in the field. *Sociometry 39*(3), 274–276.

Blascovich, J., Ginsburg, G. P., and Veach, T. L. (1975). A pluralistic explanation of choice shifts on the risk dimension. *Journal of Personality and Social Psychology 31*, 422–429.

Blascovich, J., Veach, T. L., and Ginsburg, G. P. (1973). Blackjack and the risky shift. *Sociometry 36*(1), 42–55.

Blaszczynski, A. P. (1996, April). *Impulsivity, SOGS scores, and impaired control.* Paper presented at the 1996 National Conference on Gambling, Crime and Gaming Enforcement. Illinois State University, Normal, Illinois.

Blaszczynski, A. P., and McConaghy, N. (1987). Demographic and clinical data on compulsive gambling. In Walker, M. (Ed.) *Faces of gambling: Proceedings of the Second National Conference of the National Association for Gambling Studies (1986).* Sydney, Australia: National Association for Gambling Studies.

Blaszczynski, A. P., and McConaghy, N. (1988). SCL-90 assessed psychopathology in pathological gamblers. *Psychological Reports 62*(2), 547–552.

Blaszczynski, A. P., and McConaghy, N. (1989a). Anxiety and/or depression in the pathogenesis of addictive gambling. *International Journal of the Addictions 24*(4), 337–350.

Blaszczynski, A. P., and McConaghy, N. (1989b). The medical model of pathological gambling: Current shortcomings. *Journal of Gambling Behavior 5*(1), 42–52.

Blaszczynski, A. P., and McConaghy, N. (1993). A two to nine year treatment follow-up study of pathological gambling. In Eadington, W. R., and Cornelius, J. (Eds.) *Gambling behavior and problem gambling* (pp. 215–234). Reno, Nevada: Bureau of Business and Economic Research, College of Business Administration, University of Nevada.

Blaszczynski, A. P., and McConaghy, N. (1994). Antisocial personality disorder and pathological gambling. *Journal of Gambling Studies 10*(2), 129–145.

Blaszczynski, A., and Silove, D. (1995). Cognitive and behavioral therapies for pathological gambling. *Journal of Gambling Studies 11*(2), 195–220.

Blaszczynski, A., and Steel, D. (1998). Personality disorders among pathological gamblers. *Journal of Gambling Studies 14*(1), 51–71.

Blaszczynski, A. P., Buhrich, N., and McConaghy, N. (1985). Pathological gamblers, heroin addicts and controls compared on the EPQ "addiction scale." *British Journal of Addiction 80*(3), 315–319.

Blaszczynski, A. P., McConaghy, N., and Frankova, A. (1989). Crime, antisocial personality and pathological gambling. *Journal of Gambling Behavior 5*(2), 137–152.

Blaszczynski, A. P., McConaghy, N., and Frankova, A. (1990). Boredom proneness in pathological gamblers. *Psychological Reports 67*(1), 35–42.

Blaszczynski, A. P., McConaghy, N., and Frankova, A. (1991a). A comparison of relapsed and non-relapsed abstinent pathological gamblers following behavioral treatment. *British Journal of Addiction 86*(11), 1485–1489.

Blaszczynski, A. P., McConaghy, N., and Frankova, A. (1991b). Control versus abstinence in the treatment of pathological gambling: A two to nine year follow-up. *British Journal of Addiction 86*(11), 299–306.

Blaszczynski, A., Steel, Z., and McConaghy, N. (1997). Impulsivity in pathological gambling: The antisocial impulsivist. *Addictions 92*(1), 75–87.

Blaszczynski, A. P., Wilson, A. C., and McConaghy, N. (1986). Sensation seeking and pathological gambling. *British Journal of Addiction 81*(1), 109–113.

Blaszczynski, A. P., Winter, S. W., and McConaghy, N. (1986). Plasma endorphin levels in pathological gambling. *Journal of Gambling Behavior 2*(1), 3–14.

Blume, S. B. (1994). Pathological gambling and switching addictions: Report of a case. *Journal of Gambling Studies 10*(1), 87–96.

Blume, S. B., and Lesieur, H. R. (1987). Pathological gambling in cocaine abusers. In Washton, A. M. and Gold, M. S. (Eds.) *Cocaine: A clinician's handbook.* New York: The Guilford Press.

Bolen, D. W. (1976). Gambling: Historical highlights and trends and their implications for contemporary society. In Eadington, W. R. (Ed.) *Gambling and society: Interdisciplinary studies on the subject of gambling* (pp. 7–38). Springfield, IL: Charles C Thomas.

Bolen, E. W., and Boyd, W. H. (1968). Gambling and the gambler: A review and preliminary findings. *Archives of General Psychiatry 18*(5), 617–630.

Bolen, D. W., Caldwell, A. B., and Boyd, W. H. (1975). Personality traits of pathological gamblers. In Eadington, W. R. (Ed.) *The gambling papers: Proceedings of the 1975 Conference on Gambling.* Reno, Nevada: Bureau of Business and Economic Research, College of Business Administration, University of Nevada.

Bolles, R. C. (1972). Reinforcement, expectancy, and learning. *Psychological Review 79,* 394–409.

Boyd, W. H. (1976). Excitement: The gambler's drug. In Eadington, W. R. (Ed.) *Gambling and society: Interdisciplinary studies on the subject of gambling* (pp. 371–375). Springfield, IL: Charles C Thomas.

Boyd, W,. and Bolen, D. (1970). The compulsive gambler and spouse in group psychotherapy. *International Journal of Group Psychotherapy 20*(1), 77–90.

Boyatzis, R. E. (1974). The effect of alcohol consumption on the aggressive behavior of men. *Quarterly Journal of Studies on Alcohol 35*(3), 959–972.

Breen, R. B., and Frank, M. L. (1993). The effects of statistical fluctuations and perceived status of a competitor on the illusion of control in experienced gamblers. *Journal of Gambling Studies 9*(3), 265–276.

Briggs, J. R., Goodin, B. J., and Nelson, T. (1996). Pathological gamblers and alcoholics: Do they share the same additions? *Addictive Behaviors 21*(4), 515-519.

Brockner, H. M., Shaw, M. C., and Rubin, J. Z. (1979). Factors affecting withdrawal from an escalating conflict: Quitting before it's too late. *Journal of Experimental Social Psychology 7,* 492–503.

Brown, R. I. F. (1985). The effectiveness of gamblers anonymous. In W. R. Eadington (Ed.) *The gambling studies: Proceedings of the Sixth National Conference on Gambling and Risk Taking, Vol 5* (pp. 258–284). Reno, NV: University of Nevada, Reno.

Brown, R. I. F. (1986). Arousal and sensation-seeking components in the general explanation of gambling and gambling addictions. *International Journal of the Addictions 21*(9 & 10), 1001–1016.

Brown, R. I. F. (1987a). Classical and operant paradigms in the management of compulsive gamblers. *Behavioural Psychotherapy 15,* 111–122.

Brown, R. I. F. (1987b). Dropouts and continuers in Gamblers Anonymous: Part 3. Some possible specific reasons for dropout. *Journal of Gambling Behavior 3*(2), 137–151.

Brown, R. I. F. (1987c). Gambling addictions, arousal, and an affective/decision-making explanation of behavioral reversions or relapses. *International Journal of the Addictions 22*(11), 1053–1067.

Brown, R. I. F. (1987d). Models of gambling and gambling addictions as perceptual filters. *Journal of Gambling Behavior 3*(4), 224–236.

Brown, R. I. F. (1987e). Pathological gambling and associated patterns of crime: Comparisons with alcohol and drug addiction. *Journal of Gambling Behavior 3*(2), 98–114.

Brown, R. I. F. (1988). Reversal theory and subjective experience in the explanation of addiction and relapse. In Apter, M. J., Kerr,

J. H., and Cowles, M. P. (Eds.) *Progress in reversal theory* (pp. 191–211). Amsterdam: North-Holland.

Brown, R. I. F. (1989). Relapses from a gambling perspective. In Gossop, M. (Ed.) *Relapse and addictive behaviour* (pp. 107–132). London: Tavistock/Routledge.

Brown, R. I. F. (1991). Gaming, gambling, and other addictive play. In Kerr, J. and Apter, M. (Eds.). *Adult play: A reversal theory approach* (pp. 101–118). Amsterdam: Swets and Zeitlinger.

Brown, R. I. F. (1993). Some contributions of the study of gambling to other addictions. In William R. Eadington and Judy Cornelius (Eds.) *Gambling behavior and problem gambling* (pp. 241–272). Reno, Nevada: Bureau of Business and Economic Research, College of Business Administration, University of Nevada.

Browne, B. (1989). Going on tilt: Frequent poker players and control. *Journal of Gambling Behavior 5*(1), 3–21.

Browne, B. A., and Brown, D. J. (1994). Predictors of lottery gambling among American college students. *Journal of Social Psychology 134*(3), 339–347.

Bühringer, G., and Konstanty, R. (1992). Intensive gamblers on German-style slot machines. *Journal of Gambling Studies 8*(1), 21–38.

Burger, J. M. (1986). Desire for control and the illusion of control: The effects of familiarity and sequence of outcomes. *Journal of Research in Personality 20*(1), 66–76.

Burger, J. M. (1991). The effects of desire for control in situations with chance-determined outcomes: Gambling behavior in lotto and bingo players. *Journal of Research in Personality 25*(2), 196–204.

Burger, J. M., and Cooper, H. M. (1979). The desirability of control. *Motivation and Emotion 3*(4), 381–393.

Burger, J. M., and Schnerring, D. A. (1982). The effects of desire for control and extrinsic rewards on the illusion of control and gambling. *Motivation and Emotion 6*, 329–335.

Burger, J. M., and Smith, N. G. (1985). Desire for control and gambling behavior among problem gamblers. *Personality and Social Psychology Bulletin 11*(2), 145–152.

Burglass, M. E. (1989). Compulsive gambling: Forensic update and commentary. In Shaffer, H. J., Stein, A., Gambino, B., and Cummings, J. N. (Eds.) *Compulsive gambling: Theory, research, and practice* (pp. 205–222). Lexington, MA: Lexington Books.

Caillois, R. (1961). *Man, games, and play*, Barash, M. (Trans.) New York: The Free Press.

Cain, A. H. (1964). *The cured alcoholic: New concepts in alcoholism treatment and research.* New York: John Day.

Caldwell, G. (1985). Poker machine playing in NSW and ACT clubs. In Caldwell, G., Haig, B., Dickerson, M., and Sylvan, L. (Eds.) *Gambling in Australia* (pp. 261–268). Sydney: Croom Helm.

Camerer, C. (1989). Does the basketball market believe in the "hot hand"? *American Economic Review 79*, 1257–1261.

Cameron, B., and Myers, J. (1966). Some personality correlates of risktaking. *The Journal of General Psychology 74*, 51–60.

Campbell, F. F. (1976). Gambling: A positive view. In Eadington, W. R. (Ed.) *Gambling and society: Interdisciplinary studies on the subject of gambling* (pp. 218–228). Springfield, IL: Charles C Thomas.

Campbell, H. J. (1973). *The pleasure areas.* London: Methuen.

Cappell, H., and Herman, C. P. (1972) Alcohol and tension reduction: A review. *Quarterly Journal of Studies on Alcohol 33*(1), 33–64.

Carlton, P. L., and Goldstein, L. (1987). Physiological determinants of pathological gambling. In Galski, T. (Ed.) *The handbook of pathological gambling* (pp. 111–122). Springfield, IL: Charles C Thomas.

Carlton, P. L., and Manowitz, P. (1987). Physiological factors as determinants of pathological gambling. *Journal of Gambling Behavior 3*(4), 274–285.

Carlton, P. L., and Manowitz, P. (1992). Behavioral restraint and symptoms of attention deficit disorder in alcoholics and pathological gamblers. *Neuropsychology 25*(1), 44–48.

Carlton, P. L., and Manowitz, P. (1994). Factors

determining the severity of pathological gambling in males. *Journal of Gambling Studies 10*(2), 147–157.

Carlton, P. L., Manowitz, P., McBride, H., Nora, R., Swartzburg, M., and Goldstein, L. (1987). Attention deficit disorder and pathological gambling. *Journal of Clinical Psychiatry 48*(12), 487–488.

Carnes, P. (1983). *The sexual addiction.* Minneapolis: Comp Care.

Carroll, D., and Huxley, J. A. A. (1994). Cognitive, dispositional, and psychophysiological correlates of dependent slot machine gambling in young people. *Journal of Applied Social Psychology 24*(12), 1070–1083.

Carroll, E. N., and Zuckerman, M. (1977). Psychopathology and sensation seeking in "downers," "speeders" and "trippers": A study of the relationship between personality and drug choice. *International Journal of the Addictions 12*(4), 591–601.

Carroll, E. N., Zuckerman, M., and Vogel, W. H. (1982). A test of the optimal level of arousal theory of sensation seeking. *Journal of Personality and Social Psychology 42*(3), 572–575.

Castellani, B., and Rugle, L. (1995). A comparison of pathological gamblers to alcoholics and cocaine misusers on Impulsivity, sensation seeking, and craving. *International Journal of the Addictions 30*(3), 275–289.

Ceci, S. J., and Liker, J. K. (1986). A day at the races: A study of IQ, expertise, and cognitive complexity. *Journal of Experimental Psychology: General 115*(3), 255–266.

Ceci, S. J., and Liker, J. K. (1987). Correction to Ceci and Liker (1986). *Journal of Experimental Psychology: General 116*(2), 90.

Chafetz, M. (1970). The alcoholic symptom and its therapeutic relevance. *Quarterly Journal of Studies on Alcohol 31*(2), 441–445.

Chantal, Y,. and Vallerand, R. J. (1996). Skill versus luck: A motivational analysis of gambling involvement. *Journal of Gambling Studies 12*(4), 407–418.

Chantal, Y., Vallerand, R. J., and Valliéres, E. F. (1995). Motivation and gambling involvement. *Journal of Social Psychology 125*, 755–763.

Ciarrocchi, J. (1987). Severity of impairment in dually addicted gamblers. *Journal of Gambling Behavior 3*(1), 16–26.

Ciarrocchi, J., and Richardson, R. (1989). Profile of compulsive gamblers in treatment: Update and comparisons. *Journal of Gambling Behavior 5*(1), 53–65.

Ciarrocchi, J. W., Kirschner, N. M., and Fallik, F. (1991). Personality dimensions of male pathological gamblers, alcoholics, and dually addicted gamblers. *Journal of Gambling studies 7*(2), 133–141.

Clotfelter, C. T., and Cook, P. J. (1989). *Selling hope: State lotteries in America.* Cambridge, Mass.: Harvard University Press.

Cocco, N., Sharpe, L., and Blaszczynski, A. (1995). Differences in preferred level of arousal in two sub-groups of problem gamblers: A preliminary report. *Journal of Gambling Studies 11*(2), 221–229.

Cofer, C. N., and Appley, M. H. (1964). *Motivation: Theory and research.* New York: John Wiley and Sons.

Cohen, J. (1964). *Behavior in uncertainty and its social implications.* London: Allen and Unwin.

Cohen, J. (1970). The nature of gambling. *Scientia 105*, 445–469.

Cohen, J. (1972). *Psychological probability.* London: Allen and Unwin.

Cohen, J. (1975). The psychology of gambling. *New Scientist 68*(973), 266–268.

Cohen, J., Boyle, L. E., and Shubsachs, A. P. (1969). Rouge et noir: Influence of previous play on choice of binary event outcome and size of stake in a gambling situation. *Acta Psychologica 31*, 340–352.

Conger, J. (1951). The effects of alcohol on conflict behavior in the albino rat. *Quarterly Journal of Studies on Alcohol 12*(1), 1–29.

Conrad, E. L. (1978). *The identification of three types of gamblers and related personality characteristics and gambling experiences.* Doctoral dissertation, Loyola University of Chicago. Dissertation Abstracts International 38, 5561B.

Coopersmith, S. (1964). Adaptive reactions of alcoholics and non-alcoholics. *Quarterly Journal of Studies on Alcohol 25*, 262–278.

Corless, T., and Dickerson, M. G. (1989).

Gamblers' self-perceptions of the determinants of impaired control. *British Journal of Addiction 84*(12), 1527–1537.

Corney, W. J., and Cummings, W. T. (1992). Poker tournament attributions. In Eadington, W. R., and Cornelius, J. A. (Eds.) *Gambling and commercial gaming: Essays in business, economics, philosophy, and science* (pp. 499–504). Reno, Nevada: Bureau of Business and Economic Research, College of Business Administration, University of Nevada.

Cornish, D. B. (1978). *Gambling: A review of the literature and its implications for policy and research.* London: Home Office Research Study 42.

Coulombe, A., Ladouceur, R., Desharnais, R., and Jobin, J. (1992). Erroneous perceptions and arousal among regular and occasional video poker players. *Journal of Gambling Studies 8*(3), 235–244.

Coventry, K. R., and Brown, R. I. F. (1993). Sensation seeking, gambling and gambling addictions. *Addiction 88*(4), 541–554. Reprinted (1993) as, Sensation seeking in gamblers and non-gamblers and its relation to preference for gambling activities, chasing, arousal and loss of control in regular gamblers. In Eadington, W. R., and Cornelius, J. (Eds.) *Gambling behavior and problem gambling* (pp. 25–49). Reno, Nevada: Bureau of Business and Economic Research, College of Business Administration, University of Nevada.

Coventry, K., and Norman, A. C. (1997). Arousal, sensation seeking and frequency of gambling in off-course horse racing bettors. *British Journal of Psychology 88*(4), 671–681.

Cox, W. M. (1985). Personality correlates of substance abuse. In Galizio, M. and Maisto, S. A. (Eds.) *Determinants of substance abuse. Biological, psychological, and environmental factors.* New York: Plenum Press.

Cox, W. M. (1987). Personality theory and research. In Blane, H. T. and Leonard, K. E. (Eds.) *Psychological theories of drinking and alcoholism.* New York: Guilford Press.

Coyle, C., and Kinney, W. (1990). A comparison of leisure and gambling motives of compulsive gamblers. *Therapeutic Recreation Journal 24*(1), 32–39.

Cressey, D. (1971). *Other people's money.* Belmont, CA: Wadsworth Publishing.

Cummings, C., Gordon, J. R., and Marlatt, G. A. (1980). Relapse: prevention and prediction. In Miller, W. R. (Ed.) *The addictive behaviors* (pp. 291–321). Oxford: Pergamon Press.

Custer, R. L. (1982). An overview of compulsive gambling. In Carone, P. A., Yolles, S. F., Kieffer, S. N., and Krinsky, L. W. (Eds.) *Addictive disorders update: Alcoholism/drug abuse/gambling* (pp. 107–124). New York: Human Sciences Press.

Custer, R. L. (1984). Profile of the pathological gambler. *Journal of Clinical Psychiatry 45*, 35–38.

Custer, R. L., and Custer, L. F. (1978, December). *Characteristics of the recovering compulsive gambler: A survey of 150 members of Gamblers Anonymous.* Paper presented at the fourth annual Conference on Gambling, Reno, Nevada.

Custer, R. L., and Milt, H. (1985). *When luck runs out.* New York: Warner Books.

Custer, R. L., Meeland, T., and Krug, S. E. (1984). Differences between social gamblers and pathological gamblers. In Eadington, W. R. (Ed.) *The gambling papers: Proceedings of the 1984 Conference on Gambling.* Reno, Nevada: Bureau of Business and Economic Research, College of Business Administration, University of Nevada.

Cutter, H. S. G., Boyatzis, R. E., and Clancy, D. D. (1977). Effectiveness of power motivation training in rehabilitating alcoholics. *Quarterly Journal of Studies of Alcohol 38*, 131–141.

Daghestani, A. N., Elenz, E., and Crayton, J. W, (1996). Pathological gambling in hospitalized substance abusing veterans. *Journal of Clinical Psychiatry 57*(8), 360–363.

Davis, G., and Brissett, D. (1995). *Comparing the pathological and recreational gambler: An exploratory study.* St. Paul: Minnesota Department of Human Services, Mental Health Division.

Dell, L. J., Ruzicka, M. F., and Palisi, A. T. (1981). Personality and other factors associated with the gambling addiction. *International Journal of the Addictions 16*, 149–151.

Detterman, D. K., and Spry, K. M. (1988). Is it smart to play the horses? Comment on "A day at the races: A study of IQ, expertise, and cognitive complexity." (Ceci and Liker, 1986). *Journal of Experimental Psychology: General 117*(1), 91–95.

Devereux, E. C. (1949). *Gambling and the social structure: A sociological study of lotteries and horseracing in contemporary America.* Doctoral dissertation, Harvard University.

Devereux, G. (1947). Mojave orality: An analysis of nursing and weaning customs. *Psychoanalytic Quarterly 16*, 519–546.

Devereux, G. (1950). Psychodynamics of Mohave gambling. *American Imago 7*(1), 55–64.

Devereux, G. (1961). *Mojave ethnopsychiatry and suicide: The psychiatric knowledge and the psychic disturbances of an Indian tribe.* Washington, D.C.: United States Government Printing Office.

Devinney, R. B. (1979). Gamblers: A personality study. *Dissertation Abstracts International, 40*(1-B), 429–430.

Dickerson, M. G. (1977a). "Compulsive" gambling as an addiction: Dilemmas. *Scottish Medical Journal 22*, 251–252.

Dickerson, M. G. (1977b). The role of the betting shop environment in the training of compulsive gamblers. *Behavioural Psychotherapy 5*, 3–8.

Dickerson, M. G. (1979). FI schedules and persistence at gambling in the UK Betting Office. *Journal of Applied Behavioral Analysis 12*, 315–323.

Dickerson, M. G. (1984). *Compulsive gamblers.* London: Longman.

Dickerson, M. G. (1985). The characteristics of the compulsive gambler: A rejection of a typology. In Caldwell, G., Haig, B., Dickerson, M., and Sylvan, L. (Eds.) *Gambling in Australia* (pp. 139–145). Sydney: Croom Helm.

Dickerson, M. G. (1987). The future of gambling research–Learning from the lessons of alcoholism. *Journal of Gambling Behavior 3*(4), 248–256.

Dickerson, M. G. (1989). Gambling: A dependence without a drug. *International Review Journal of Psychiatry 1*, 157–171.

Dickerson, M. G. (1991). Internal and external determinants of persistent gambling: Implications for treatment. In Heather, N., Miller, W. R., and Greeley, J. (Eds.) *Self-control and the addictive behaviors* (pp. 317–328). Australia: Maxwell Macmillan Publishing.

Dickerson, M. G. (1993a). Internal and external determinants of persistent gambling: Problems in generalizing from one form of gambling to another. In Eadington, W. R., and Cornelius, J. A. (Eds.) *Gambling behavior and problem gambling* (pp. 3–24). Reno, Nevada: Institute for the Study of Gambling and Commercial Gaming, College of Business Administration, University of Nevada.

Dickerson, M. (1993b). A preliminary exploration of a two-stage methodology in the assessment of the extent and degree of gambling related problems in the Australian population. In Eadington, W. R., and Cornelius, J. A. (Eds.) *Gambling behavior and problem gambling* (pp. 347–363). Reno, Nevada: Bureau of Business and Economic Research, College of Business Administration, University of Nevada.

Dickerson, M. and Adcock, S. (1987). Mood, Arousal and cognitions in persistent gambling: Preliminary investigation of a theoretical model. *Journal of Gambling Behavior 3*(1), 3–15.

Dickerson, M. G., Bayliss, D. and Head, P. (1984). *Survey of a social club population of poker machine players.* Unpublished research paper.

Dickerson, M., Hinchy, J., and Fabre, J. (1987). Chasing, arousal and sensation seeking in off-course gamblers. *British Journal of Addiction 82*, 673–680.

Dickerson, M., Cunningham, R., Legg England, S., and Hinchy, J. (1991). On the determinants of persistent gambling. III. Personality, prior mood, and poker machine play. *International Journal of the Addictions 26*(5), 531–548.

Dickerson, M., Walker, M., Legg England, S., and Hinchy, J. (1990). Demographic, personality, cognitive and behavioral correlates of off-course betting involvement. *Journal of Gambling Studies 6*(2), 165–182.

Dickerson, M., Hinchy, J., Legg England, S.,

Fabre, J., and Cunningham, R. (1992). On the determinants of persistent gambling behaviour. I. High-frequency poker machine players. *British Journal of Psychology 83*, 237–248.

Dickerson, M., Hinchy, J., Schaefer, M., Whitworth, N., and Fabre, J. (1988). The use of hand-held microcomputer in the collection of physiological, subjective and behavioral data in ecologically valid gambling settings. *Journal of Gambling Behavior 4*(2), 92–98.

Dollard, J., and Miller, N. E. (1950). *Personality and psychotherapy*. New York: McGraw-Hill.

Dostoevsky, F. (1914 [1866]). *The gambler and other short stories*. Garnett, C. (Trans.). London: Heinemann and Zsolnay.

Dostoevsky, F. (1972 [1866]). *The gambler*, Terras, V. (Trans.) Chicago: University of Chicago Press.

Downes, D. M., Davies, B. P., David, M., and Stone, P. (1976). *Gambling, work and leisure: A study across three areas*. London: Routledge and Kegan Paul.

Dumont, M., and Ladouceur, R. (1990). Evaluation of motivation among video-poker players. *Psychological Reports 66*, 95–98.

Dykstra, S. P., and Dollinger, S. J. (1990). Model competence, depression, and the illusion of control. *Bulletin of the Psychonomic Society 28*(3), 235–238.

Edwards, G., and Gross, M. (1976). Alcohol dependence: Provisional description of a clinical syndrome. *British Medical Journal 1*, 1058–1061.

Edwards, W. (1955). The prediction of decisions among bets. *Journal of Experimental Psychology 51*(3), 201–214.

Elia, C., and Jacobs, D. F. (1993). The incidence of pathological gambling among Native Americans treated for alcohol dependence. *International Journal of the Addictions, 28*(7), 659–666.

Fabian, T. (1995). Pathological gambling: A comparison of gambling at German-style slot machines and "classical" gambling. *Journal of Gambling Studies 11*(3), 249–263.

Fachinelli, E. (1974 [1965]). Anal money-time. In Halliday, J. and Fuller, P. (Eds.) *The psychology of gambling* (pp. 273–296). New York: Harper and Row.

Farmer, R., and Sundberg, N. D. (1986). Boredom proneness: The development of a new scale. *Journal of Personality Assessment 50*, 4–17.

Feigelman, W., Wallisch, L., and Lesieur, H. R. (1998). Problem gamblers, Problem substance users, and dual-problem individuals: An epidemiological study. *American Journal of Public Health 88*(3), 467–470.

Feigelman, W., Kleinman, P. H., Lesieur, H. R., Millman, R. B., Lesser, M. L. (1995). Pathological gambling among methadone patients. *Drug and Alcohol Dependence 39*(2), 75–81.

Fenichel, O. (1945). *The psychoanalytic theory of neurosis*. New York: Norton.

Ferenczi, S. (1952 [1914]). The ontogenesis of the interest in money. In Jones, E. (Trans.) *First contributions to psycho-analysis* (pp. 319–331). London: Hogarth Press. Reprinted (1974) In Halliday, J., and Fuller, P. (Eds.) *The psychology of gambling* (pp. 264–272). New York: Harper and Row.

Ferrioli, M., and Ciminero, A. R. (1981). The treatment of pathological gambling as an addictive behavior. In Eadington, W. R. (Ed.) *The gambling papers: Proceedings of the Fifth National Conference on Gambling and Risk Taking*. Reno, Nevada: Bureau of Business and Economic Research, College of Business Administration, University of Nevada.

Ferster, C. B., and Skinner, B. F. (1957). *Schedules of reinforcement*. New York: Appleton-Century-Crofts.

Fink, H. K. (1961). Compulsive gambling. *Acta Psychotherapeutica 9*(4), 251–261.

Fisher, S. (1993a). The pull of the fruit machine: A sociological typology of young players. *The Sociological Review 41*(3), 446–474.

Fisher, S. (1993b). Towards a sociological understanding of slot machine gambling in young people. In Eadington, W. R., and Cornelius, J. (Eds.) *Gambling behavior and problem gambling* (pp. 395–403). Reno, Nevada: Bureau of Business and Economic Research, College of Business Administration, University of Nevada.

France, C. J. (1902). The gambling impulse. *American Journal of Psychology 13*(3), 64–407.

Frank, M. L. (1979). Why people gamble: A behavioral perspective. In Lester, D. (Ed.) *Gambling today* (pp. 71–83). Springfield, IL: Charles C Thomas.

Frank, M. L. (1993). Underage gambling in New Jersey. In Eadington, W. R., and Cornelius, J. (Eds.) *Gambling behavior and problem gambling* (pp. 387–394). Reno, Nevada: Bureau of Business and Economic Research, College of Business Administration, University of Nevada.

Frank, M. L., and Smith, C. (1989). Illusion of control and gambling in children. *Journal of Gambling Behavior 5*(2), 127–136.

Freed, E. X. (1978). Alcohol and mood: An updated review. *International Journal of the Addictions 13*, 173–200.

Freud, S. (1905). Infantile sexuality. In Strachey, J. (Ed.) *Three essays on the theory of sexuality.* The complete works of Sigmund Freud, standard edition. London: Hogarth Press.

Freud, S. (1907). Obsessive actions and religious practices. In Strachey, J. (Ed.) *The standard edition of the complete works of Sigmund Freud, Vol. 9.* London: Hogarth Press.

Freud, S. (1913). Totem and taboo. In Strachey, J. (Ed.) *The standard edition of the complete works of Sigmund Freud, Vol. 13.* London: Hogarth Press.

Freud, S. (1917). On transformations of instinct as exemplified in anal eroticism. In Strachey, J. (Ed.) *The standard edition of the complete works of Sigmund Freud, Vol. 17.* London: Hogarth Press.

Freud, S. (1927). The future of an illusion. In Strachey, J. (Ed.) *The standard edition of the complete works of Sigmund Freud, Vol. 21.* London: Hogarth Press.

Freud, S. (1938). *The basic writings of Sigmund Freud*, Brill, D. A. (Trans.) New York: The Modern Library.

Freud, S. (1943 [1920]). *A general introduction to psychoanalysis*, Riviere, J. (Trans.) Garden City, N.Y.: Garden City Publishing.

Freud, S. (1949). *An outline of psychoanalysis*, Strachey, J. (Trans.) New York: Norton.

Freud, S. (1950 [1928]). Dostoevsky and parricide. In Strachey, J. (Ed.) *Collected papers, Vol. 5: Miscellaneous papers 1888–1938* (pp. 222–242). London: Hogarth Press and The Institute of Psychoanalysis.

Freud, S. (1954 [1897]). Letter no. 79, dated Dec. 22, 1897. In Bonaparte, M., Freud, A., and Kris, E. (Eds.) *The origins of psychoanalysis: Letters to Wilhelm Fleiss, drafts and notes: 1887–1902.* New York: Basic Books.

Freud, S. (1959 [1908]). Character and anal eroticism. In Strachey, J. (Ed.) *The standard edition of the complete works of Sigmund Freud, Vol. 9.* London: Hogarth Press.

Fuller, P. (1974). Introduction. In Halliday, J., and Fuller, P. (Eds.) *The psychology of gambling.* New York: Harper and Row.

Gaboury, A., and Ladouceur R. (1988). Irrational thinking and gambling. In Eadington, W. R. (Ed.) *Gambling research: Proceedings of the Seventh International Conference on Gambling and Risk Taking, Volume. 3* (pp. 142–163). Reno, Nevada: Bureau of Business and Economic Research, College of Business Administration, University of Nevada.

Gaboury, A., and Ladouceur, R. (1989). Erroneous perceptions and gambling. *Journal of Social Behavior and Personality 4*, 411–420.

Gaboury, A., and Ladouceur, R. (1993). Preventing pathological gambling among teenagers. In Eadington, W. R. and Cornelius, J. (Eds.) *Gambling behavior and problem gambling* (pp. 443–450). Reno, Nevada: Bureau of Business and Economic Research, College of Business Administration, University of Nevada.

Galdston, I. (1951). The psychodynamics of the triad: Alcoholism, gambling, and superstition. *Mental Hygiene 35*, 589–598.

Galdston, I. (1960). The gambler and his love. *American Journal of Psychiatry 35*, 553–555.

Galski, T. (1987). Psychological testing of pathological gamblers: Research, uses and new directions. In Galski, T. (Ed.) *The handbook of pathological gambling* (pp. 123–135). Springfield, IL: Charles C Thomas.

Gambino, B., Fitzgerald, R., Shaffer, H., Renner, J., and Courtnage, P. (1993). Perceived family history of problem gambling and scores on SOGS. *Journal of Gambling Studies 9*(2),

169–184.

Geha, R. (1970). Dostoevsky and "The Gambler": A contribution to the psychogenics of gambling. *Psychoanalytic Review 57*(1), 298–302.

Gendreau, P., and Gendreau, L. P. (1970). The "addiction-prone" personality: A study of Canadian heroin addicts. *Canadian Journal of Behavior Science 2*(1), 18–25.

Gilovich, T. (1983). Biased evaluation and persistence in gambling. *Journal of Personality and Social Psychology 44*(6), 1110–1126.

Gilovich, T., and Douglas, C. (1986). Biased evaluations of randomly determined gambling outcomes. *Journal of Experimental and Social Psychology 22*(3), 228–241.

Glasser, W. (1976). *Positive addictions.* New York: Harper and Row.

Glen, A. (1979, September). *Psychometric analysis of the compulsive gambler.* Paper presented at The 87th Annual Convention of the American Psychological Association, New York.

Goddard, L. L. (1993). Alcohol and other drug abuse literature, 1980-1989: Selected abstracts. In Goddard, Lawford L. (Ed.) *An African-centered model of prevention for African-American youth at high risk* (pp. 47–56). Center for Substance Abuse Prevention (CSAP) Technical Report No. 6. Rockville, MD.: U.S. Department of Health and Human Services, Public Health Services, Substance Abuse and Mental Health Services Administration.

Goffman, E. (1967). *Interaction ritual: Essays on face-to-face behavior.* New York: Anchor Books.

Goffman, E. (1969). *Where the action is.* London: Allen Lane.

Goldstein, L., and Carlton, P. L. (1988). Hemispheric EEG correlates of compulsive behavior: The case of pathological gamblers. *Research Communications in Psychology, Psychiatry and Behavior 13*(1 & 2), 103–111.

Goldstein, L, Manowitz, P., Nora, R., Swartzburg, M., and Carlton, P. (1985). Differential EEG activation and pathological gambling. *Biological psychiatry 20*(11), 1232–1234.

Gonzalez-Ibanez, A., Mercade, P. V., Ayman, N., Saldana, C., and Vallejo-Ruiloba, J. (1991, July). *Pathological gambling and impulsivity.* Paper presented at the 5th National Conference on Gambling Behavior. Duluth, Minnesota.

Goodman, A. (1990). Addiction: Definition and implications. *British Journal of Addiction, 85,* 1403–1408.

Graham, J. R., and Lowenfeld, B. H. (1986). Personality dimensions of the pathological gambler. *Journal of Gambling Behavior 2*(1), 58–66.

Greenberg, H. R. (1980). Psychology of gambling. In Kaplan, H. I., Freeman, A. M., and Sadock, B. J. (Eds.) *Comprehensive textbook of psychiatry, Third edition, Vol. 3* (pp. 3274–3283). New York: Williams and Wilkins.

Greenberg, M., and Weiner, B. (1966). Effects of reinforcement history upon risk-taking behavior. *Journal of Experimental Psychology 71,* 587–592.

Greene, J. (1982). The gambling trap. *Psychology Today 16,* 50–55.

Greenson, R. R. (1948). On gambling. *The Yearbook of Psychoanalysis 4,* 110–123. Orig. *American Imago 4,* 61–77.

Griffith, R. M. (1949). Odds adjustments by American horse-race bettors. *American Journal of Psychology 62*(2), 290–294.

Griffiths, M. D. (1989). Gambling in children and adolescents. *Journal of Gambling Behavior 5*(1), 66–83.

Griffiths, M. D. (1990a). The cognitive psychology of gambling. *Journal of Gambling Studies 6*(1), 31–42.

Griffiths, M. D. (1990b). Addiction to fruit machines: A preliminary study among young males. *Journal of Gambling Studies 6*(2), 113–126.

Griffiths, M. D. (1990c). The acquisition, development and maintenance of fruit machine gambling in adolescence. *Journal of Gambling Studies 6*(3), 193–204.

Griffiths, M. D. (1990d). The role of cognitive bias and skill in fruit machine gambling. In Lea, S. E. G., Webley, P., and Young, B. M. (Eds.) *Applied economic psychology in the 1990s, Vol 1* (pp. 228–253). Exeter: Washington Singer Press.

Griffiths, M. (1991a). Fruit machine addiction: Two brief case studies. *British Journal of*

Addiction 86(4), 465.

Griffiths, M. (1991b). Psychobiology of the near-miss in fruit machine gambling. *Journal of Psychology 125*(3), 347–357.

Griffiths, M. (1993a). A study of the cognitive activity of fruit machine players. In Eadington, W. R., and Cornelius, J. (Eds.) *Gambling behavior and problem gambling* (pp. 85–109). Reno, Nevada: Bureau of Business and Economic Research, College of Business Administration, University of Nevada.

Griffiths, M. (1993b). Fruit machine gambling: The importance of structural characteristics. *Journal of Gambling Studies 9*(2), 101–120.

Griffiths, M. (1993c). Factors in problem adolescent fruit machine gambling: Results of a small postal survey. *Journal of Gambling Studies 9*(1), 31–45.

Griffiths, M. (1994). An exploratory study of gambling cross addictions. *Journal of Gambling Studies 10*(4), 371–383.

Griffiths, M. (1995). The role of subjective mood states in the maintenance of fruit machine gambling behaviour. *Journal of Gambling Studies 11*(2), 123–135.

Gross, W. F., and Carpenter, L. L. (1971). Alcoholic personality: Reality or fiction? *Psychological Reports 28*, 375–378.

Gupta, R., and Derevensky, J. (1997). Familial and social influences on juvenile gambling behavior. *Journal of Gambling Studies 13*(3), 179–192.

Gupta, R., and Derevensky, J. (1998). An empirical examination of Jacobs' General Theory of Addictions: Do adolescent gamblers fit the theory? *Journal of Gambling Studies 14*(1), 17–49.

Haberman, P. W. (1969). Drinking and other self-indulgences: Complements or counter-attractions? *International Journal of the Addictions 4*(2), 157–167.

Harris, H. (1964). Gambling addiction in an adolescent male. *Psychoanalytic Quarterly 33*, 513–525.

Haustein, J., and Schürgers, G. (1992). Therapy and male pathological gamblers: Between self help and group therapy–report on developmental process. *Journal of Gambling Studies 8*(2), 131–142.

Havemann, E. (1952). Gambling's many mansions. In Marx, H. L. (Ed.) *Gambling in America.* New York: H. W. Wilson.

Henslin, J. M. (1967). Craps and magic. *American Journal of Sociology 73*, 316–330.

Herman, R. D. (1967). Gambling as work: A sociological study of the race track. In Herman, R. D. (Ed.) *Gambling.* New York: Harper and Row.

Herman, R. D. (1976a). *Gamblers and gambling.* Lexington, Mass.: Lexington Books.

Herman, R. D. (1976b). Motivations to gamble: The model of Roger Caillois. In Eadington, W. R. (Ed.) *Gambling and society: Interdisciplinary studies on the subject of gambling,* pp. 207–217. Springfield, IL: Charles C Thomas.

Hesselbrock, M. N. (1991). Gender comparison of antisocial personality and depression in alcoholism. *Journal of Substance Abuse 3*, 205–219.

Hesselbrock, M. N., and Hesselbrock, V. M. (1992). Relationship of family history, antisocial personality disorder and personality traits in young men at risk for alcoholism. *Journal of Studies on Alcohol 53*(6), 619–625.

Hickey, J. E., Haertzen, C. A., and Henningfield, J. E. (1986). Simulation of gambling responses on the Addiction Research Center Inventory. *Addictive Behaviors 11*(3), 345–349.

Hochauer, B. (1970). Decision-making in roulette. *Acta Psychologica 34*(2-3), 357–366.

Hong, Y. I., and Chiu, C.-Y. (1988). Sex, locus of control, and illusion of control in Hong Kong as correlates of gambling involvement. *Journal of Social Psychology 128*(5), 667–673.

Hopper, V. F. (1970). *Chaucer's Canterbury tales (selected), An interlinear translation.* Woodbury, NY: Barron's Educational Series.

Hraba, J., and Lee, G. (1995). Problem gambling and policy advice: The mutability and relative effects of structural, associational, and attitudinal variables. *Journal of Gambling Studies 11*(2), 105–121.

Hraba, J., Mok, W. P., and Huff, D. (1990). Lottery play and problem gambling. *Journal of Gambling Studies 6*(4), 355–377. Reprinted (1993) as Tonight's numbers are . . . Lottery play and problem gambling. In Eadington, W. R., and Cornelius, J. (Eds.) *Gambling behavior and problem gambling* (pp. 177–196). Reno, Nevada: Bureau of Business and Economic Research, College of Business Administration, University of Nevada.

Huizinga, J. (1950). *Homo ludens: A study of the play-element in culture.* New York: Roy Publishers.

Hunter, J., and Brunner, R. (1928). Emotional outlets of gamblers. *Journal of Abnormal and Social Psychology 23,* 76–89.

Ibàñez, A. G., Mercadé, P. V., Aymami Sanromà, M. N., and Cordero, C. P. (1992). Clinical and behavioral evaluation of pathological gambling in Barcelona, Spain. *Journal of Gambling Studies 8*(3), 299–310.

Inglis, K. (1985). Gambling and culture in Australia. In Caldwell, G., Haig, B., Dickerson, M., and Sylvan, L. (Eds.) *Gambling in Australia* (pp. 5–17). Sydney: Croom Helm.

Israeli, J. (1935). Outlook of a depressed patient, interested in planned gambling, before and after his attempt at suicide. *American Journal of Orthopsychiatry 5*(1), 57–63.

Jacobs, D. F. (1982). The Addictive Personality Syndrome (APS), A new theoretical model for understanding and treating addictions. In Eadington, W. R. (Ed.) *The gambling papers: Proceedings of the Fifth National Conference on Gambling and Risk Taking.* Reno, Nevada: Bureau of Business and Economic Research, College of Business Administration, University of Nevada.

Jacobs, D. F. (1986). A general theory of addictions: A new theoretical model. *Journal of Gambling Behavior 2*(1), 15–31.

Jacobs, D. F. (1987). A general theory of addictions: Application to treatment and rehabilitation planning for pathological gamblers. In Galski, T. (Ed.) *The handbook of pathological gambling* (pp. 169–194). Springfield, IL: Charles C Thomas.

Jacobs, D. F. (1988). Evidence for a common dissociative-like reaction among addicts. *Journal of Gambling Behavior 4*(1), 27–37.

Jacobs, D. F. (1989). A general theory of addictions: Rationale for and evidence supporting a new approach for understanding and treating addictive bahviors. In Shaffer, H. J., Stein, S. A., Gambino, G., and Cummings, T. N. (Eds.) *Compulsive gambling: Theory, research, and practice* (pp. 35–64). Lexington, MA: Lexington Books.

Jellinek, E. M. (1960). *The disease concept of alcoholism.* New Haven, CT: College and University Press.

Johnson, E. E., Nora, R. M., and Bustos, N. (1992). The Rotter I-E scale as a predictor of relapse in a population of compulsive gamblers. *Psychological Reports 70*(3, Pt. 1), 691–696.

Kagan, D. M. (1987). Addictive personality factors. *The Journal of Psychology 121*(6), 533–538.

Kallick, M., Suits, D., Dielman, T., and Hybels, J. (1976). Appendix 2: Survey of American gambling attitudes and behavior. In *Gambling in America.* U.S. Department of Justice. Washington, D.C.: U.S. Government Printing Office.

Kallick, M., Suits, D., Dielman, T., and Hybels, J. (1979). *A survey of American gambling attitudes and behavior.* Ann Arbor, Mich.: Survey Research Center, Institute of Social Research, University of Michigan.

Kaplan, H. R. (1978). *Lottery winners: How they won and how winning changed their lives.* New York: Harper and Row.

Kaplan, H. R. (1988). Gambling among lottery winners: Before and after the big score. *Journal of Gambling Behavior 4*(3), 171–182.

Kearney, C., and Drabman, R. S. (1992). Risk-taking/gambling-like behavior in preschool children. *Journal of Gambling Studies 8*(3), 287–297.

Keren, G., and Lewis, C. (1994). The two fallacies of gamblers: Type I and Type II. *Organizational Behavior and Human Decision Processes 60*(1), 75–89.

Keren, G., and Wagenaar, W. A. (1985). On the psychology of playing blackjack: Normative and descriptive considerations with implications for decision theory. *Journal of Experimental Psychology: General 114*(2), 133–158.

King, K. M. (1990). Neutralizing marginally deviant behavior: Bingo players and superstition. *Journal of Gambling Studies 6*(1), 43–61.

Knapp, T. J. (1976). A functional analysis of gambling behavior. In Eadington, W. R. (Ed.) *Gambling and society: Interdisciplinary studies on the subject of gambling* (pp. 276–294). Springfield, IL: Charles C Thomas.

Knapp, T. J., and Lech, B. C. (1987). Pathological gambling: A review with recommendations. *Behavioral Research and Theory 9*(1), 21–49.

Koller, K. M. (1972). Treatment of poker-machine addicts by aversion therapy. The Medical *Journal of Australia 59*, 742–745.

Kozlowski, C. (1977). Demand for stimulation and probability preferences in gambling decisions. *Polish Psychological Bulletin 8*(2), 67–73.

Kris, E. (1938). Ego development and the comic. *International Journal of Psychoanalysis 19*(1), 77–90.

Kroeber, A. L. (1963). *Anthropology: Culture patterns and processes.* New York: Harcourt, Brace, and World.

Kroeber, H.-L. (1992). Roulette gamblers and gamblers at electronic game machines: Where are the differences? *Journal of Gambling Studies 8*(1), 79–92.

Kruglanski, A. W. (1980). Lay epistemologic process and contents. *Psychological Review 87*, 70–87.

Kruglanski, A. W., and Ajzen, I. (1983). Bias and error in human judgment. *European Journal of Social Psychology 13*, 1–44.

Krystal, H., and Raskin, H. A. (1970). *Drug dependence: Aspects of ego functions.* Detroit: Wayne State University.

Kuley, N. B., and Jacobs, D. F. (1988). The relationship between dissociative-like experiences and sensation seeking among social and problem gamblers. *Journal of Gambling Behavior 4*(3), 197–207.

Kusyszyn, I. (1972). The gambling addict versus the gambling professional: A difference in character? *International Journal of the Addictions 7*, 387–393.

Kusyszyn, I. (1976). How gambling saved me from a misspent sabbatical. In Eadington, W. R. (Ed.) *Gambling and society: Interdisciplinary studies on the subject of gambling* (pp. 255–264). Springfield, IL: Charles C Thomas.

Kusyszyn, I. (1978). "Compulsive" gambling: The problem of definition. *International Journal of the Addictions 13*(7), 1095–1101.

Kusyszyn, I. (1984). The psychology of gambling. *Annals of the American Academy of Political and Social Science 474 (July)*, 133–145.

Kusyszyn, I. (1990). Existence, effectance, esteem: From gambling to a new theory of human motivation. *International Journal of the Addictions 25*, 159–177.

Kusyszyn, I., and Kallai, C. (1975). *The gambling person: Healthy or sick?* Paper presented at the Second Annual Conference on Gambling, South Lake Tahoe, Nevada.

Kusyszyn, I., and Rubenstein, L. (1985). Locus of control and race track betting behaviors: A preliminary investigation. *Journal of Gambling Behavior 1*(2), 106–110.

Kusyszyn, I., and Rutter, R. (1985). Personality characteristics of male heavy gamblers, light gamblers, nongamblers, and lottery players. *Journal of Gambling Behavior 1*(1), 106–110.

Kweitel, R. A., and Felicity C. L. (1998). Cognitive processes associated with gambling behaviour. *Psychological Reports 82*(1), 147–153.

Ladouceur, R. (1993). Causes of pathological gambling. In Eadington, W. R., and Cornelius, J. (Eds.) *Gambling behavior and problem gambling* (pp. 333–336). Reno, Nevada: Bureau of Business and Economic Research, College of Business Administration, University of Nevada.

Ladouceur, R., and Dubé, D. (1997). Erroneous perceptions in generating random sequences: Identification and strength of a basic misconception in gambling behavior. Journal of Psychology - Schweizerische Zeitschrift Fuer Psychologie - Revue Suisse de Psychologie 56(4), 256–259.

Ladouceur, R., and Gaboury, A. (1988). Effects of limited and unlimited stakes on gambling behavior. *Journal of Gambling Behavior 4*(2), 119–126.

Ladouceur, R., and Mayrand, M. (1984). Evaluation of the "illusion of control": Type of feedback, outcome sequence, and number of trials among regular and occasional gamblers. *The Journal of Psychology 117*(1), 37–46.

Ladouceur, R. and Mayrand, M. (1986). Charactéristiques psychologiques de la prise de risque monétaire des joueurs et des nonjoueurs à la roulette. *International Journal of Psychology 21*(415), 433–443.

Ladouceur, R., and Mayrand, M. (1987). The level of involvement and the timing of betting in roulette. *The Journal of Psychology 121*(2), 169–176.

Ladouceur, R., Gaboury, A., et Duval, C. (1988). Modification des verbalisations irrationnelles pendent le jeu de roulette américaine et prise de risque monétaire. *Science et Comportement 18*(1 & 2), 58–68.

Ladouceur, R., Mayrand, M., and Tourigny, Y. (1987). Risk-taking behavior in gamblers and non-gamblers during prolonged exposure. *Journal of Gambling Behavior 3*(2), 115–122.

Ladouceur, R., Tourigny, Y., and Mayrand, M. (1986). Familiarity, group exposure, and risk-taking behavior in gambling. *Journal of Psychology 120*(1), 45–49.

Ladouceur, R., Gaboury, A., Dumont, M., and Rochette, P. (1988). Gambling: Relationship between the frequency of wins and irrational thinking. *Journal of Psychology 122*(4), 409–414.

Ladouceur, R., Gaboury, A., Bujold, A., Lachance, N., and Tremblay, S. (1991). Ecological validity of laboratory studies of videopoker gaming. *Journal of Gambling Studies 7*(2), 109–116.

Ladouceur, R., Mayrand, M., Dussault, R., Letarte, A., and Tremblay, J. (1984). Illusion of control: Effects of participation and involvement. *Journal of Psychology 117*(1)(1), 47–52.

Ladouceur, R., Boisvert, J.-M., Pépin, M., Loranger, M., and Sylvain, C. (1994). Social cost of pathological gambling. *Journal of Gambling Studies 10*(4), 399–409.

Laforgue, R. (1930). On the eroticization of anxiety. *International Journal of Psychoanalysis 11*(3), 312–321.

Lancet (1982). Gambling–Crave or craze? *Lancet 1*(8269), 434.

Lang, A. R. (1983). Addictive personality: A viable construct? In Levinson, P. K., Gerstein, D. R., and Maloff, D. R., (Eds.) *Commonalities in substance abuse and habitual behavior* (pp. 3–28). Lexington: D. C. Heath.

Landis, C. (1945). Theories of the alcoholic personality. In Jellinek, E. M. (Ed.) *Alcohol, science, and society.* New Haven, CT: Quarterly Journal of Studies on Alcohol.

Langer, E. J. (1975). The illusion of control. *Journal of Personality and Social Psychology, 32*(2), 311–328.

Langer, E. J., and Roth, J. (1975). Heads I win, tails it's chance: The illusion of control as a function of the sequence of outcomes in a purely chance task. *Journal of Personality and Social Psychology 32*(6), 951–955.

Larkin, M., and Griffiths, M. (1998). Response to Shaffer (1996), The case for a "Complex Systems" conceptualisation of addiction. *Journal of Gambling Studies 14*(1), 73–82.

Laundergan, J. C., Schaefer, J. M., Eckhoff, K. F., and Pirie, P. L. (1990). *Adult survey of Minnesota gambling behavior: A benchmark, 1990.* Duluth, MN: University of Minnesota Center for Addiction Studies.

Lea, S. E. G., Tarpy, R. M., and Webley, P. (1987). *The individual in the economy: A textbook of economic psychology.* London: Cambridge University Press.

Leary, K., and Dickerson, M. (1985). Levels of arousal in high and low frequency gamblers. *Behaviour Research and Therapy 23*, 635–640.

Leopard, A. (1978). Risk preference in consecutive gambling. *Journal of Experimental Psychology: Human Perception and Performance 4*(3), 521–528.

Legarda, J. J., Babio, R., and Abreu, J. M. (1992). Prevalence estimates of pathological gambling in Seville (Spain). *British Journal of Addiction 87*, 767–770.

Lemert, E. (1953). An isolation and closure theory of naive check forgery. *Journal of Criminal Law, Criminology, and Police Science 44*, 296–307.

Lesieur, H. R. (1979). The compulsive gambler's spiral of options and involvement. *Psychiatry: Journal for the Study of Interpersonal Processes 42*, 79–87.

Lesieur, H. R. (1984). *The chase: Career of the compulsive gambler.* Cambridge, MA: Schenkman Publishing Co.

Lesieur, H. R. (1987). Gambling, pathological gambling, and crime. In Galski, T. (Ed.) *The handbook of pathological gambling* (pp. 89–110). Springfield, IL: Charles C Thomas.

Lesieur, H. R. (1988a). Altering the DSM-III criteria for pathological gambling. *Journal of Gambling Behavior 4*(1), 38–47.

Lesieur, H. R. (1988b). The female pathological gambler. In Eadington, W. R. (Ed.) *Gambling research: Proceedings of the Seventh International Conference on Gambling and Risk Taking* (pp. 230–258). Reno, Nevada: Bureau of Business and Economic Research, College of Business Administration, University of Nevada.

Lesieur, H. R. (1988c). Report on pathological gambling in New Jersey. In *Report and recommendations of the Governor's Advisory Commission on Gambling.* Trenton: New Jersey Governor's Advisory Commission on Gambling.

Lesieur, H. R. (1989). Current research into pathological gambling and gaps in the literature. In Shaffer, H. J., Stein, S. A., Gambino, G., and Cummings, T. N. (Eds.) *Compulsive gambling: Theory, research, and practice* (pp. 225–248). Lexington, MA: Lexington Books.

Lesieur, H. R. (1990). *Compulsive gambling: Documenting the social and economic costs.* Paper presented at Gambling in Minnesota: An Issue for Policy Makers. Humphrey Institute of Public Affairs, University of Minnesota, Minneapolis, December, 1990.

Lesieur, H. R. (1992). *Compulsive gambling. Society 29*(4), 43–50.

Lesieur, H. R. (1993). Female pathological gamblers and crime. In Eadington, W. R., and Cornelius, J. (Eds.) *Gambling behavior and problem gambling* (pp. 495–515). Reno, Nevada: Bureau of Business and Economic Research, College of Business Administration, University of Nevada.

Lesieur, H. R., and Blume, S. B. (1990). Characteristics of pathological gamblers identified among patients on a psychiatric admissions service. *Hospital and Community Psychiatry 41*(9), 1009–1112.

Lesieur, H. R., and Blume, S. B. (1991). When lady luck loses: Women and compulsive gambling. In van den Bergh, N. (Ed.) *Feminist perspectives on treating addictions* (pp. 181–197). New York: Springer.

Lesieur, H. R., and Blume, S. B. (1993). Pathological gambling, eating disorders, and the psychoactive substance abuse disorders. *Journal of Addictive Diseases 12*(3), 89–102.

Lesieur, H. R., and Custer, R. L. (1984). Pathological gambling: Roots, phases, and treatment. *Annals of the American Academy of Political and Social Science 474 (July)*, 147–156.

Lesieur, H. R., and Heineman, M. (1988). Pathological gambling among youthful multiple substance abusers in a therapeutic community. *British Journal of Addiction 83*(7), 765–771.

Lesieur, H. R., and Klein, R. (1987). Pathological gambling among high school students. *Addictive Behaviors 12*(2), 129–134.

Lesieur, H. R., and Rosenthal, R. J. (1991). Pathological gambling: A review of the literature. *Journal of Gambling Studies 7*(1), 5–39.

Lesieur, H. R., Blume, S. G., and Zoppa, R. M. (1986). Alcoholism, drug abuse, and gambling. *Alcoholism: Clinical and Experimental Research 10*(1), 33–38.

Lester, D. (1979). *Gambling today.* Springfield, IL: Charles C Thomas.

Letarte, A., Ladouceur, R., and Mayrand, M. (1986). Primary and secondary control and risk-taking behavior in gambling (roulette). *Psychological Reports 58*(1), 299–302.

Levitz, L. S. (1971). The experimental induction of compulsive gambling behaviours. *Dissertation Abstracts International, 32, B,* 1216–1217.

Levy, M., and Feinberg, M. (1991). Psychopathology and pathological gambling among males: Theoretical and clinical concerns. *Journal of Gambling Studies 7*(1), 41–53.

Lewis, D. J., and Duncan, C. P. (1956). Effect of different percentages of money reward on extinction of a lever-pulling response. *Journal of Experimental Psychology 52*, 23–27.

Lewis, D. J., and Duncan, C. P. (1957). Expectation and resistance to extinction of a lever-pulling response as functions of percentage of reinforcement and amount of reward. *Journal of Experimental Psychology 54*, 115–120.

Lewis, D. J., and Duncan, C. P. (1958). Expectation and resistance to extinction of a lever-pulling response as a function of percentage of reinforcement and number of acquisition trials. *Journal of Experimental Psychology 55,* 121–128.

Li, W. L., and Smith, M. H. (1976). The propensity to gamble: Some structural determinants. In Eadington, W. R. (Ed.) *Gambling and society: Interdisciplinary studies on the subject of gambling* (pp. 347–370). Springfield, IL: Charles C Thomas.

Liker, J. K., and Ceci, S. J. (1987). IQ and reasoning complexity: The role of experience. *Journal of Experimental Psychology: General 116*(3), 304–306.

Linden, R. D., Pope, H. G., and Jonas, J. M. (1986). Pathological gambling and major affective disorder: Preliminary findings. *Journal of Clinical Psychiatry 47*(4), 201–203.

Lindner, R. M. (1950). The psychodynamics of gambling. *Annals of the American Academy of Political and Social Science 269 (May),* 93–107.

Lisansky, E. S. (1960). The etiology of alcoholism: The role of psychological predisposition. *Quarterly Journal of Studies on Alcohol 21*(2), 314–343.

Lisansky, E. S. (1967). Clinical research in alcoholism and the use of psychological tests: A re-evaluation. In Fox, R. (ed.) *Alcoholism: Behavioral research, therapeutic approaches.* New York: Springer.

Liverant, S., and Scodel, A. (1960). Internal and external control as determinants of decision making under conditions of risk. *Psychological Reports* 7(1), 59–67.

Livingston, J. (1974a). *Compulsive gamblers: Observations on action and abstinence.* New York: Harper and Row.

Livingston, J. (1974b). Compulsive gambling: A culture of losers. *Psychology Today* 7(10), 51–55.

Lolli, G. (1949). The addictive drinker. *Quarterly Journal of Studies on Alcohol 10,* 404–414.

Lolli, G. (1961). *Social drinking: The effects of alcohol.* New York: Collier Books.

Lorenz, V. C. (1981). Differences among Catholic, Protestant, and Jewish families of pathological gamblers. In Eadington, W. R. (Ed.) *The gambling papers: Proceedings of the 1981 Conference on Gambling.* Reno, Nevada: Bureau of Business and Economic Research, College of Business Administration, University of Nevada.

Lorenz, V. C. (1993). Compulsive gambling hotline: A source for help and information. In Eadington, W. R., and Cornelius, J. (Eds.) *Gambling behavior and problem gambling* (pp. 605–626). Reno, Nevada: Bureau of Business and Economic Research, College of Business Administration, University of Nevada.

Lorenz, V. C., and Politzer, R. M. (1990). *Final report on the task force on gambling addiction in Maryland.* Report to the Maryland Department of Health and Mental Hygiene. Baltimore, MD.

Lorenz, V. C., and Yaffee, R. A. (1986). Pathological gambling: Psychosomatic, emotional, and marital difficulties as reported by the gambler. *Journal of Gambling Behavior, 2*(1), 40–49.

Lowenfeld, B. H. (1979). Personality dimensions of the pathological gambler. Doctoral dissertation, Kent State University. *Dissertation Abstracts International 40,* 456B.

Lowenhar, J. A., and Boykin, S. (1985). Casino gaming behavior and the psychology of winning and losing: How gamers overcome persistent failure. In Eadington, W. R. (Ed.) *Proceedings of the Sixth National Conference on Gambling and Risk Taking, Vol. 3* (pp. 182–205). Reno, Nevada: Bureau of Business and Economic Research, College of Business Administration, University of Nevada.

Ludwig, A. W. (1972). On and off the wagon: Reasons for drinking and abstaining in alcoholics. *Quarterly Journal of Studies on Alcohol 3*(1), 91–96.

Lumley, M. A. and Roby, K. J. (1995). Alexithymia and pathological gambling. *Psychotherapy and Psychosomatics 63*(3-4), 201–206.

Lyons, J. C. (1985). Differences in sensation seeking and in depression levels between male social gamblers and male compulsive gamblers. In Eadington, W. R. (Ed.) *Proceedings of the Sixth National Conference on Gambling and Risk Taking* (pp. 76–100). Reno, Nevada: Bureau of Business and Economic Research, College of Business Administration, University of Nevada.

McClelland, D. C. (1977). The impact of power

motivation training on alcoholics. *Journal of Studies on Alcohol 38*(1), 142–144.

McClelland, D. C., and Davis, W. N. (1972). The influence of unrestrained power concerns in working-class men. In McClelland, D. C. and Davis, W. N., and Wanner, E. (Eds.) *The drinking man.* New York: The Free Press.

McClelland, D. C., Davis, W. N., Wanner, E., and Kalin, R. (1966). A cross-cultural study of folk-tale content and drinking. *Sociometry 29,* 308–333.

McConaghy, N. (1980). Behavior completion mechanisms rather than primary drives maintain behavioral patterns. *Activitas Nervosa Superior (Praha) 22,* 138–151.

McConaghy, N. (1991). A pathological or a compulsive gambler? *Journal of Gambling Studies 7*(1), 55–64.

McConaghy, N., Armstrong, M., Blaszczynski, A., and Allcock, C. (1983). Controlled comparison of aversive therapy and imaginal desensitization in compulsive gambling. *British Journal of Psychiatry 142* (Apr.), 366–372.

McCormack, P. J. (1994). *Minnesota's programs for troubled gamblers.* St. Paul. Minn.: Senate Counsel and Research.

McCormick, R. A. (1987). Pathological gambling: A parsimonious need state model. *Journal of Gambling Behavior 3*(4), 257–263.

McCormick, R. A. (1993). Disinhibition and negative affectivity in substance abusers with and without a gambling problem. *Addictive Behaviors 18*(3), 331–336.

McCormick, R. A., and Ramirez, L. F. (1988). Pathological gambling. In Howells, J. G. (Ed.) *Modern perspectives in psychosocial pathology* (pp. 135–157). New York: Brunner/Mazel.

McCormick, R. A., and Taber, J. I. (1987). The pathological gambler: Salient personality variables. In Galski, T. (Ed.) *The handbook of pathological gambling* (pp. 9–39). Springfield, IL: Charles C Thomas.

McCormick, R. A., and Taber, J. I. (1988). Attributional style in pathological gamblers in treatment. *Journal of Abnormal Psychology 97,* 368–370.

McCormick, R. A., Taber, J. I., Kruedelbach, N. (1989). The relationship between attributional style and post-traumatic stress disorder in addicted patients. *Journal of Traumatic Stress 2*(4), 477–487.

McCormick, R. A., Russo, A. M., Ramirez, L. F., and Taber, J. I. (1984). Affective disorders among pathological gamblers seeking treatment. *American Journal of Psychiatry 141*(2), 215–218.

McCormick, R. A., Taber, J. I., Kruedelbach, N., and Russo, A. (1987). Personality profiles of hospitalized pathological gamblers: The California Personality Inventory. *Journal of Clinical Psychology 43,* 521–527.

McGlothlin, W. H. (1954). A psychometric study of gambling. *Journal of Consulting Psychology 18,* 145–149.

McGlothlin, W. H. (1956). Stability of choices among uncertain alternatives. *American Journal of Psychology 69,* 604–615.

Madsen, W. (1974). *The American alcoholic: The nature-nurture controversy in alcoholism research and therapy.* Springfield, IL: Charles C Thomas.

Malinowski, B. (1948). *Magic, science, and religion.* Garden City, N.J.: Doubleday.

Malkin, D., and Syme, G. J. (1986). Personality and problem gambling. *International Journal of the Addictions 21,* 267–272.

Mark, M. E., and Lesieur, H. R. (1992). A feminist critique of problem gambling research. *British Journal of Addiction 87*(4), 549–565.

Markowitz, M. (1984). Alcohol misuse as a response to perceived powerlessness in the organization. *Journal of Studies on Alcohol 45*(3), 225–227.

Marks, I. (1990). Behavioural (non-chemical) addictions. *British Journal of Addiction 85,* 1389–1394.

Marlatt, G. A. (1985a). Lifestyle modification. In Marlatt, G. A. and Gordon, J. R. (Eds.) *Relapse prevention.* New York: Guilford Press.

Marlatt, G. A. (1985b). Relapse prevention: Theoretical rationale and overview of the model. In Marlatt, G. A., and Gordon, J. R. (Eds.) *Relapse prevention.* New York: Guilford Press.

Marlatt, G. A. (1985c). Cognitive factors in the relapse process. In Marlatt, G. A. and Gordon, J. R. (Eds.) *Relapse prevention.* New

York: Guilford Press.

Marlatt, G. A., and Gordon, J. R. (Eds.) (1985). *Relapse prevention.* New York: Guilford Press.

Martinez, T. (1976). Compulsive gambling and the conscious mood perspective. In Eadington, W. R. (Ed.) *Gambling and society: Interdisciplinary studies on the subject of gambling* (pp. 347–370). Springfield, IL.: Charles C Thomas.

Martinez-Pina, A., Guirao de Parga, J. L., Fuste i Vallverdu, R., Serrat Planas, X., Martin Mateo, M., and Moreno Auguado, V. (1991). The Catalonia survey: Personality and intelligence structure in a sample of compulsive gamblers. *Journal of Gambling Studies 7*(4), 275–299. Reprinted (1993) in Eadington, W. R., and Cornelius J. (Eds.) *Gambling behavior and problem gambling.* Reno, Nevada: Bureau of Business and Economic Research, College of Business Administration, University of Nevada.

Marty, H., Zoppa, R., and Lesieur, H. (1985). Dual addiction: Pathological gambling and alcoholism. In Eadington, W. R. (Ed.) *Proceedings of the Sixth National Conference on Gambling and Risk-Taking.* Reno, Nevada: Bureau of Business and Economic Research, College of Business Administration, University of Nevada.

Masserman, J. H. (1961). *Principles of dynamic psychiatry.* Philadelphia: Saunders.

Matussek, P. (1953). Zur psychodynamik des Gluckspielers (On the psychodynamics of the gambler). *Jahrbuck fur Psychology und Psychotherapie 1*, 232–252. English abstract *Psychological Abstracts 27b*, 78–79.

Maurer, D. D. (1974). *The American confidence man.* Springfield, IL: Charles C Thomas.

Maze, J. (1987). Lady luck is a gambler's mother. In Walker, M. (Ed.) *Faces of gambling: Proceedings of the Second National Conference of the National Association for Gambling Studies* (1986) (pp. 209–213). Sydney, Australia: National Association for Gambling Studies.

Menninger, K. A. (1938). *Man against himself.* New York: Harcourt, Brace, and World.

Meyer, G. (1989). *Glucksspieler in Selfsthilfegruppen–erste Ergebnisse einer empirischen Untersuchung.* Hamburg: Neuland.

Miller, M. A., and Westermeyer, J. (1996). Gambling in Minnesota. *American Journal of Psychiatry 153*(6), 845.

Miller, P. M. (1980). Theoretical and practical issues in substance abuse assessment and treatment. In Miller, W. R. (Ed.) *The addictive behaviors: Treatment of alcoholism, drug abuse, smoking, and obesity* (pp. 265–290). Oxford: Pergamon.

Miller, P. M., Hersen, M., Eisler, R. M., and Hilsman, G. (1975). Effects of social stress on operant drinking of alcoholics and social drinkers. *Behaviour Research and Therapy 12*, 67–72.

Miller, W. R. (1980). The addictive behaviors. In Miller, W. R. (Ed.) *The addictive behaviors: Treatment of alcoholism, drug abuse, smoking, and obesity* (pp. 3–7). Oxford: Pergamon.

Miller, W. R., and Hester, R. K. (1980). Treating the problem drinker: Modern approaches. In Miller, W. R. (Ed.) *The addictive behaviors: Treatment of alcoholism, drug abuse, smoking, and obesity.* Oxford: Pergamon.

Moody, G. E. (1985). Playing with chance. In Eadington, W. R. (Ed.) *The gambling studies: Proceedings of the Sixth National Conference on Gambling and Risk Taking, Vol. 5* (pp. 317–329). Reno, Nevada: Bureau of Business and Economic Research, College of Business Administration, University of Nevada.

Moore, A. (1968). The conception of alcoholism as a mental illness: Implications for treatment and research. *Quarterly Journal of Studies on Alcohol 29*(1), 172–175.

Moran, E. (1969). Taking the final risk. *Mental Health (London) 2*, 21–22.

Moran, E. (1970a). Varieties of pathological gambling. *British Journal of Psychiatry 116*, 593–597.

Moran, E. (1970b). Gambling as a form of dependence. *British Journal of Addiction 64*, 419–428.

Moran, E. (1970c). Clinical and social aspects of risk taking. *Proceedings of the Royal Society of Medicine 63*(12), 1273–1277.

Moran, E. (1970d). Pathological gambling. *British Journal of Hospital Medicine 4*(1), 59–70. Reprinted (1975) *British Journal of Psychiatry, Special Publication No. 9*, 127, 416–428.

Moran, E. (1993). The growing presence of pathological gambling in society: What we know now. In Eadington. W. R., and Cornelius, J. (Eds.) *Gambling behavior and problem gambling* (pp. 135–142). Reno, Nevada: Bureau of Business and Economic Research, College of Business Administration, University of Nevada.

Moravec, J. D., and Munley, P. H. (1983). Psychological test findings on pathological gamblers in treatment. *International Journal of the Addictions 18*(7), 1003–1009.

Morris, R. P. (1957). An exploratory study of some personality characteristics of gamblers. *Journal of Clinical Psychology 13*, 191–193.

Moskowitz, J. (1980). Lithium and lady luck. *New York State Journal of Medicine 80*, 785–788.

Murray, J. B. (1993). Review of research on pathological gambling. *Psychological Reports, 72*(3), 791–810.

Myerson, A. (1940). Alcohol: A study of social ambivalence. *Quarterly Journal of Studies on Alcohol 1*(1), 13–20.

Nathan, P. E. (1988). The addictive personality is the behavior of the addict. *Journal of Consulting and Clinical Psychology 56*(2), 183–188.

Newman, O. (1972). *Gambling: Hazard and reward.* London: The Athelone Press.

Newmark, D. L. (1992). Covert religious aspects of gambling. In Eadington, W. R., and Cornelius, J. A. (Eds.) *Gambling and commercial gaming: Essays in business, economics, philosophy, and science* (pp. 449–456). Reno, Nevada: Bureau of Business and Economic Research, College of Business Administration, University of Nevada.

Niederland, W. G. (1967). A contribution to the psychology of gambling. *Psychoanalytic Forum 2*, 175–179.

Nora, R. M. (1989). Inpatient treatment programs for pathological gambling. In Shaffer, H. J., Stein, S. A., Gambino, G., and Cummings, T. N. (Eds.) *Compulsive gambling: Theory, research, and practice* (pp. 127–134). Lexington, MA: Lexington Books.

Oldman, D. (1974). Chance and skill: A study of roulette. *Sociology 8*(3), 407–426.

Oldman, D. (1978). Compulsive gamblers. *Sociological Review 26*, 349–370.

Olmstead, C. (1962). *Heads I win–tails you lose.* New York: McMillan.

Orford, J. (1978). Hypersexuality: Implications for a theory of dependence. *British Journal of Addiction 73*, 299–310.

Orford, J. (1985). *Excessive appetites: A psychological view of addictions.* New York: John Wiley and Sons.

Orford, J., and McCartney, J. (1990). Is excessive gambling seen as a form of dependence? Evidence from the community and the clinic. *Journal of Gambling Behavior 6*(2), 139–152.

Paulson, R. A. (1994). A comment on the misperception of streaks. *Journal of Gambling Studies 10*(2), 199–205.

Pavlov, I. P. (1927). *Conditioned reflexes: An investigation of the physiological activity of the cerebral cortex.* Anrep, G. V. (Ed. and Trans.). London: Oxford University Press.

Peck, C. P. (1986). Risk-taking behavior and compulsive gambling. *American Psychologist, 41*(4), 461–465.

Peele, S. (1985). *The meaning of addiction: Compulsive experience and its interpretation.* Lexington, MA: Lexington Books.

Peele, S. (1989). Out of the habit trap. In Rucker, W. B,. and Rucker, M. B. (Eds.) *Drugs, society, and behavior.* Guilford, CT: Dushkin.

Peele, S. and Brodsky, A. (1975). *Love and addiction.* New York: Signet.

Pihl, R. O., and Smith S. (1983). On affect and alcohol. In Pohorecky, L. A., and Brick, J. (Eds.) *Stress and alcohol use.* New York: Elsevier.

Polich, J. M., Armor, D. J., and Braiker, H. B. (1981). *The course of alcoholism: Four years after treatment.* New York: John Wiley and Sons.

Popkin, J. (1994, March 14). Tricks of the trade: The many modern ways casinos try to part bettors from their cash. *U.S. News and World Report 116*(10), 48–52.

Popper, K. R. (1962). *Conjectures and refutations: The growth of scientific knowledge.* New York: Basic Books.

Preston, M. G., and Baratta, P. (1948). An experimental study of the auction-value of an uncertain outcome. *American Journal of Psychology 61*, 183–193.

Price, J. A. (1972). *Gambling in traditional Asia. Anthropologica 14*(2), 157–180.

Rabow, J., Comess, L., Donovan, N., and Hollos, C. (1984). Compulsive gambling: Psychoanalytic and sociological perspectives. *Israel Journal of Psychiatry and Related Sciences 21*(3), 189–207.

Rachlin, H. (1990). Why do people gamble and keep gambling despite heavy losses? *Psychological Science 1*(5), 294–297.

Rado, S. (1926). The psychic effects of intoxicants: An attempt to evolve a psychoanalytic theory of morbid cravings. *International Journal of Psychoanalysis 7*, 396–413.

Rado, S. (1933). The psychoanalysis of pharmacothymia (drug addiction). *Psychoanalytic Quarterly 2*, 1–23.

Ramirez, L. F., McCormick, R. A., Russo, A. M., and Taber, J. I. (1983). Patterns of substance abuse in pathological gamblers undergoing treatment. *Addictive Behaviors, 8*(4), 425–428.

Radin, D. I., and Rebman, J. M. (1998). Seeking psi in the casino. *Journal of the Society for Psychical Research 62*(850), 193–219.

Raviv, M. (1993). Personality characteristics of sexual addicts and pathological gamblers. *Journal of Gambling Studies 9*(1), 17–30.

Reagan, R. T. (1987). Complexity of IQ: Comment on Ceci and Liker (1986). *Journal of Experimental Psychology: General 116*(3), 302–303.

Reid, R. L. (1986). The psychology of the near miss. *Journal of Gambling Behavior 2*(1), 32–39.

Reid, S. A. (1985). The churches' campaign against casinos and poker machines in Victoria. In Caldwell, G., Haig, B., Dickerson, M., and Sylvan, L. (Eds.) *Gambling in Australia* (pp. 195–216). Sydney: Croom Helm.

Reik, T. (1940). *From thirty years with Freud.* New York: International University Press.

Roberts, J. M., and Sutton-Smith, B. (1966). Cross-cultural correlates of games of chance. *Behavior Science Notes 1*(1), 131–144.

Robins, L. N., Helzer, J. E., Weissman, M. M., Orvaschel, H., Gruenberg, E., Burke, J. D., and Regier, D. (1984). Lifetime prevalence of specific psychiatric disorders in three sites. *Archives of General Psychiatry 41*, 949–958.

Roebuck, J. (1967). *Criminal typology.* Springfield, IL: Charles C Thomas.

Rogers, P. (1999). The cognitive psychology of lottery gambling: A theoretical review. *Journal of Gambling Studies 14*(2), 111–134.

Rosecrance, J. (1986a). Why regular gamblers don't quit: A sociological perspective. *Sociological Perspectives 29*, 357–378.

Rosecrance, J. (1986b). Attributions and the origins of problem gambling. *The Sociological Quarterly 27*, 463–477.

Rosecrance, J. (1988). *Gambling without guilt.* Pacific Grove, Calif.: Brooks/Cole Publishing.

Rosenthal, R. J. (1970). *Genetic theory and abnormal behavior.* New York: McGraw-Hill.

Rosenthal, R. J. (1985). The pathological gambler's system for self-deception. In Eadington, W. R. (Ed.) *The gambling papers: Proceedings of the 1985 Conference on Gambling.* Reno, Nevada: Bureau of Business and Economic Research, College of Business.

Rosenthal, R. J. (1986). The pathological gambler's system of self-deception. *Journal of Gambling Behavior 2*(2), 108–120.

Rosenthal, R. J. (1987). The psychodynamics of pathological gambling: A review of the literature. In Galski, T. (Ed.) *The handbook of pathological gambling* (pp. 41–70). Springfield, IL: Charles C Thomas.

Rosenthal, R. J. (1989). Pathological gambling and problem gambling: Problems of definition and diagnosis. In Shaffer, H. J., Stein, S. A., Gambino, G., and Cummings, T. N. (Eds.) *Compulsive gambling: Theory, research, and practice* (pp. 101–125). Lexington, MA: Lexington Books.

Rosenthal, R. J. (1992). Pathological gambling. *Psychiatric Annals 22*(2), 72–78.

Rosenthal, R. J. (1993). Some causes of pathological gambling. In Eadington, W. R., and Cornelius, J. (Eds.) *Gambling behavior and problem gambling* (pp. 143–148). Reno, Nevada: Bureau of Business and Economic Research, College of Business Administration, University of Nevada.

Rosenthal, R. J., and Lesieur, H. R. (1992). Self-reported withdrawal symptoms and pathological gambling. *American Journal of the*

Addictions 1(2), 150–154. Reprinted (1993) in Eadington, W. R. and Cornelius, J. (Eds.) *Gambling behavior and problem gambling* (pp. 337–344). Reno, Nevada: Bureau of Business and Economic Research, College of Business Administration, University of Nevada.

Roston, R. A. (1961). *Some personality characteristics of compulsive gamblers.* Doctoral dissertation, University of California, Los Angeles.

Roston, R. A. (1965). Some personality characteristics of male compulsive gamblers. In *Proceedings of the 73rd Annual Convention of the American Psychological Association* (pp. 263–264).

Rothbaum, F. M., Weitz, R. R., Snyder, S. S. (1982). Changing the world and changing the self; A two-process model of perceived control. *Journal of Personality and Social Psychology 42*(1), 5–37.

Rotter, J. B. (1954). *Social learning and clinical psychology.* New York: Prentice-Hall.

Rotter, J. B. (1966). Generalized expectancies for internal versus external control of reinforcement. *Psychological Monographs 80,* 1–28.

Roy, A., DeJong, J., and Linnoila, M. (1989). Extraversion in pathological gamblers: Correlates with indexes of noradrenergic function. *Archives of General Psychiatry, 46*(8), 679–681.

Roy, A., Smelson, D., and Lindeken, S. (1996). Screening for pathological gambling among substance misusers. *British Journal of Psychiatry 169*(4), 523.

Roy, A., Custer, R., Lorenz, V., and Linnoila, M. (1988). Depressed pathological gamblers. *Acta Psychiatrica Scandinavica 77*(2), 163–165.

Roy, A., Custer, R., Lorenz, V., and Linnoila, M. (1989). Personality factors and pathological gambling. *Acta Psychiatrica Scandinavica 80*(1), 37–39.

Roy, A., Adinoff, B., Roehrich, L., Lamparski, D., Custer, R., Lorenz, V., Barbaccia, M., Guidotti, A., Costa, E., and Linnoila, M. (1988). Pathological gambling: A psychobiological study. *Archives of General Psychiatry 45*(4), 369–373.

Rozin, P. and Stoess, C. (1993). Is there a general tendency to become addicted? *Addictive Behaviors 18*(1), 81–87.

Rugle, L. J. (1996, April 2). *Adult attention deficit hyperactivity disorder, conduct disorder, and pathological gambling.* Paper presented at the 1996 National Conference on Gambling, Crime and Gaming Enforcement. Illinois State University, Normal, Illinois.

Rugle, L. J., and Melamed, L. (1993). Neuropsychological assessment of attention deficit disorder in pathological gamblers. *Journal of Nervous and Mental Disease 181*(2), 107–112. Reprinted (1993) in Eadington, W. R., and Cornelius, J. (Eds.) *Gambling behavior and problem gambling* (pp. 309–332). Reno, Nevada: Bureau of Business and Economic Research, College of Business Administration, University of Nevada.

Rule, B. G., and Fischer, D. G. (1970). Impulsivity, subjective probability, cardiac response and risk-taking: Correlates and factors. *Personality 1*(3), 251–260.

Rule, B. G., Nutter, R. W., and Fischer, D. G. (1971). The effect of arousal on risk-taking. *Personality 2*(3), 239–247.

Salzman, L. (1981). Psychodynamics and the addictions. In Mule, S. J. (Ed.) *Behavior in excess: An examination of the volitional disorders* (pp. 338–349). New York: The Free Press.

Saunders, D. M. (1981). The late betting phenomenon in relation to types of bet and type of race. *Behavioural Psychotherapy 9,* 330–337.

Saunders, D. M., and Wookey, P. E. (1980). Behavioral analyses of gambling. *Behavioural Psychotherapy 8,* 1–6.

Scarne, J. (1975). *Scarne's new complete guide to gambling.* London: Constable.

Schachter, S. (1971). *Emotion, obesity, and crime.* New York: Academic Press.

Schneider, J. M. (1968). Skill versus chance activity preference and locus of control. *Journal of Consulting and Clinical Psychology 32*(3), 333–337.

Schneider, J. M. (1972). Relationship between locus of control and activity preferences: Effects of masculinity, activity, and skill. *Journal of Consulting and Clinical Psychology 38,* 225–230.

Schuckit, M. A. (1985). The clinical implications of primary diagnostic groups among alcoholics. *Archives of General Psychiatry 42,*

1043–1049.
Schuckit, M. A., and Monteiro, M. (1988). Alcoholism, anxiety, and depression. *British Journal of Addiction 83*, 1373–1380.
Schwartz, R. M., Burkhart, B. R., and Green, S. B. (1978). Turning on and turning off: Sensation seeking or tension reduction as motivational determinants of alcohol use. *Journal of Consulting and Clinical Psychology 46*(5), 1144–1145.
Schwarz, J., and Lindner, A. (1992). Inpatient treatment of male pathological gamblers in Germany. *Journal of Gambling Studies 8*(1), 93–109.
Scott, M. B. (1968). *The racing game.* Chicago: Aldine Publishing Co.
Scoufis, P., and Walker, M. (1982). Heavy drinking and the need for power. *Journal of Studies on Alcohol 43*(9), 1010–1019.
Seager, C. P. (1970). Treatment of compulsive gambling using electrical aversion. *British Journal of Psychiatry 117*(540), 545–553.
Seixas, F. A., Omenn, G. S., and Burk, D. (1972). Nature and nurture in alcoholism. *Annals of the New York Academy of Sciences, Vol. 197*, May 25.
Seliger, R. V. and Rosenberg, S. J. (1941). Personality of the alcoholic. *Medical Record, 54*, 418–421.
Shaffer, H. J. (1989). Conceptual crises in the addictions: The role of models in the field of compulsive gambling. In Shaffer, H. J., Stein, S. A., Gambino, G., and Cummings, T. N. (Eds.) *Compulsive gambling: Theory, research, and practice* (pp. 3–33). Lexington, MA: Lexington Books.
Shaffer, H. J. (1996). Understanding the means and objects of addiction: Technology, the internet, and gambling. *Journal of Gambling Studies 12*(4), 461–469.
Shaffer, H. J. (1997). The most important unresolved issue in the addictions: conceptual chaos. *Substance Use & Misuse 32*(11), 1573–1580.
Shaffer, H. J., and Gambino, B. (1989). The epistemology of "addictive disease": Gambling as predicament. *Journal of Gambling Behavior 5*(3), 211–229.
Shaffer, H. J., and Schneider R. J. (1984). Trends in the behavioral psychology and the addictions. In Milkman, H. B., and Shaffer, H. J. (Eds.) *The addictions: Multidisciplinary perspectives and treatments* (pp. 39–55). Lexington, MA: Lexington Books.
Shaffer, H. J., Hall, M. N., and Vander Bilt, J. (1997). *Estimating the prevalence of disordered gambling behavior in the United States and Canada: A meta-analysis.* Boston: Harvard Medical School Division on Addictions.
Shaffer, H. J., Stein, S. A., Gambino, B., and Cummings, T. N. (1989). Introduction. In Shaffer, H. J., Stein, S. A., Gambino, G., and Cummings, T. N. (Eds.) *Compulsive gambling: Theory, research, and practice* (pp. xv–xviii). Lexington, MA: Lexington Books.
Sharpe, L., and Tarrier, N. (1993). Towards a cognitive-behavioural model of problem gambling behaviour. *British Journal of Psychiatry 162*, 407–412.
Sharpe, L., Tarrier, N., Schotte, D., and Spence, S. H. (1995). The role of autonomic arousal in problem gambling. *Addiction 90*(11), 1529–1540).
Shepherd, R.-M. (1996). Clinical obstacles in administrating the South Oaks Gambling Screen in a methadone and alcohol clinic. *Journal of Gambling Studies 12*(1), 21–32.
Shewan, D., and Brown, R. I. F. (1993). The role of fixed interval conditioning in promoting involvement in off-course betting. In Eadington, W. R., and Cornelius, J. (Eds.) *Gambling behavior and problem gambling* (pp. 111–132). Reno, Nevada: Bureau of Business and Economic Research, College of Business Administration, University of Nevada.
Shiffman, S., Read, L., Maltese, J., Rapkin, D., and Jarvik, M. (1985). Preventing relapse in ex-smokers: A self-management approach. In Marlatt, G. A. and Gordon, J. R. (Eds.) *Relapse prevention.* New York: Guilford Press.
Shipley, T. E., Jr. (1987). Opponent process theory. In Blane, H. T. and Leonard, K. E. (Eds.) *Psychological theories of drinking and alcoholism.* New York: Guilford Press.
Siegel, S. (1979). The role of conditioning in drug tolerance and addiction. In Keehn, J. D. (Ed.) *Psychopathology in animals: Research and treatment implication.* New York: Academic Press.

Siegel, S. (1983). Classical conditioning in drug tolerance and dependence. In Smart, R. G., et al. (Eds.) *Research advances in alcohol and drug problems.* New York: Plenum.

Siegel, S. (1988). Drug anticipation and the treatment of dependence. In Ray, B. A. (Ed.) *Learning factors in substance abuse, NIDA Research Monograph 84.* Washington D.C.: U.S. Government Printing Office.

Simmel, E. (1920). Psychoanalysis of the gambler. *International Journal of Psychoanalysis 1*, 352–353.

Simmel, E. (1948). Alcoholism and addiction. *Psychoanalytic Quarterly 17*, 6–31.

Sjoberg, L. (1969). Alcohol and gambling. *Psychopharmacologia 14*, 284–289.

Skinner, B. F. (1938). *The behavior of organisms: An experimental analysis.* New York: Appleton-Century-Crofts.

Skinner, B. F. (1948). "Superstition" in the pigeon. *Journal of Experimental Psychology 38*, 168–172.

Skinner, B. F. (1953). *Science and human behavior.* New York: The Free Press.

Skinner, B. F. (1969). *Contingencies of reinforcement: A theoretical analysis.* New York: Appleton-Century-Crofts.

Skinner, B. F. (1971). *Beyond freedom and dignity.* New York: Alfred A. Knopf.

Skinner, B. F. (1974). *About behaviorism.* New York: Alfred A. Knopf.

Slovic, P. (1962). Convergent validation of risk-taking measures. *Journal of Abnormal and Social Psychology 65*, 68–71.

Slovic, P. (1964). Assessment of risk-taking behavior. *Psychological Bulletin 61*, 220–233.

Smith, J. F., and Abt, V. (1984). Gambling as play. *Annals of the American Academy of Political and Social Science 474* (July), 122–132.

Smith, R. W., and Preston, F. (1984). Vocabularies of motives for gambling behavior. *Sociological Perspectives 27*, 325–348.

Sobell, M. B. (1978). Goals in the treatment of alcohol problems. *American Journal of Drug Abuse 5*(3), 283–291.

Sobell, M. B., and Sobell, L. C. (1977). *Individualized behavioral treatment of alcohol problems.* New York: Plenum.

Sommers, I. (1988). Pathological gambling: Estimating prevalence and group characteristics. *International Journal of the Addictions 23*, 477–490.

Spanier, D. (1994). *Inside the gambler's mind.* Reno: University of Nevada Press.

Specker, S. M., Carlson, G. A., Edmonson, K. M., Johnson, P. E., and Marcotte, M. (1996). Psychopathology in pathological gamblers seeking treatment. *Journal of Gambling Studies 12*(1), 67–81.

Sprowls, R. C. (1953). Psychological-mathematical probability in relationships of lottery gambles. *American Journal of Psychology 66*, 126–130.

Spunt, B., Lesieur, H., Hunt, D., and Cahill, D. (1995). Gambling among methadone patients. *International Journal of the Addictions 30*(8), 929–962.

Spunt, B., Lesieur, H., Liberty, H. J., and Hunt, D. (1996). Pathological gamblers in methadone treatment: A comparison between men and women. *Journal of Gambling Studies 12*(4), 431–449.

Spunt, B., Dupont, I., Lesieur, H., Liberty, H. J., and Hunt, D. (1998). Pathological gambling and substance misuse: A review of the literature. *Substance Use & Misuse 33*(13), 2535–2560.

Steinberg, M. A. (1990). Sexual addiction and compulsive gambling. *American Journal of Preventive Psychiatry and Neurology 2*, 39–41.

Steinberg, M. A. (1993). Pathological gambling and couple relationship issues. In Eadington, W. R. and Cornelius, J. A. (Eds.) *Gambling behavior and problem gambling* (pp. 197–214). Reno, Nevada: Bureau of Business and Economic Research, College of Business Administration, University of Nevada.

Steinberg, M. A., Kosten, T. A., and Rounsaville, B. J. (1992). Cocaine abuse and pathological gambling. *American Journal on Addictions 1*(2), 121–132.

Steinmetz, A. (1870). *The gaming table: Its votaries and victims, Volume 1.* London: Tinsley.

Stekel, W. (1929). The gambler. In Van Teslaar, S. (Ed.) *Peculiarities of behavior* (pp. 233–255). New York: Liveright.

Strachan, M. L., and Custer, R. L. (1993). Female compulsive gamblers in Las Vegas. In Eadington, W. R., and Cornelius, J. A. (Eds.)

Gambling behavior and problem gambling (pp. 235–238). Reno, Nevada: Bureau of Business and Economic Research, College of Business Administration, University of Nevada.

Steel, Z., and Blaszczynski, A. (1996). The factorial structure of pathological gambling. *Journal of Gambling Studies 12*(1), 3–20.

Steel, Z., and Blaszczynski, A. (1998). Impulsivity, personality disorders and pathological gambling severity. *Addiction 93*(6), 895–905.

Strickland, L. H., and Grote, F. W. (1967). Temporal presentation of winning symbols and slot machine playing. *Journal of Experimental Psychology 74*, 10–13.

Strickland, L. H., Lewicki, R, J., and Katz, A. M. (1966). Temporal orientation and perceived control as determinants of risk-taking. *Journal of Experimental Social Psychology 2*(2), 143–151.

Sutker, P. B., and Allain, A. N. (1988). Issues in personality conceptualizations of addictive behaviors. *Journal of Consulting and Clinical Psychology 56*, 172–182.

Swyhart, P. R. (1976). *The relationship of pathological gambling to money management, impulsiveness, and wager preferences.* Doctoral dissertation, California School of Professional Psychology, Los Angeles.

Symes, B. A., and Nicki, R. M. (1997). A preliminary consideration of cue-exposure, response-prevention treatment for pathological gambling behavior: Two case studies. *Journal of Gambling Studies 13*(2), 145–157.

Szasz, T. S. (1961). *The myth of mental illness: Foundations of a theory of personal conduct.* New York: Hoeber-Harper.

Taber, J. I. (1982). Group psychotherapy with pathological gamblers. In Eadington, W. R. (Ed.) *The gambling papers: Proceedings of the Fifth National Conference on Gambling and Risk-Taking.* Reno, Nevada: Bureau of Business and Economic Research, College of Business Administration, University of Nevada.

Taber, J. I. (1993). Addictive behavior: An informal clinical view. In Eadington, W. R,. and Cornelius, J. A. (Eds.) *Gambling behavior and problem gambling* (pp. 273–286). Reno, Nevada: Bureau of Business and Economic Research, College of Business Administration, University of Nevada.

Taber, J. I., and McCormick, R. A. (1987). The pathological gambler in treatment. In Galski, T. (Ed.) *The handbook of pathological gambling* (pp. 137–168). Springfield, IL: Charles C Thomas.

Taber, J. I., McCormick, R. A., and Ramirez, L. F. (1987). The prevalence and impact of major life stressors among pathological gamblers. *International Journal of the Addictions 22*, 71–79.

Taber, J. I., Russo, A. M., Adkins, B. J., and McCormick, R. A. (1986). Ego strength and achievement motivation in pathological gamblers. *Journal of Gambling Behavior 2*(2), 69–80.

Tarter, R. E. (1990). Vulnerability to alcoholism: From individual differences to different individuals. In Cloninger, C. R., and Begleiter, H. (Eds.) *Genetics and biology of alcoholism, Banbury Report No. 33.* Plainview, N.Y.: Cold Springs Harbor Laboratory Press.

Tarter, R. E., and Schneider, D. U. (1976). Models and theories of alcoholism. In Tarter, R. E. and Sugerman, A. A. (Eds.) *Alcoholism: Interdisciplinary approaches to an enduring problem.* Reading, MA: Addison-Wesley.

Tarter, R. E., Alterman, A. I., and Edwards, K. I. (1985). Vulnerability to alcoholism in men: A behavior-genetic perspective. *Journal of Studies on Alcohol 46*(4), 329–356.

Tarter, R. E., Hegedus, A. M., and Gavaler, J. S. (1985). Hyperactivity in sons of alcoholics. *Journal of Studies on Alcohol 46*(3), 259–261.

Tarter, R. E., Kabene, M., Escallier, E., Laird, S., and Jacob, T. (1990). Temperament deviations and risk for alcoholism. *Alcoholism: Clinical and Experimental Research, 14*, 380–382.

Tec, N. (1964). *Gambling in Sweden.* Totawa, N.J.: Bedminster Press.

Templer, D. I., Kaiser, G., and Siscoe, K. (1993). Correlates of pathological gambling propensity in prison inmates. *Comprehensive Psychiatry 34*(5), 347–351.

Tepperman, J. H. (1977). The effectiveness of short term group therapy upon the pathological gambler and his wife. Doctoral Dissertation, California School of Professional Psychology, Los Angeles. *Dissertation Abstracts 37*, 5383B.

Thomas, W. I. (1901). The gaming instinct. *American Journal of Sociology 6*, 750–763.

Thorson, J. A., Powell, P. C., and Hilt, M. (1994). Epidemiology of gambling and depression in an adult sample. *Psychological Reports 74*(3), 987–994.

Tonneatto, T., Blitz-Miller, T., Calderwood, K., Dragonetti, R., and Tsanos, A. (1997). Cognitive distortions in heavy gambling. *Journal of Gambling Studies 13*(3), 253–266.

Törne, I. V., and Konstanty, R. (1992). Gambling behavior and psychological disorders of gamblers on German-style slot-machines. *Journal of Gambling Studies 8*(1), 39–58.

Tucker, J. A., Vuchinich, R. B., and Sobell. M. B. (1982). Alcohol's effects on human emotions: A review of the stimulation/depression hypothesis. *International Journal of the Addictions 17*, 155–180.

Tylor, E. B. (1958 [1871]). *Primitive culture, Volume 1.* New York: Harper Torchbooks.

Tyndel, M. (1963). Gambling: An addiction. *Addictions 10*, 40–48.

Victor, R. G. (1981). Gambling. In Mulé, S. J. (Ed.) *Behavior in excess: An examination of the volitional disorders* (pp. 271–281). New York: The Free Press.

Vitaro, F. Arseneault, L., and Tremblay, R. E. (1997). Dispositional predictors of problem gambling in male adolescents. *American Journal of Psychiatry 154*(12), 1769–1770.

Vitaro, F., Ferland, F., Jacques, C., and Ladouceur, R. (1998). Gambling, substance use, and impulsivity during adolescence. *Psychology of Addictive Behaviors 12*(3), 185–194.

Vitaro, F., Ladouceur, R., and Bujold, A. (1996). Predictive and concurrent correlates of gambling in early adolescent boys. *Journal of Early Adolescence 16*(2), 211–228.

Volberg, R. A. (1993). Estimating the prevalence of pathological gambling in the United States. In Eadington, W. R., and Cornelius, J. A. (Eds.) *Gambling behavior and problem gambling* (pp. 365–378). Reno: University of Nevada Press.

Volberg, R. A. (1994). The prevalence and demographics of pathological gamblers: Implications for public health. *American Journal of Public Health 84*(2), 237–241.

Volberg, R. A., and Steadman, H. J. (1988). Refining prevalence estimates of pathological gamblers. *American Journal of Psychiatry 145*(4), 502–505.

Volberg, R. A., and Steadman, H. J. (1989). Prevalence estimates of pathological gambling in New Jersey and Maryland. *American Journal of Psychiatry 146*(12), 1618–1619.

Volberg, R. A., Reitzes, D. C., and Boles, J. (1997). Exploring the links between gambling, problem gambling, and self-esteem. *Deviant Behavior 18*(4), 321–342.

Volger, R. E., and Bartz, W. R. (1982). *The better way to drink.* New York: Simon and Schuster.

Von Hattingberg, H. (1914). Analerotic, angstlust and eigensinn. Internationale Zeitschrift für *Psychoanalyse 2*, 244–258.

Wagenaar, W. A. (1970). Subjective randomness and the capacity to generate information. *Acta Psychologica 33*, 233–242.

Wagenaar, W. A. (1988). *Paradoxes of gambling behavior.* London: Hove Erlbaum Associates.

Wagenaar, W. A., Keren, G., and Pleit-Kuiper, A. (1984). The multiple objectives of gamblers. *Acta Psychologica 56*(1-3), 167–178.

Wagner, W. (1972). *To gamble or not to gamble.* New York: World Publishing.

Walker, M. B. (1985). Explanations for gambling. In Caldwell, G., Haig, B., Dickerson, M., and Sylvan, L. (Eds.) *Gambling in Australia* (pp. 146–162). Sydney: Croom Helm.

Walker, M. B. (1988). Betting shops and slot machines: Comparisons among gamblers. In Eadington, W. R. (Ed.) *Gambling research: Proceedings of the Seventh International Conference on Gambling and Risk Taking, Volume 3* (pp. 65–82). Reno, Nevada: Bureau of Business and Economic Research, College of Business Administration, University of Nevada.

Walker, M. B. (1989). Some problems with the concept of "gambling addiction": Should theories of addiction be generalized to include excessive gambling? *Journal of Gambling Behavior 5*(3), 179–200.

Walker, M. B. (1992a). A sociocognitive theory of gambling involvement. In Eadington, W. R., and Cornelius, J. A. (Eds.) *Gambling and com-*

mercial gaming: Essays in business, economics, philosophy, and science (pp. 371–398). Reno, Nevada: Bureau of Business and Economic Research, College of Business Administration, University of Nevada.

Walker, M. B. (1992b). The presence of irrational thinking among poker machine players. In Eadington, W. R. and Cornelius, J. A. (Eds.) *Gambling and commercial gaming: Essays in business, economics, philosophy, and science* (pp. 485–498). Reno, Nevada: Bureau of Business and Economic Research, College of Business Administration, University of Nevada.

Walker, M. B. (1992c). *The psychology of gambling.* Oxford: Pergamon Press.

Walker, M. B. (1992d). Irrational thinking among slot machine players. *Journal of Gambling Studies 8*(3), 245–261.

Walters, G. D. (1994a). The gambling lifestyle: I. Theory. *Journal of Gambling Studies, 10*(2), 159–182.

Walters, G. D. (1994b). The gambling lifestyle: II. Treatment. *Journal of Gambling Studies, 10*(3), 219–235.

Waters, L. K., and Kirk, W. (1968). Stimulus-seeking motivation and risk-taking behavior in a gambling situation. *Educational and Psychological Measurement 28*(2), 549–550.

Weddige, R. L., and Ostrom, M. B. (1990). Affective disorders and affective symptoms in alcoholism. *Journal of Chemical Dependency Treatment 3*, 139–162.

Whiting, J. W. M., and Child, I. L. (1953). *Child training and personality: A cross-cultural study.* New Haven, CT: Yale University Press.

Whitman-Raymond, R. G. (1988). Pathological gambling as a defense against loss. *Journal of Gambling Behavior 4*(2), 99–109.

Wilson, A. N. (1965). *The casino gambler's guide.* New York: Harper and Row.

Witkin, H. A., Carp, S., and Goodenough, D. R. (1959). Dependence in alcoholics. *Quarterly Journal of Studies on Alcohol 20*(3), 493–504.

Wittman, G. W., Fuller, N. P., and Taber, J. I. (1988). Patterns of polyaddictions in alcoholism patients and high school students. In Eadington, W. R. (Ed.) *Gambling research: Proceedings of the Seventh International Conference on Gambling and Risk Taking.* Reno, Nevada: Bureau of Business and Economic Research, College of Business Administration, University of Nevada.

Wolkowitz, O. M., Roy, A. and Doran, A. R. (1985). Pathological gambling and other risk-taking pursuits. *Psychiatric Clinics of North America 8*(2), 311–322.

Wood, G. (1992). Predicting outcomes: Sports and stocks. *Journal of Gambling Studies, 8*(2), 201–222.

World Health Organization (1991). *The international classification of diseases, 9th revision, clinical modification; ICD-9-CM, fourth edition, volume 1, diseases, tabular list.* Washington, D.C.: DHHS Publication No. (DHS) 91-1260, U.S. Dept. of Health and Human Services, U.S. Govt. Printing Office.

World Health Organization (1992). *International Statistical Classification of Diseases and related health problems, tenth revision, ICD-10, volume 1.* Geneva: World Health Organization.

Wolfgang, A. K. (1988). Gambling as a function of gender and sensation seeking. *Journal of Gambling Behavior 4*(2), 71–77.

Wortman, C. B (1975). Some determinants of perceived control. *Journal of Personality and Social Psychology 31*(2), 282–294.

Wortman, C. B. (1976). Causal attributions and personal control. In Havey, J. H., Ickes, W. J., and Kidd, R. F. (Eds.) *New directions in attributional research* (pp. 23–52). Hillsdale, N.J.: Erlbaum.

Wray, I., and Dickerson, M. G. (1981). Cessation of high frequency gambling and "withdrawal" symptoms. *British Journal of Addiction 76*(4), 401–405.

Yaffee, R. A., Lorenz, V. C., and Politzer, R. M. (1993). Models explaining gambling severity among patients undergoing treatment in Maryland: 1983 through 1989. In Eadington, W. R., and Cornelius, J. A. (Eds.) *Gambling behavior and problem gambling* (pp. 657–667). Reno, Nevada: Bureau of Business and Economic Research, College of Business Administration, University of Nevada.

Zenker, S. I., and Wolfgang, A. K. (1982). Relationship of Machiavellianism and locus of control to preferences for leisure activity by college men and women. *Psychological*

Reports 50, 583–586.

Zimmerman, M. A., Meeland, T. G., and Krug, S. E. (1963). Measurement and structure of gambling behavior. *Journal of Personality Assessment 49*, 76–81.

Zinberg, N. (1984). *Drug, set, and setting: The basis for controlled intoxicant use.* New Haven, CT: Yale University Press.

Zola, I. K. (1963). Observations on gambling in a lower-class setting. *Social Problems 10*, 353–361.

Zuckerman, M. (1974). The sensation seeking motive. In Maher, B. A. (Ed.) *Progress in experimental personality research, Vol. 7.* New York: Academic Press.

Zuckerman, M. (1978). The search for high sensation. *Psychology Today 11*, 38–46; 96–99.

Zuckerman, M. (1979). *Sensation seeking: Beyond the optimal level of arousal.* Hillsdale, N. J.: Lawrence Erlbaum Associates.

Zuckerman, M. (1983). A biological theory of sensation seeking. In Zuckerman, M. (Ed.) *Biological bases of sensation seeking, impulsivity, and anxiety.* Hillsdale, N.J.: Lawerence Erlbaum.

Zuckerman, M., Kolin, E., Price, L., and Zoob, I. (1964). Development of a sensation-seeking scale. *Journal of Consulting Psychology 28*, 477–482.

Zwerling, I. (1959). Psychiatric findings in an interdisciplinary study of forty-six alcoholic patients. *Quarterly Journal of Studies on Alcohol 20*(3), 543–554.

INDEX

O

P

R

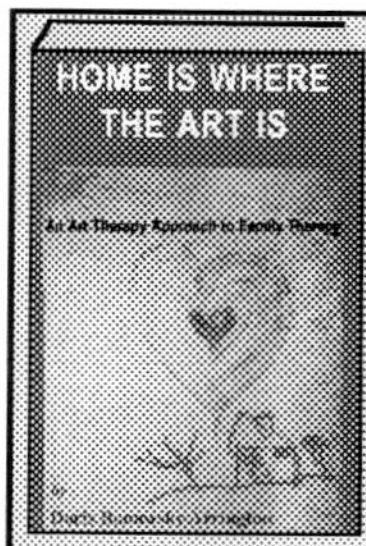

HOME IS WHERE THE ART IS
An Art Therapy Approach to Family Therapy

Published 2001, 224 pages
Doris Banowsky Arrington
$61.95, hard ISBN 0-398-07160-8
$42.95, paper ISBN 0-398-07161-6

PROBLEM GAMBLING AND ITS TREATMENT
An Introduction

To be published 2001, 186 pages
Ronald M. Pavalko
$39.96, hard ISBN 0-398-07229-9
$25.95, paper ISBN 0-398-07230-2

PSYCHOLOGICAL AND EDUCATIONAL TEST SCORES
What Are They?

To be published 2002, 196 pages
Marty Sapp
hard, ISBN 0-398-07258-2
paper, ISBN 0-398-07259-0

WORKING WITH IMAGES: THE ART OF ART THERAPISTS

To be published 2001, 244 pages
Bruce L. Moon
hard ISBN 0-398-07243-4
paper ISBN 0-398-07244-2

A HANDBOOK FOR CORRECTIONAL PSYCHOLOGISTS
Guidance for the Prison Practitioner

Published 2001, 178 pages
Kevin M. Correia
$44.95, hard ISBN 0-398-07186-1
$29.95, paper ISBN 0-398-07219-1 (displayed)

HOW WE SEE GOD AND WHY IT MATTERS
A Multicultural View Through Children's Drawings and Stories

Published 2001, 230 pages
Robert J. Landy
$58.95, hard ISBN 0-398-07170-5
$41.95, paper ISBN 0-398-07171-3

IMAGE AND MIRAGE
Art Therapy with Dissociative Clients

To be published 2001, 288 pages
Dee Spring
hard, ISBN 0-398-07247-7
paper, ISBN 0-398-07248-5

RESEARCH WRITING IN EDUCATION AND PSYCHOLOGY—FROM PLANNING TO PUBLICATION
A Practical Handbook

Published 2001, 176 pages
Herbert J. Klausmeier
$40.95, hard ISBN 0-398-07156-X
$25.95, paper ISBN 0-398-07157-8

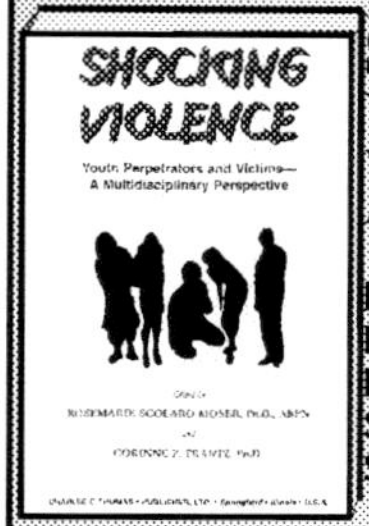

SHOCKING VIOLENCE
Youth Perpetrators and Victims—A Multidisciplinary Perspective

Published 2000, 230 pages
Rosemarie Scolaro Moser & Corinne E. Frantz
$50.95, hard ISBN 0-398-07120-9
$33.95, paper ISBN 0-398-07121-7

NEW ESSAYS IN DRAMA THERAPY
Unfinished Business

To be published 2001, 204 pages
Robert J. Landy
hard, ISBN 0-398-07235-3
paper, ISBN 0-398-07236-1

THE POWER SERIAL RAPIST
A Criminology-Victimology Typology of Female Victim Selection

To be published 2001 190 pages
Dawn J. Graney & Bruce A. Arrigo
(cloth) ISBN 0-398-07249-3
(paper) ISBN 0-398-07250-7

CREATIVE SPIRITUALITY FOR WOMEN
Developing a Positive Sense of Self Through Spiritual Growth Exercises

Published 2000, 180 pages
Iris St. John
$26.95, spiral paper ISBN 0-398-07051-2

CHARLES C THOMAS • PUBLISHER, LTD. • P.O. Box 19265, Springfield, IL 62794-9265

Call 1-800-258-8980 or 1-217-789-8980 or Fax 1-217-789-9130
Complete catalog available at www.ccthomas.com • books@ccthomas.com

Books sent on approval • Shipping charges: $5.95 U.S. / Outside U.S., actual shipping fees will be charged • Prices subject to change without notice